Praise for

TITAN

"A GRIPPING, KNOTTY, EPIC TALE of exploitation and solidarity, and a stern reminder that rights are never given, only taken."
—CORY DOCTOROW, author of *RADICALIZED*

"*TITAN* IS A GEM. It's a thrilling and compact space-adventure story, a smart look on certain enduring political realities, and—surprisingly, delightfully—a romance, an honest-to-God love story that keeps us anchored through the plot's many swift surprises. Were *TITAN* simply a novel, it would be great; as a piece of graphic art, with its richly imagined backgrounds and bold character portraiture, IT IS SUBLIME."
—BEN H. WINTERS, author of *UNDERGROUND AIRLINES*

"An IMMENSELY ENGAGING poli-sci-fi thriller with a satisfying mix of action, romance, and ideological nuance."
—EZRA CLAYTAN DANIELS, author of *UPGRADE SOUL*

"IN THE GREATEST TRADITION OF GOLDEN AGE SCI-FI, François Vigneault creates a future rich with detail and technology, yet socially all too familiar. From dialect to economics, *TITAN* is a masterclass in world building."
—JASON SHIGA, author of *DEMON*

"In *TITAN*, François Vigneault FULFILLS EVERY POTENTIAL OF SCIENCE FICTION. There is a fully realized and socially relevant future world, a suspenseful story gliding through that setting, and beautiful, believable characters at the center of it all. A story this sharp and nuanced is what makes comics excellent."
—MALACHI WARD, author of *ANCESTOR*

"A SMART, STYLISH, POLITICAL sci-fi romance thriller[...] a solid example of genre fiction that doesn't insult the reader's intelligence and has multiple layers..."
—THE COMICS JOURNAL

"Hard sci-fi usually prioritizes technology over characters, but Vigneault beautifully illustrates interclass dynamics, and, in doing so, foregrounds the VERY HUMAN RELATIONSHIPS that make *TITAN* more than a bushel of techno-babble."
—*PASTE MAGAZINE*

"ONE OF THE MOST REALISTIC SCI-FI WEBCOMICS WE'VE READ IN AGES[...] it's that blend of the human moments with the plausible futuristic technology that leaves us so invested in *TITAN* and the ultimate fate of its labor force."
—*IO9*

"Any science fiction fan can quickly find themselves comfortable in the setting of this tension-filled moon. But the setting[...] feels unfamiliar because it's so specific, so unique to Vigneault's imagination and so FULL-FLEDGED IN ITS VISION."
—*THE COMICS BULLETIN*

Finalist

JOE SHUSTER AWARD · *PRIX DES LIBRARIES* · *PRIX BÉDÉLYS QUÉBEC*
PRIX BÉDÉIS CAUSA · *PRIX BD DES COLÉGIENS* · *PRIX AURORA-BORÉAL*

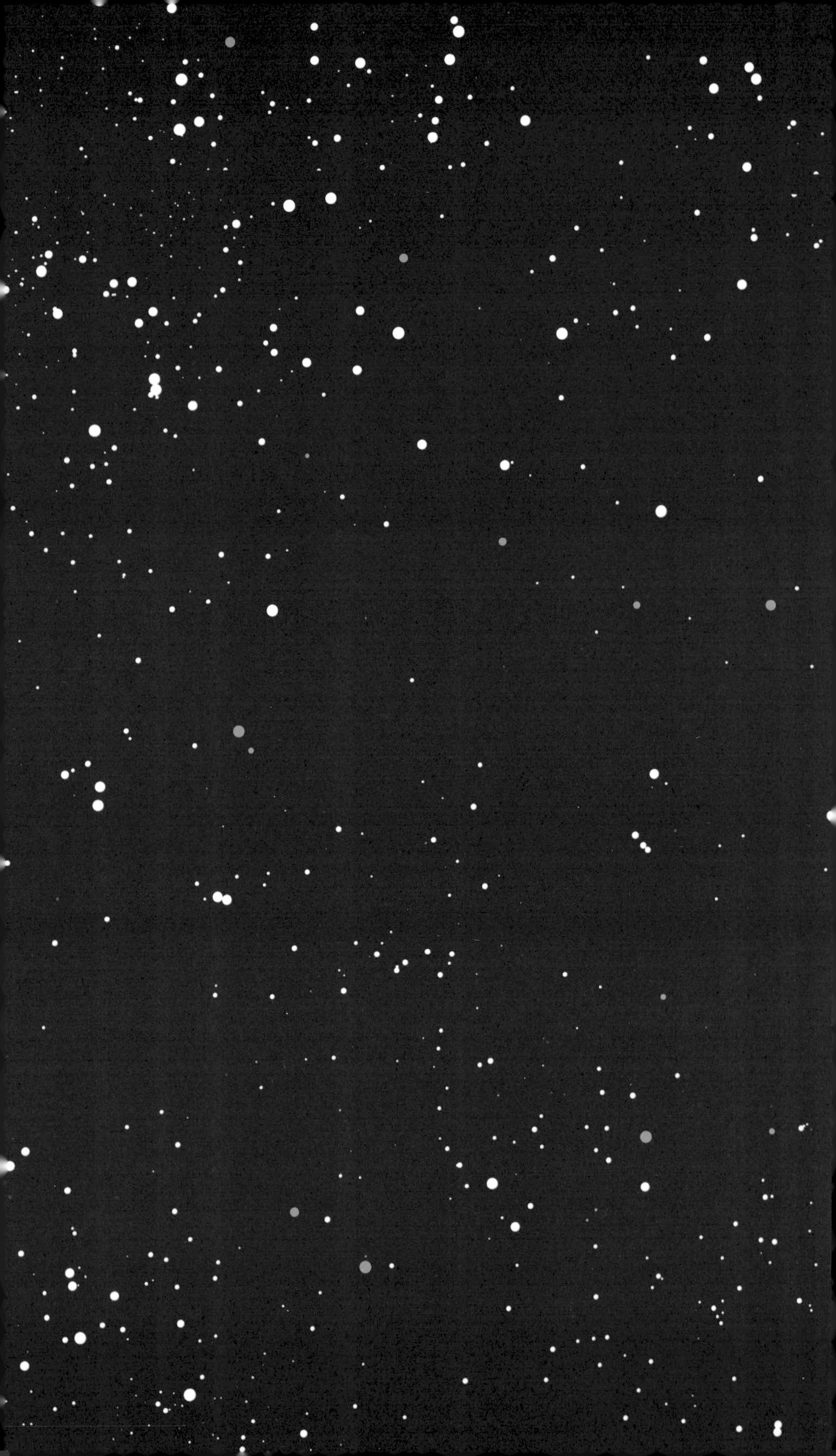

TITAN

ONI PRESS

FRANÇOIS VIGNEAULT

TITAN

TITAN

Created by François Vigneault
Edited by Grace Bornhoft
3D Visualization by Brandi Benkert

Published by
Oni-Lion Forge Publishing Group, LLC
James Lucas Jones, *president & publisher*
Sarah Gaydos, *editor in chief*
Charlie Chu, *e.v.p. of creative*
            & business development
Brad Rooks, *director of operations*
Amber O'Neill, *special projects manager*
Harris Fish, *events manager*
Margot Wood, *director of marketing & sales*
Devin Funches, *sales & marketing manager*
Katie Sainz, *marketing manager*
Tara Lehmann, *publicist*
Troy Look, *director of design & production*
Kate Z. Stone, *senior graphic designer*
Sonja Synak, *graphic designer*
Hilary Thompson, *graphic designer*
Sarah Rockwell, *junior graphic designer*
Angie Knowles, *digital prepress lead*
Vincent Kukua, *digital prepress technician*
Jasmine Amiri, *senior editor*
Shawna Gore, *senior editor*
Amanda Meadows, *senior editor*
Robert Meyers, *senior editor, licensing*
Grace Bornhoft, *editor*
Zack Soto, *editor*
Chris Cerasi, *editorial coordinator*
Steve Ellis, *vice president of games*
Ben Eisner, *game developer*
Michelle Nguyen, *executive assistant*
Jung Lee, *logistics coordinator*

Joe Nozemack, *publisher emeritus*

francois-vigneault.com

onipress.com
facebook.com/onipress
twitter.com/onipress
instagram.com/onipress

lionforge.com
facebook.com/lionforge
twitter.com/lionforge
instagram.com/lionforge

First Edition: September 2020

ISBN 978-1-62010-779-9
eISBN 978-1-62010-800-0

Published previously by
Éditions Pow Pow (2017, editor Luc Bossé)
and Study Group Comics
(2012-2016, editor Zack Soto).

TITAN, September 2020. Published by
Oni-Lion Forge Publishing Group, LLC,
1319 SE Martin Luther King Jr. Blvd., Suite 240,
Portland, OR 97214.

Printed in South Korea through
Four Colour Print Group, Louisville, KY.

Library of Congress Control Number: 2020934175

1 2 3 4 5 6 7 8 9 10

PART 01: FAR, FAR AWAY

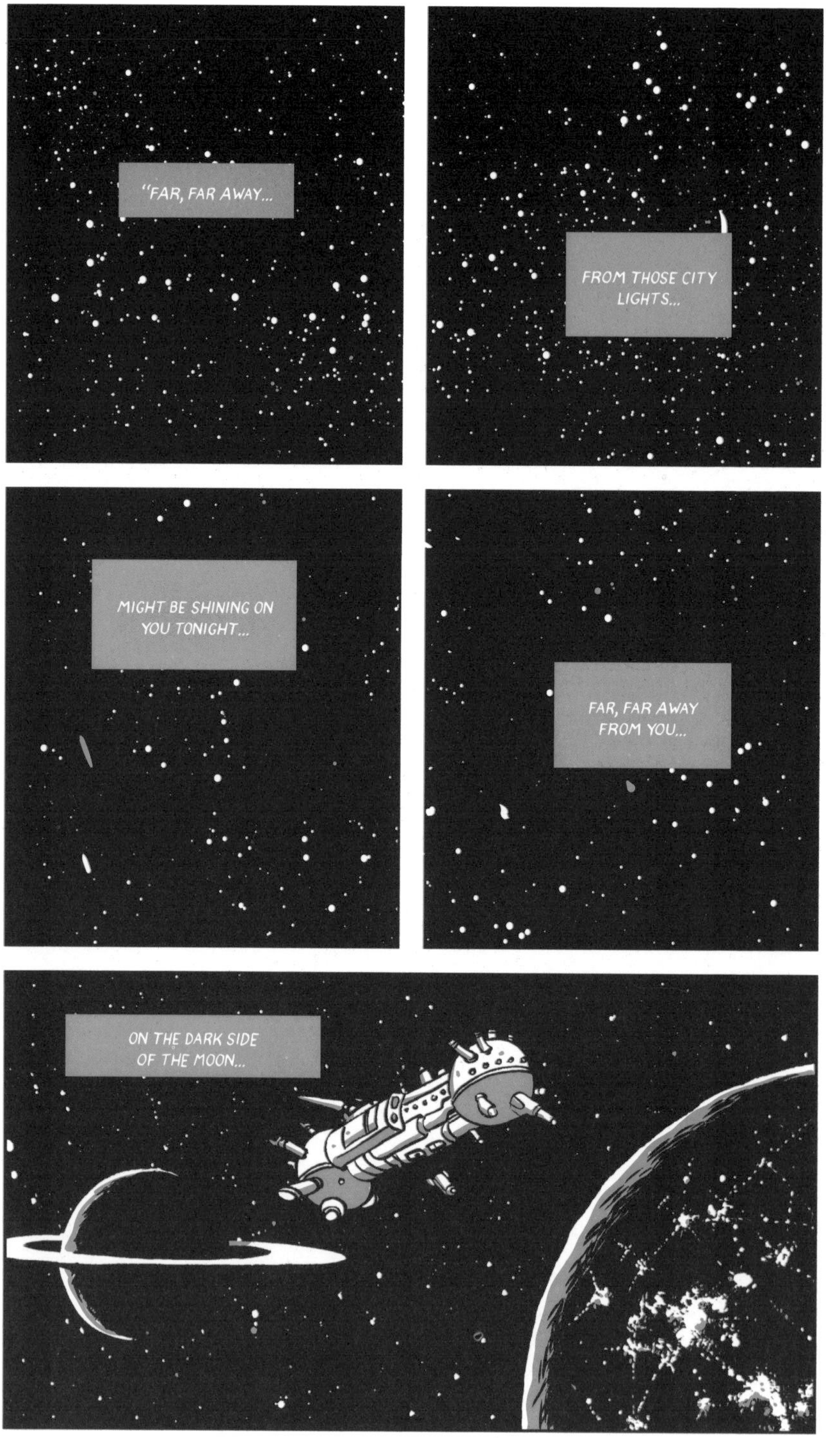
"FAR, FAR AWAY...
FROM THOSE CITY LIGHTS...
MIGHT BE SHINING ON YOU TONIGHT...
FAR, FAR AWAY FROM YOU...
ON THE DARK SIDE OF THE MOON...

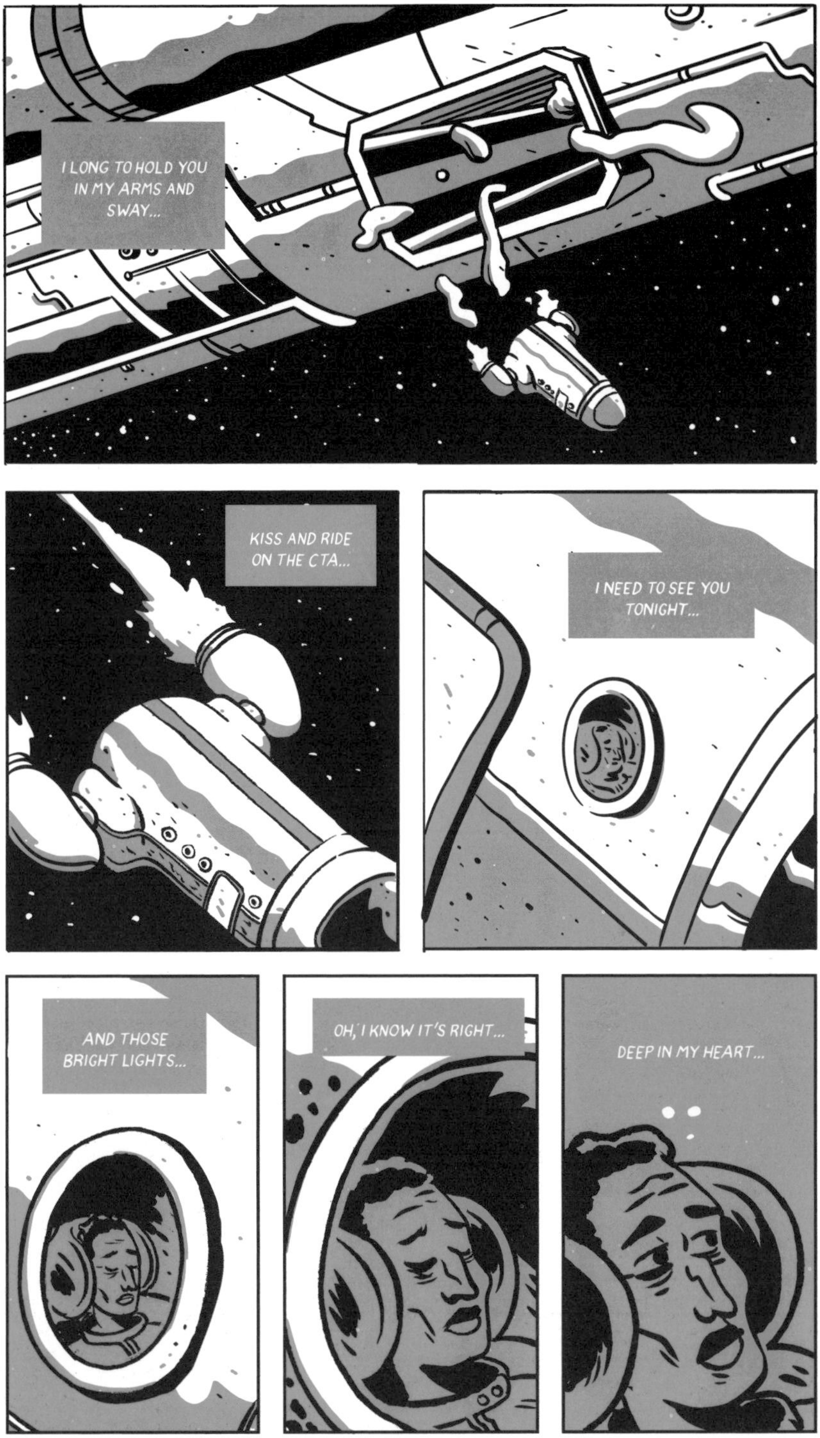
I LONG TO HOLD YOU IN MY ARMS AND SWAY...
KISS AND RIDE ON THE CTA...
I NEED TO SEE YOU TONIGHT...
AND THOSE BRIGHT LIGHTS...
OH, I KNOW IT'S RIGHT...
DEEP IN MY HEART...

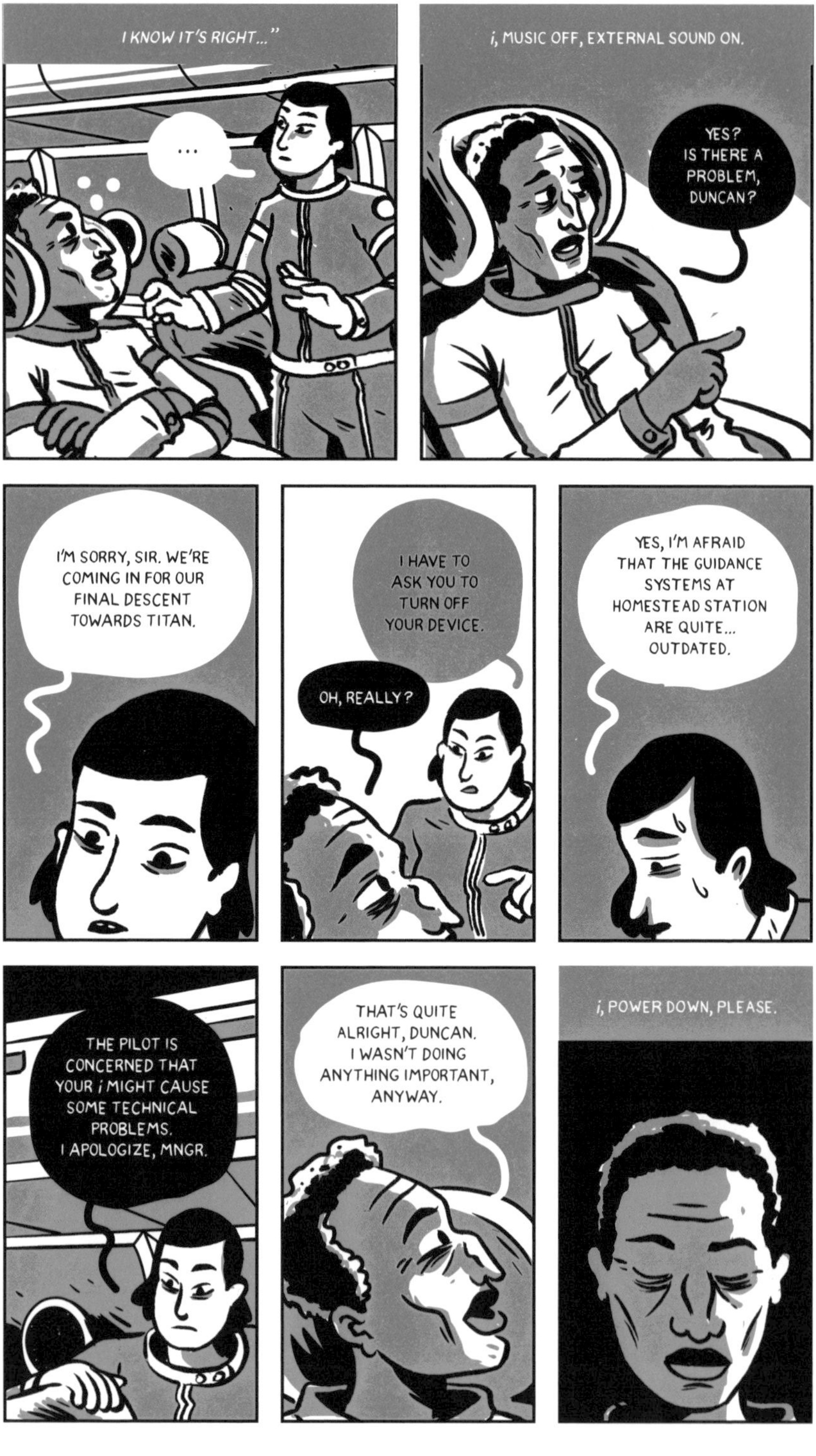
I KNOW IT'S RIGHT..."
...
i, MUSIC OFF, EXTERNAL SOUND ON.
YES? IS THERE A PROBLEM, DUNCAN?
I'M SORRY, SIR. WE'RE COMING IN FOR OUR FINAL DESCENT TOWARDS TITAN.
I HAVE TO ASK YOU TO TURN OFF YOUR DEVICE.
OH, REALLY?
YES, I'M AFRAID THAT THE GUIDANCE SYSTEMS AT HOMESTEAD STATION ARE QUITE... OUTDATED.
THE PILOT IS CONCERNED THAT YOUR i MIGHT CAUSE SOME TECHNICAL PROBLEMS. I APOLOGIZE, MNGR.
THAT'S QUITE ALRIGHT, DUNCAN. I WASN'T DOING ANYTHING IMPORTANT, ANYWAY.
i, POWER DOWN, PLEASE.

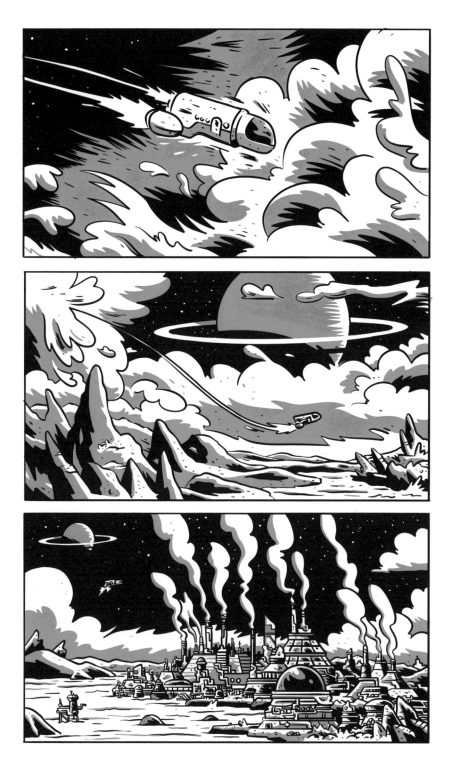

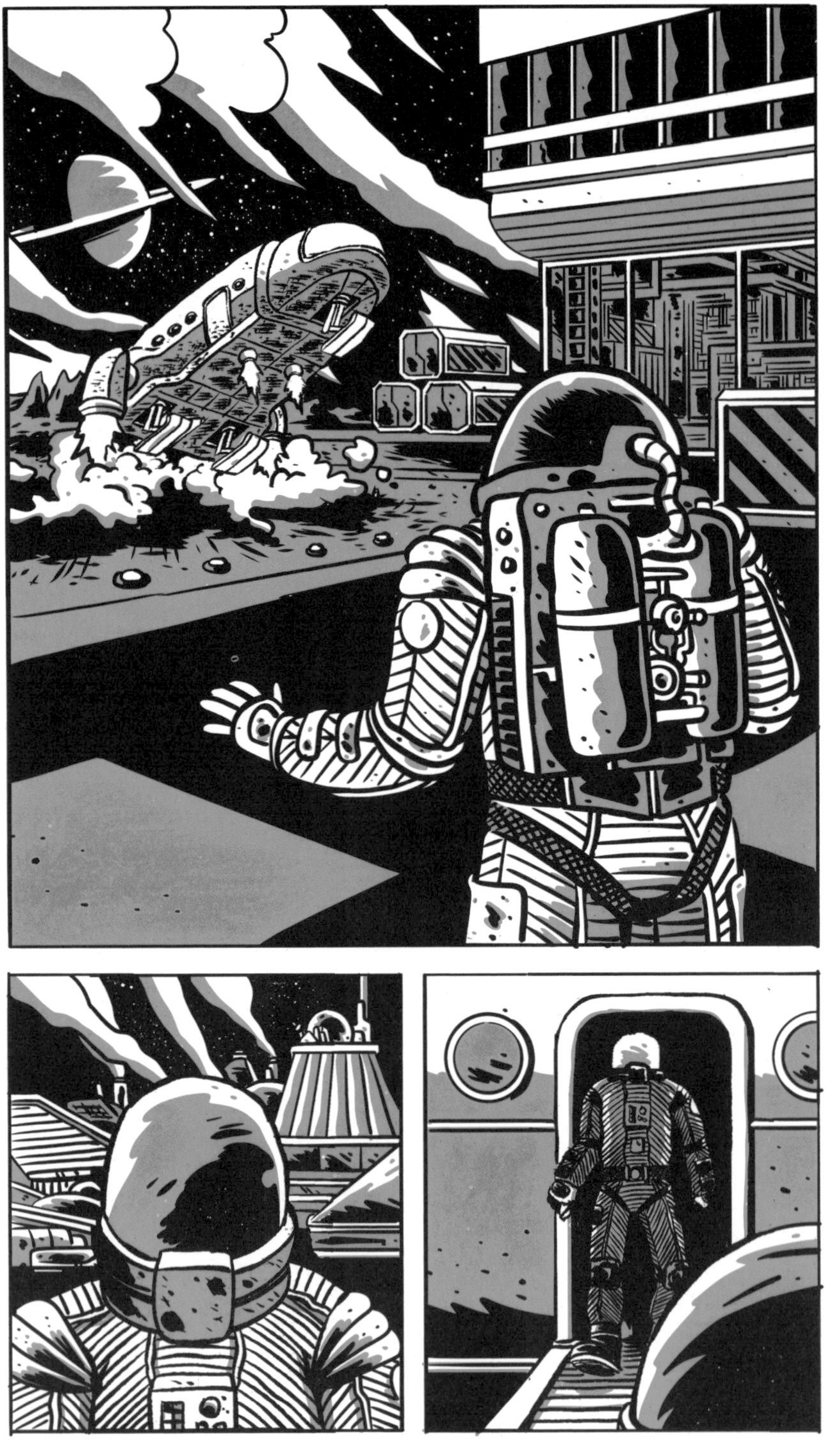

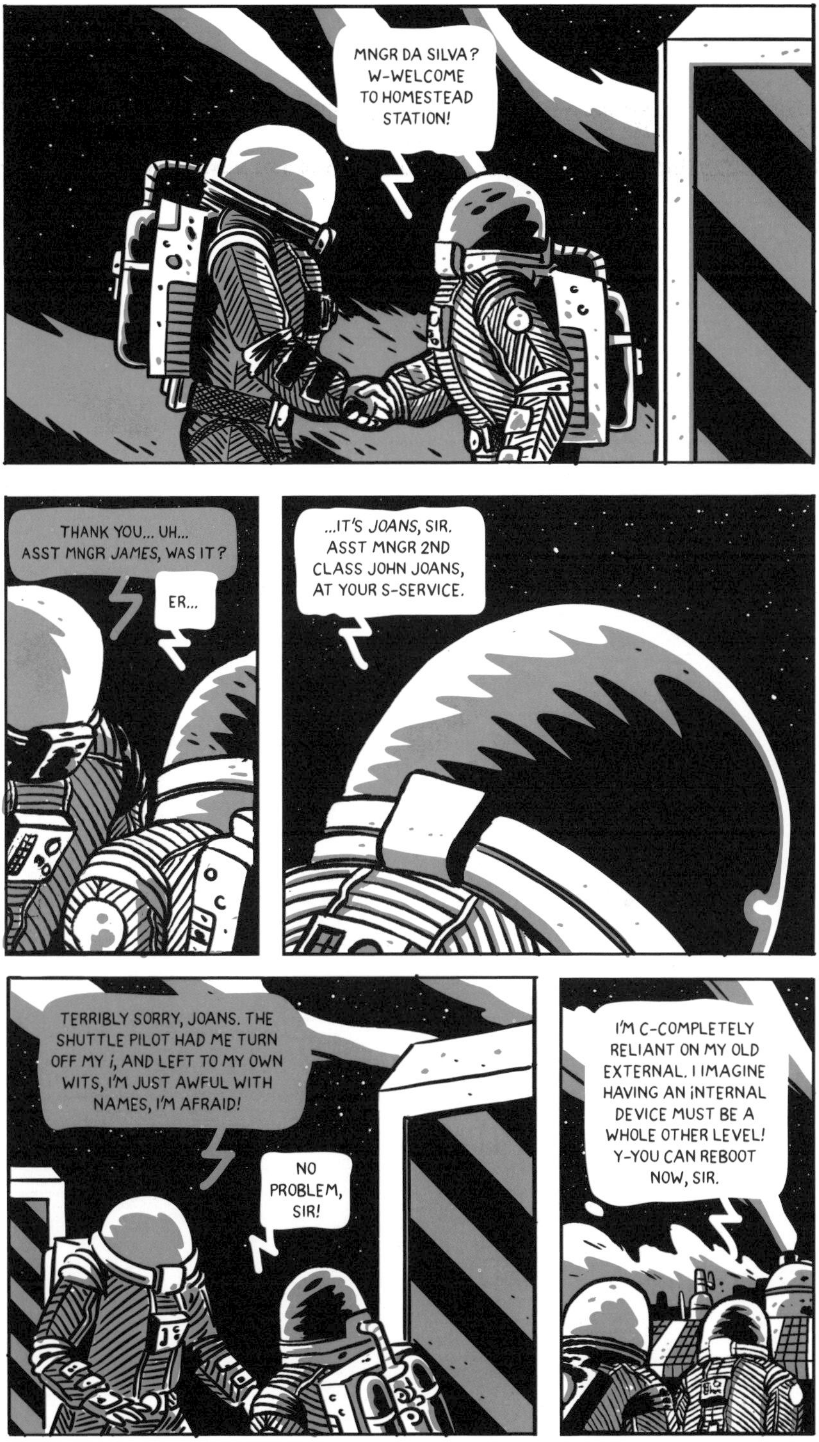
MNGR DA SILVA? W-WELCOME TO HOMESTEAD STATION!
THANK YOU... UH... ASST MNGR *JAMES*, WAS IT?
ER...
...IT'S *JOANS*, SIR. ASST MNGR 2ND CLASS JOHN JOANS, AT YOUR S-SERVICE.
TERRIBLY SORRY, JOANS. THE SHUTTLE PILOT HAD ME TURN OFF MY *i*, AND LEFT TO MY OWN WITS, I'M JUST AWFUL WITH NAMES, I'M AFRAID!
NO PROBLEM, SIR!
I'M C-COMPLETELY RELIANT ON MY OLD EXTERNAL. I IMAGINE HAVING AN *i*NTERNAL DEVICE MUST BE A WHOLE OTHER LEVEL! Y-YOU CAN REBOOT NOW, SIR.

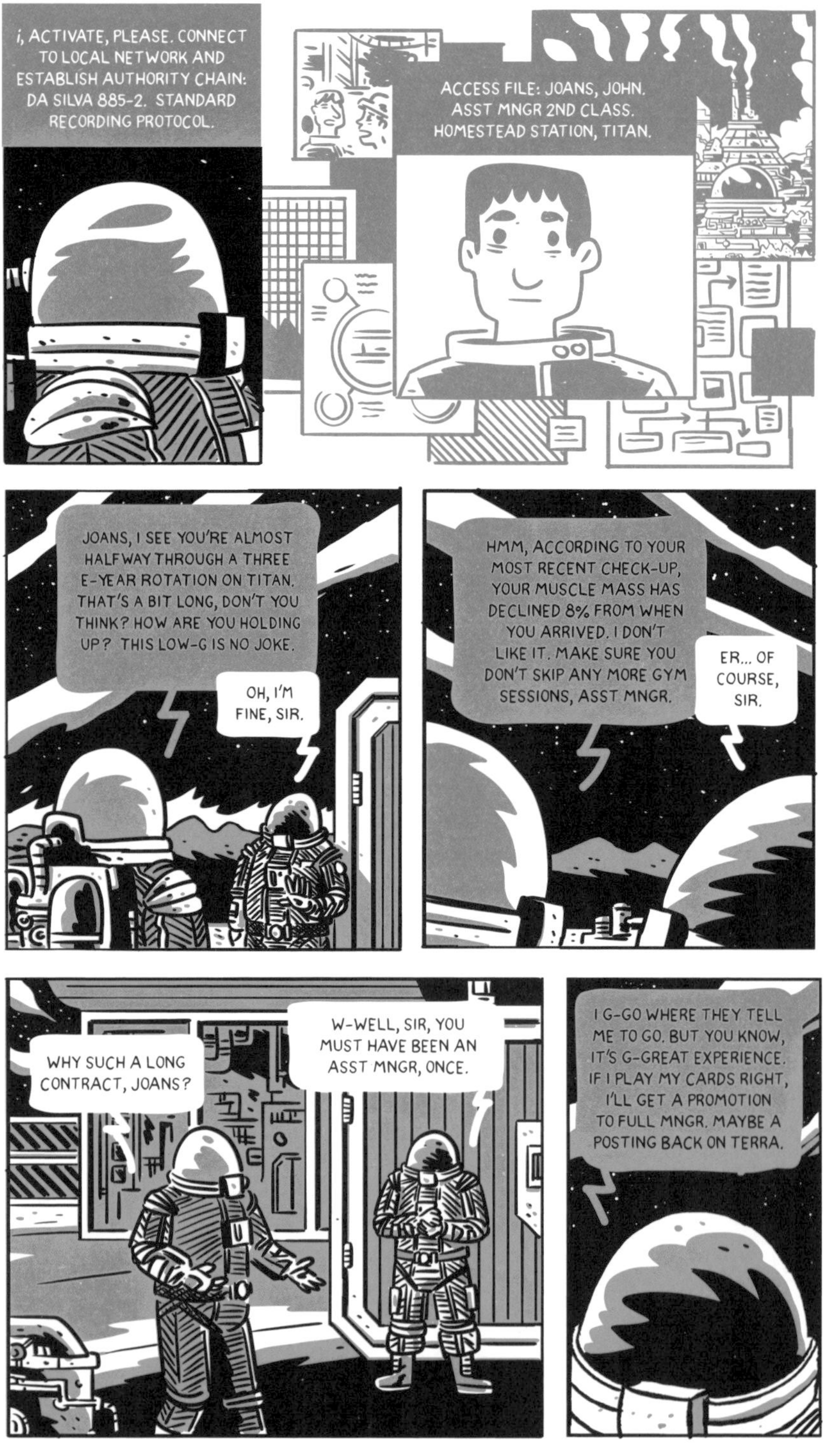

i, ACTIVATE, PLEASE. CONNECT TO LOCAL NETWORK AND ESTABLISH AUTHORITY CHAIN: DA SILVA 885-2. STANDARD RECORDING PROTOCOL.
ACCESS FILE: JOANS, JOHN. ASST MNGR 2ND CLASS. HOMESTEAD STATION, TITAN.
JOANS, I SEE YOU'RE ALMOST HALFWAY THROUGH A THREE E-YEAR ROTATION ON TITAN. THAT'S A BIT LONG, DON'T YOU THINK? HOW ARE YOU HOLDING UP? THIS LOW-G IS NO JOKE.
OH, I'M FINE, SIR.
HMM, ACCORDING TO YOUR MOST RECENT CHECK-UP, YOUR MUSCLE MASS HAS DECLINED 8% FROM WHEN YOU ARRIVED. I DON'T LIKE IT. MAKE SURE YOU DON'T SKIP ANY MORE GYM SESSIONS, ASST MNGR.
ER... OF COURSE, SIR.
WHY SUCH A LONG CONTRACT, JOANS?
W-WELL, SIR, YOU MUST HAVE BEEN AN ASST MNGR, ONCE.
I G-GO WHERE THEY TELL ME TO GO. BUT YOU KNOW, IT'S G-GREAT EXPERIENCE. IF I PLAY MY CARDS RIGHT, I'LL GET A PROMOTION TO FULL MNGR. MAYBE A POSTING BACK ON TERRA.

CARACA! THREE E-YEARS... THANK GOD I'VE ONLY GOT SIX E-MONTHS BEFORE I SHIP BACK HOME TO TERRA.

AND WITH ANY LUCK, THIS WILL BE MY LAST OFF-WORLD POSTING.

THAT'S THE SPIRIT, JOANS. WELL, SHALL WE HEAD IN?

AH, OF COURSE, SIR.

A-ACTUALLY THE HEAD OF THE TITAN UNION WANTED TO MEET YOU RIGHT AWAY.

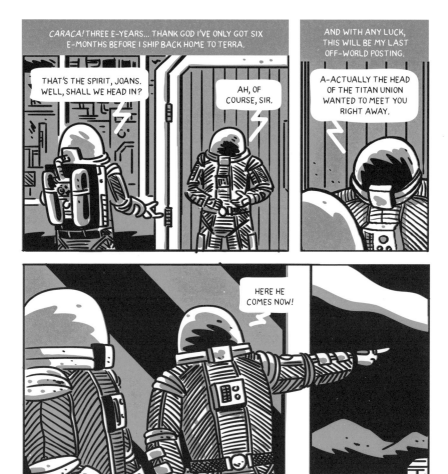

HERE HE COMES NOW!

I'M NO STRANGER TO THIS WORK. I'M A FULL MNGR 2ND CLASS. AN EXPERT ON PRODUCTIVITY. I'VE WORKED AT OR VISITED DOZENS OF THESE OFF-WORLD FACILITIES OVER THE YEARS.

I KNOW ALL ABOUT THE TITANS. THE DESCENDANTS OF GENETICALLY MODIFIED COLONISTS WHO WERE ALTERED TO WORK IN HARSH, LOW-GRAVITY CONDITIONS.

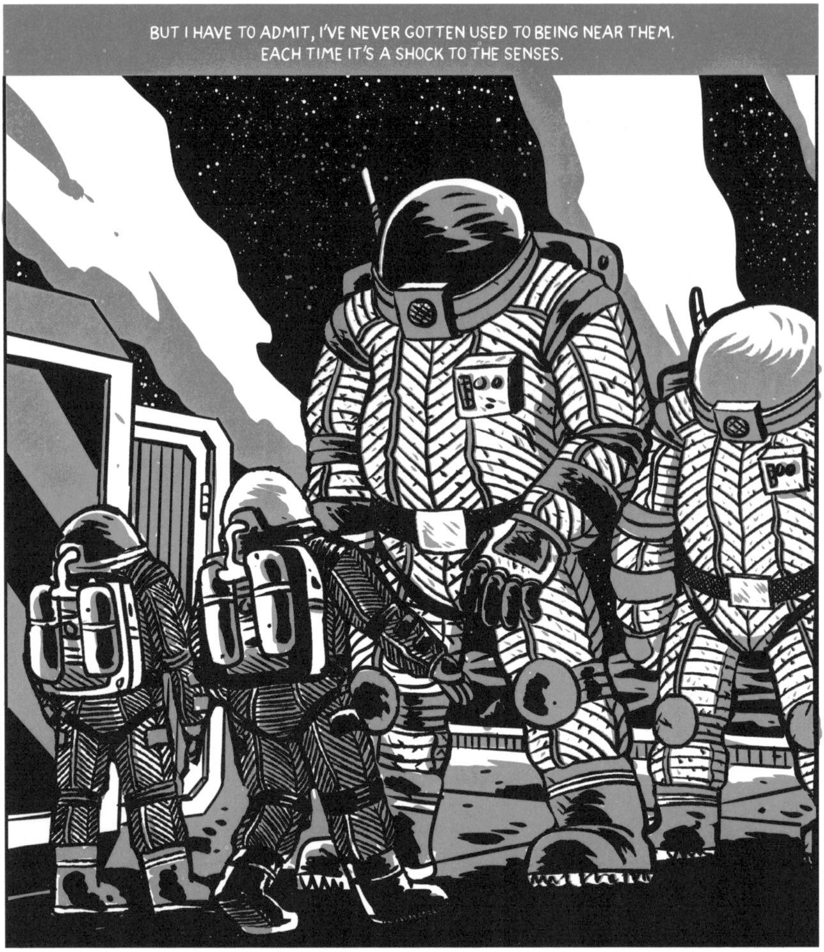
BUT I HAVE TO ADMIT, I'VE NEVER GOTTEN USED TO BEING NEAR THEM. EACH TIME IT'S A SHOCK TO THE SENSES.

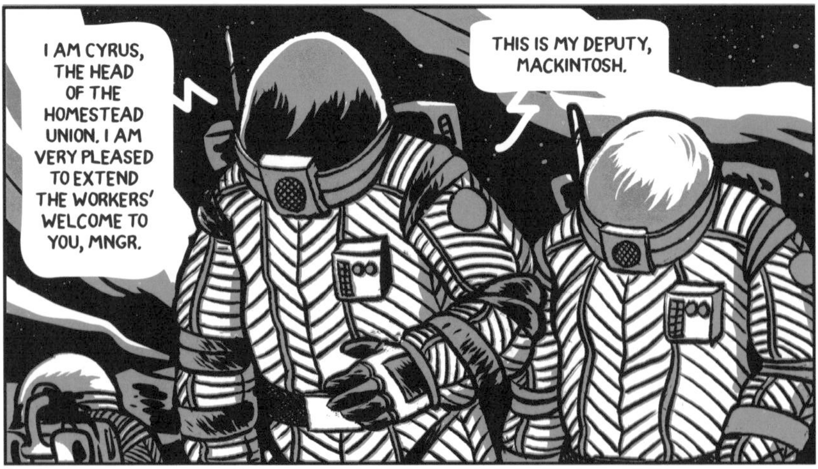
I AM CYRUS, THE HEAD OF THE HOMESTEAD UNION. I AM VERY PLEASED TO EXTEND THE WORKERS' WELCOME TO YOU, MNGR.
THIS IS MY DEPUTY, MACKINTOSH.

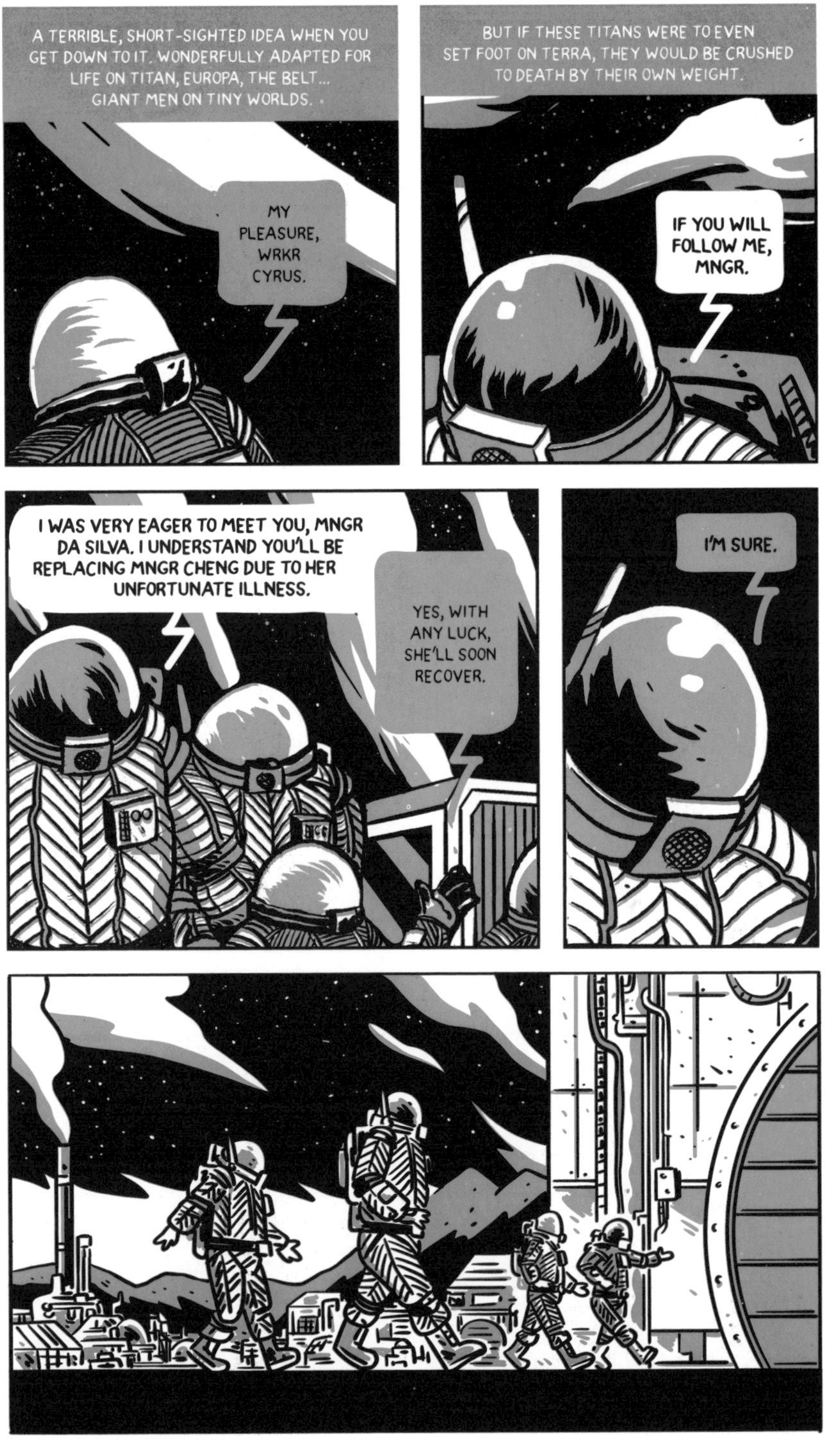
A TERRIBLE, SHORT-SIGHTED IDEA WHEN YOU GET DOWN TO IT. WONDERFULLY ADAPTED FOR LIFE ON TITAN, EUROPA, THE BELT... GIANT MEN ON TINY WORLDS.
MY PLEASURE, WRKR CYRUS.
BUT IF THESE TITANS WERE TO EVEN SET FOOT ON TERRA, THEY WOULD BE CRUSHED TO DEATH BY THEIR OWN WEIGHT.
IF YOU WILL FOLLOW ME, MNGR.
I WAS VERY EAGER TO MEET YOU, MNGR DA SILVA. I UNDERSTAND YOU'LL BE REPLACING MNGR CHENG DUE TO HER UNFORTUNATE ILLNESS.
YES, WITH ANY LUCK, SHE'LL SOON RECOVER.
I'M SURE.

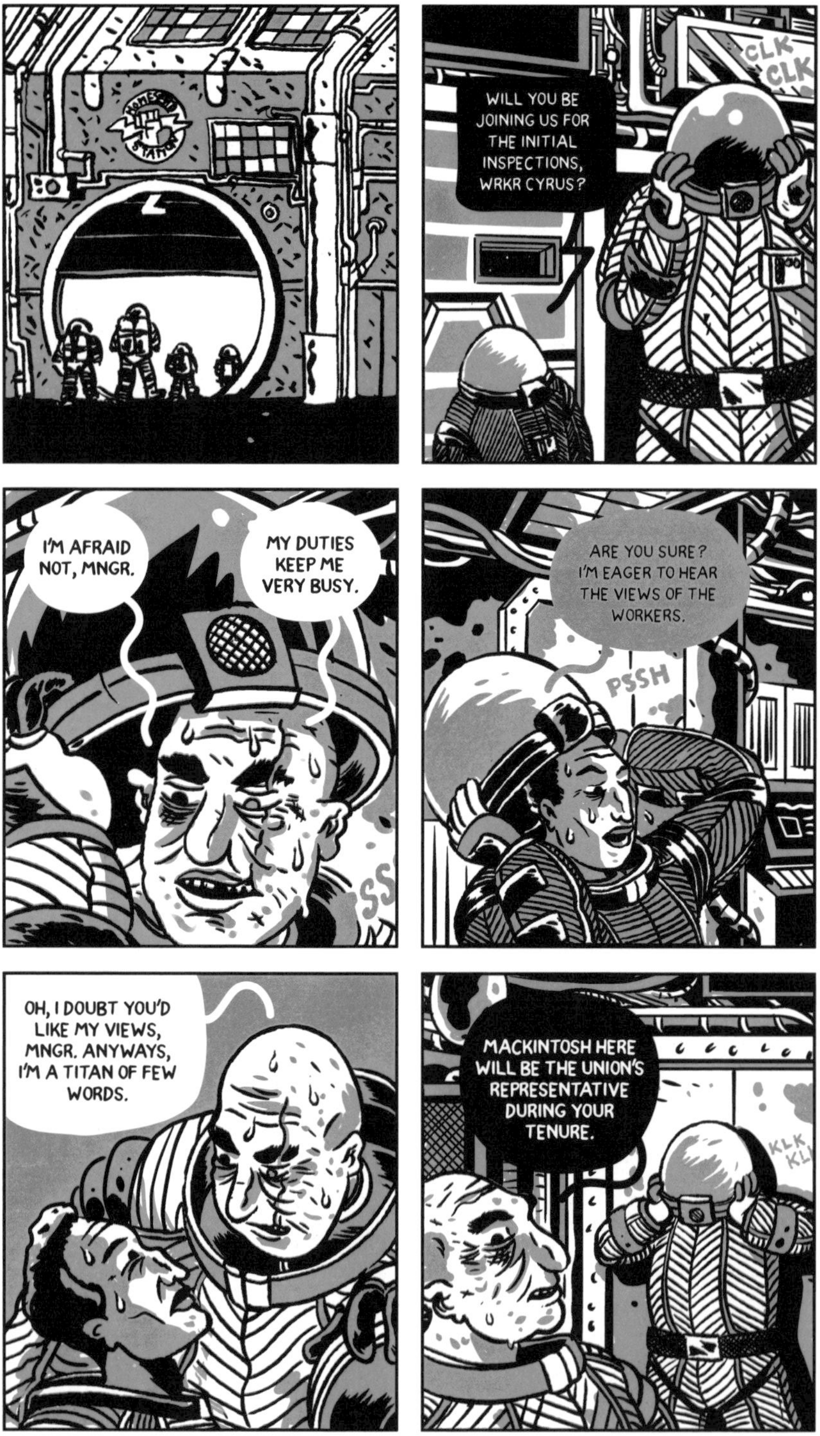
CLK CLK
WILL YOU BE JOINING US FOR THE INITIAL INSPECTIONS, WRKR CYRUS?
I'M AFRAID NOT, MNGR.
MY DUTIES KEEP ME VERY BUSY.
ARE YOU SURE? I'M EAGER TO HEAR THE VIEWS OF THE WORKERS.
PSSH
OH, I DOUBT YOU'D LIKE MY VIEWS, MNGR. ANYWAYS, I'M A TITAN OF FEW WORDS.
MACKINTOSH HERE WILL BE THE UNION'S REPRESENTATIVE DURING YOUR TENURE.
KLK

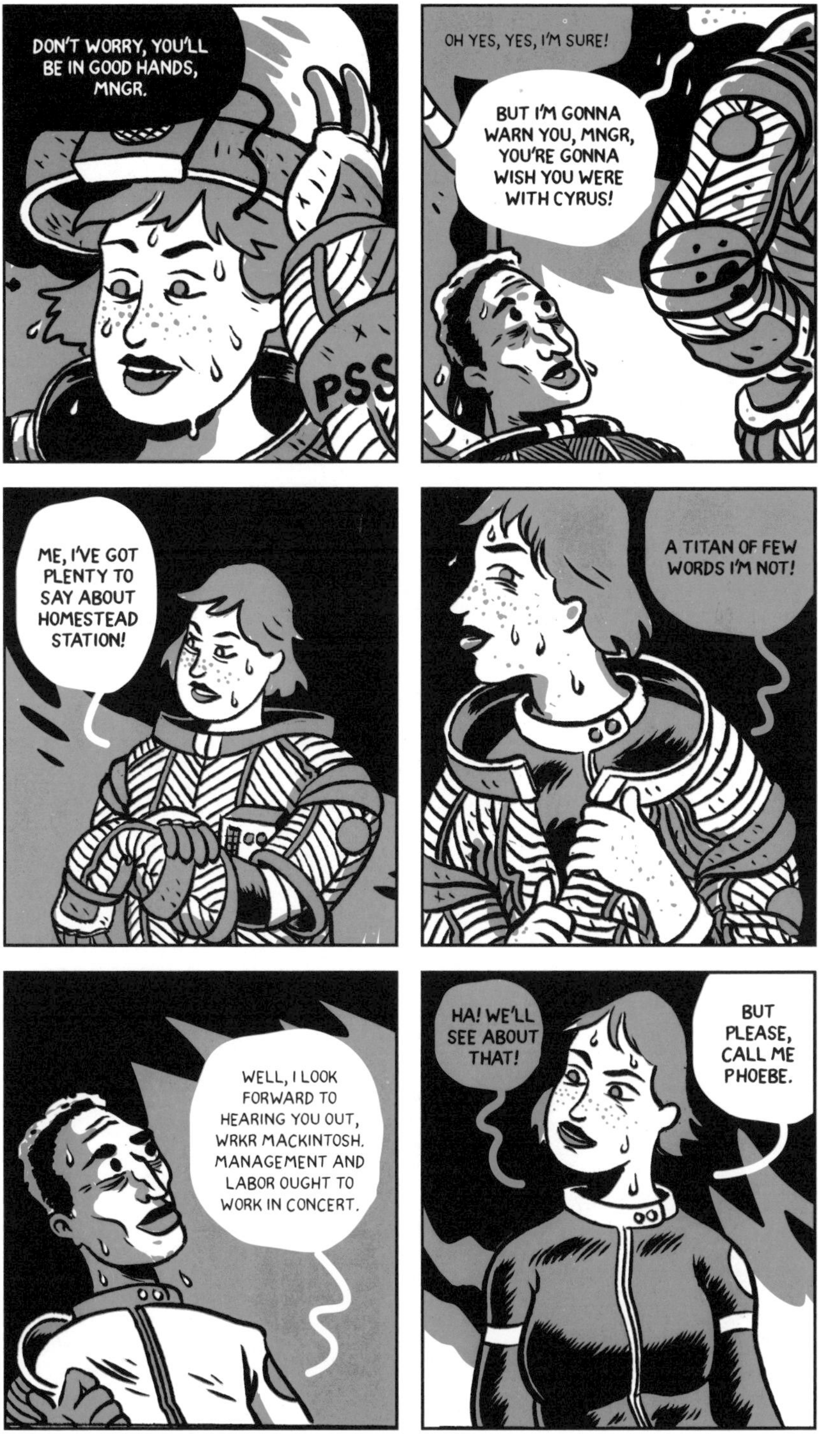
DON'T WORRY, YOU'LL BE IN GOOD HANDS, MNGR.
PSS
OH YES, YES, I'M SURE!
BUT I'M GONNA WARN YOU, MNGR, YOU'RE GONNA WISH YOU WERE WITH CYRUS!
ME, I'VE GOT PLENTY TO SAY ABOUT HOMESTEAD STATION!
A TITAN OF FEW WORDS I'M NOT!
WELL, I LOOK FORWARD TO HEARING YOU OUT, WRKR MACKINTOSH. MANAGEMENT AND LABOR OUGHT TO WORK IN CONCERT.
HA! WE'LL SEE ABOUT THAT!
BUT PLEASE, CALL ME PHOEBE.

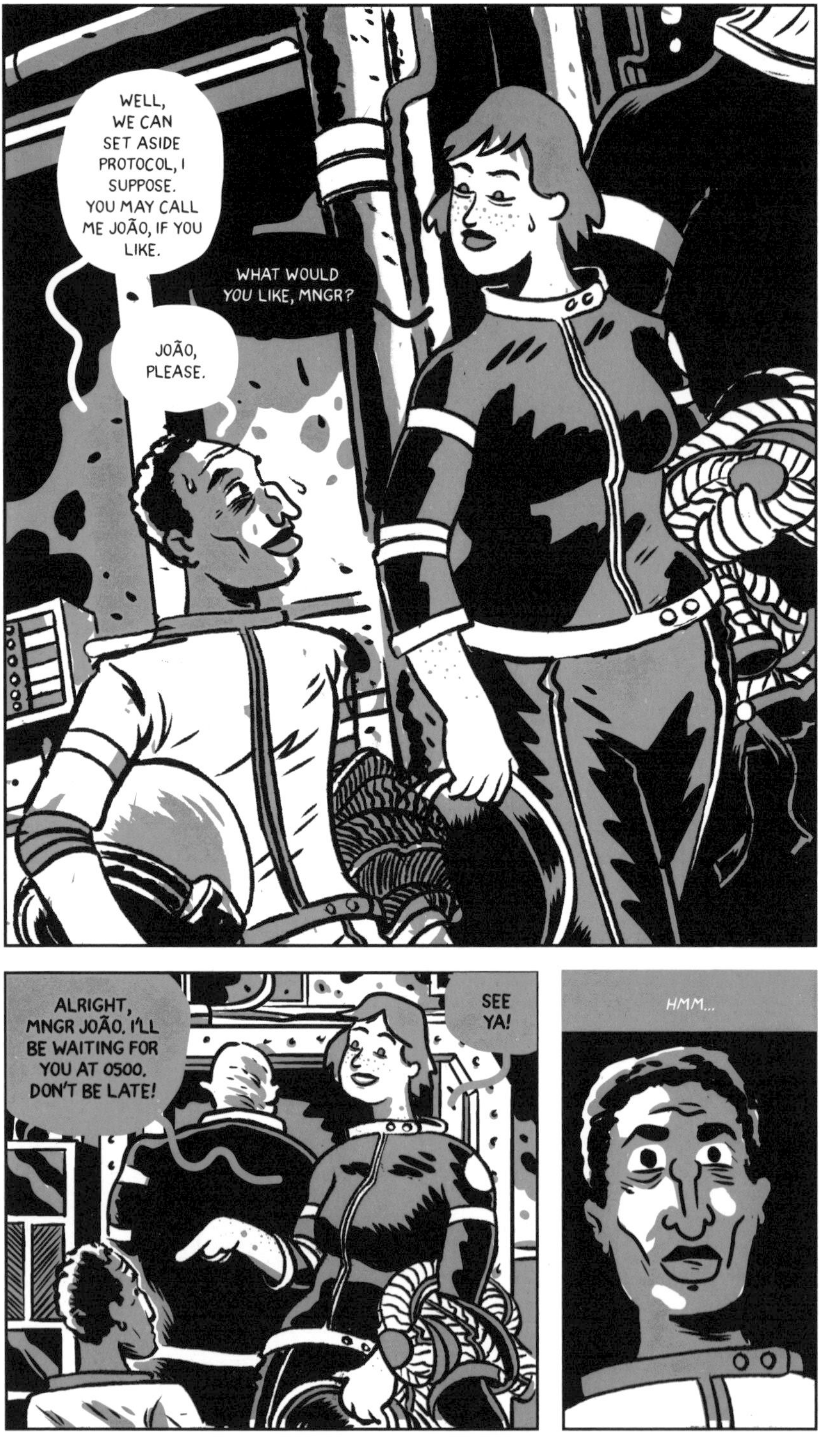
WELL, WE CAN SET ASIDE PROTOCOL, I SUPPOSE. YOU MAY CALL ME JOÃO, IF YOU LIKE.
WHAT WOULD YOU LIKE, MNGR?
JOÃO, PLEASE.
ALRIGHT, MNGR JOÃO. I'LL BE WAITING FOR YOU AT 0500. DON'T BE LATE!
SEE YA!
HMM...

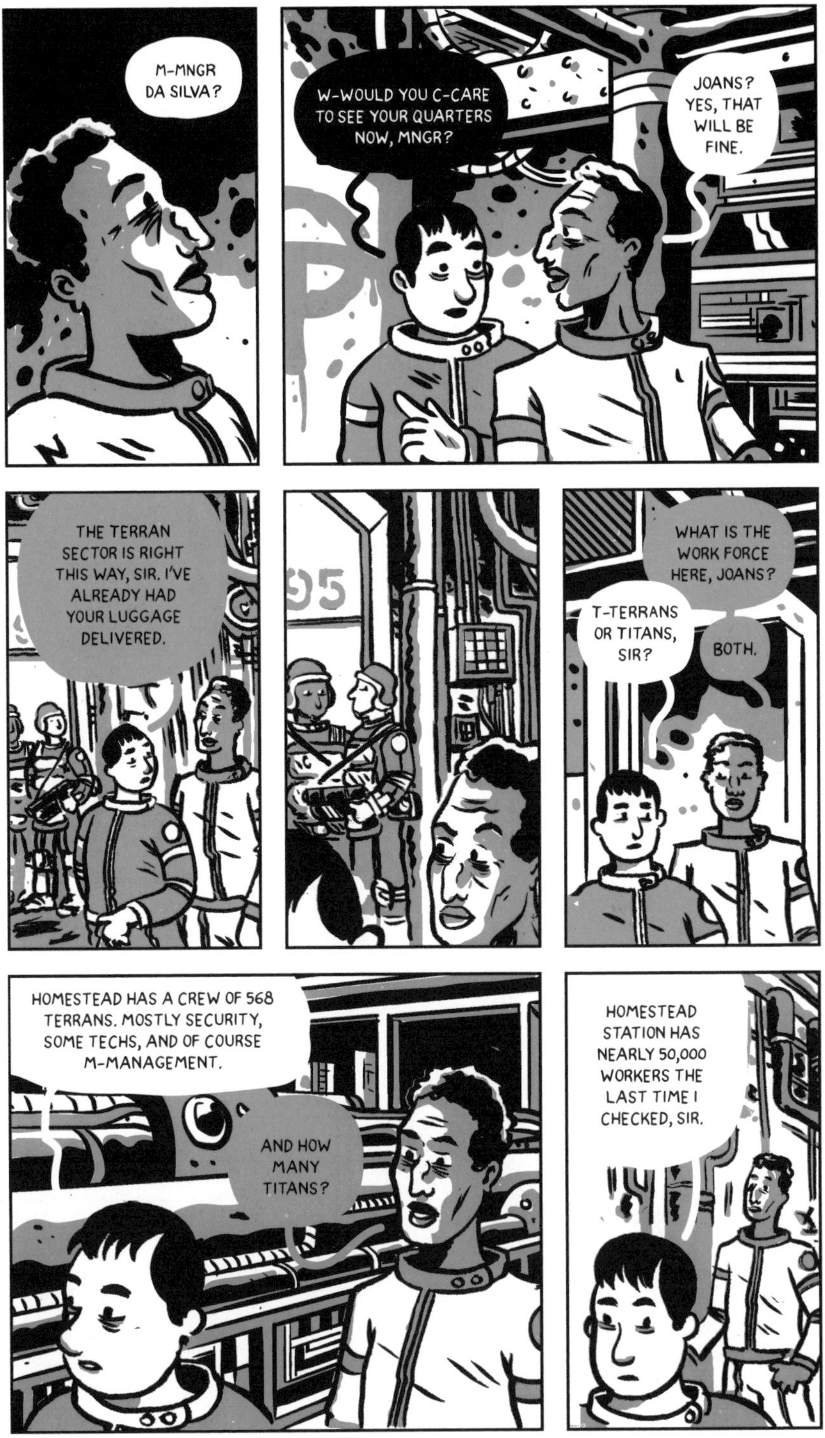
M-MNGR DA SILVA?
W-WOULD YOU C-CARE TO SEE YOUR QUARTERS NOW, MNGR?
JOANS? YES, THAT WILL BE FINE.
THE TERRAN SECTOR IS RIGHT THIS WAY, SIR. I'VE ALREADY HAD YOUR LUGGAGE DELIVERED.
95
WHAT IS THE WORK FORCE HERE, JOANS?
T-TERRANS OR TITANS, SIR?
BOTH.
HOMESTEAD HAS A CREW OF 568 TERRANS. MOSTLY SECURITY, SOME TECHS, AND OF COURSE M-MANAGEMENT.
AND HOW MANY TITANS?
HOMESTEAD STATION HAS NEARLY 50,000 WORKERS THE LAST TIME I CHECKED, SIR.

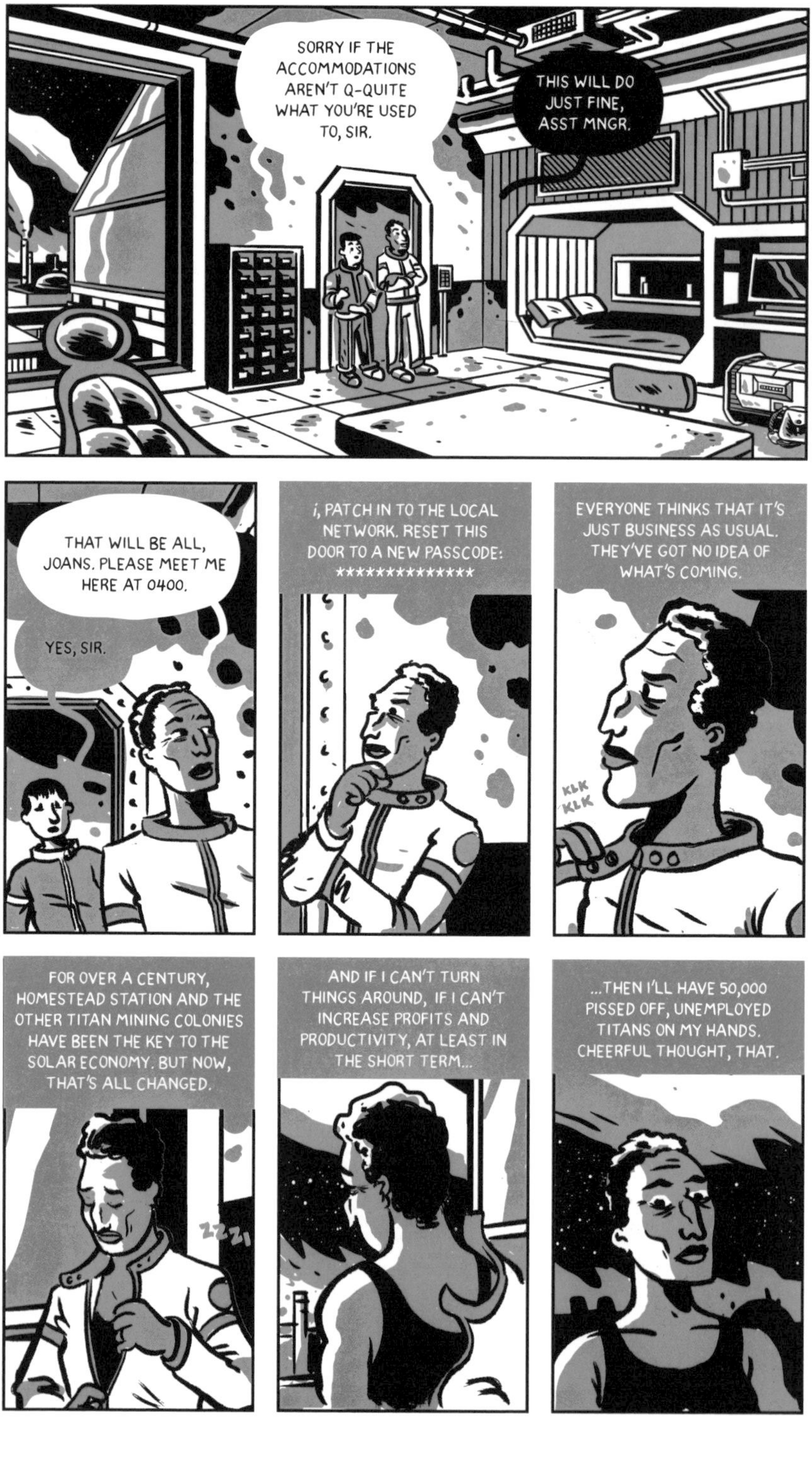
SORRY IF THE ACCOMMODATIONS AREN'T Q-QUITE WHAT YOU'RE USED TO, SIR.
THIS WILL DO JUST FINE, ASST MNGR.
THAT WILL BE ALL, JOANS. PLEASE MEET ME HERE AT 0400.
YES, SIR.
i, PATCH IN TO THE LOCAL NETWORK. RESET THIS DOOR TO A NEW PASSCODE: **************
EVERYONE THINKS THAT IT'S JUST BUSINESS AS USUAL. THEY'VE GOT NO IDEA OF WHAT'S COMING.
KLK KLK
FOR OVER A CENTURY, HOMESTEAD STATION AND THE OTHER TITAN MINING COLONIES HAVE BEEN THE KEY TO THE SOLAR ECONOMY. BUT NOW, THAT'S ALL CHANGED.
ZZZZ
AND IF I CAN'T TURN THINGS AROUND, IF I CAN'T INCREASE PROFITS AND PRODUCTIVITY, AT LEAST IN THE SHORT TERM...
...THEN I'LL HAVE 50,000 PISSED OFF, UNEMPLOYED TITANS ON MY HANDS. CHEERFUL THOUGHT, THAT.

PART 02: 99 PROBLEMS

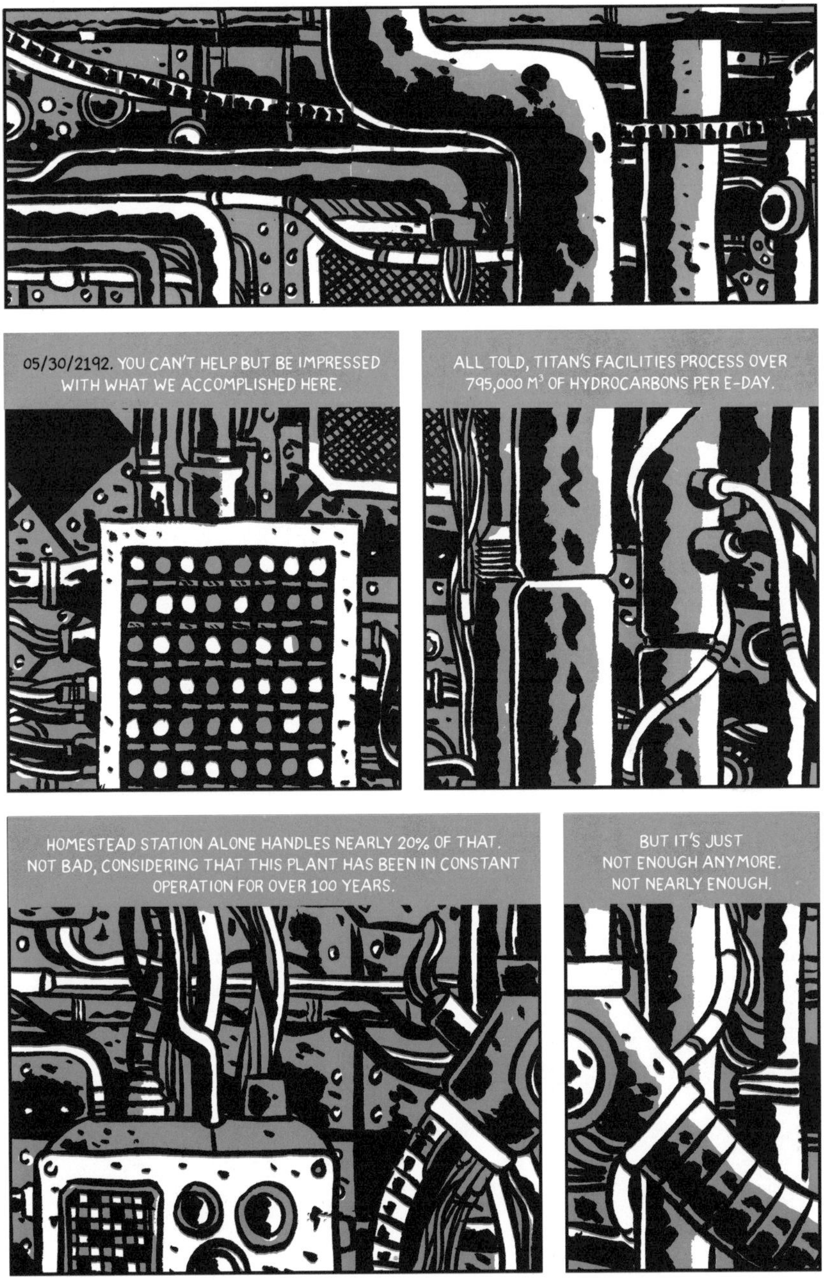

05/30/2192. YOU CAN'T HELP BUT BE IMPRESSED WITH WHAT WE ACCOMPLISHED HERE.

ALL TOLD, TITAN'S FACILITIES PROCESS OVER 795,000 M³ OF HYDROCARBONS PER E-DAY.

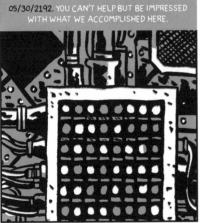

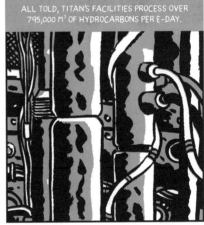

HOMESTEAD STATION ALONE HANDLES NEARLY 20% OF THAT. NOT BAD, CONSIDERING THAT THIS PLANT HAS BEEN IN CONSTANT OPERATION FOR OVER 100 YEARS.

BUT IT'S JUST NOT ENOUGH ANYMORE. NOT NEARLY ENOUGH.

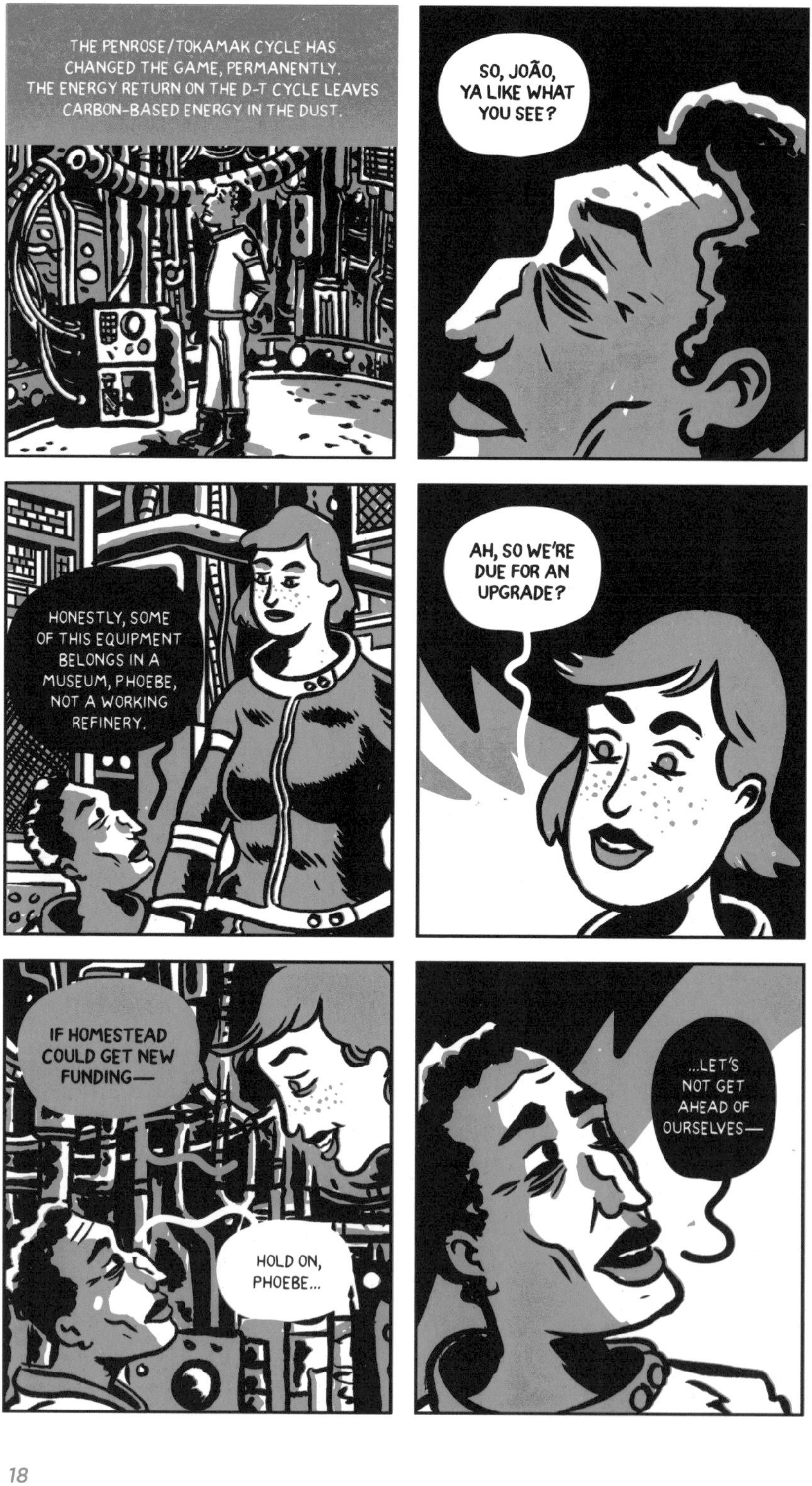
THE PENROSE/TOKAMAK CYCLE HAS CHANGED THE GAME, PERMANENTLY. THE ENERGY RETURN ON THE D-T CYCLE LEAVES CARBON-BASED ENERGY IN THE DUST.
SO, JOÃO, YA LIKE WHAT YOU SEE?
HONESTLY, SOME OF THIS EQUIPMENT BELONGS IN A MUSEUM, PHOEBE, NOT A WORKING REFINERY.
AH, SO WE'RE DUE FOR AN UPGRADE?
IF HOMESTEAD COULD GET NEW FUNDING—
HOLD ON, PHOEBE...
...LET'S NOT GET AHEAD OF OURSELVES—

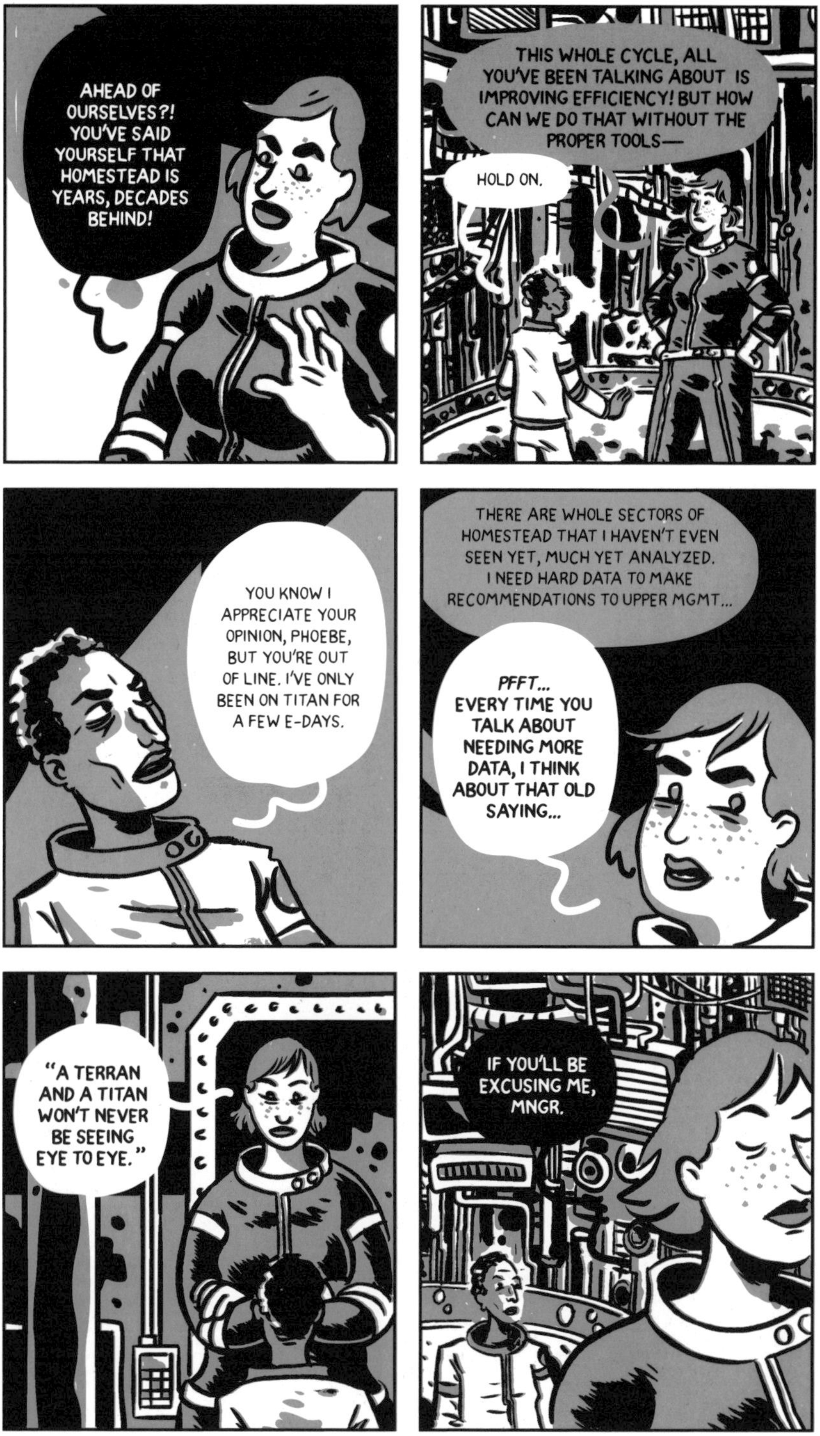
AHEAD OF OURSELVES?! YOU'VE SAID YOURSELF THAT HOMESTEAD IS YEARS, DECADES BEHIND!
THIS WHOLE CYCLE, ALL YOU'VE BEEN TALKING ABOUT IS IMPROVING EFFICIENCY! BUT HOW CAN WE DO THAT WITHOUT THE PROPER TOOLS—
HOLD ON.
YOU KNOW I APPRECIATE YOUR OPINION, PHOEBE, BUT YOU'RE OUT OF LINE. I'VE ONLY BEEN ON TITAN FOR A FEW E-DAYS.
THERE ARE WHOLE SECTORS OF HOMESTEAD THAT I HAVEN'T EVEN SEEN YET, MUCH YET ANALYZED. I NEED HARD DATA TO MAKE RECOMMENDATIONS TO UPPER MGMT...
PFFT... EVERY TIME YOU TALK ABOUT NEEDING MORE DATA, I THINK ABOUT THAT OLD SAYING...
"A TERRAN AND A TITAN WON'T NEVER BE SEEING EYE TO EYE."
IF YOU'LL BE EXCUSING ME, MNGR.

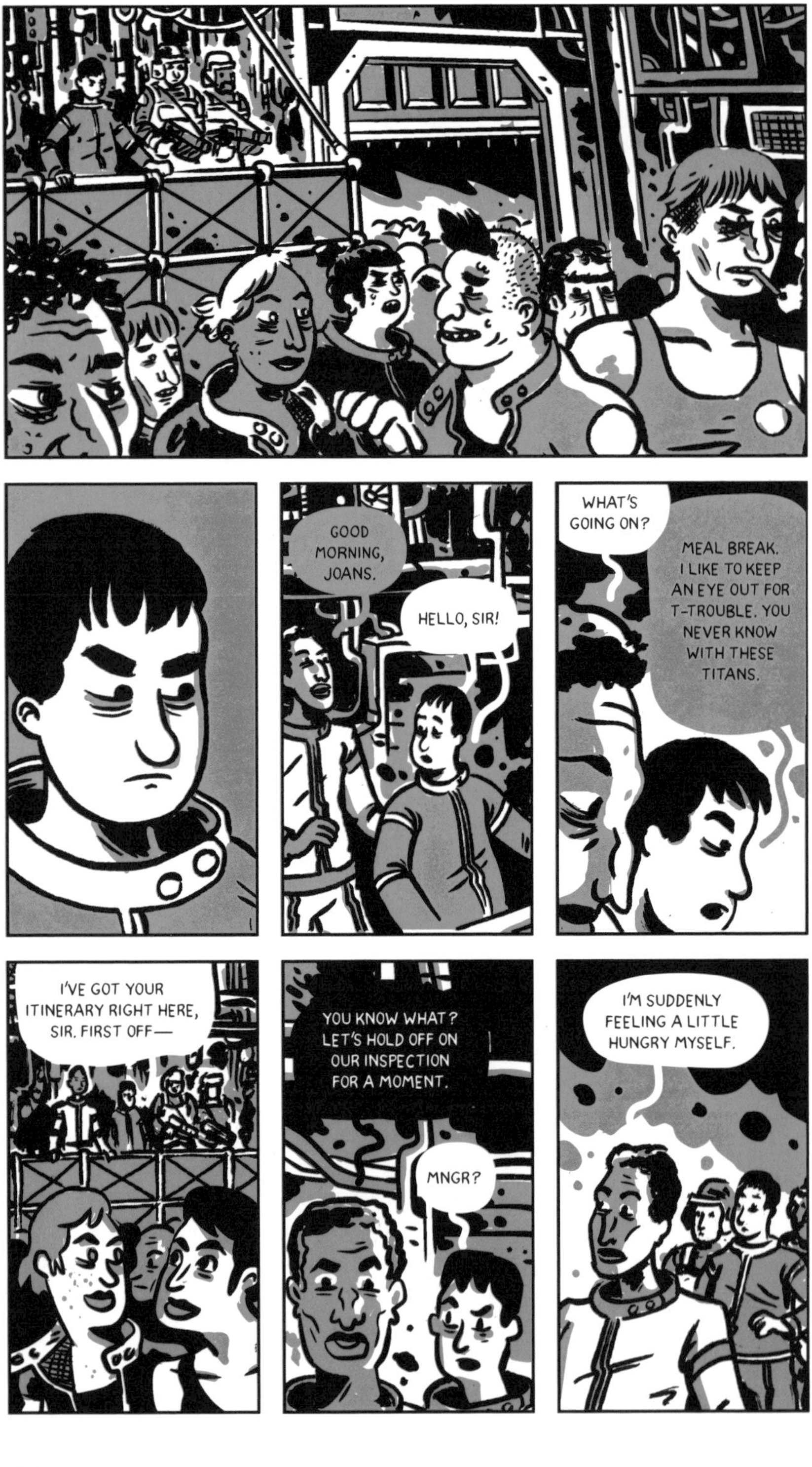
GOOD MORNING, JOANS.
HELLO, SIR!
WHAT'S GOING ON?
MEAL BREAK. I LIKE TO KEEP AN EYE OUT FOR T-TROUBLE. YOU NEVER KNOW WITH THESE TITANS.
I'VE GOT YOUR ITINERARY RIGHT HERE, SIR. FIRST OFF—
YOU KNOW WHAT? LET'S HOLD OFF ON OUR INSPECTION FOR A MOMENT.
MNGR?
I'M SUDDENLY FEELING A LITTLE HUNGRY MYSELF.

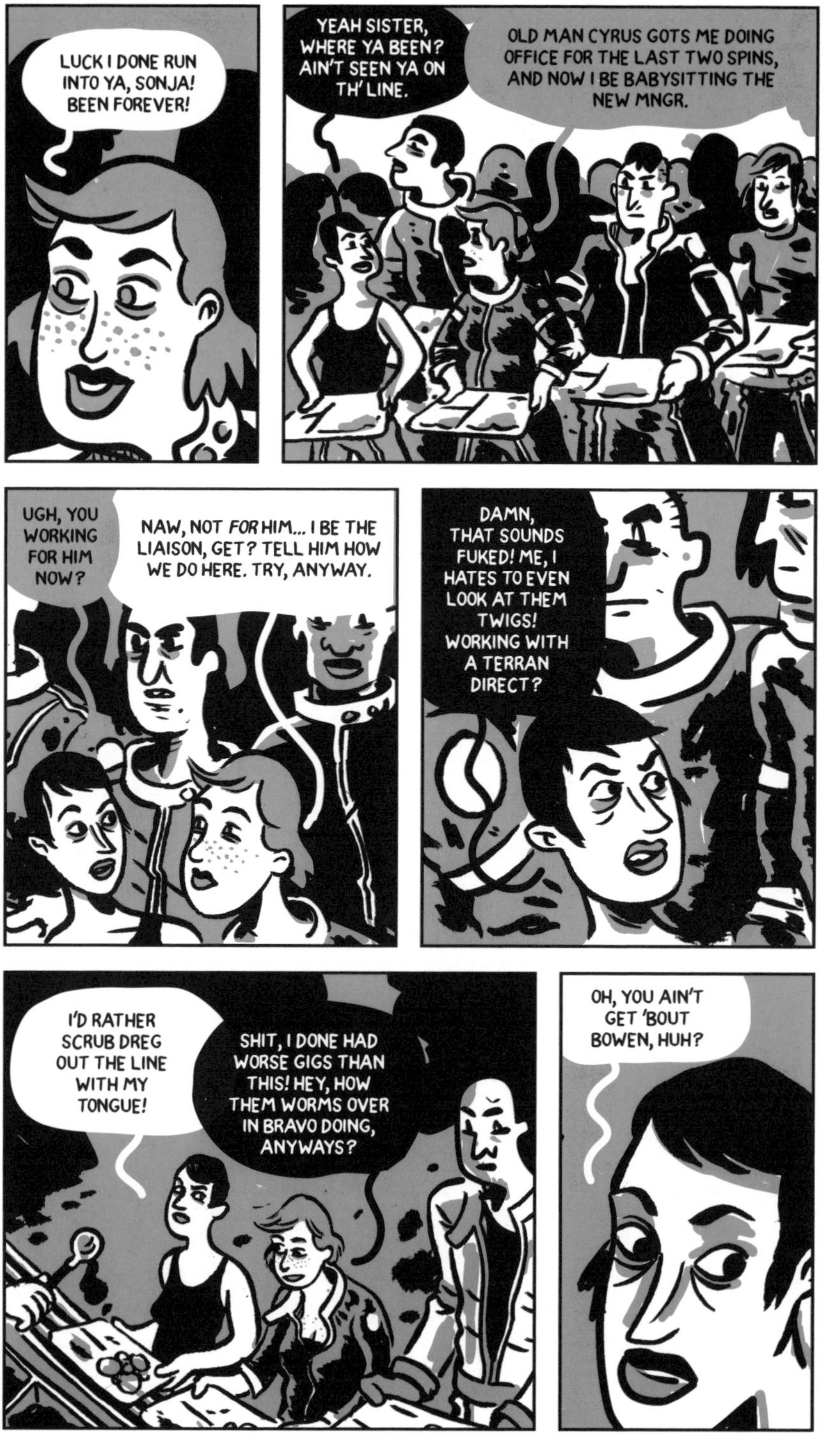
LUCK I DONE RUN INTO YA, SONJA! BEEN FOREVER!
YEAH SISTER, WHERE YA BEEN? AIN'T SEEN YA ON TH' LINE.
OLD MAN CYRUS GOTS ME DOING OFFICE FOR THE LAST TWO SPINS, AND NOW I BE BABYSITTING THE NEW MNGR.
UGH, YOU WORKING FOR HIM NOW?
NAW, NOT *FOR* HIM... I BE THE LIAISON, GET? TELL HIM HOW WE DO HERE. TRY, ANYWAY.
DAMN, THAT SOUNDS FUKED! ME, I HATES TO EVEN LOOK AT THEM TWIGS! WORKING WITH A TERRAN DIRECT?
I'D RATHER SCRUB DREG OUT THE LINE WITH MY TONGUE!
SHIT, I DONE HAD WORSE GIGS THAN THIS! HEY, HOW THEM WORMS OVER IN BRAVO DOING, ANYWAYS?
OH, YOU AIN'T GET 'BOUT BOWEN, HUH?

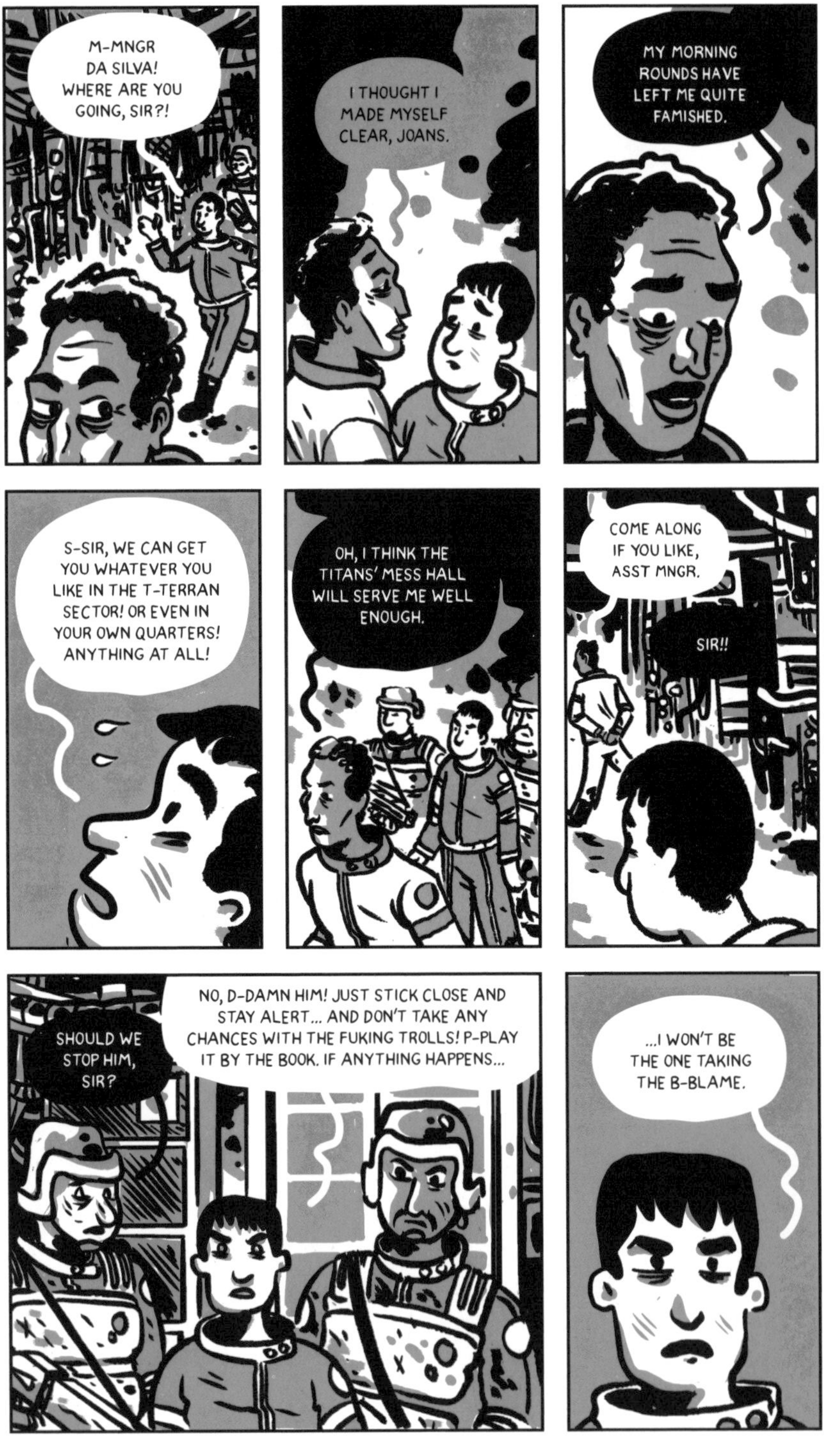
M-MNGR DA SILVA! WHERE ARE YOU GOING, SIR?!
I THOUGHT I MADE MYSELF CLEAR, JOANS.
MY MORNING ROUNDS HAVE LEFT ME QUITE FAMISHED.
S-SIR, WE CAN GET YOU WHATEVER YOU LIKE IN THE T-TERRAN SECTOR! OR EVEN IN YOUR OWN QUARTERS! ANYTHING AT ALL!
OH, I THINK THE TITANS' MESS HALL WILL SERVE ME WELL ENOUGH.
COME ALONG IF YOU LIKE, ASST MNGR.
SIR!!
SHOULD WE STOP HIM, SIR?
NO, D-DAMN HIM! JUST STICK CLOSE AND STAY ALERT... AND DON'T TAKE ANY CHANCES WITH THE FUKING TROLLS! P-PLAY IT BY THE BOOK. IF ANYTHING HAPPENS...
...I WON'T BE THE ONE TAKING THE B-BLAME.

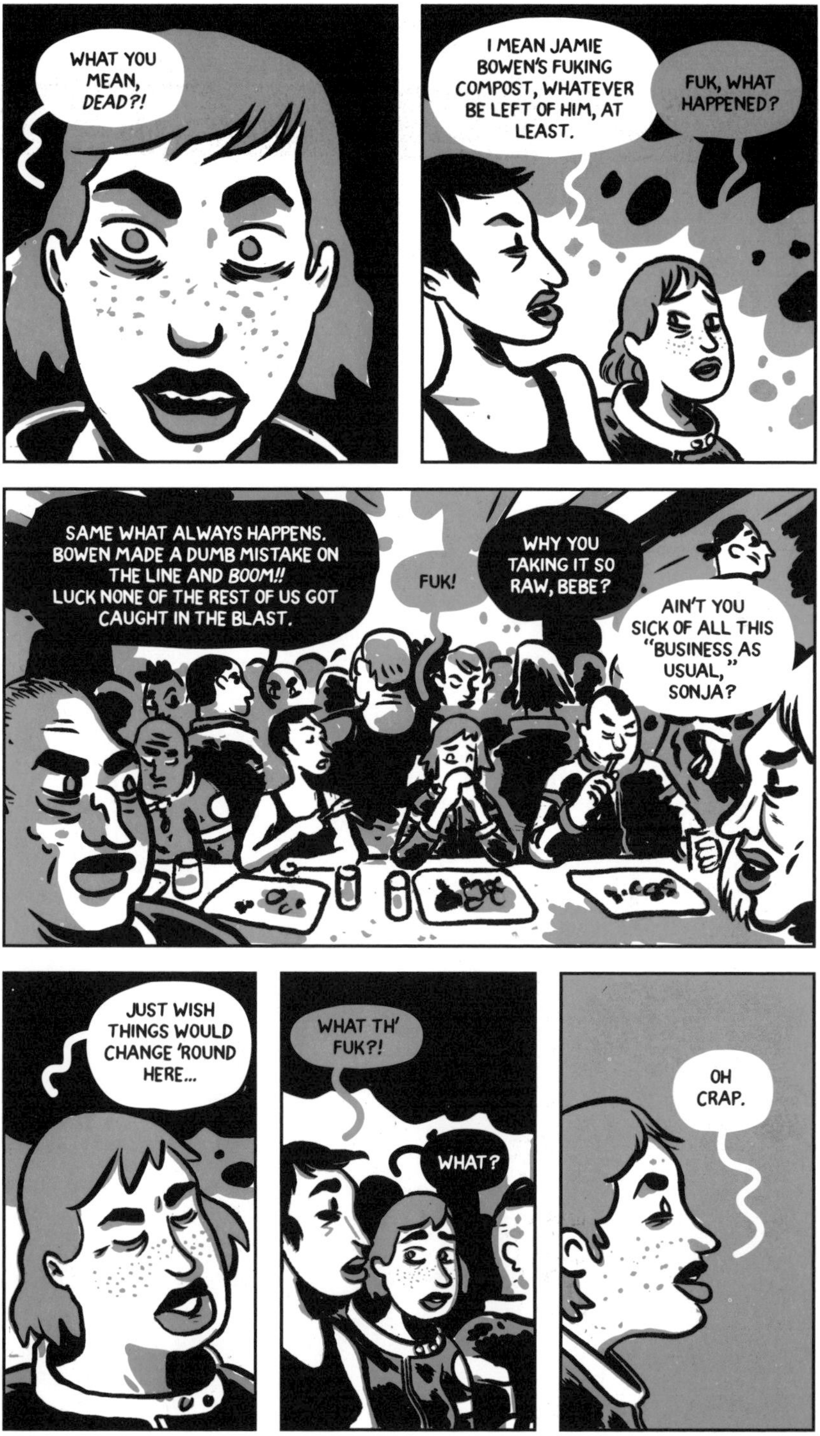
WHAT YOU MEAN, *DEAD?!*
I MEAN JAMIE BOWEN'S FUKING COMPOST, WHATEVER BE LEFT OF HIM, AT LEAST.
FUK, WHAT HAPPENED?
SAME WHAT ALWAYS HAPPENS. BOWEN MADE A DUMB MISTAKE ON THE LINE AND *BOOM!!* LUCK NONE OF THE REST OF US GOT CAUGHT IN THE BLAST.
FUK!
WHY YOU TAKING IT SO RAW, BEBE?
AIN'T YOU SICK OF ALL THIS "BUSINESS AS USUAL," SONJA?
JUST WISH THINGS WOULD CHANGE 'ROUND HERE...
WHAT TH' FUK?!
WHAT?
OH CRAP.

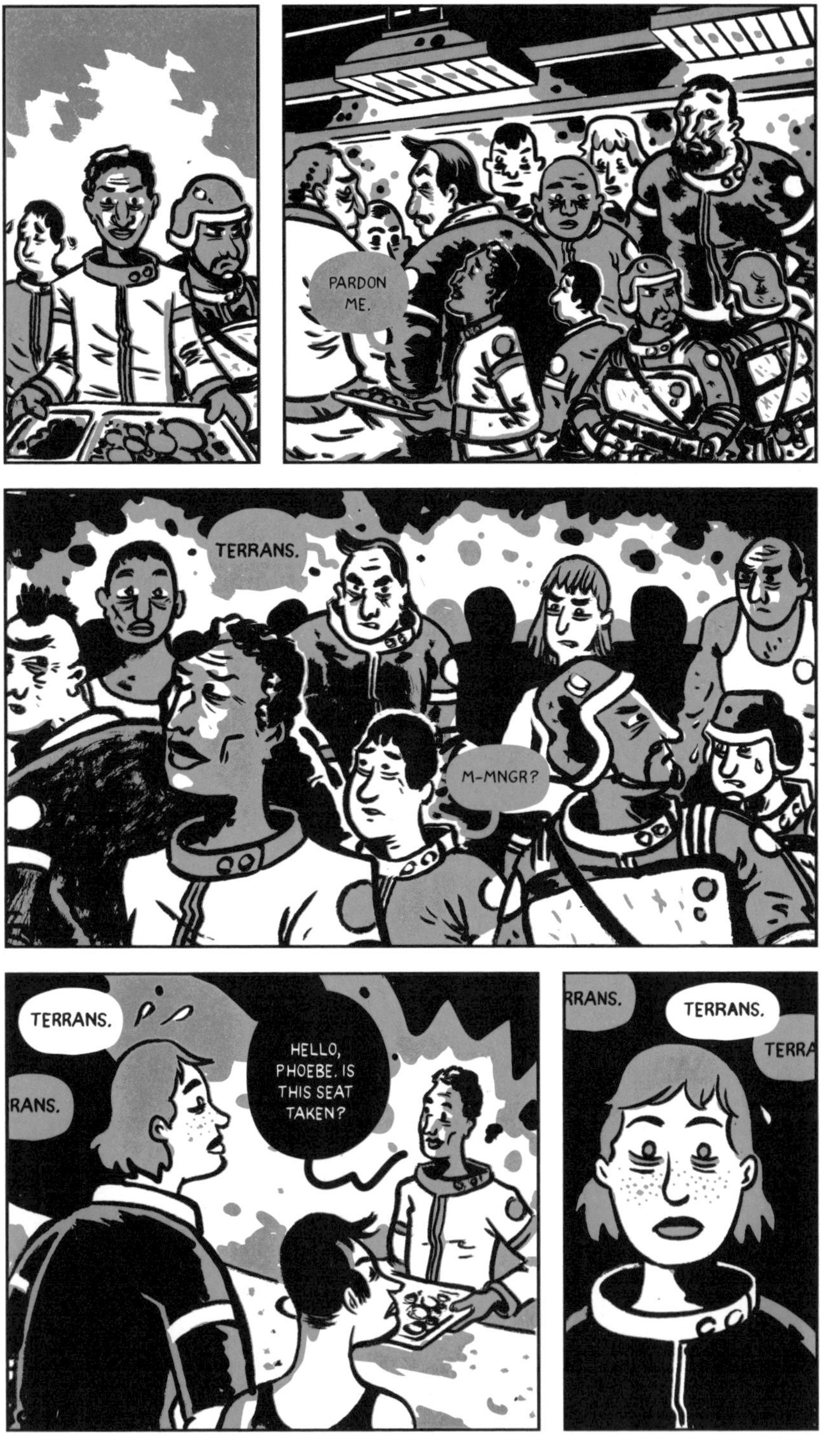
PARDON ME.
TERRANS.
M-MNGR?
TERRANS.
RANS.
HELLO, PHOEBE. IS THIS SEAT TAKEN?
RRANS.
TERRANS.
TERRA

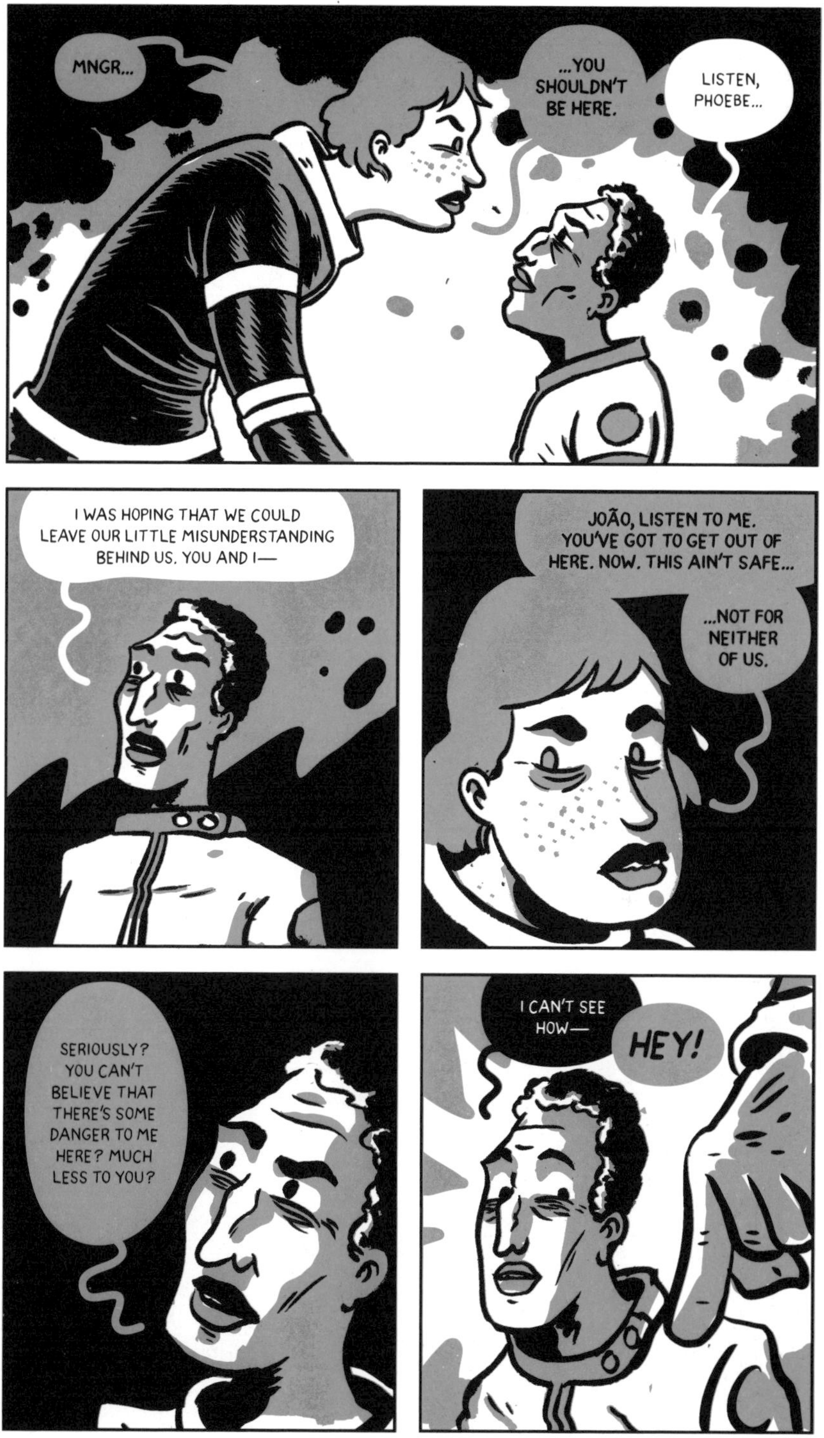
MNGR...
...YOU SHOULDN'T BE HERE.
LISTEN, PHOEBE...
I WAS HOPING THAT WE COULD LEAVE OUR LITTLE MISUNDERSTANDING BEHIND US. YOU AND I—
JOÃO, LISTEN TO ME. YOU'VE GOT TO GET OUT OF HERE. NOW. THIS AIN'T SAFE...
...NOT FOR NEITHER OF US.
SERIOUSLY? YOU CAN'T BELIEVE THAT THERE'S SOME DANGER TO ME HERE? MUCH LESS TO YOU?
I CAN'T SEE HOW—
HEY!

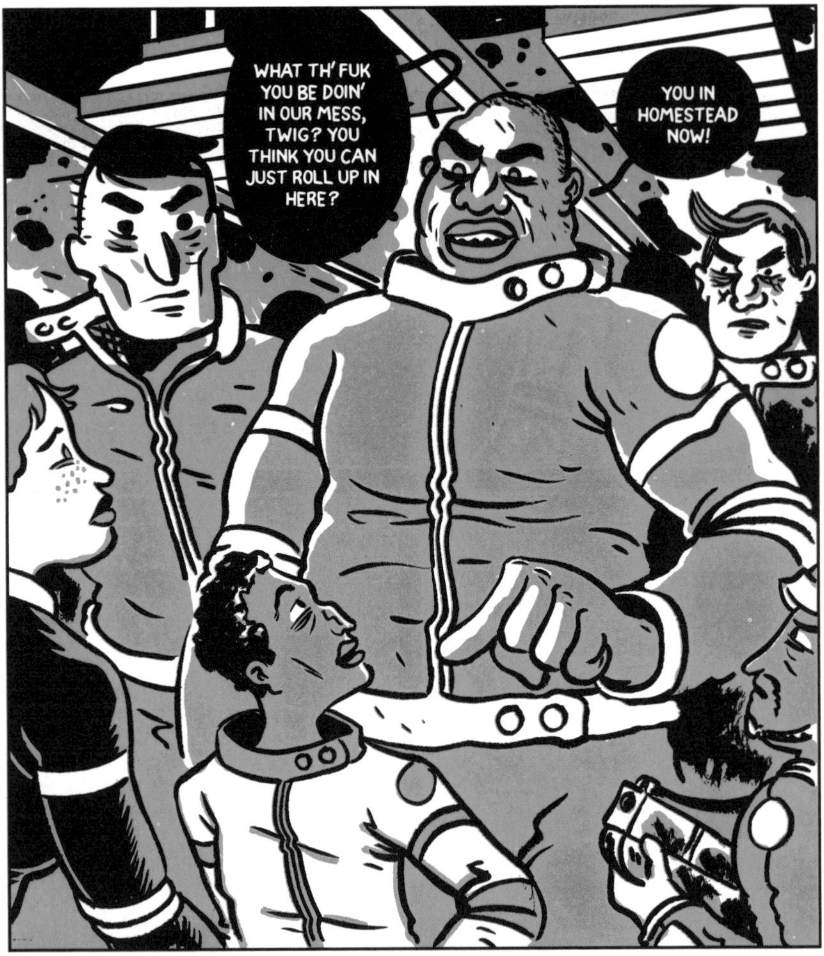
WHAT TH' FUK YOU BE DOIN' IN OUR MESS, TWIG? YOU THINK YOU CAN JUST ROLL UP IN HERE?
YOU IN HOMESTEAD NOW!

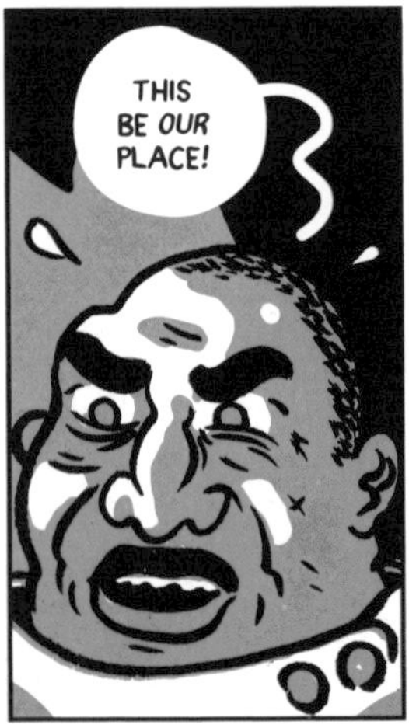
THIS BE *OUR* PLACE!

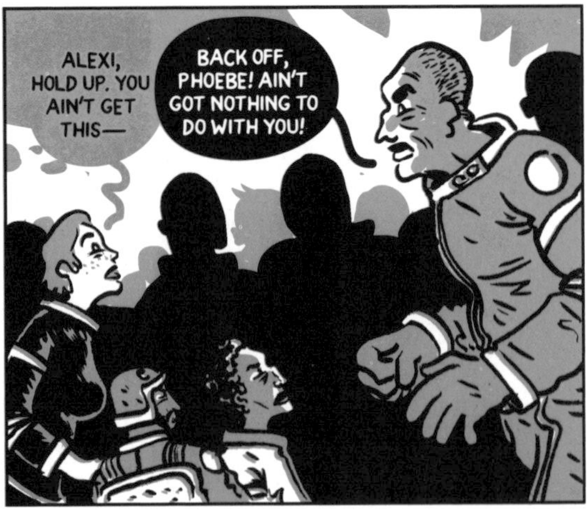
ALEXI, HOLD UP. YOU AIN'T GET THIS—
BACK OFF, PHOEBE! AIN'T GOT NOTHING TO DO WITH YOU!

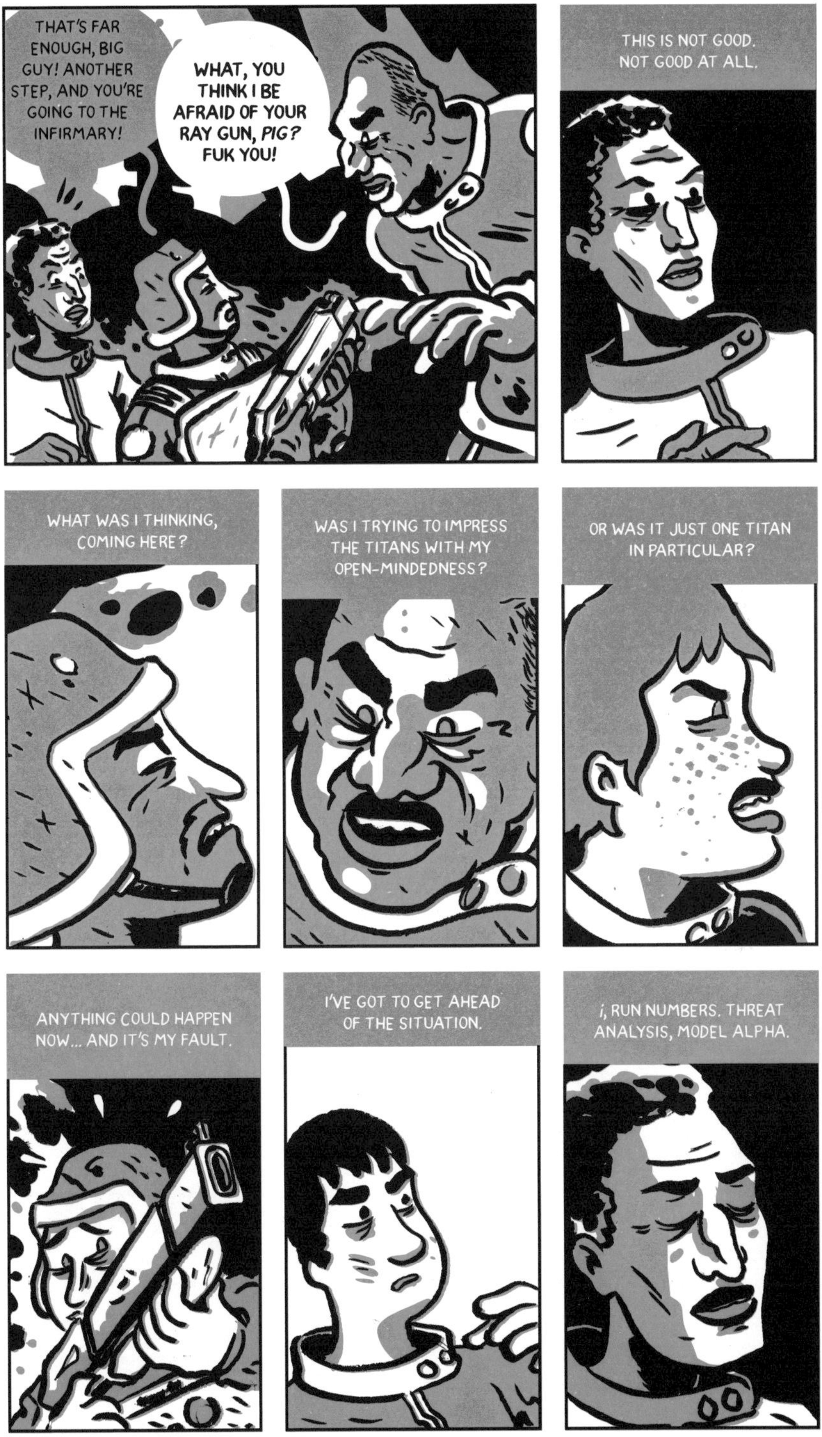
THAT'S FAR ENOUGH, BIG GUY! ANOTHER STEP, AND YOU'RE GOING TO THE INFIRMARY!
WHAT, YOU THINK I BE AFRAID OF YOUR RAY GUN, *PIG?* FUK YOU!
THIS IS NOT GOOD. NOT GOOD AT ALL.
WHAT WAS I THINKING, COMING HERE?
WAS I TRYING TO IMPRESS THE TITANS WITH MY OPEN-MINDEDNESS?
OR WAS IT JUST ONE TITAN IN PARTICULAR?
ANYTHING COULD HAPPEN NOW... AND IT'S MY FAULT.
I'VE GOT TO GET AHEAD OF THE SITUATION.
i, RUN NUMBERS. THREAT ANALYSIS, MODEL ALPHA.

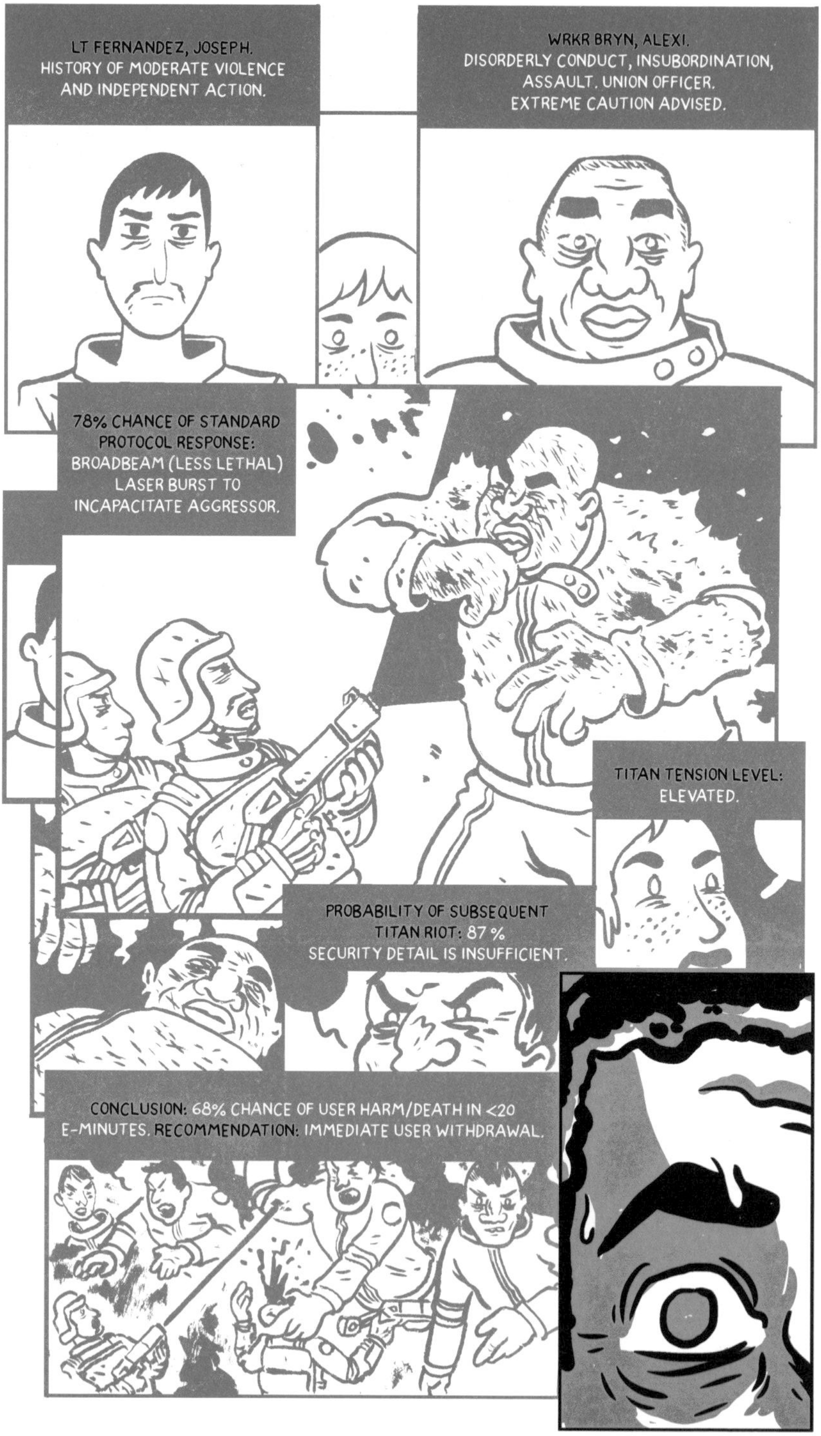
LT FERNANDEZ, JOSEPH.
HISTORY OF MODERATE VIOLENCE AND INDEPENDENT ACTION.
WRKR BRYN, ALEXI.
DISORDERLY CONDUCT, INSUBORDINATION, ASSAULT. UNION OFFICER.
EXTREME CAUTION ADVISED.
78% CHANCE OF STANDARD PROTOCOL RESPONSE: BROADBEAM (LESS LETHAL) LASER BURST TO INCAPACITATE AGGRESSOR.
TITAN TENSION LEVEL: ELEVATED.
PROBABILITY OF SUBSEQUENT TITAN RIOT: 87 %
SECURITY DETAIL IS INSUFFICIENT.
CONCLUSION: 68% CHANCE OF USER HARM/DEATH IN <20 E-MINUTES. RECOMMENDATION: IMMEDIATE USER WITHDRAWAL.

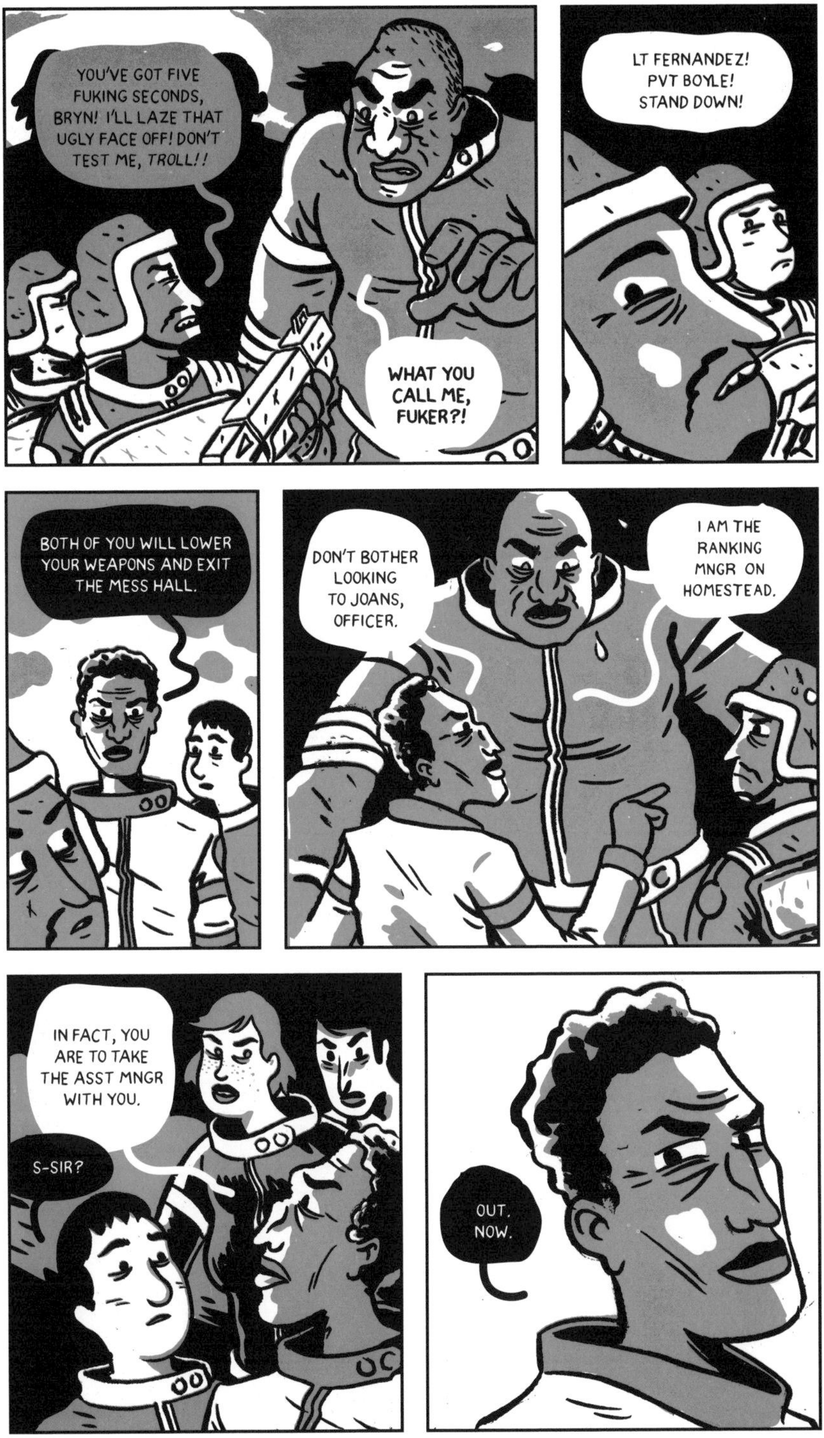
YOU'VE GOT FIVE FUKING SECONDS, BRYN! I'LL LAZE THAT UGLY FACE OFF! DON'T TEST ME, TROLL!!
WHAT YOU CALL ME, FUKER?!
LT FERNANDEZ! PVT BOYLE! STAND DOWN!
BOTH OF YOU WILL LOWER YOUR WEAPONS AND EXIT THE MESS HALL.
I AM THE RANKING MNGR ON HOMESTEAD.
DON'T BOTHER LOOKING TO JOANS, OFFICER.
IN FACT, YOU ARE TO TAKE THE ASST MNGR WITH YOU.
S-SIR?
OUT. NOW.

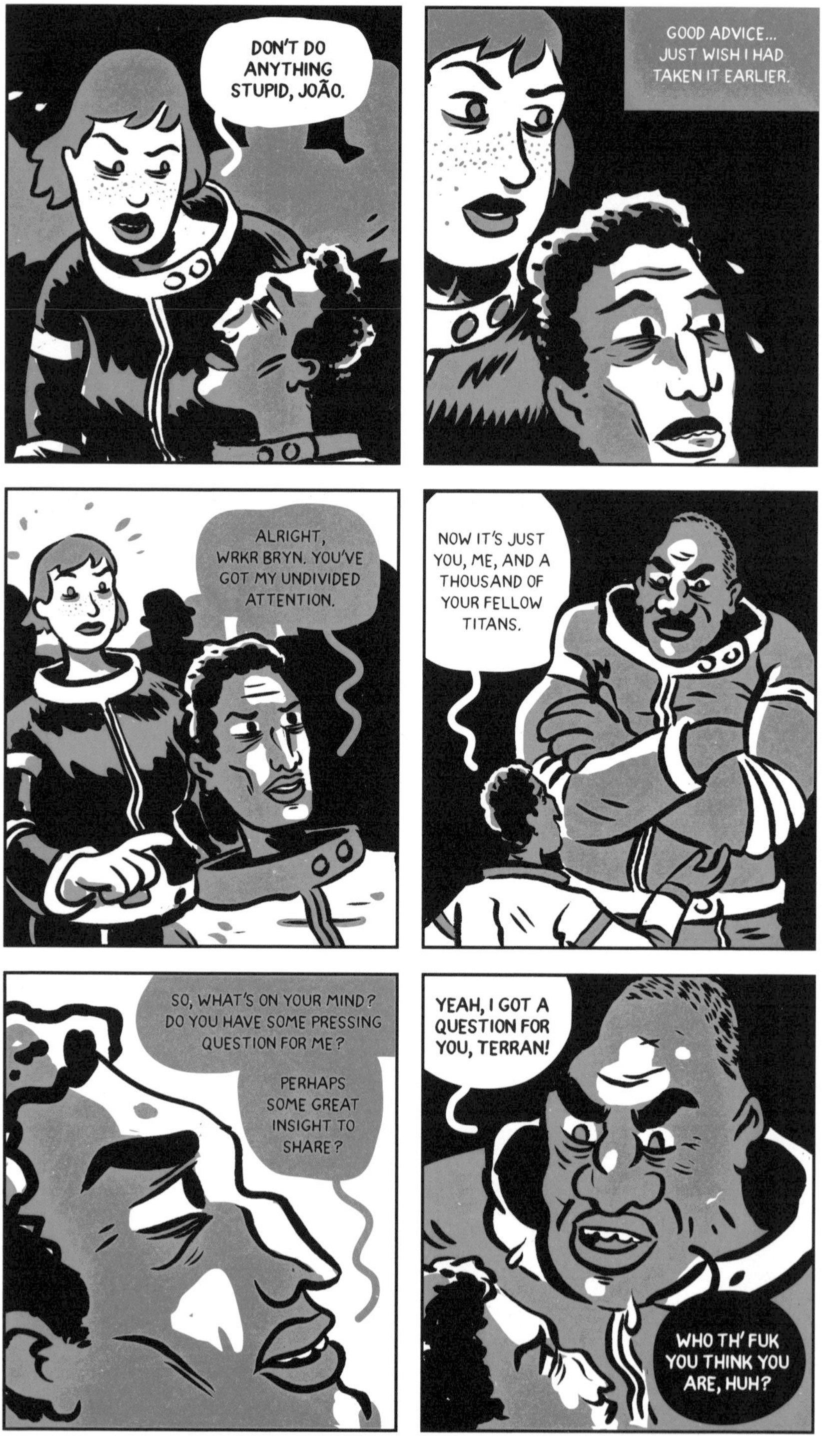
DON'T DO ANYTHING STUPID, JOÃO.
GOOD ADVICE... JUST WISH I HAD TAKEN IT EARLIER.
ALRIGHT, WRKR BRYN. YOU'VE GOT MY UNDIVIDED ATTENTION.
NOW IT'S JUST YOU, ME, AND A THOUSAND OF YOUR FELLOW TITANS.
SO, WHAT'S ON YOUR MIND? DO YOU HAVE SOME PRESSING QUESTION FOR ME?
PERHAPS SOME GREAT INSIGHT TO SHARE?
YEAH, I GOT A QUESTION FOR YOU, TERRAN!
WHO TH' FUK YOU THINK YOU ARE, HUH?

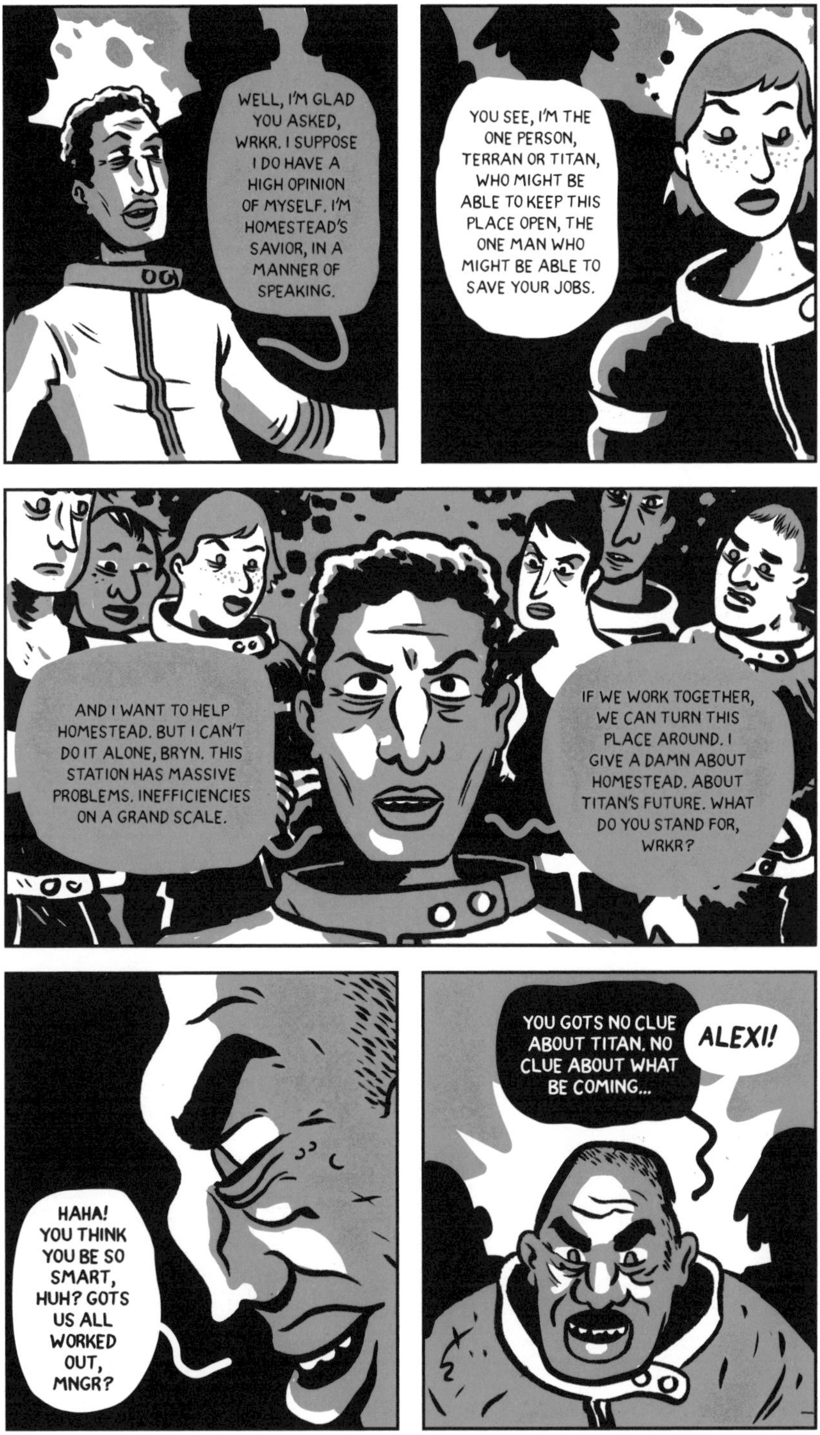
WELL, I'M GLAD YOU ASKED, WRKR. I SUPPOSE I DO HAVE A HIGH OPINION OF MYSELF. I'M HOMESTEAD'S SAVIOR, IN A MANNER OF SPEAKING.
YOU SEE, I'M THE ONE PERSON, TERRAN OR TITAN, WHO MIGHT BE ABLE TO KEEP THIS PLACE OPEN, THE ONE MAN WHO MIGHT BE ABLE TO SAVE YOUR JOBS.
AND I WANT TO HELP HOMESTEAD. BUT I CAN'T DO IT ALONE, BRYN. THIS STATION HAS MASSIVE PROBLEMS. INEFFICIENCIES ON A GRAND SCALE.
IF WE WORK TOGETHER, WE CAN TURN THIS PLACE AROUND. I GIVE A DAMN ABOUT HOMESTEAD. ABOUT TITAN'S FUTURE. WHAT DO YOU STAND FOR, WRKR?
HAHA! YOU THINK YOU BE SO SMART, HUH? GOTS US ALL WORKED OUT, MNGR?
YOU GOTS NO CLUE ABOUT TITAN. NO CLUE ABOUT WHAT BE COMING...
ALEXI!

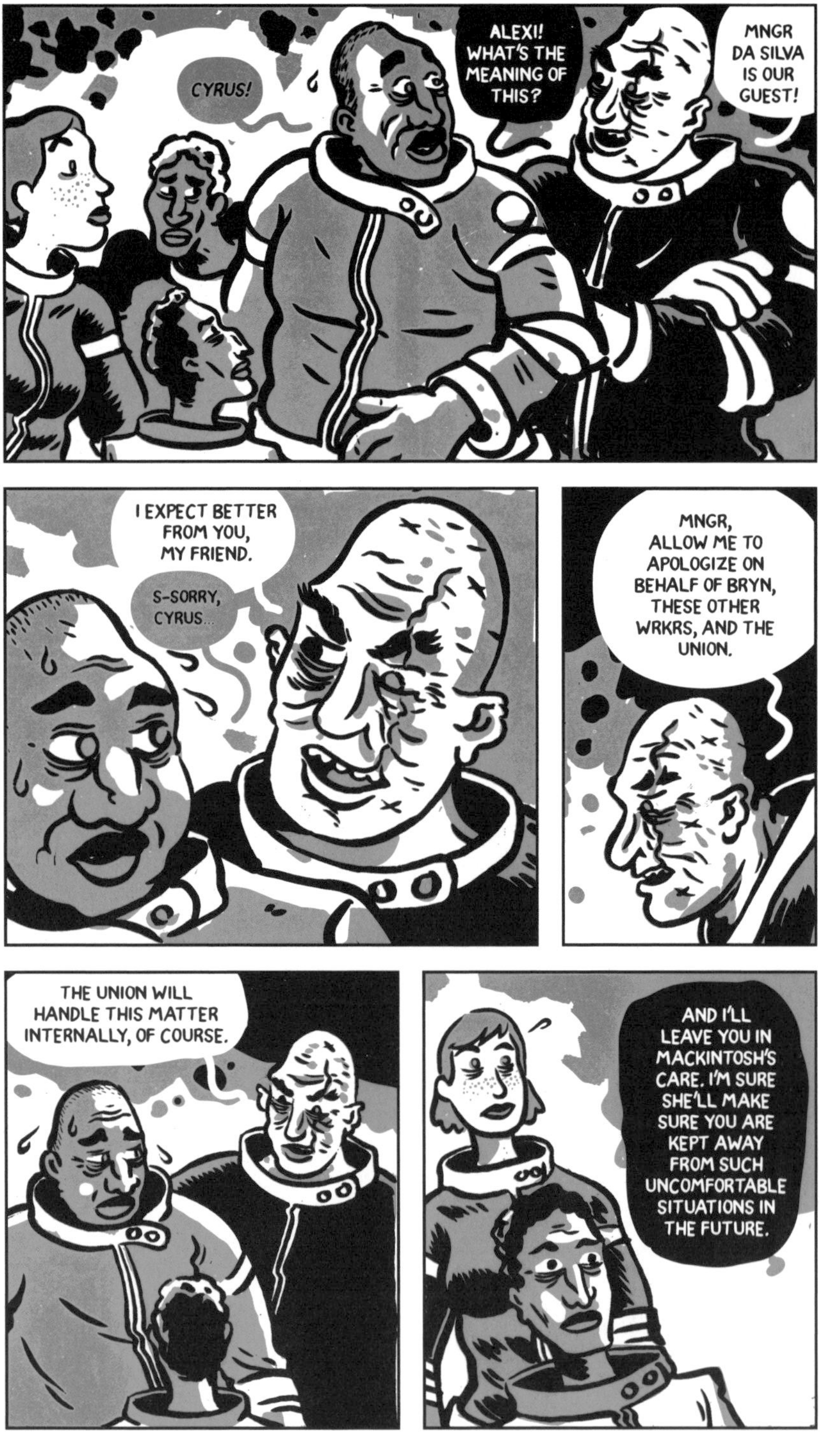
CYRUS!
ALEXI! WHAT'S THE MEANING OF THIS?
MNGR DA SILVA IS OUR GUEST!
I EXPECT BETTER FROM YOU, MY FRIEND.
S-SORRY, CYRUS...
MNGR, ALLOW ME TO APOLOGIZE ON BEHALF OF BRYN, THESE OTHER WRKRS, AND THE UNION.
THE UNION WILL HANDLE THIS MATTER INTERNALLY, OF COURSE.
AND I'LL LEAVE YOU IN MACKINTOSH'S CARE. I'M SURE SHE'LL MAKE SURE YOU ARE KEPT AWAY FROM SUCH UNCOMFORTABLE SITUATIONS IN THE FUTURE.

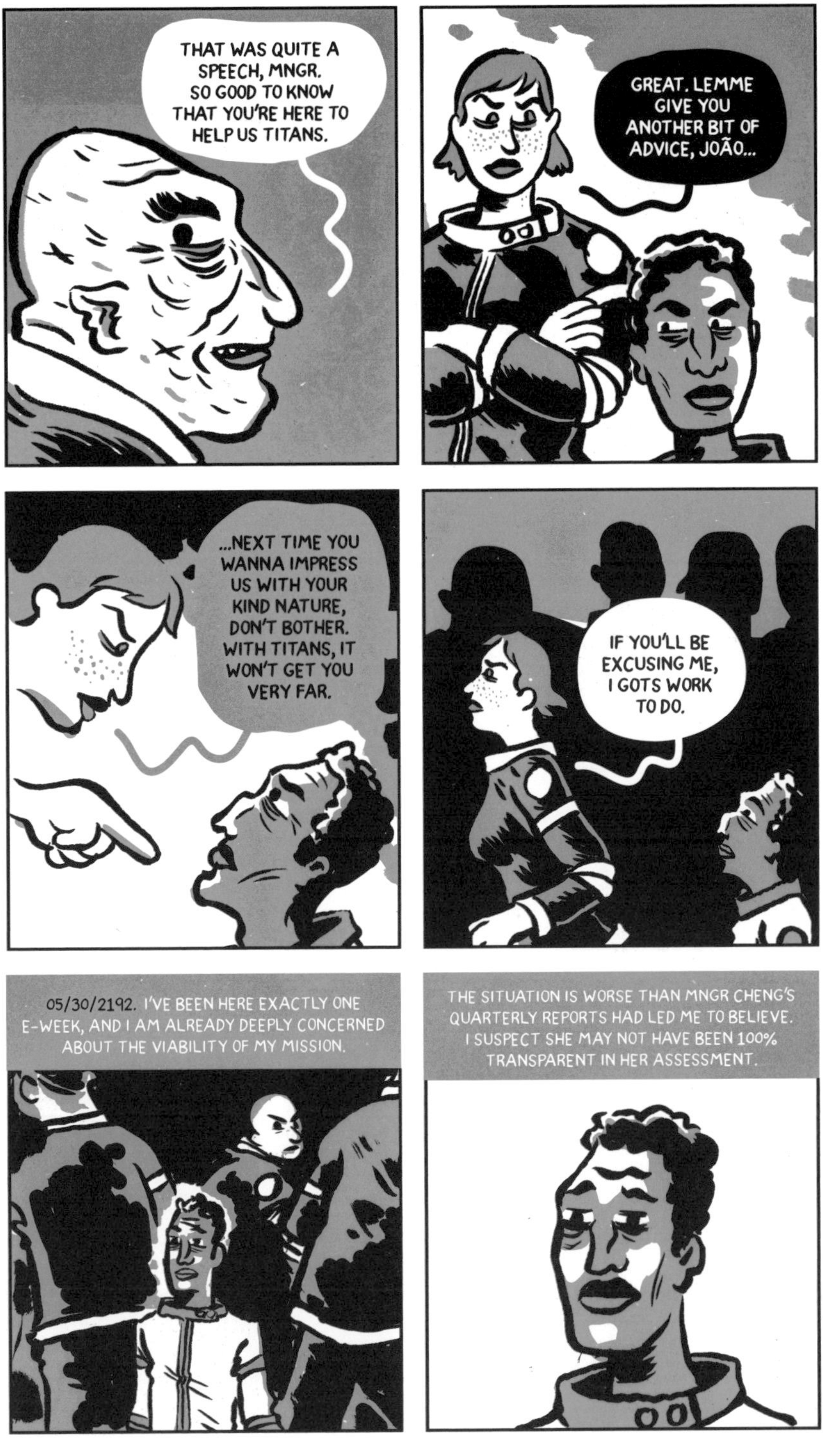
THAT WAS QUITE A SPEECH, MNGR. SO GOOD TO KNOW THAT YOU'RE HERE TO HELP US TITANS.
GREAT. LEMME GIVE YOU ANOTHER BIT OF ADVICE, JOÃO...
...NEXT TIME YOU WANNA IMPRESS US WITH YOUR KIND NATURE, DON'T BOTHER. WITH TITANS, IT WON'T GET YOU VERY FAR.
IF YOU'LL BE EXCUSING ME, I GOTS WORK TO DO.
05/30/2192. I'VE BEEN HERE EXACTLY ONE E-WEEK, AND I AM ALREADY DEEPLY CONCERNED ABOUT THE VIABILITY OF MY MISSION.
THE SITUATION IS WORSE THAN MNGR CHENG'S QUARTERLY REPORTS HAD LED ME TO BELIEVE. I SUSPECT SHE MAY NOT HAVE BEEN 100% TRANSPARENT IN HER ASSESSMENT.

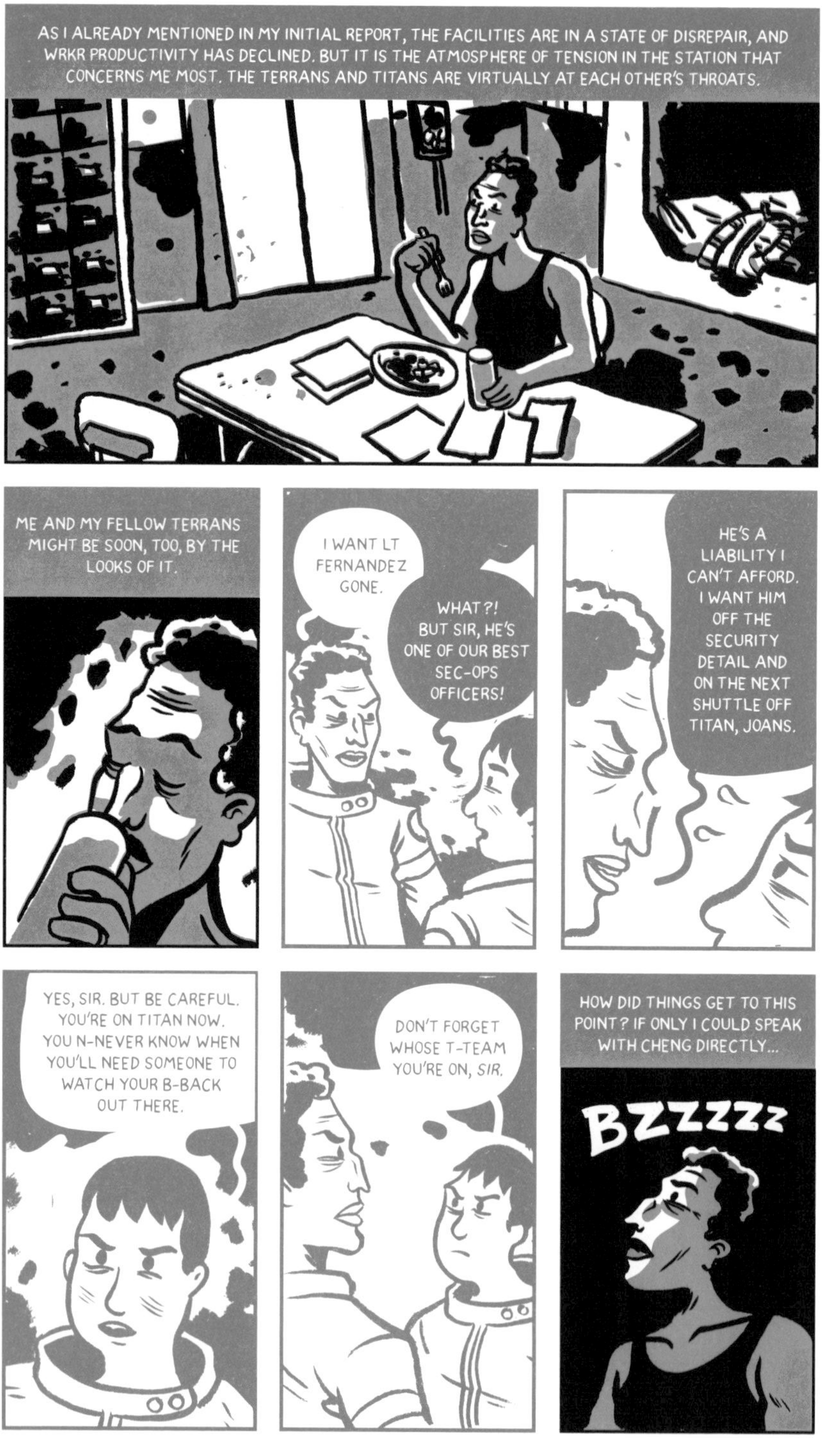
AS I ALREADY MENTIONED IN MY INITIAL REPORT, THE FACILITIES ARE IN A STATE OF DISREPAIR, AND WRKR PRODUCTIVITY HAS DECLINED. BUT IT IS THE ATMOSPHERE OF TENSION IN THE STATION THAT CONCERNS ME MOST. THE TERRANS AND TITANS ARE VIRTUALLY AT EACH OTHER'S THROATS.
ME AND MY FELLOW TERRANS MIGHT BE SOON, TOO, BY THE LOOKS OF IT.
I WANT LT FERNANDEZ GONE.
WHAT?! BUT SIR, HE'S ONE OF OUR BEST SEC-OPS OFFICERS!
HE'S A LIABILITY I CAN'T AFFORD. I WANT HIM OFF THE SECURITY DETAIL AND ON THE NEXT SHUTTLE OFF TITAN, JOANS.
YES, SIR. BUT BE CAREFUL. YOU'RE ON TITAN NOW. YOU N-NEVER KNOW WHEN YOU'LL NEED SOMEONE TO WATCH YOUR B-BACK OUT THERE.
DON'T FORGET WHOSE T-TEAM YOU'RE ON, *SIR.*
HOW DID THINGS GET TO THIS POINT? IF ONLY I COULD SPEAK WITH CHENG DIRECTLY...
BZZZZZ

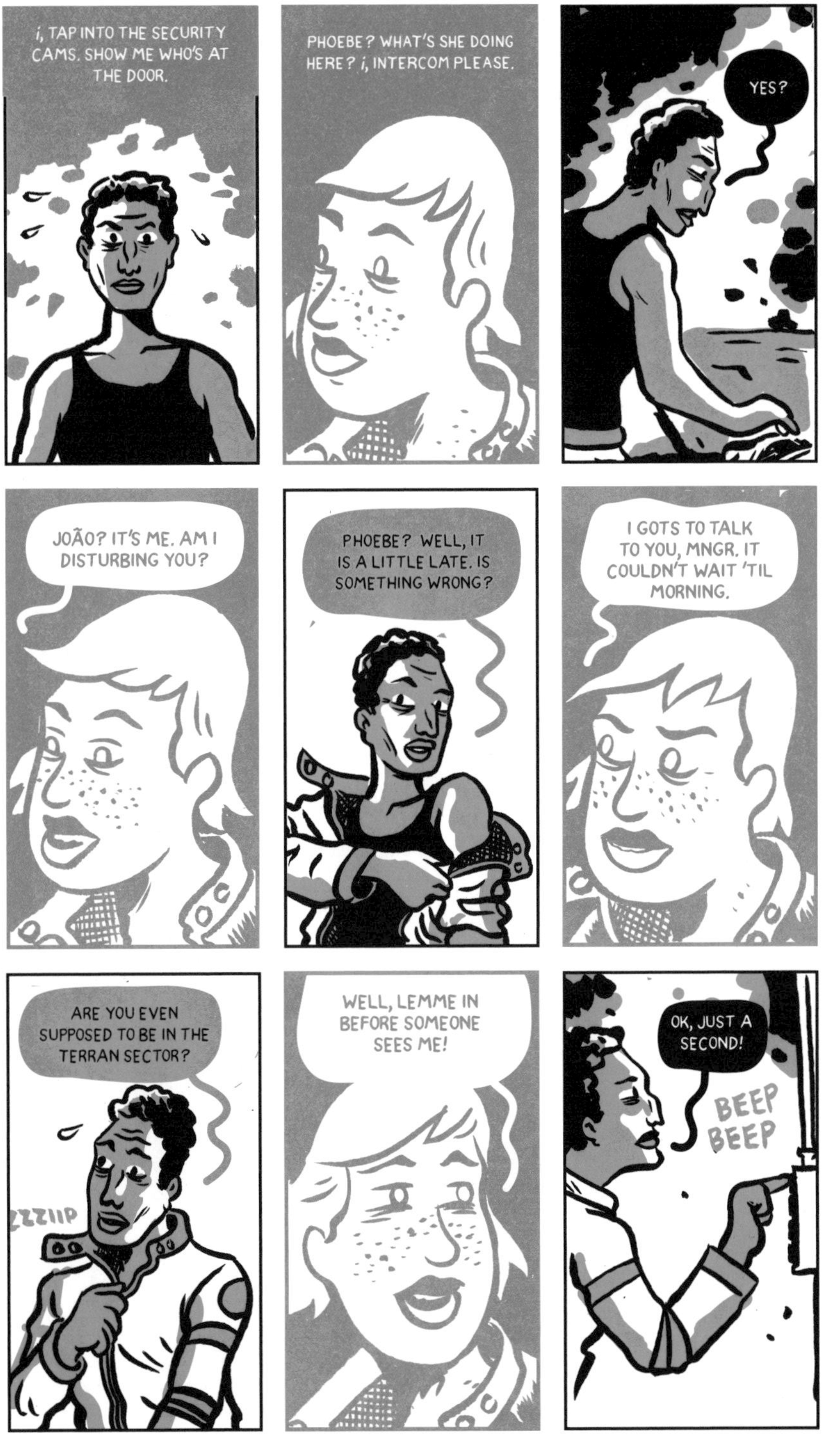
i, TAP INTO THE SECURITY CAMS. SHOW ME WHO'S AT THE DOOR.
PHOEBE? WHAT'S SHE DOING HERE? i, INTERCOM PLEASE.
YES?
JOÃO? IT'S ME. AM I DISTURBING YOU?
PHOEBE? WELL, IT IS A LITTLE LATE. IS SOMETHING WRONG?
I GOTS TO TALK TO YOU, MNGR. IT COULDN'T WAIT 'TIL MORNING.
ARE YOU EVEN SUPPOSED TO BE IN THE TERRAN SECTOR?
ZZZIIP
WELL, LEMME IN BEFORE SOMEONE SEES ME!
OK, JUST A SECOND!
BEEP BEEP

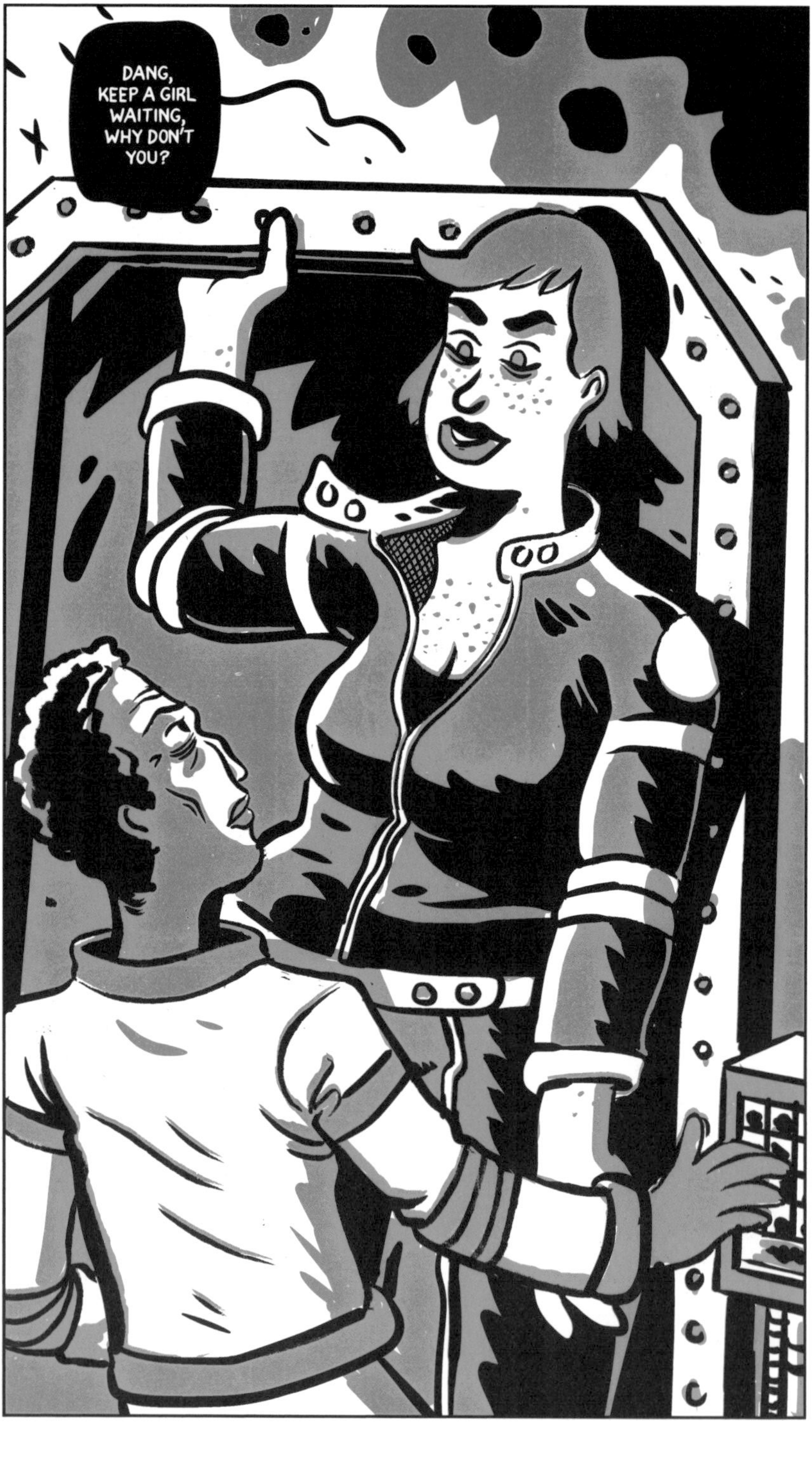
DANG, KEEP A GIRL WAITING, WHY DON'T YOU?

PART 03: HARD HEADED WOMAN

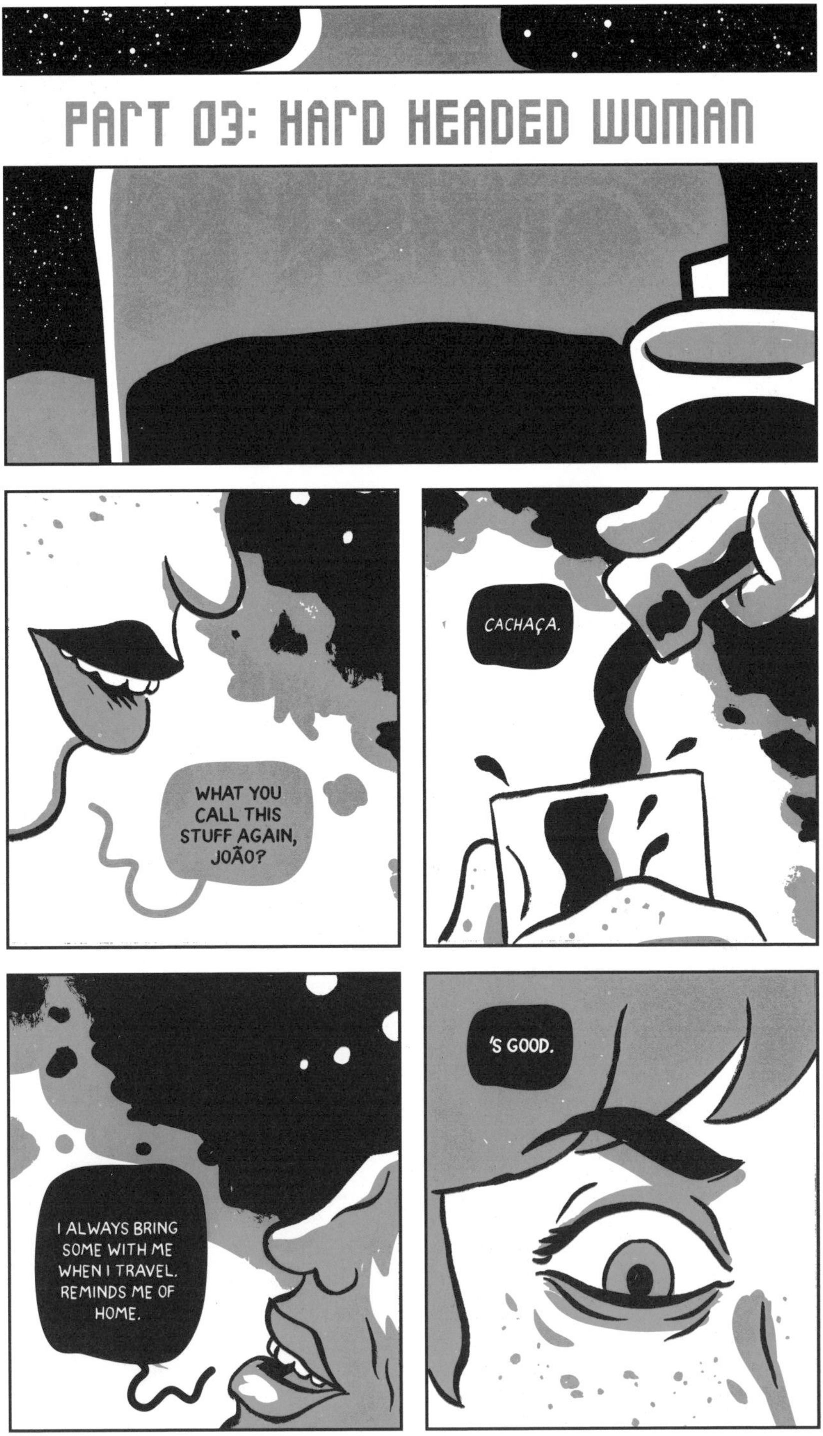
WHAT YOU CALL THIS STUFF AGAIN, JOÃO?
CACHAÇA.
I ALWAYS BRING SOME WITH ME WHEN I TRAVEL. REMINDS ME OF HOME.
'S GOOD.

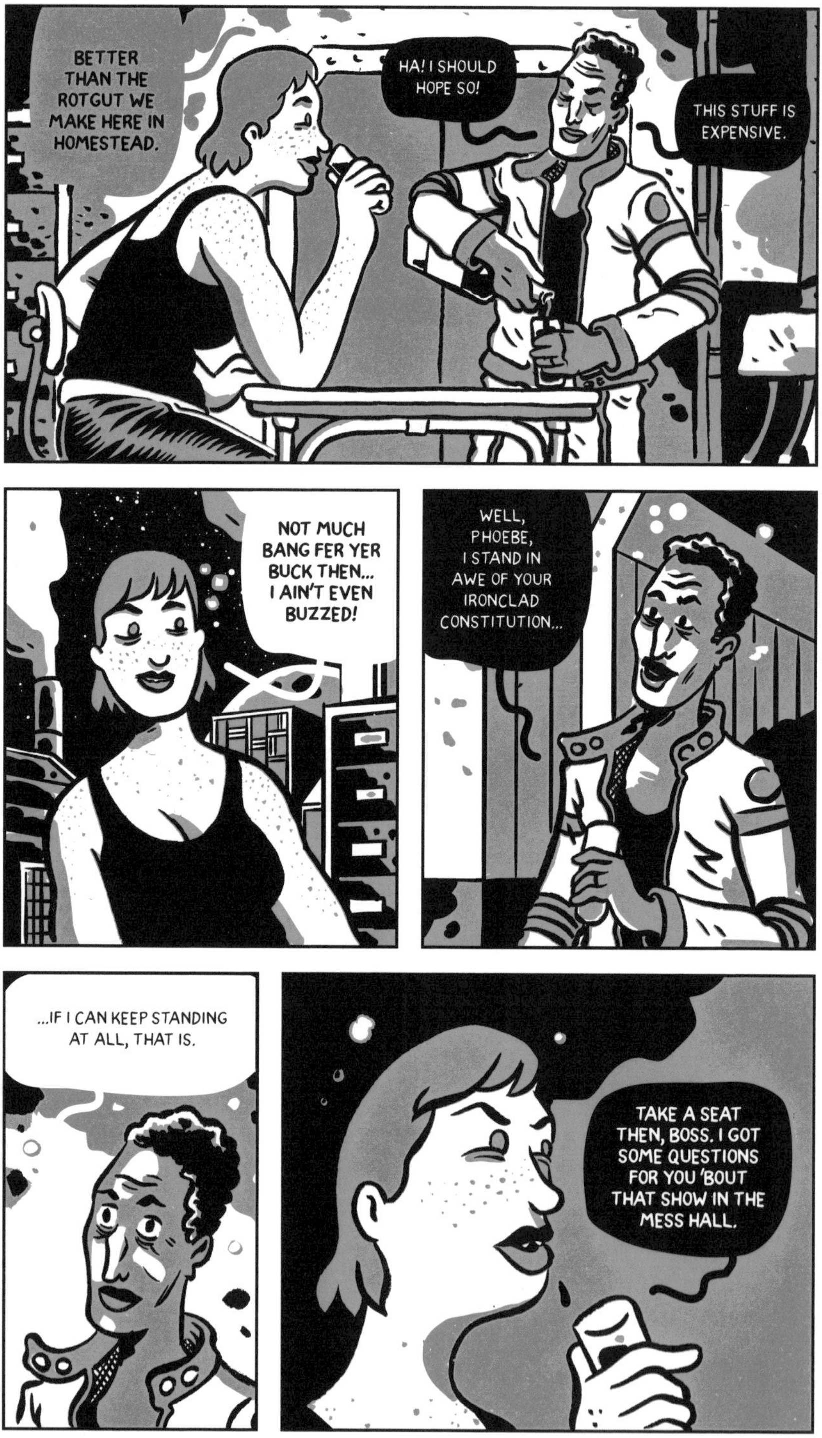
BETTER THAN THE ROTGUT WE MAKE HERE IN HOMESTEAD.
HA! I SHOULD HOPE SO!
THIS STUFF IS EXPENSIVE.
NOT MUCH BANG FER YER BUCK THEN... I AIN'T EVEN BUZZED!
WELL, PHOEBE, I STAND IN AWE OF YOUR IRONCLAD CONSTITUTION...
...IF I CAN KEEP STANDING AT ALL, THAT IS.
TAKE A SEAT THEN, BOSS. I GOT SOME QUESTIONS FOR YOU 'BOUT THAT SHOW IN THE MESS HALL.

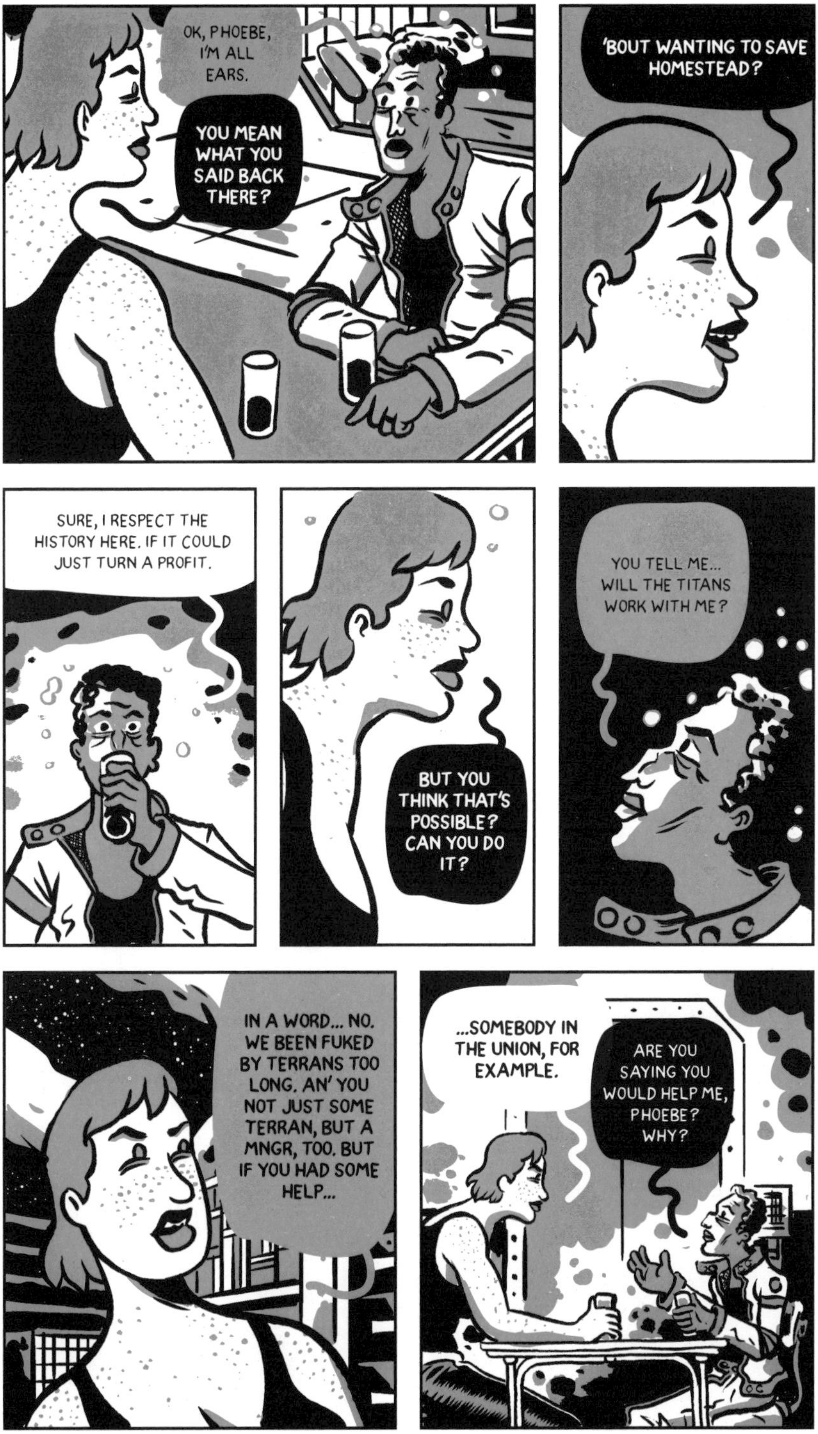

OK, PHOEBE, I'M ALL EARS.
YOU MEAN WHAT YOU SAID BACK THERE?
'BOUT WANTING TO SAVE HOMESTEAD?
SURE, I RESPECT THE HISTORY HERE. IF IT COULD JUST TURN A PROFIT.
BUT YOU THINK THAT'S POSSIBLE? CAN YOU DO IT?
YOU TELL ME... WILL THE TITANS WORK WITH ME?
IN A WORD... NO. WE BEEN FUKED BY TERRANS TOO LONG. AN' YOU NOT JUST SOME TERRAN, BUT A MNGR, TOO. BUT IF YOU HAD SOME HELP...
...SOMEBODY IN THE UNION, FOR EXAMPLE.
ARE YOU SAYING YOU WOULD HELP ME, PHOEBE? WHY?

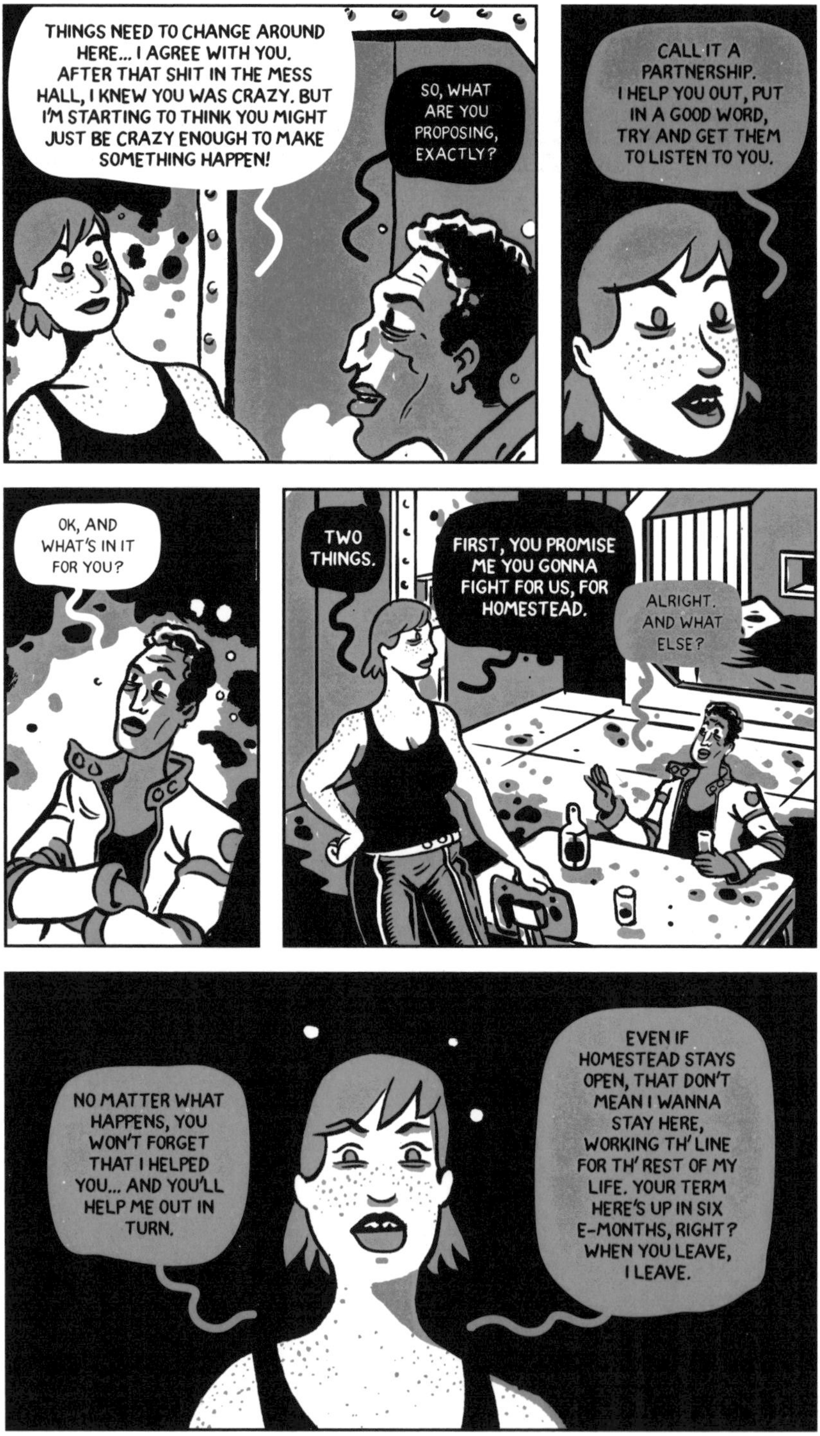
THINGS NEED TO CHANGE AROUND HERE... I AGREE WITH YOU. AFTER THAT SHIT IN THE MESS HALL, I KNEW YOU WAS CRAZY. BUT I'M STARTING TO THINK YOU MIGHT JUST BE CRAZY ENOUGH TO MAKE SOMETHING HAPPEN!
SO, WHAT ARE YOU PROPOSING, EXACTLY?
CALL IT A PARTNERSHIP. I HELP YOU OUT, PUT IN A GOOD WORD, TRY AND GET THEM TO LISTEN TO YOU.
OK, AND WHAT'S IN IT FOR YOU?
TWO THINGS.
FIRST, YOU PROMISE ME YOU GONNA FIGHT FOR US, FOR HOMESTEAD.
ALRIGHT. AND WHAT ELSE?
NO MATTER WHAT HAPPENS, YOU WON'T FORGET THAT I HELPED YOU... AND YOU'LL HELP ME OUT IN TURN.
EVEN IF HOMESTEAD STAYS OPEN, THAT DON'T MEAN I WANNA STAY HERE, WORKING TH' LINE FOR TH' REST OF MY LIFE. YOUR TERM HERE'S UP IN SIX E-MONTHS, RIGHT? WHEN YOU LEAVE, I LEAVE.

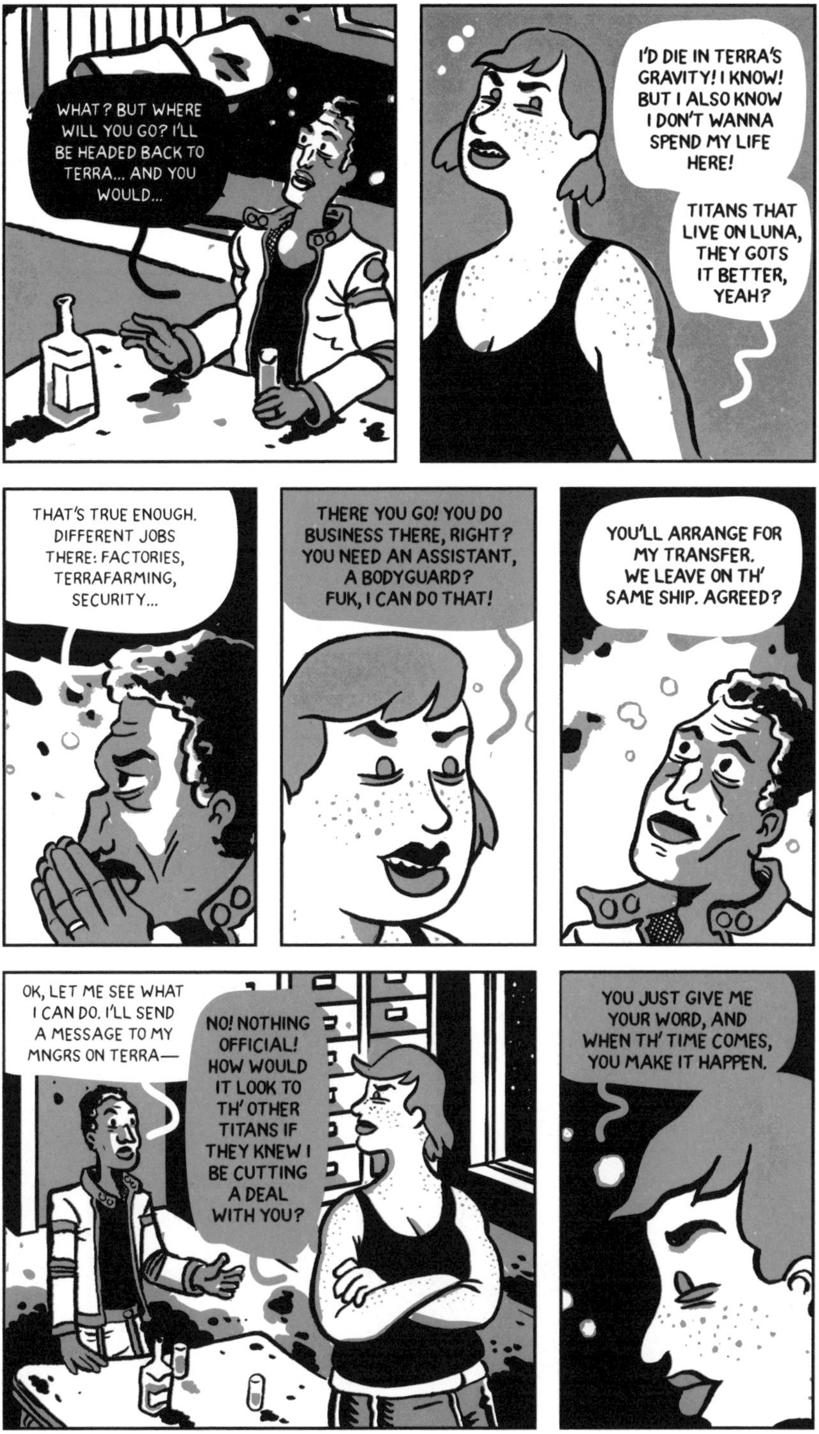
WHAT? BUT WHERE WILL YOU GO? I'LL BE HEADED BACK TO TERRA... AND YOU WOULD...
I'D DIE IN TERRA'S GRAVITY! I KNOW! BUT I ALSO KNOW I DON'T WANNA SPEND MY LIFE HERE!
TITANS THAT LIVE ON LUNA, THEY GOTS IT BETTER, YEAH?
THAT'S TRUE ENOUGH. DIFFERENT JOBS THERE: FACTORIES, TERRAFARMING, SECURITY...
THERE YOU GO! YOU DO BUSINESS THERE, RIGHT? YOU NEED AN ASSISTANT, A BODYGUARD? FUK, I CAN DO THAT!
YOU'LL ARRANGE FOR MY TRANSFER. WE LEAVE ON TH' SAME SHIP. AGREED?
OK, LET ME SEE WHAT I CAN DO. I'LL SEND A MESSAGE TO MY MNGRS ON TERRA—
NO! NOTHING OFFICIAL! HOW WOULD IT LOOK TO TH' OTHER TITANS IF THEY KNEW I BE CUTTING A DEAL WITH YOU?
YOU JUST GIVE ME YOUR WORD, AND WHEN TH' TIME COMES, YOU MAKE IT HAPPEN.

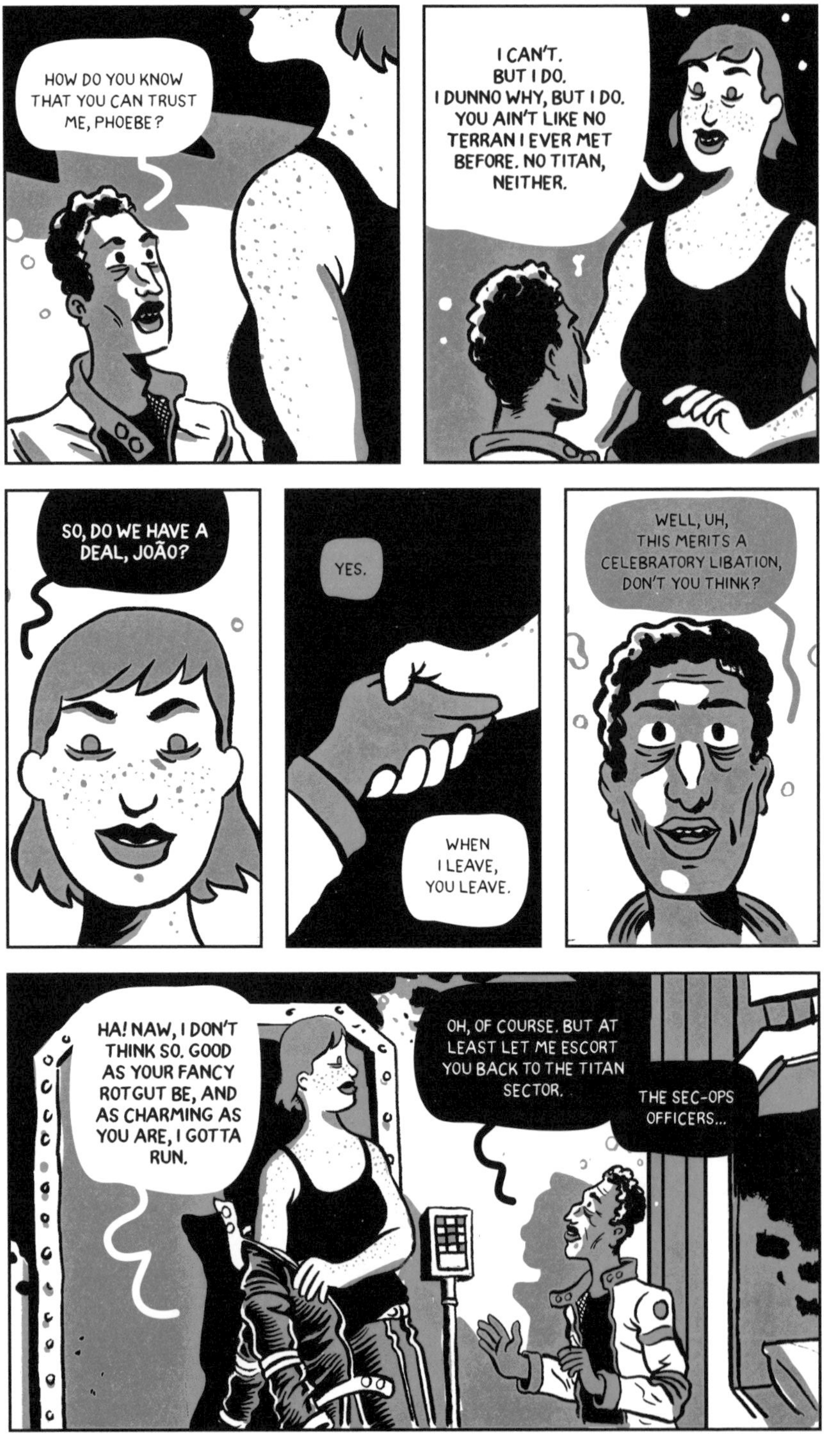
HOW DO YOU KNOW THAT YOU CAN TRUST ME, PHOEBE?
I CAN'T. BUT I DO. I DUNNO WHY, BUT I DO. YOU AIN'T LIKE NO TERRAN I EVER MET BEFORE. NO TITAN, NEITHER.
SO, DO WE HAVE A DEAL, JOÃO?
YES.
WHEN I LEAVE, YOU LEAVE.
WELL, UH, THIS MERITS A CELEBRATORY LIBATION, DON'T YOU THINK?
HA! NAW, I DON'T THINK SO. GOOD AS YOUR FANCY ROTGUT BE, AND AS CHARMING AS YOU ARE, I GOTTA RUN.
OH, OF COURSE. BUT AT LEAST LET ME ESCORT YOU BACK TO THE TITAN SECTOR.
THE SEC-OPS OFFICERS...

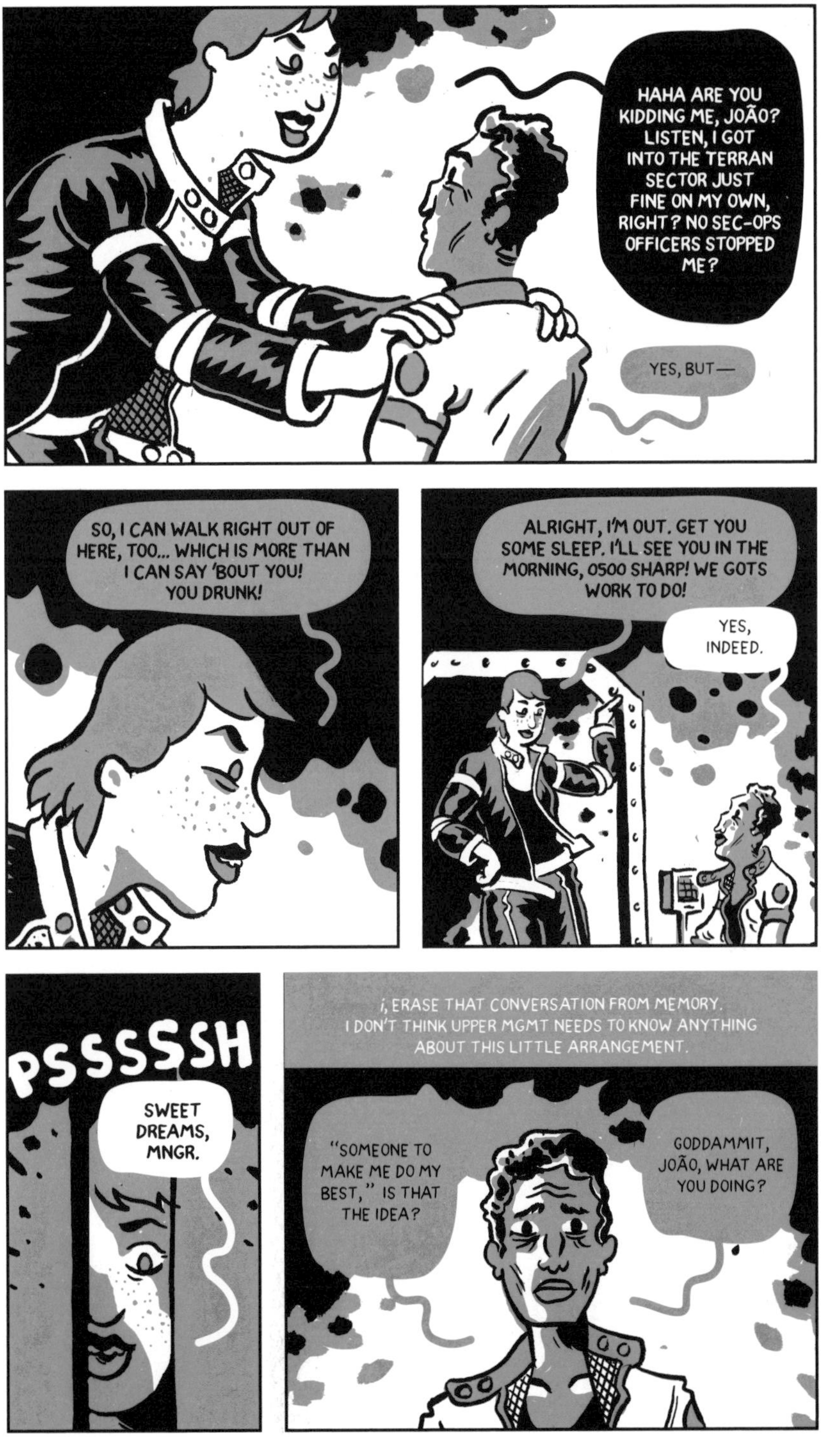
HAHA ARE YOU KIDDING ME, JOÃO? LISTEN, I GOT INTO THE TERRAN SECTOR JUST FINE ON MY OWN, RIGHT? NO SEC-OPS OFFICERS STOPPED ME?
YES, BUT—
SO, I CAN WALK RIGHT OUT OF HERE, TOO... WHICH IS MORE THAN I CAN SAY 'BOUT YOU! YOU DRUNK!
ALRIGHT, I'M OUT. GET YOU SOME SLEEP. I'LL SEE YOU IN THE MORNING, 0500 SHARP! WE GOTS WORK TO DO!
YES, INDEED.
PSSSSSH
SWEET DREAMS, MNGR.
i, ERASE THAT CONVERSATION FROM MEMORY. I DON'T THINK UPPER MGMT NEEDS TO KNOW ANYTHING ABOUT THIS LITTLE ARRANGEMENT.
"SOMEONE TO MAKE ME DO MY BEST," IS THAT THE IDEA?
GODDAMMIT, JOÃO, WHAT ARE YOU DOING?

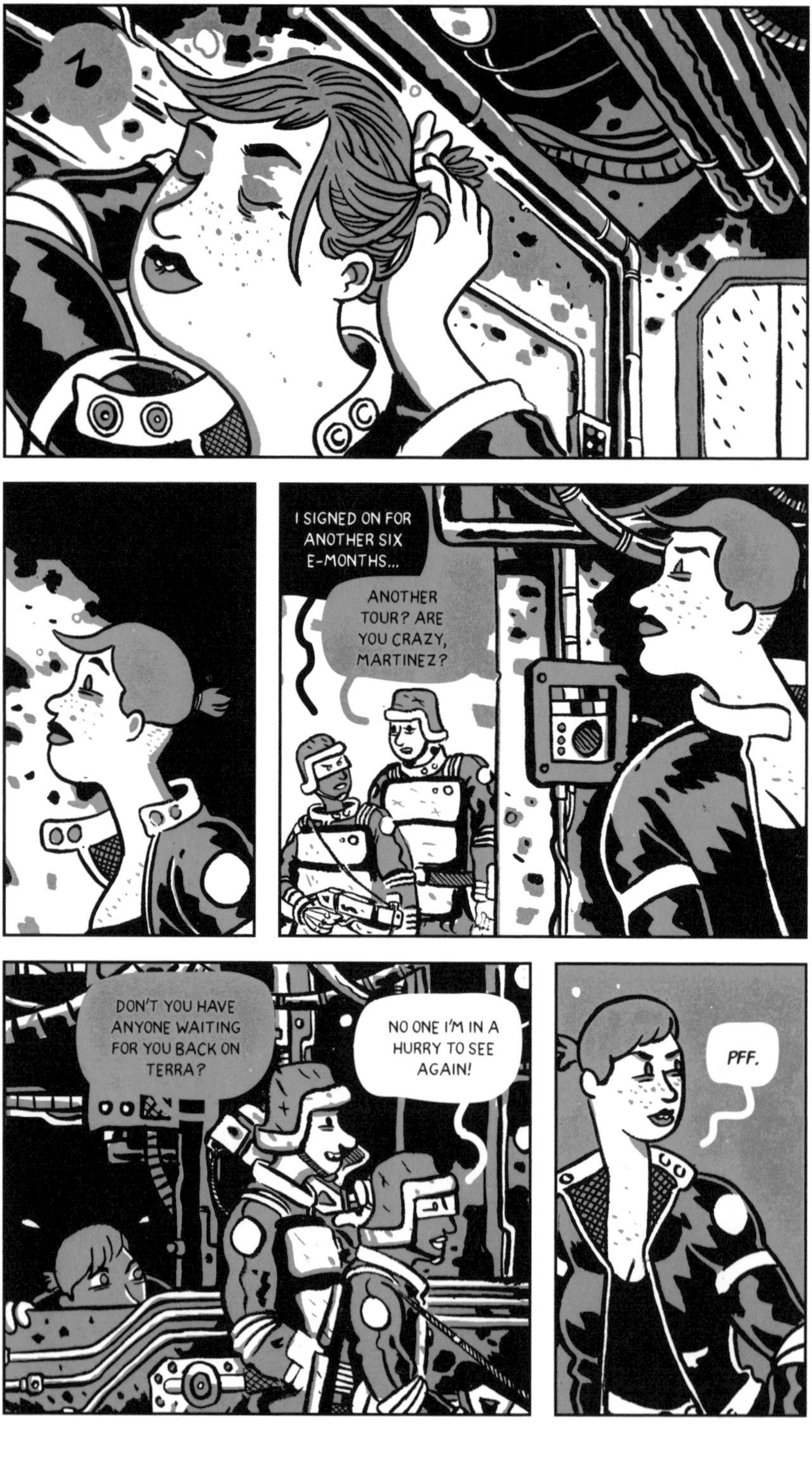
I SIGNED ON FOR ANOTHER SIX E-MONTHS...
ANOTHER TOUR? ARE YOU CRAZY, MARTINEZ?
DON'T YOU HAVE ANYONE WAITING FOR YOU BACK ON TERRA?
NO ONE I'M IN A HURRY TO SEE AGAIN!
PFF.

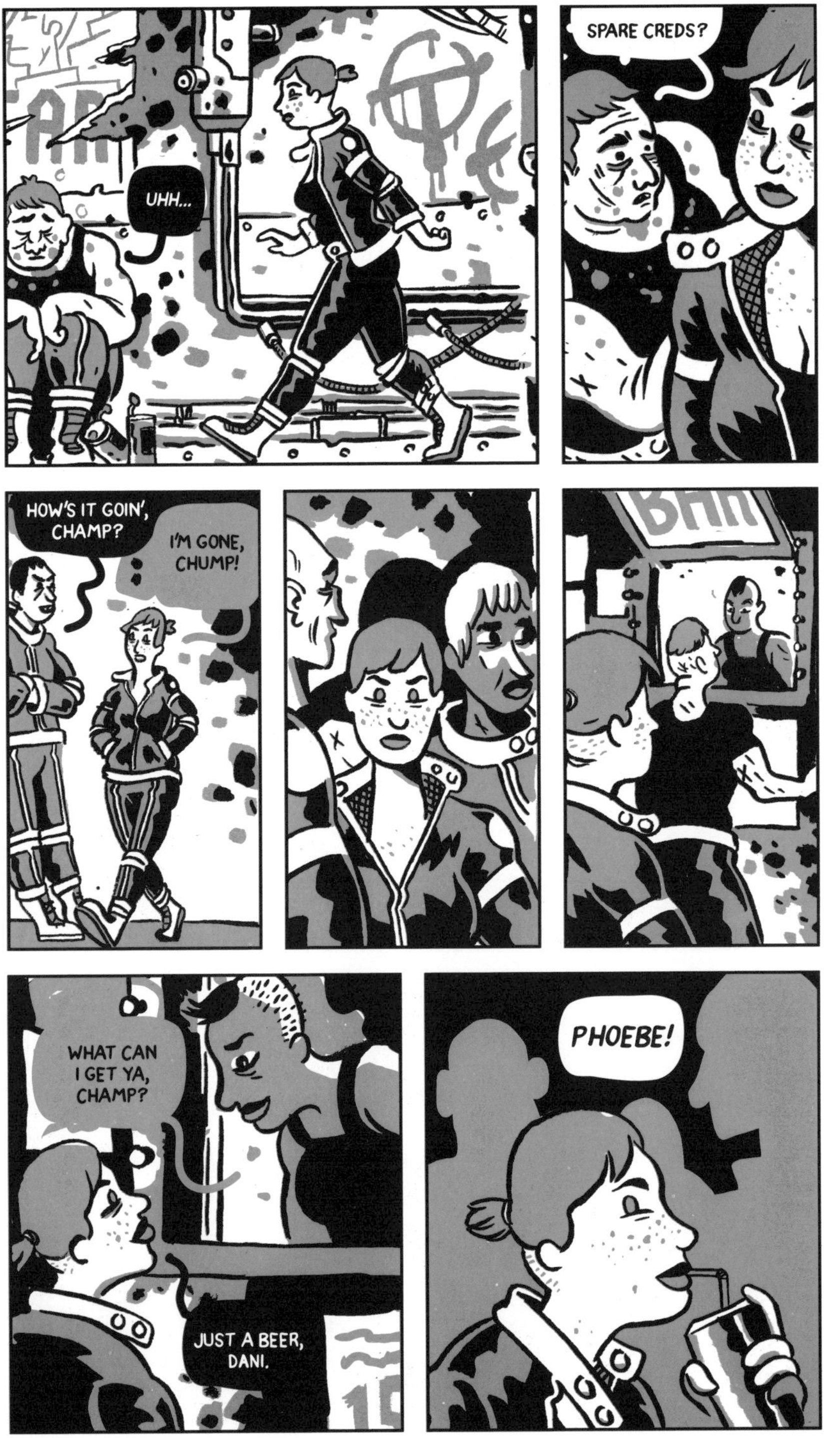
UHH...
SPARE CREDS?
HOW'S IT GOIN', CHAMP?
I'M GONE, CHUMP!
WHAT CAN I GET YA, CHAMP?
JUST A BEER, DANI.
PHOEBE!

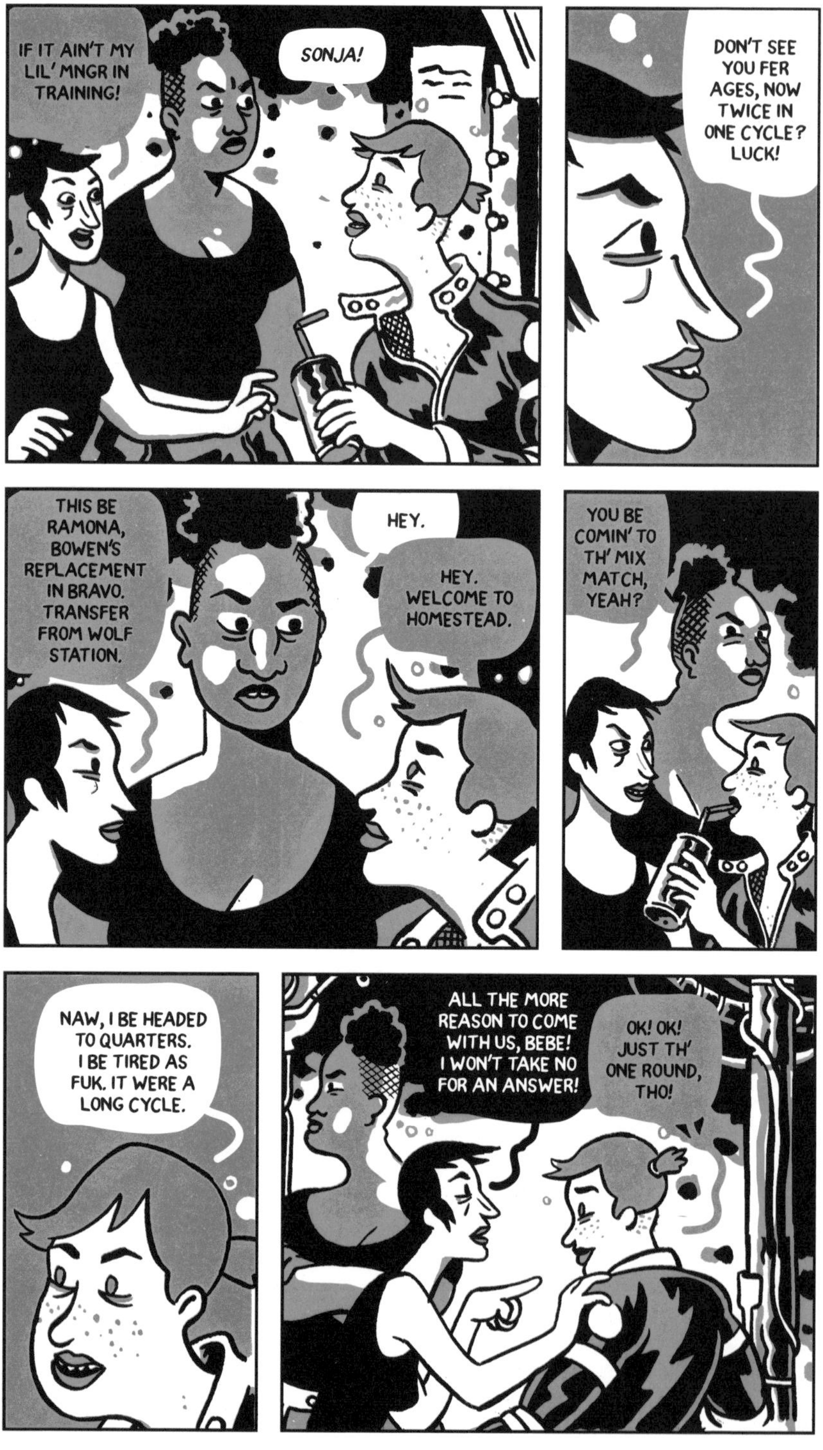
IF IT AIN'T MY LIL' MNGR IN TRAINING!
SONJA!
DON'T SEE YOU FER AGES, NOW TWICE IN ONE CYCLE? LUCK!
THIS BE RAMONA, BOWEN'S REPLACEMENT IN BRAVO. TRANSFER FROM WOLF STATION.
HEY.
HEY. WELCOME TO HOMESTEAD.
YOU BE COMIN' TO TH' MIX MATCH, YEAH?
NAW, I BE HEADED TO QUARTERS. I BE TIRED AS FUK. IT WERE A LONG CYCLE.
ALL THE MORE REASON TO COME WITH US, BEBE! I WON'T TAKE NO FOR AN ANSWER!
OK! OK! JUST TH' ONE ROUND, THO!

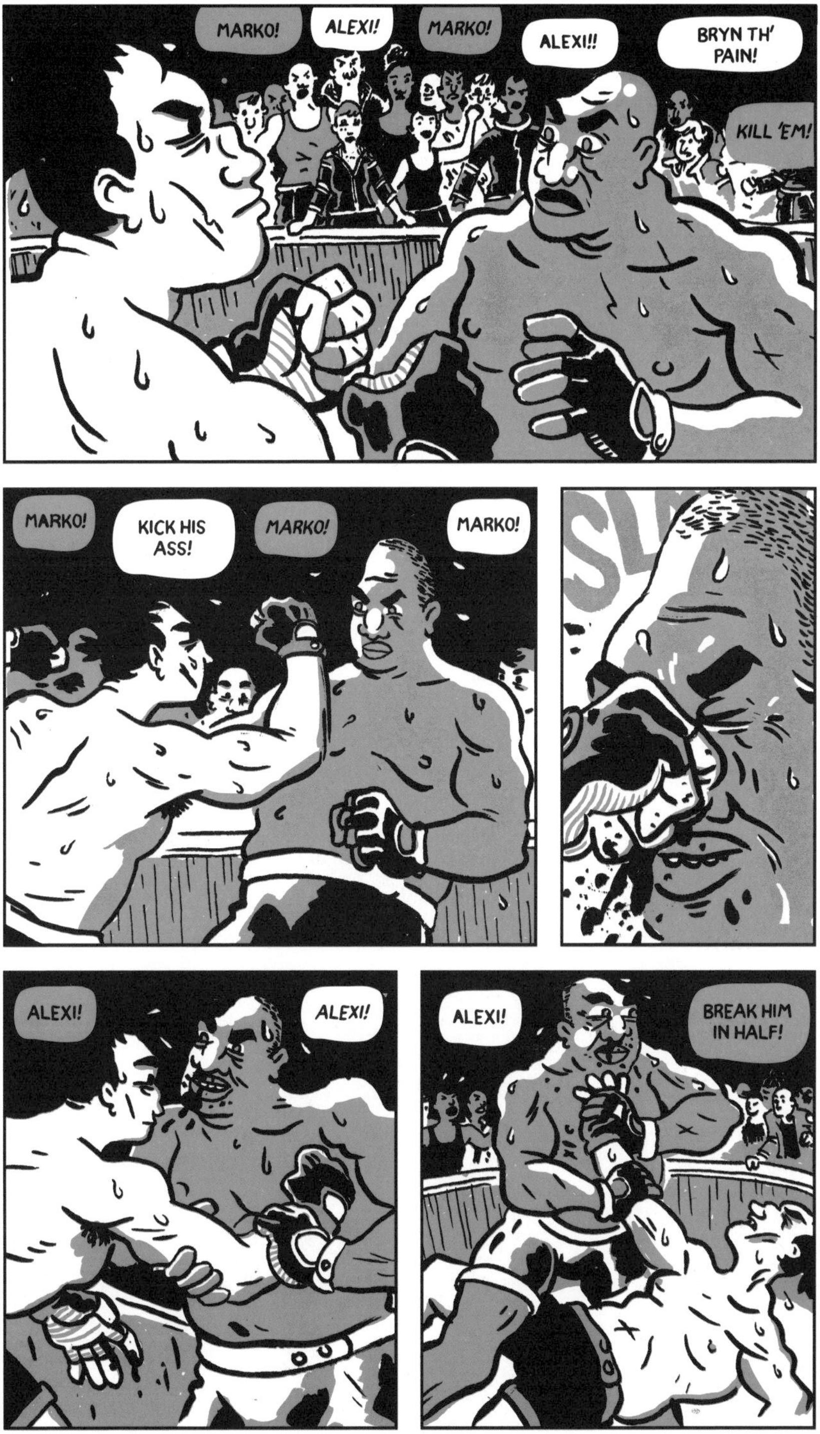
MARKO!
ALEXI!
MARKO!
ALEXI!!
BRYN TH' PAIN!
KILL 'EM!
MARKO!
KICK HIS ASS!
MARKO!
MARKO!
ALEXI!
ALEXI!
ALEXI!
BREAK HIM IN HALF!

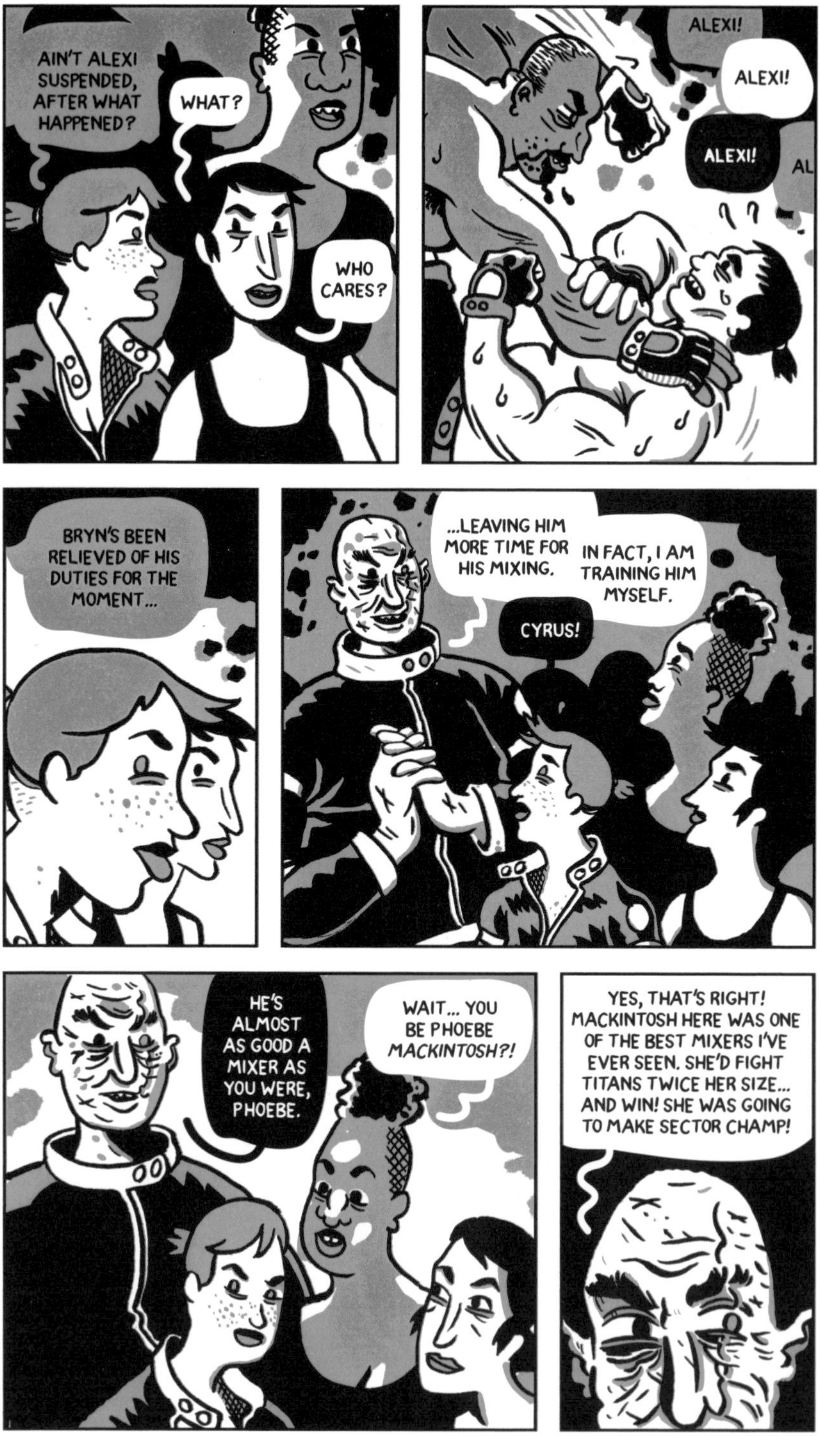
AIN'T ALEXI SUSPENDED, AFTER WHAT HAPPENED?
WHAT?
WHO CARES?
ALEXI!
ALEXI!
ALEXI!
AL
BRYN'S BEEN RELIEVED OF HIS DUTIES FOR THE MOMENT...
...LEAVING HIM MORE TIME FOR HIS MIXING.
IN FACT, I AM TRAINING HIM MYSELF.
CYRUS!
HE'S ALMOST AS GOOD A MIXER AS YOU WERE, PHOEBE.
WAIT... YOU BE PHOEBE *MACKINTOSH?!*
YES, THAT'S RIGHT! MACKINTOSH HERE WAS ONE OF THE BEST MIXERS I'VE EVER SEEN. SHE'D FIGHT TITANS TWICE HER SIZE... AND WIN! SHE WAS GOING TO MAKE SECTOR CHAMP!

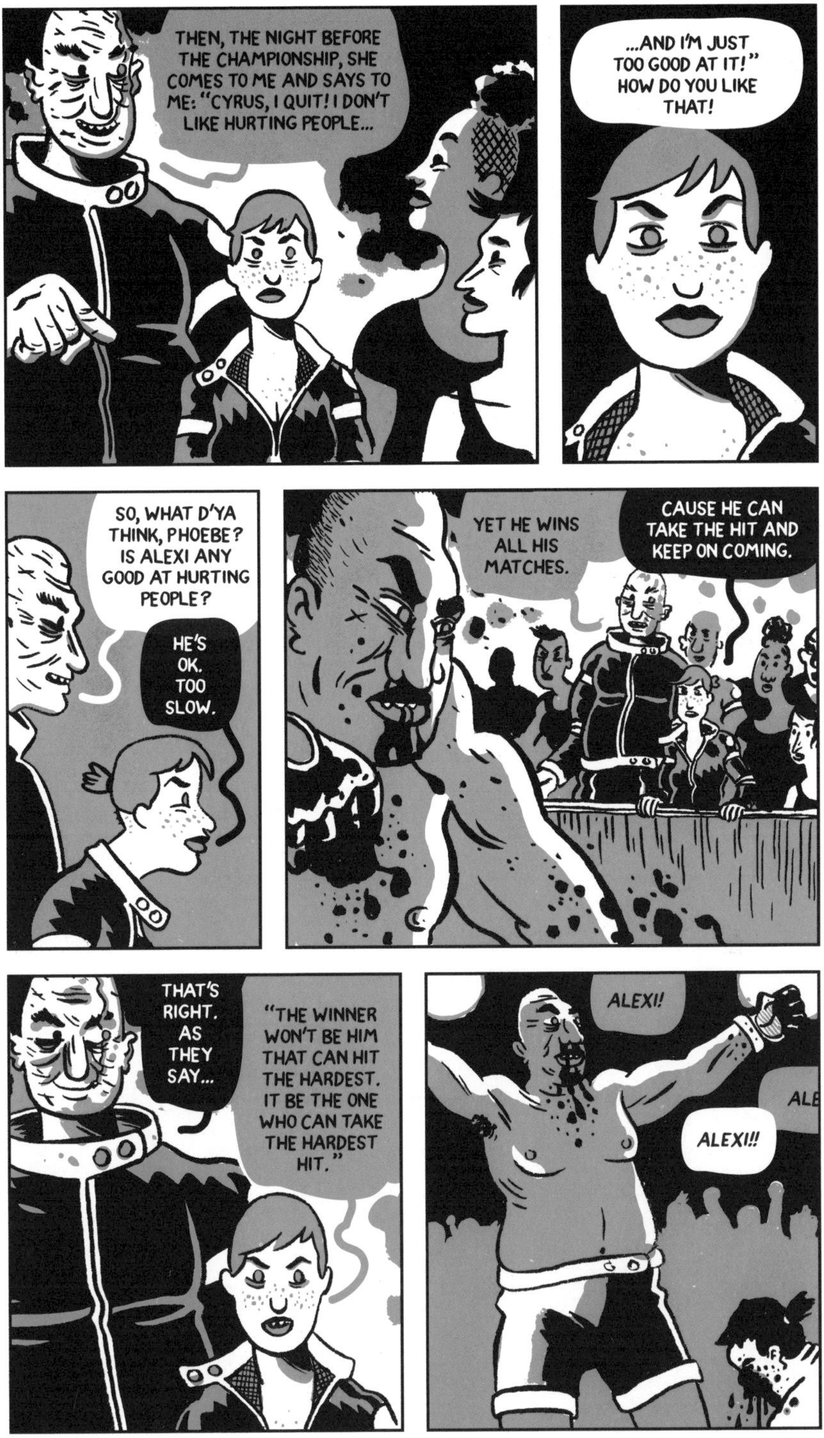
THEN, THE NIGHT BEFORE THE CHAMPIONSHIP, SHE COMES TO ME AND SAYS TO ME: "CYRUS, I QUIT! I DON'T LIKE HURTING PEOPLE...
...AND I'M JUST TOO GOOD AT IT!" HOW DO YOU LIKE THAT!
SO, WHAT D'YA THINK, PHOEBE? IS ALEXI ANY GOOD AT HURTING PEOPLE?
HE'S OK. TOO SLOW.
YET HE WINS ALL HIS MATCHES.
CAUSE HE CAN TAKE THE HIT AND KEEP ON COMING.
THAT'S RIGHT. AS THEY SAY...
"THE WINNER WON'T BE HIM THAT CAN HIT THE HARDEST. IT BE THE ONE WHO CAN TAKE THE HARDEST HIT."
ALEXI!
ALEXI!!

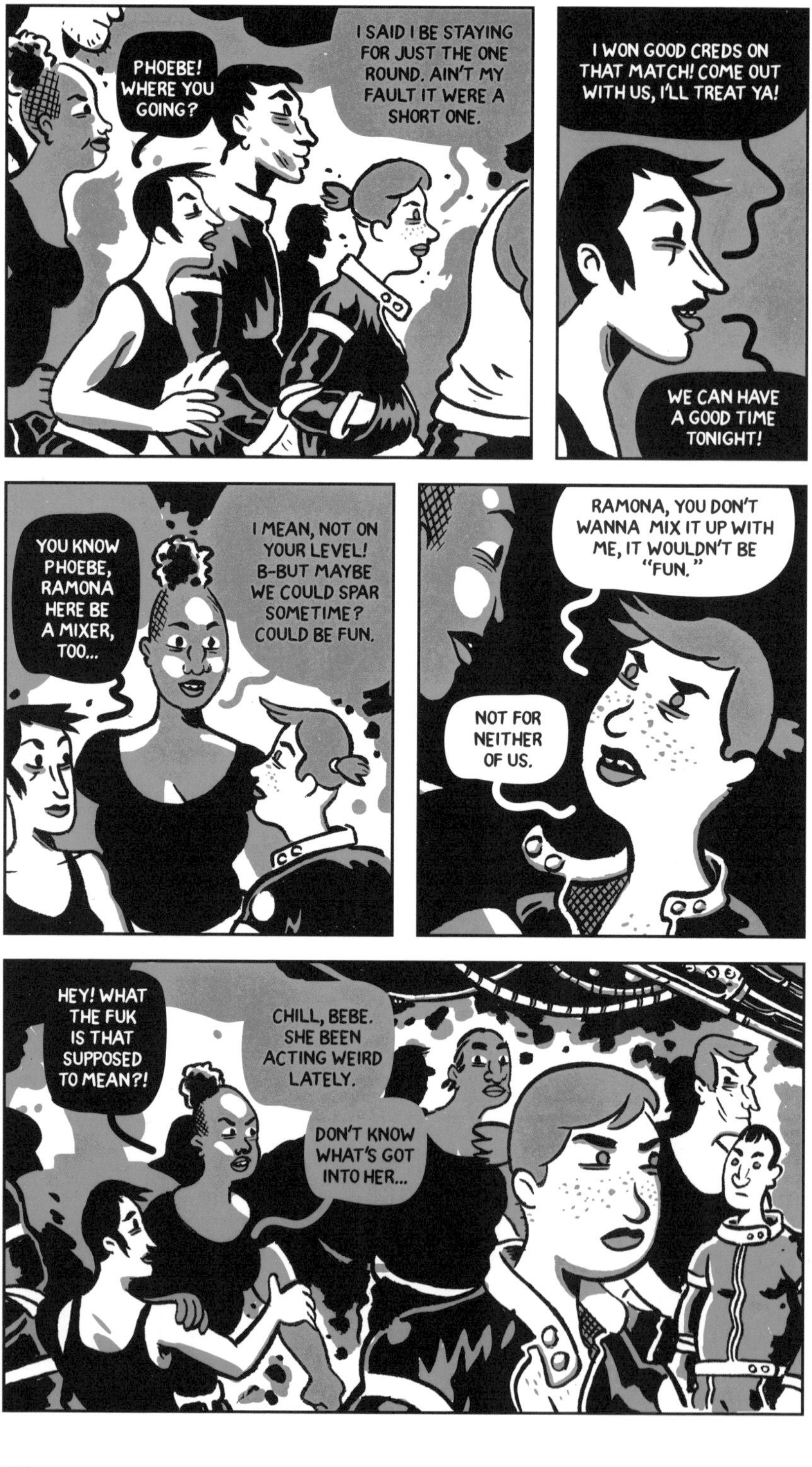
PHOEBE! WHERE YOU GOING?
I SAID I BE STAYING FOR JUST THE ONE ROUND. AIN'T MY FAULT IT WERE A SHORT ONE.
I WON GOOD CREDS ON THAT MATCH! COME OUT WITH US, I'LL TREAT YA!
WE CAN HAVE A GOOD TIME TONIGHT!
YOU KNOW PHOEBE, RAMONA HERE BE A MIXER, TOO...
I MEAN, NOT ON YOUR LEVEL! B-BUT MAYBE WE COULD SPAR SOMETIME? COULD BE FUN.
RAMONA, YOU DON'T WANNA MIX IT UP WITH ME, IT WOULDN'T BE "FUN."
NOT FOR NEITHER OF US.
HEY! WHAT THE FUK IS THAT SUPPOSED TO MEAN?!
CHILL, BEBE. SHE BEEN ACTING WEIRD LATELY.
DON'T KNOW WHAT'S GOT INTO HER...

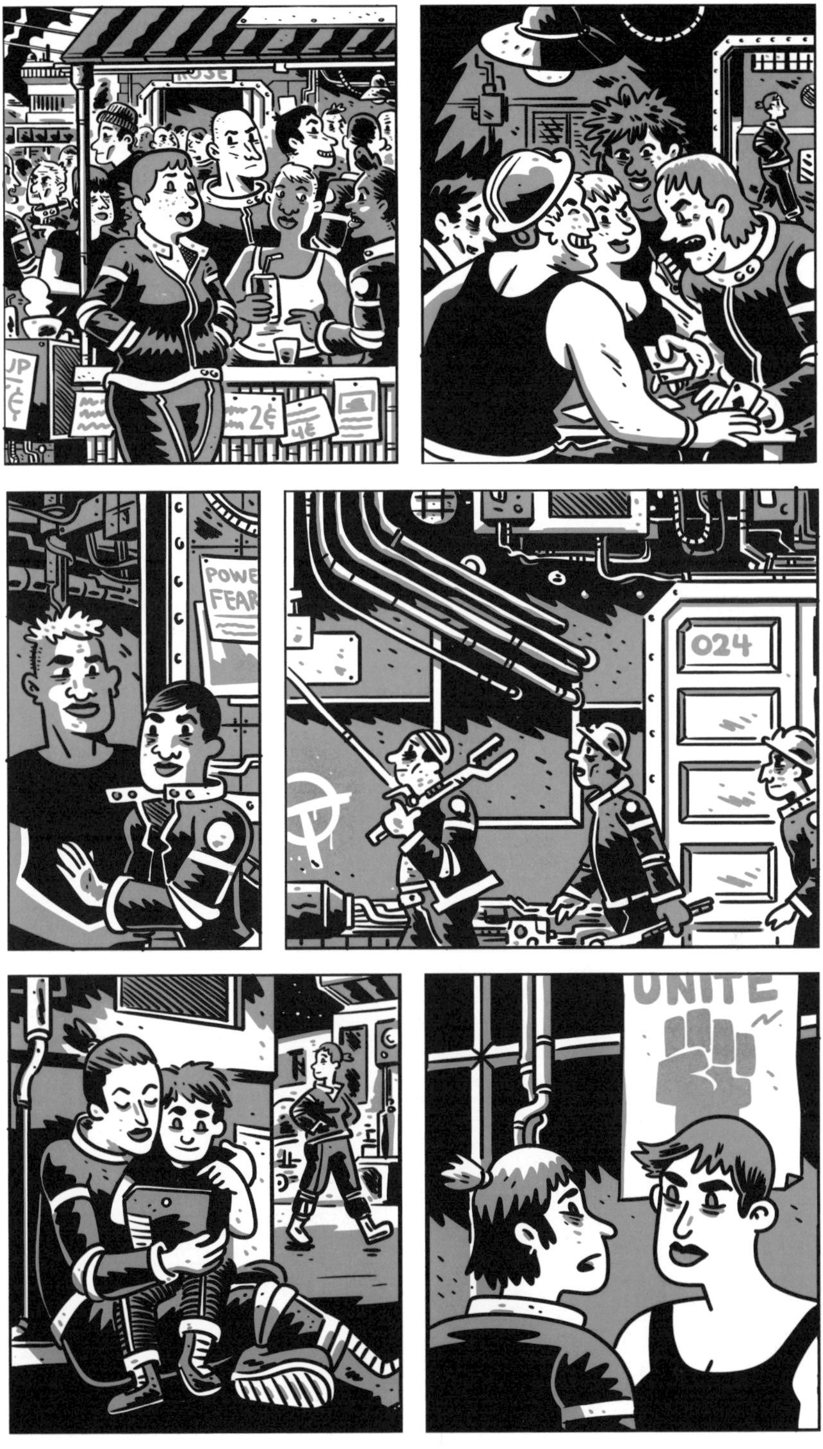
ROSE
2¢
4¢
POWE
FEAR
024
UNITE

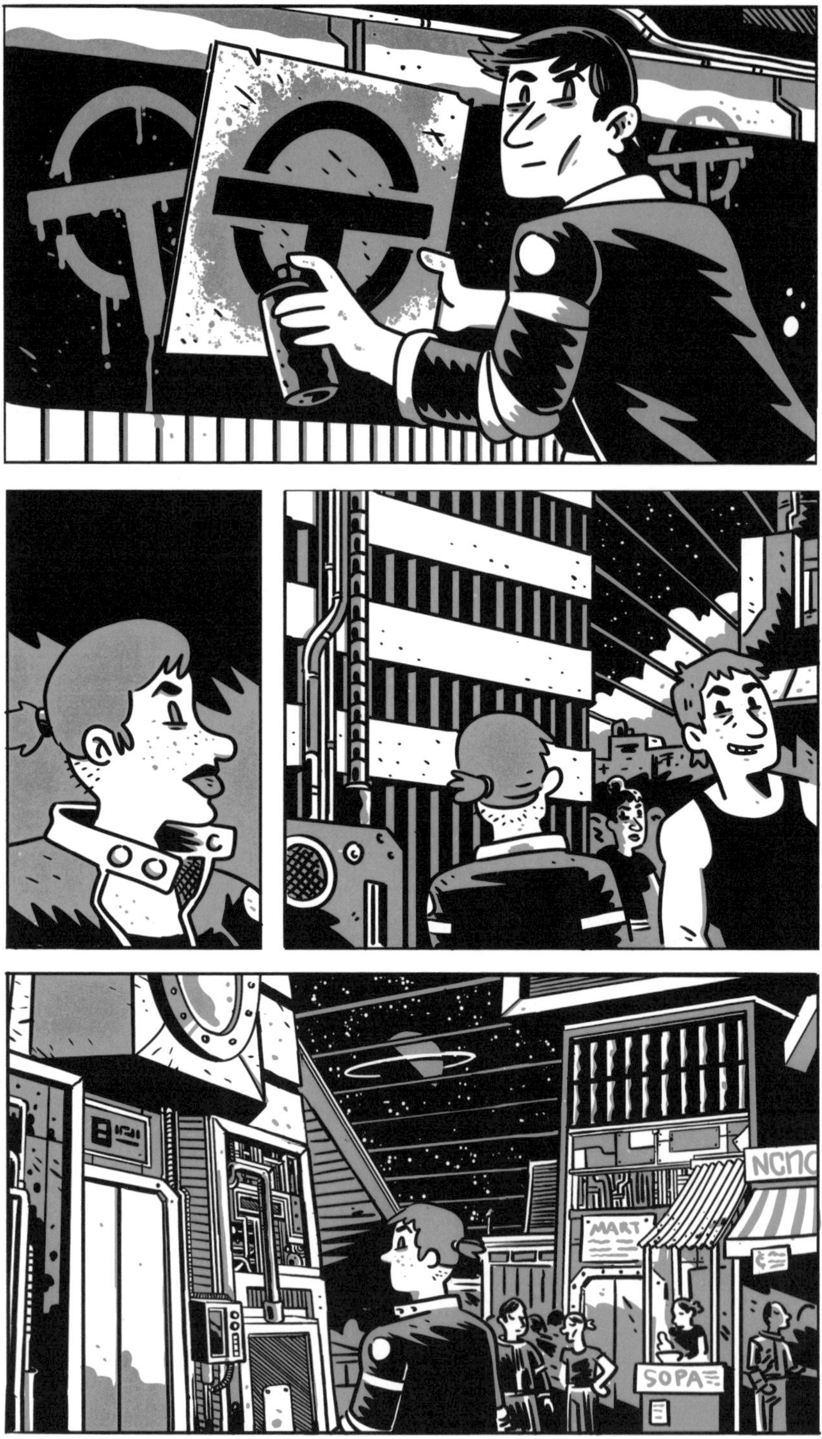
MART
SOPA

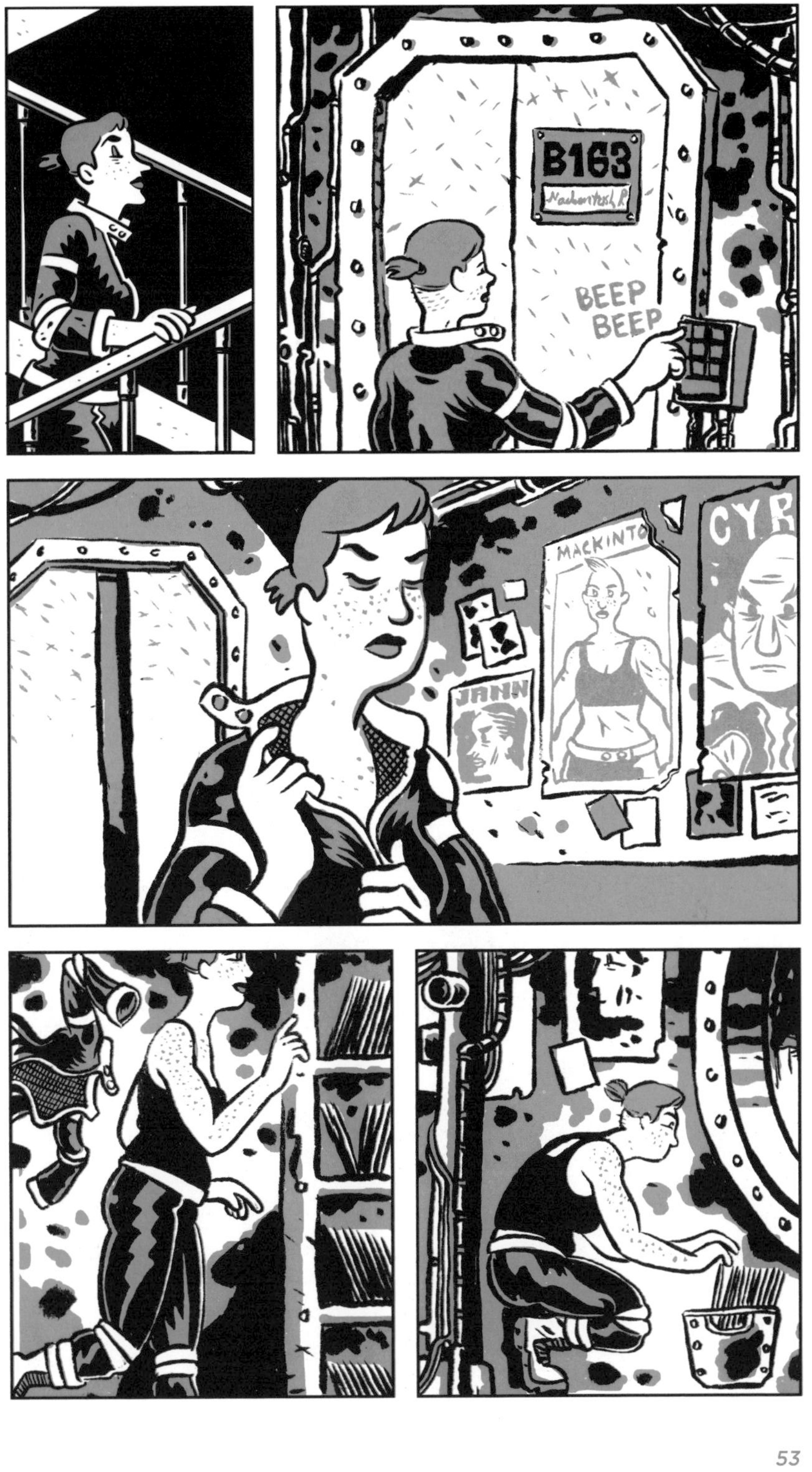
B163
BEEP BEEP
MACKINTO
JAHN
CYR

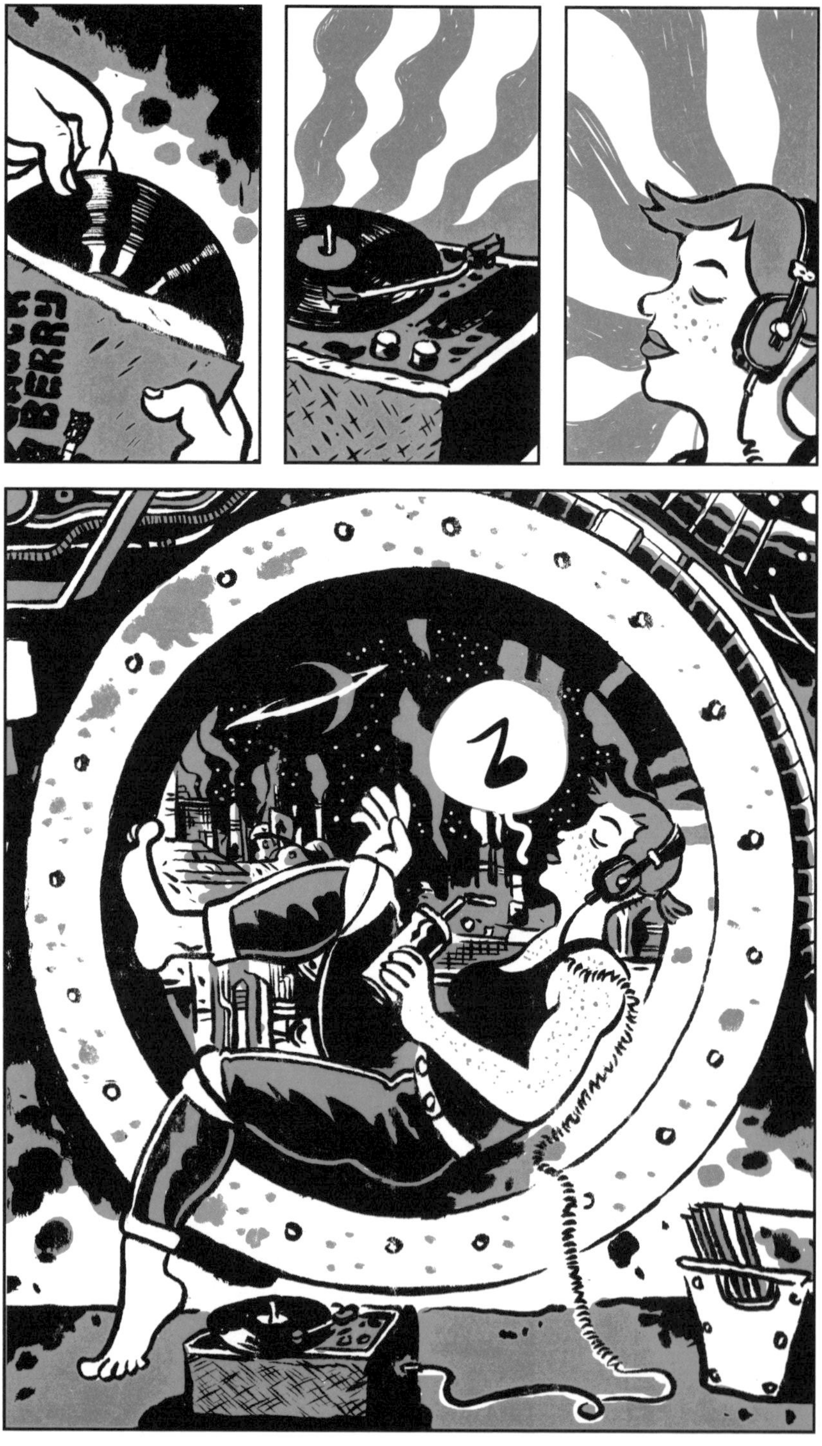
BERRY

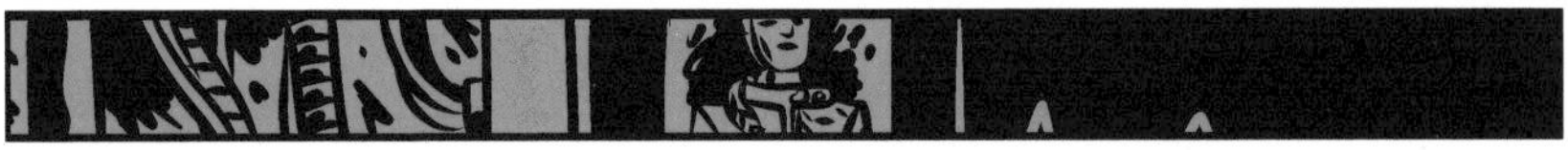

PART 04: I THINK WE'RE ALONE NOW

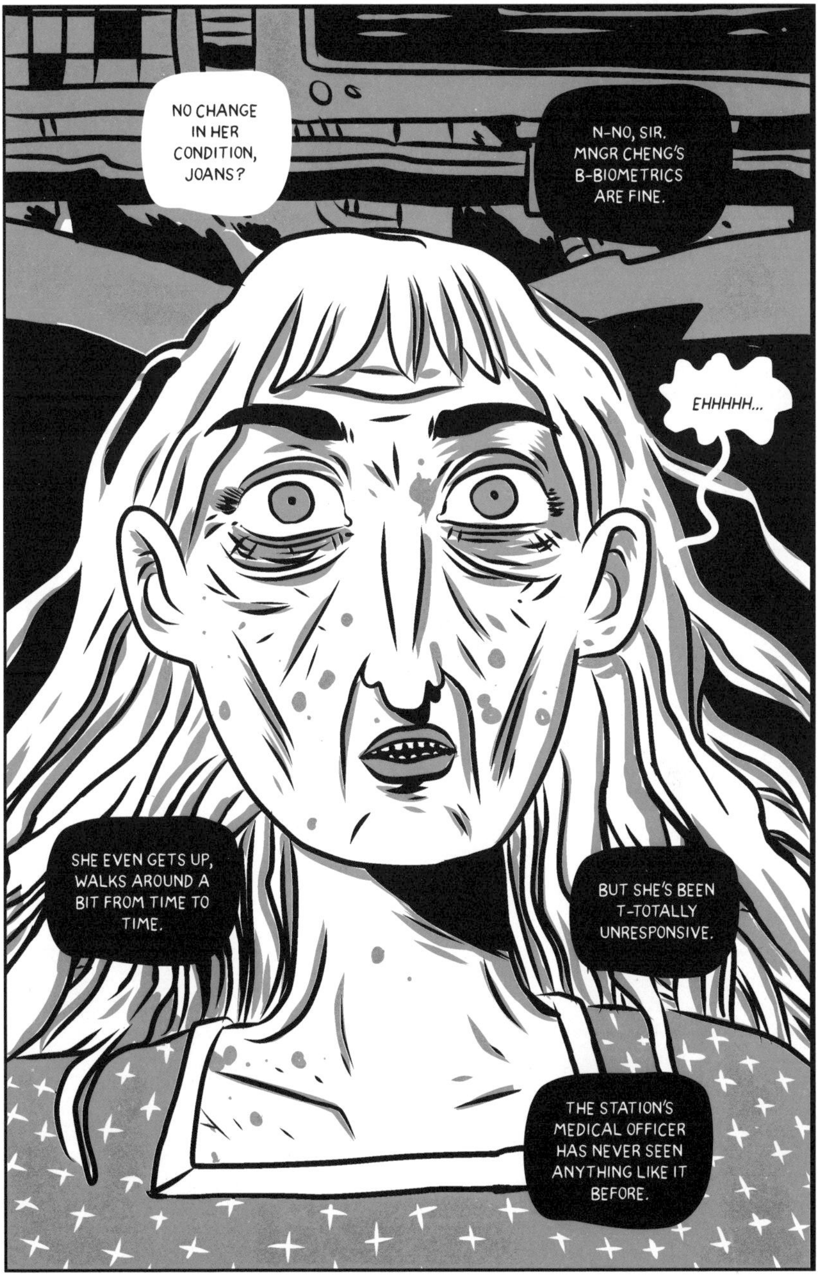
NO CHANGE IN HER CONDITION, JOANS?
N-NO, SIR. MNGR CHENG'S B-BIOMETRICS ARE FINE.
EHHHHH...
SHE EVEN GETS UP, WALKS AROUND A BIT FROM TIME TO TIME.
BUT SHE'S BEEN T-TOTALLY UNRESPONSIVE.
THE STATION'S MEDICAL OFFICER HAS NEVER SEEN ANYTHING LIKE IT BEFORE.

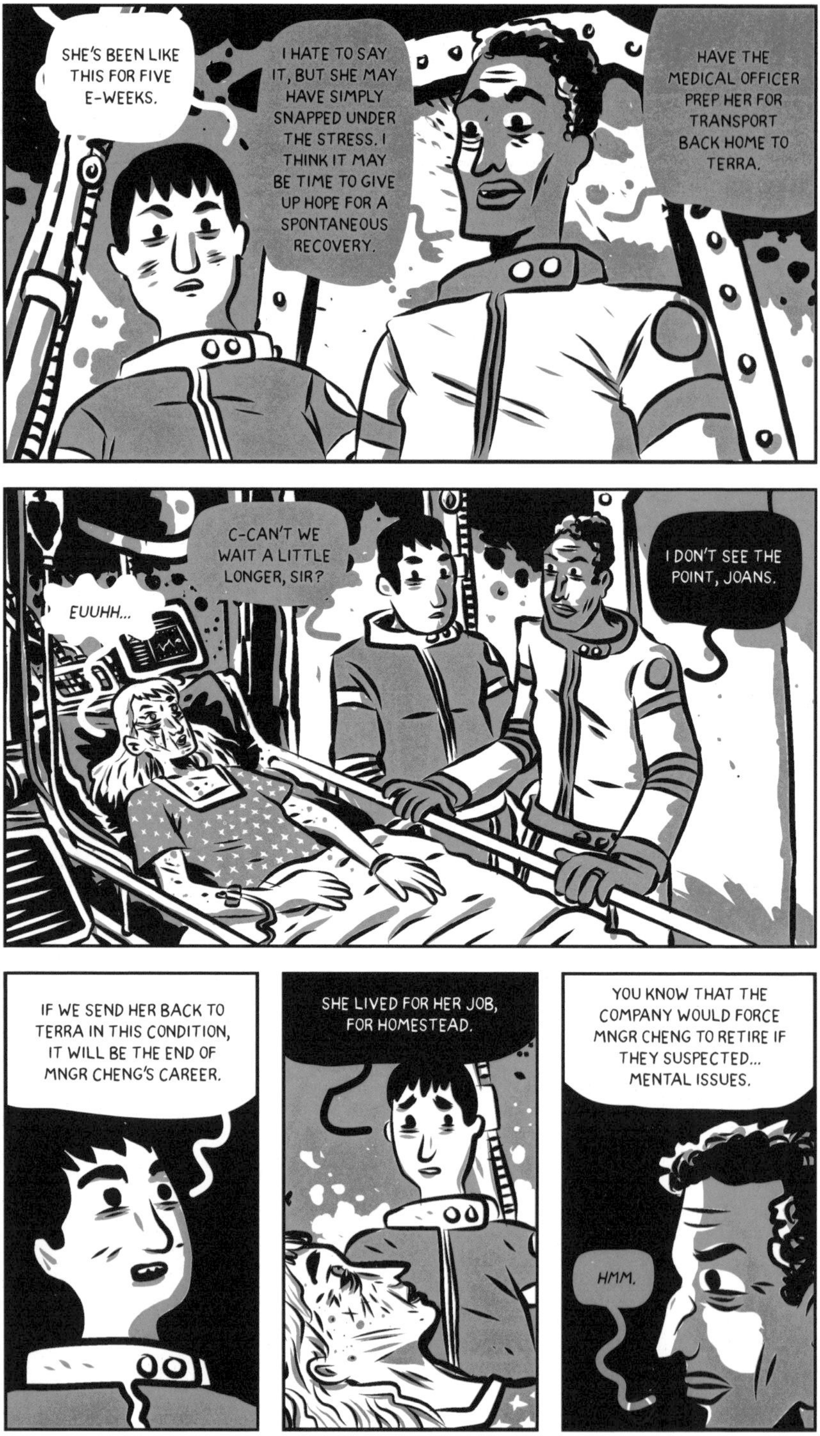
SHE'S BEEN LIKE THIS FOR FIVE E-WEEKS.
I HATE TO SAY IT, BUT SHE MAY HAVE SIMPLY SNAPPED UNDER THE STRESS. I THINK IT MAY BE TIME TO GIVE UP HOPE FOR A SPONTANEOUS RECOVERY.
HAVE THE MEDICAL OFFICER PREP HER FOR TRANSPORT BACK HOME TO TERRA.
EUUHH...
C-CAN'T WE WAIT A LITTLE LONGER, SIR?
I DON'T SEE THE POINT, JOANS.
IF WE SEND HER BACK TO TERRA IN THIS CONDITION, IT WILL BE THE END OF MNGR CHENG'S CAREER.
SHE LIVED FOR HER JOB, FOR HOMESTEAD.
YOU KNOW THAT THE COMPANY WOULD FORCE MNGR CHENG TO RETIRE IF THEY SUSPECTED... MENTAL ISSUES.
HMM.

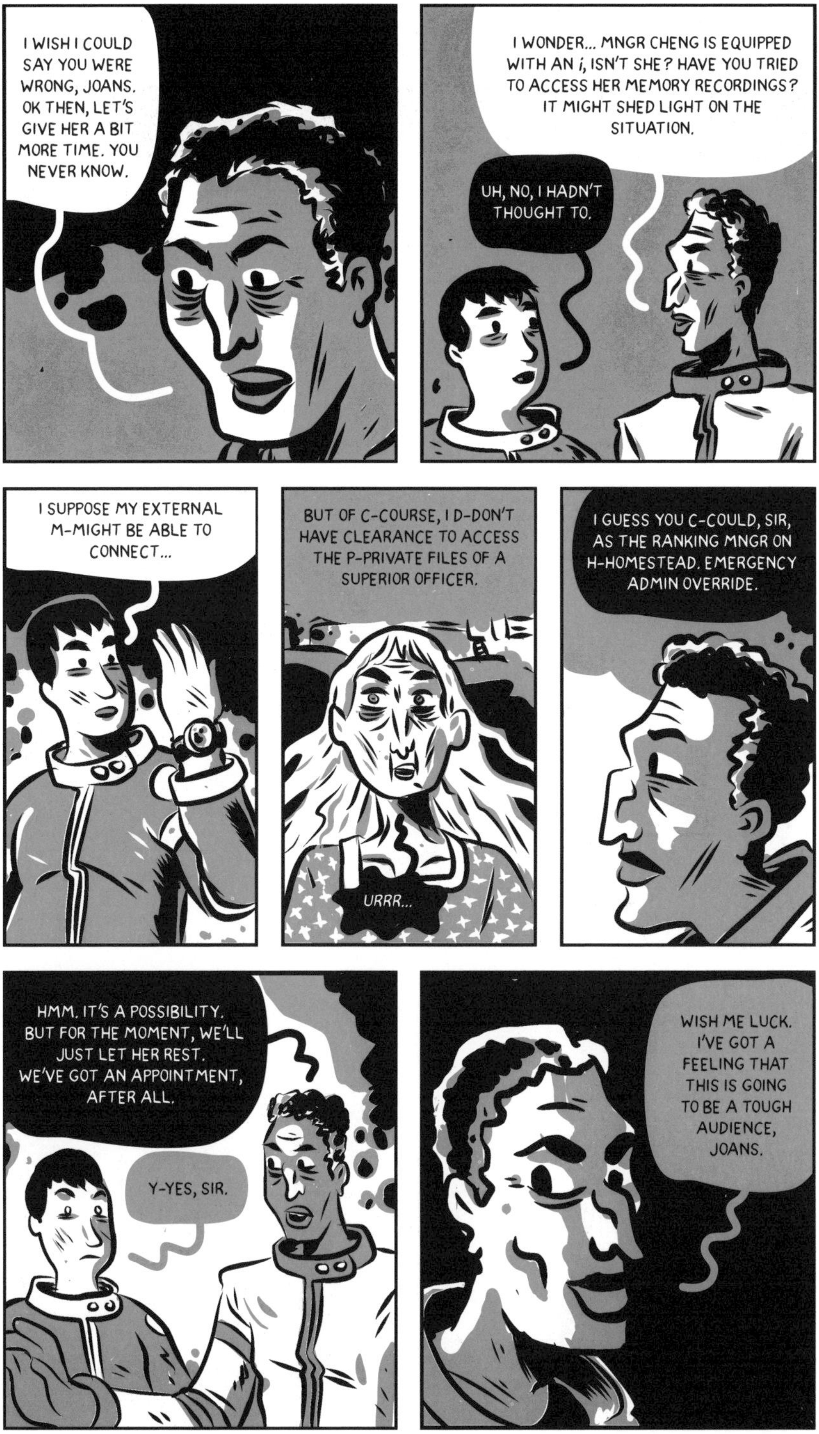
I WISH I COULD SAY YOU WERE WRONG, JOANS. OK THEN, LET'S GIVE HER A BIT MORE TIME. YOU NEVER KNOW.
I WONDER... MNGR CHENG IS EQUIPPED WITH AN *i*, ISN'T SHE? HAVE YOU TRIED TO ACCESS HER MEMORY RECORDINGS? IT MIGHT SHED LIGHT ON THE SITUATION.
UH, NO, I HADN'T THOUGHT TO.
I SUPPOSE MY EXTERNAL M-MIGHT BE ABLE TO CONNECT...
BUT OF C-COURSE, I D-DON'T HAVE CLEARANCE TO ACCESS THE P-PRIVATE FILES OF A SUPERIOR OFFICER.
URRR...
I GUESS YOU C-COULD, SIR, AS THE RANKING MNGR ON H-HOMESTEAD. EMERGENCY ADMIN OVERRIDE.
HMM. IT'S A POSSIBILITY. BUT FOR THE MOMENT, WE'LL JUST LET HER REST. WE'VE GOT AN APPOINTMENT, AFTER ALL.
Y-YES, SIR.
WISH ME LUCK. I'VE GOT A FEELING THAT THIS IS GOING TO BE A TOUGH AUDIENCE, JOANS.

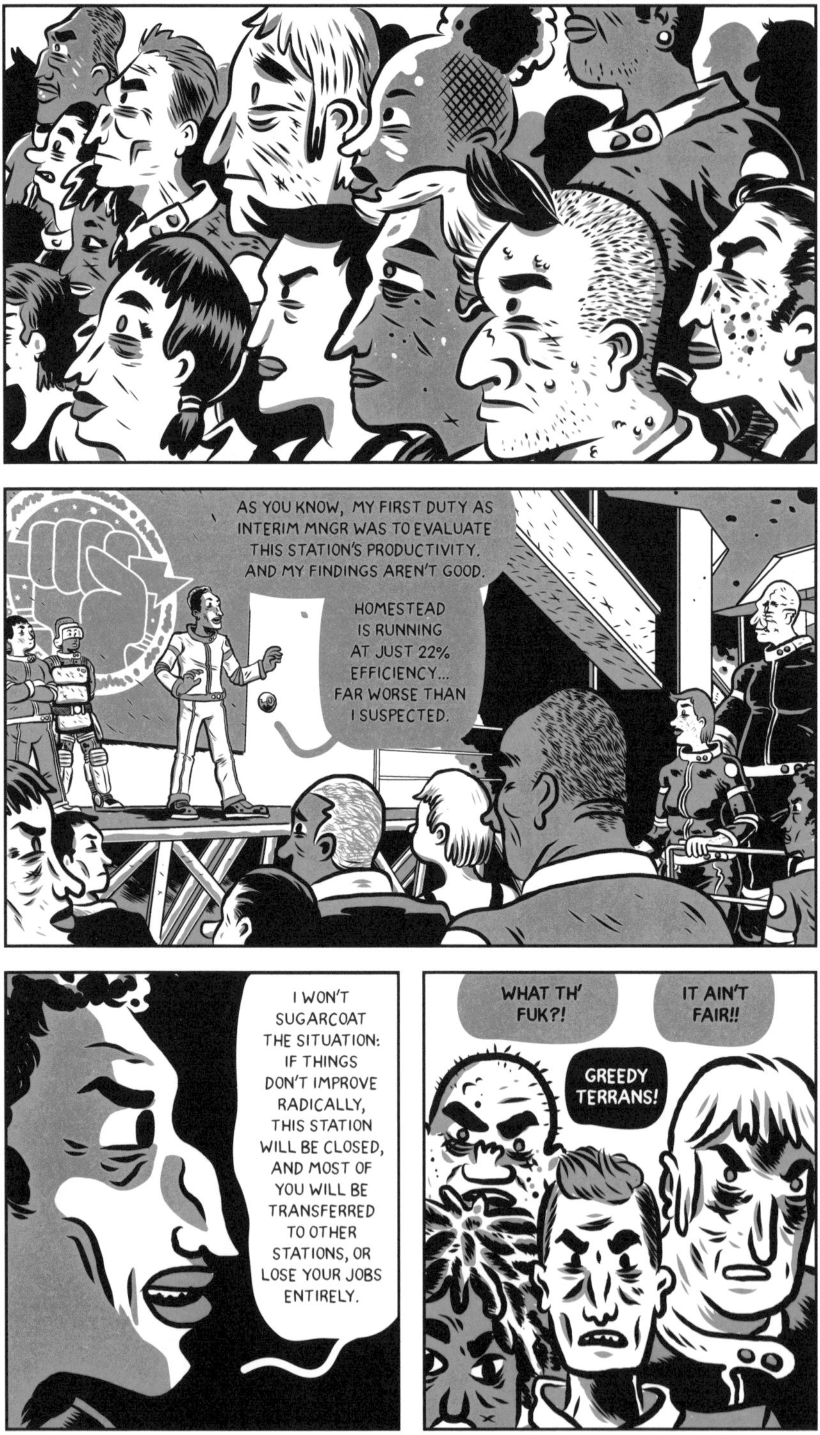
AS YOU KNOW, MY FIRST DUTY AS INTERIM MNGR WAS TO EVALUATE THIS STATION'S PRODUCTIVITY. AND MY FINDINGS AREN'T GOOD.
HOMESTEAD IS RUNNING AT JUST 22% EFFICIENCY... FAR WORSE THAN I SUSPECTED.
I WON'T SUGARCOAT THE SITUATION: IF THINGS DON'T IMPROVE RADICALLY, THIS STATION WILL BE CLOSED, AND MOST OF YOU WILL BE TRANSFERRED TO OTHER STATIONS, OR LOSE YOUR JOBS ENTIRELY.
WHAT TH' FUK?!
IT AIN'T FAIR!!
GREEDY TERRANS!

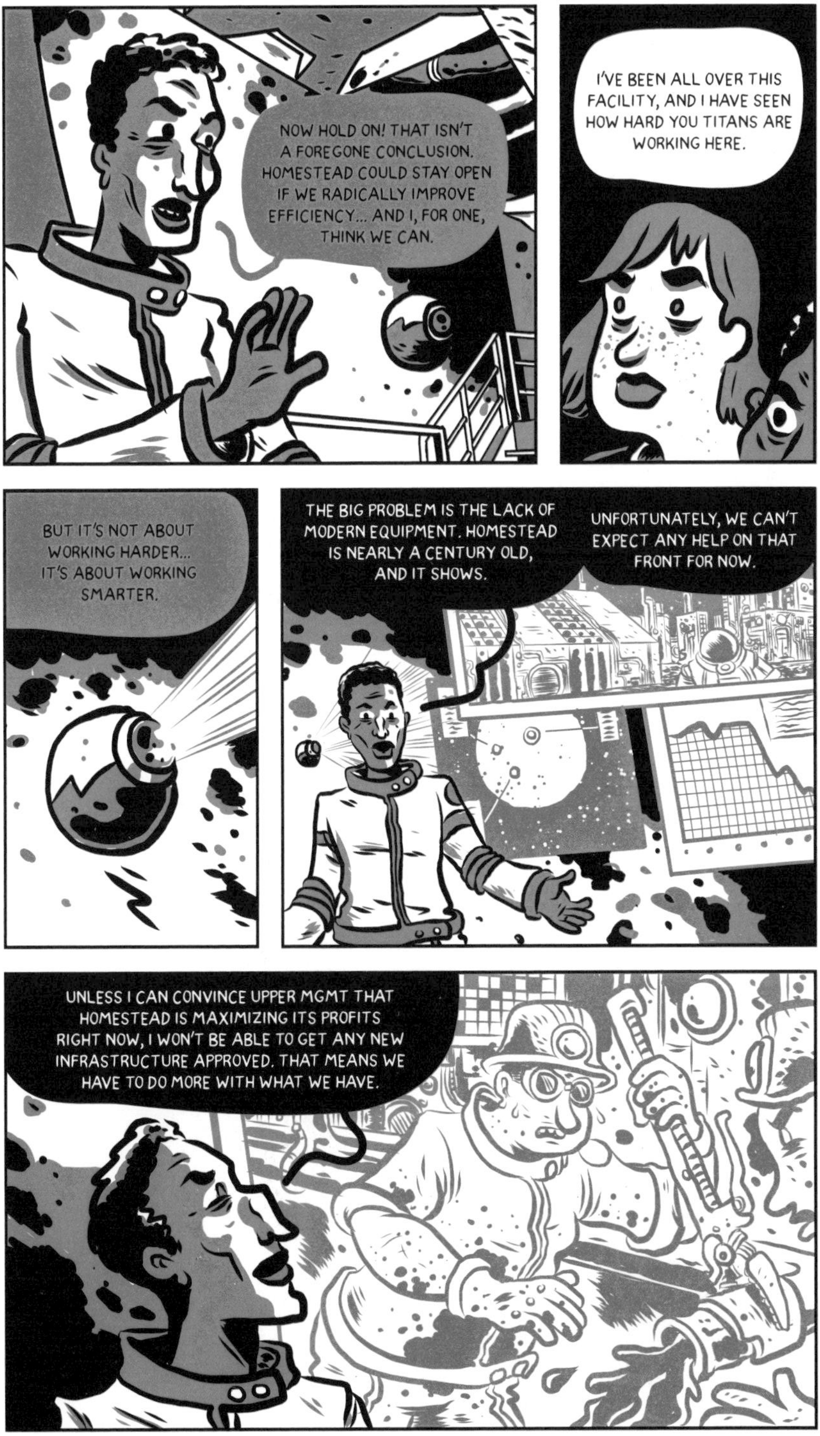
NOW HOLD ON! THAT ISN'T A FOREGONE CONCLUSION. HOMESTEAD COULD STAY OPEN IF WE RADICALLY IMPROVE EFFICIENCY... AND I, FOR ONE, THINK WE CAN.
I'VE BEEN ALL OVER THIS FACILITY, AND I HAVE SEEN HOW HARD YOU TITANS ARE WORKING HERE.
BUT IT'S NOT ABOUT WORKING HARDER... IT'S ABOUT WORKING SMARTER.
THE BIG PROBLEM IS THE LACK OF MODERN EQUIPMENT. HOMESTEAD IS NEARLY A CENTURY OLD, AND IT SHOWS.
UNFORTUNATELY, WE CAN'T EXPECT ANY HELP ON THAT FRONT FOR NOW.
UNLESS I CAN CONVINCE UPPER MGMT THAT HOMESTEAD IS MAXIMIZING ITS PROFITS RIGHT NOW, I WON'T BE ABLE TO GET ANY NEW INFRASTRUCTURE APPROVED. THAT MEANS WE HAVE TO DO MORE WITH WHAT WE HAVE.

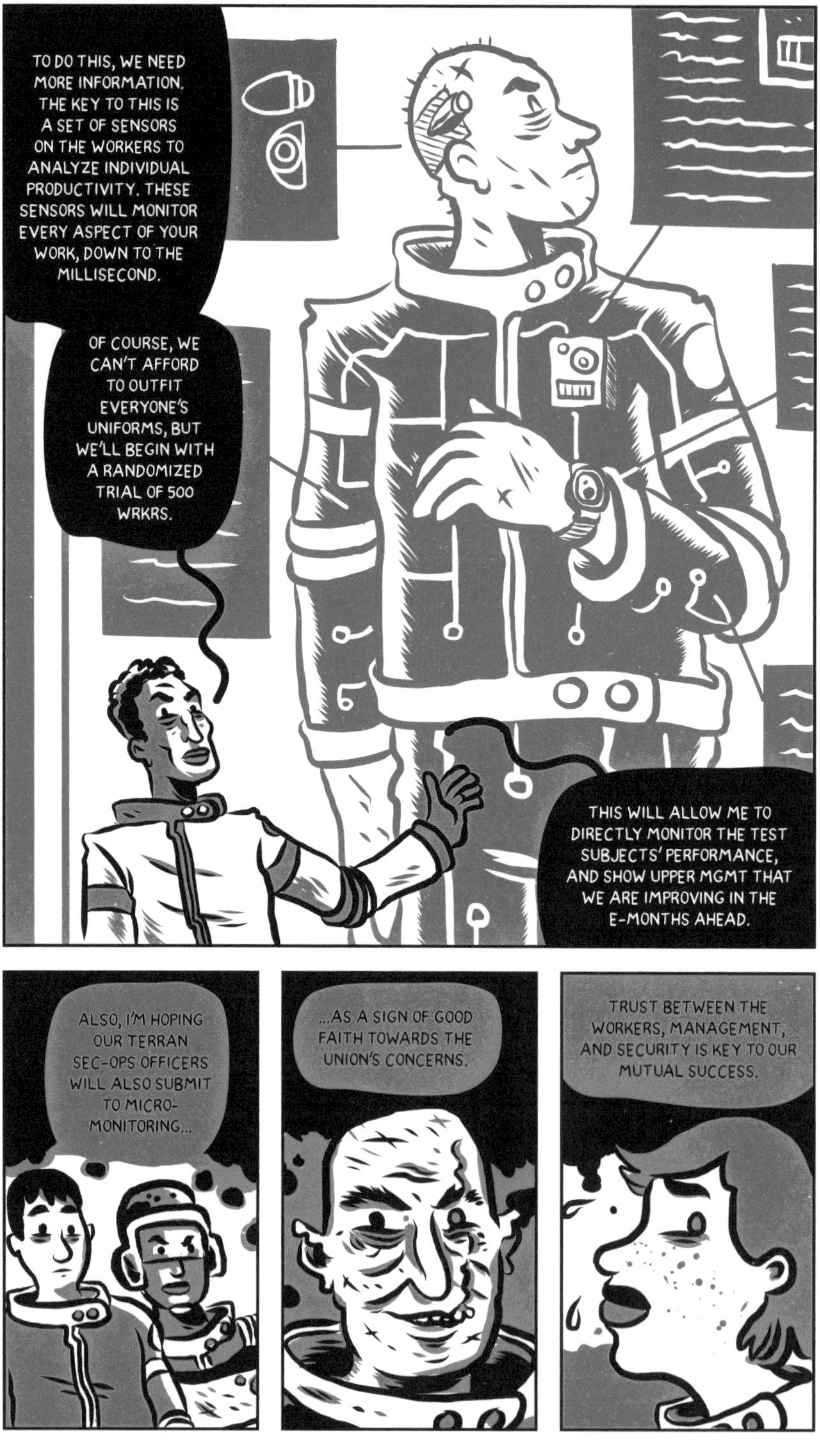

TO DO THIS, WE NEED MORE INFORMATION. THE KEY TO THIS IS A SET OF SENSORS ON THE WORKERS TO ANALYZE INDIVIDUAL PRODUCTIVITY. THESE SENSORS WILL MONITOR EVERY ASPECT OF YOUR WORK, DOWN TO THE MILLISECOND.
OF COURSE, WE CAN'T AFFORD TO OUTFIT EVERYONE'S UNIFORMS, BUT WE'LL BEGIN WITH A RANDOMIZED TRIAL OF 500 WRKRS.
THIS WILL ALLOW ME TO DIRECTLY MONITOR THE TEST SUBJECTS' PERFORMANCE, AND SHOW UPPER MGMT THAT WE ARE IMPROVING IN THE E-MONTHS AHEAD.
ALSO, I'M HOPING OUR TERRAN SEC-OPS OFFICERS WILL ALSO SUBMIT TO MICRO-MONITORING...
...AS A SIGN OF GOOD FAITH TOWARDS THE UNION'S CONCERNS.
TRUST BETWEEN THE WORKERS, MANAGEMENT, AND SECURITY IS KEY TO OUR MUTUAL SUCCESS.

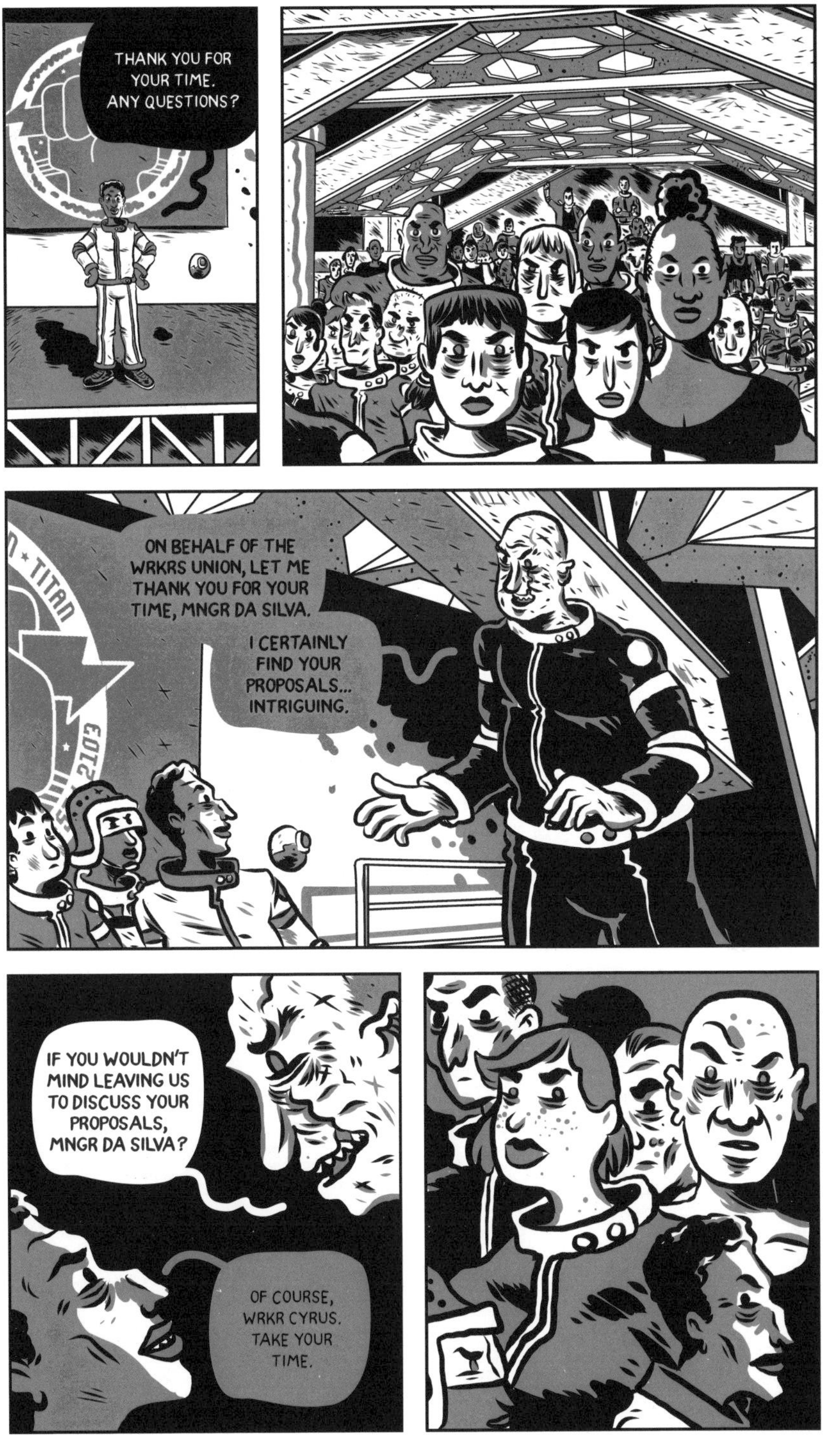
THANK YOU FOR YOUR TIME. ANY QUESTIONS?
TITAN
2103
ON BEHALF OF THE WRKRS UNION, LET ME THANK YOU FOR YOUR TIME, MNGR DA SILVA.
I CERTAINLY FIND YOUR PROPOSALS... INTRIGUING.
IF YOU WOULDN'T MIND LEAVING US TO DISCUSS YOUR PROPOSALS, MNGR DA SILVA?
OF COURSE, WRKR CYRUS. TAKE YOUR TIME.

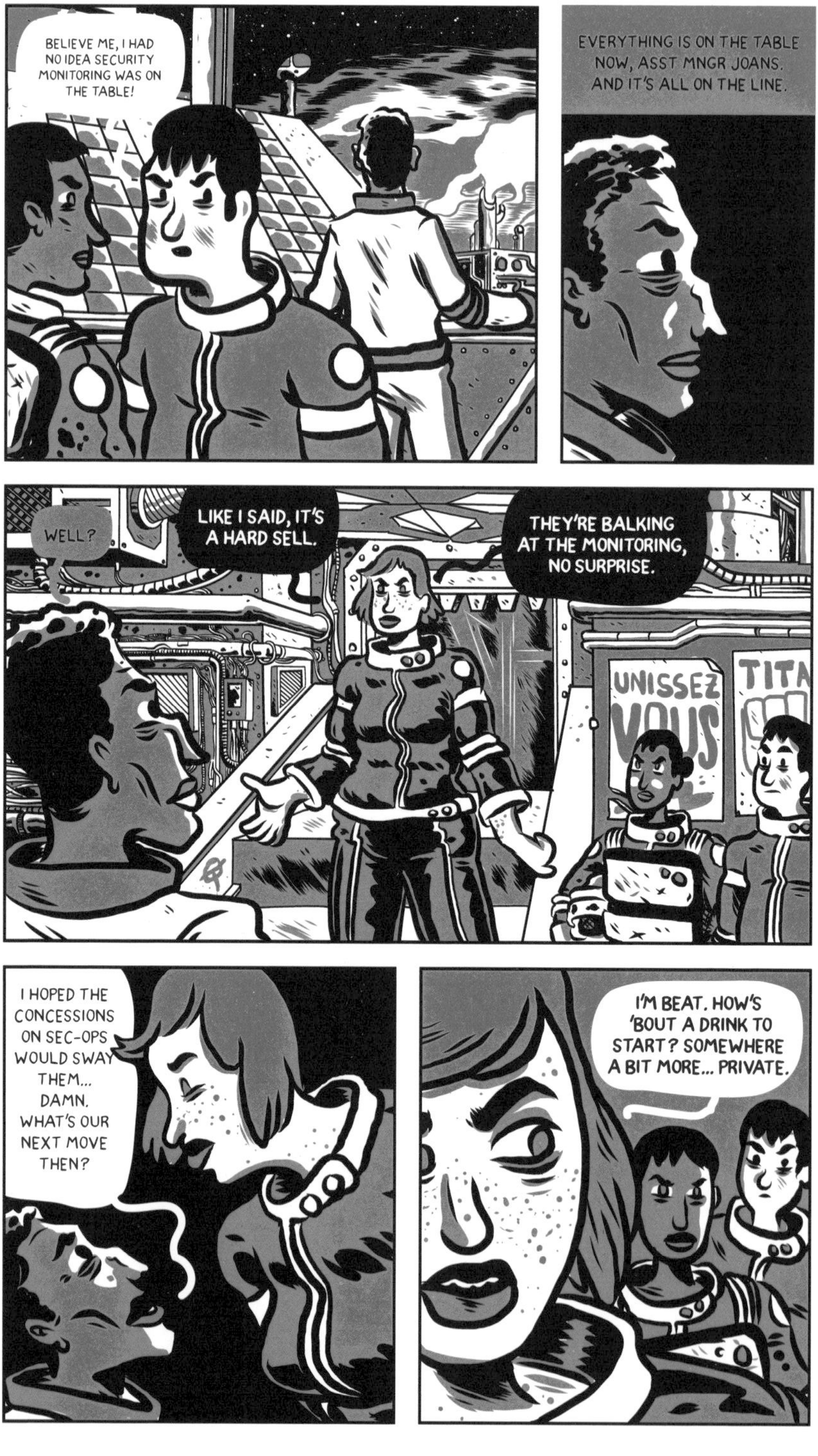
BELIEVE ME, I HAD NO IDEA SECURITY MONITORING WAS ON THE TABLE!
EVERYTHING IS ON THE TABLE NOW, ASST MNGR JOANS. AND IT'S ALL ON THE LINE.
WELL?
LIKE I SAID, IT'S A HARD SELL.
THEY'RE BALKING AT THE MONITORING, NO SURPRISE.
UNISSEZ VOUS
TITA
I HOPED THE CONCESSIONS ON SEC-OPS WOULD SWAY THEM... DAMN. WHAT'S OUR NEXT MOVE THEN?
I'M BEAT. HOW'S 'BOUT A DRINK TO START? SOMEWHERE A BIT MORE... PRIVATE.

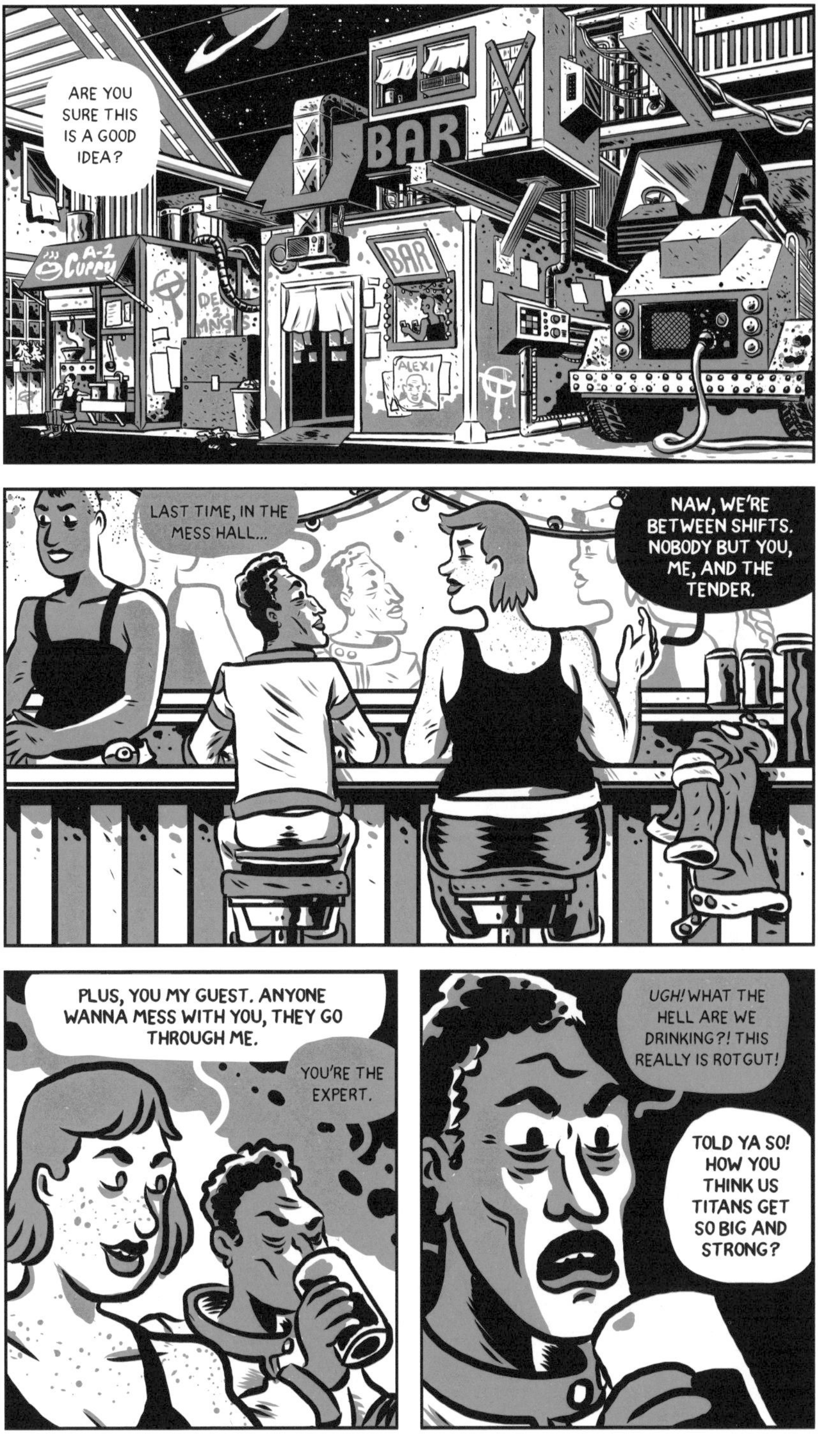
ARE YOU SURE THIS IS A GOOD IDEA?
BAR
A-1 Curry
BAR
ALEXI
LAST TIME, IN THE MESS HALL...
NAW, WE'RE BETWEEN SHIFTS. NOBODY BUT YOU, ME, AND THE TENDER.
PLUS, YOU MY GUEST. ANYONE WANNA MESS WITH YOU, THEY GO THROUGH ME.
YOU'RE THE EXPERT.
UGH! WHAT THE HELL ARE WE DRINKING?! THIS REALLY IS ROTGUT!
TOLD YA SO! HOW YOU THINK US TITANS GET SO BIG AND STRONG?

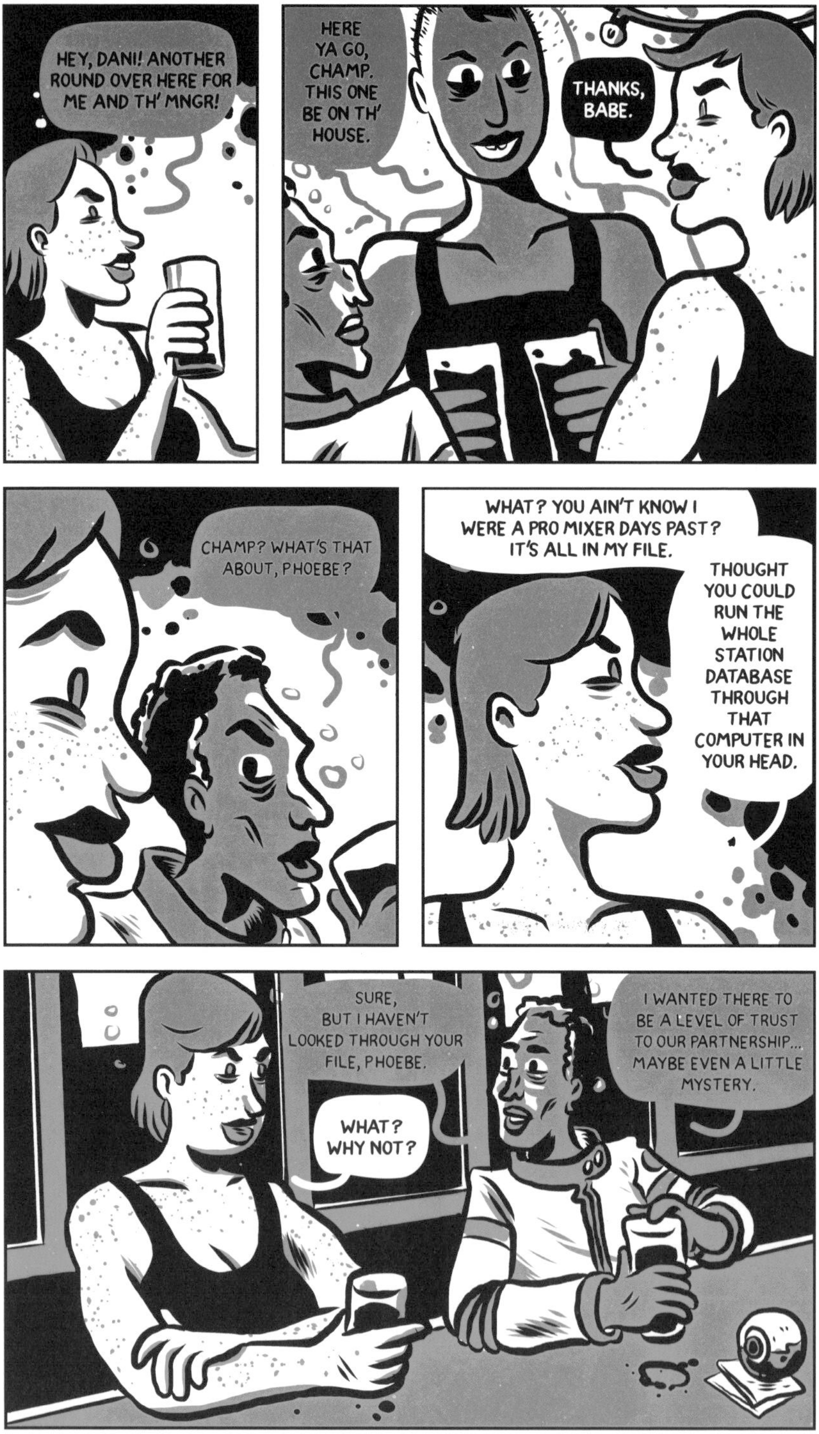
HEY, DANI! ANOTHER ROUND OVER HERE FOR ME AND TH' MNGR!
HERE YA GO, CHAMP. THIS ONE BE ON TH' HOUSE.
THANKS, BABE.
CHAMP? WHAT'S THAT ABOUT, PHOEBE?
WHAT? YOU AIN'T KNOW I WERE A PRO MIXER DAYS PAST? IT'S ALL IN MY FILE.
THOUGHT YOU COULD RUN THE WHOLE STATION DATABASE THROUGH THAT COMPUTER IN YOUR HEAD.
SURE, BUT I HAVEN'T LOOKED THROUGH YOUR FILE, PHOEBE.
WHAT? WHY NOT?
I WANTED THERE TO BE A LEVEL OF TRUST TO OUR PARTNERSHIP... MAYBE EVEN A LITTLE MYSTERY.

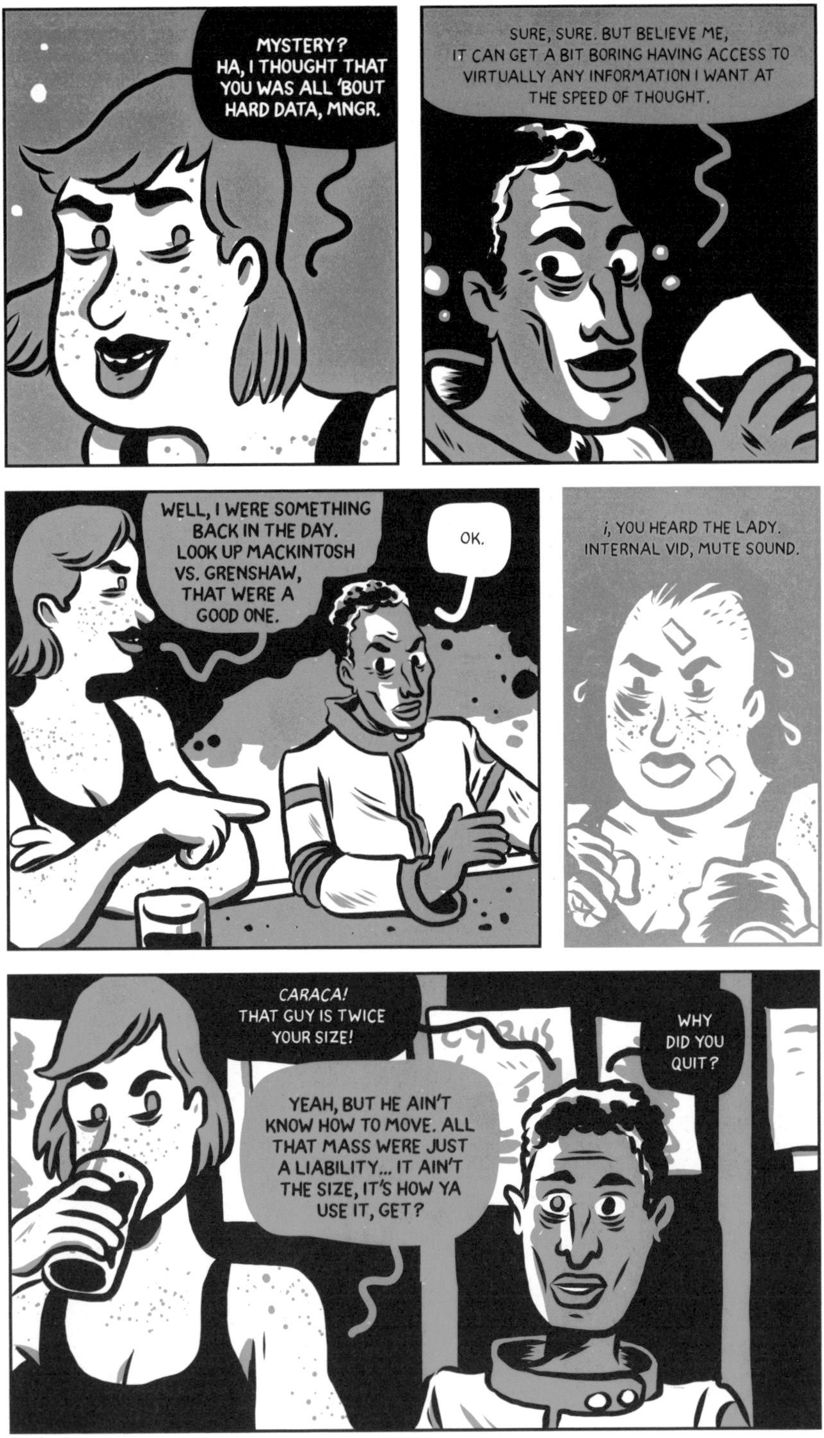
MYSTERY? HA, I THOUGHT THAT YOU WAS ALL 'BOUT HARD DATA, MNGR.
SURE, SURE. BUT BELIEVE ME, IT CAN GET A BIT BORING HAVING ACCESS TO VIRTUALLY ANY INFORMATION I WANT AT THE SPEED OF THOUGHT.
WELL, I WERE SOMETHING BACK IN THE DAY. LOOK UP MACKINTOSH VS. GRENSHAW, THAT WERE A GOOD ONE.
OK.
i, YOU HEARD THE LADY. INTERNAL VID, MUTE SOUND.
CARACA! THAT GUY IS TWICE YOUR SIZE!
YEAH, BUT HE AIN'T KNOW HOW TO MOVE. ALL THAT MASS WERE JUST A LIABILITY... IT AIN'T THE SIZE, IT'S HOW YA USE IT, GET?
WHY DID YOU QUIT?

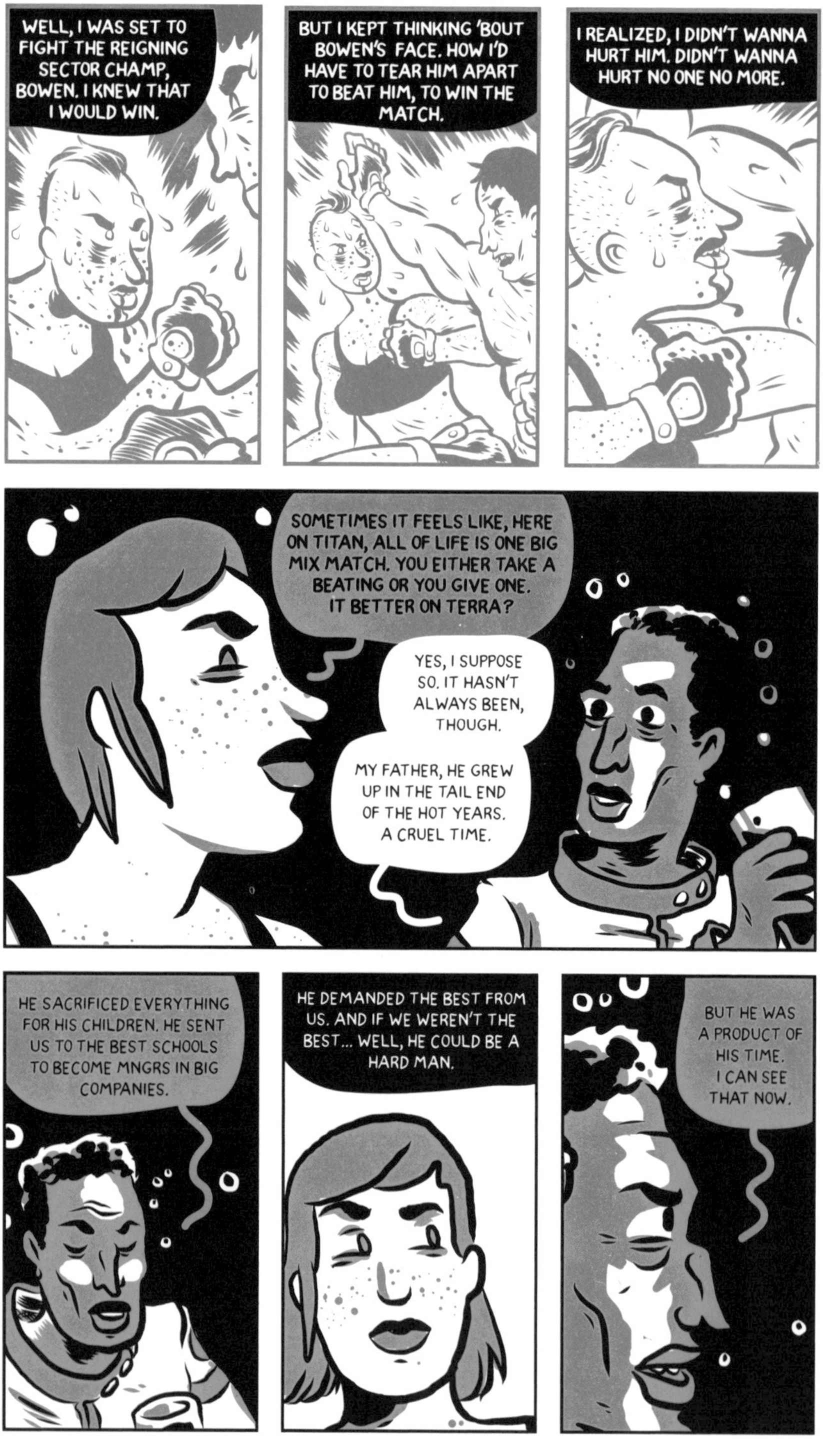
WELL, I WAS SET TO FIGHT THE REIGNING SECTOR CHAMP, BOWEN. I KNEW THAT I WOULD WIN.
BUT I KEPT THINKING 'BOUT BOWEN'S FACE. HOW I'D HAVE TO TEAR HIM APART TO BEAT HIM, TO WIN THE MATCH.
I REALIZED, I DIDN'T WANNA HURT HIM. DIDN'T WANNA HURT NO ONE NO MORE.
SOMETIMES IT FEELS LIKE, HERE ON TITAN, ALL OF LIFE IS ONE BIG MIX MATCH. YOU EITHER TAKE A BEATING OR YOU GIVE ONE. IT BETTER ON TERRA?
YES, I SUPPOSE SO. IT HASN'T ALWAYS BEEN, THOUGH.
MY FATHER, HE GREW UP IN THE TAIL END OF THE HOT YEARS. A CRUEL TIME.
HE SACRIFICED EVERYTHING FOR HIS CHILDREN. HE SENT US TO THE BEST SCHOOLS TO BECOME MNGRS IN BIG COMPANIES.
HE DEMANDED THE BEST FROM US. AND IF WE WEREN'T THE BEST... WELL, HE COULD BE A HARD MAN.
BUT HE WAS A PRODUCT OF HIS TIME. I CAN SEE THAT NOW.

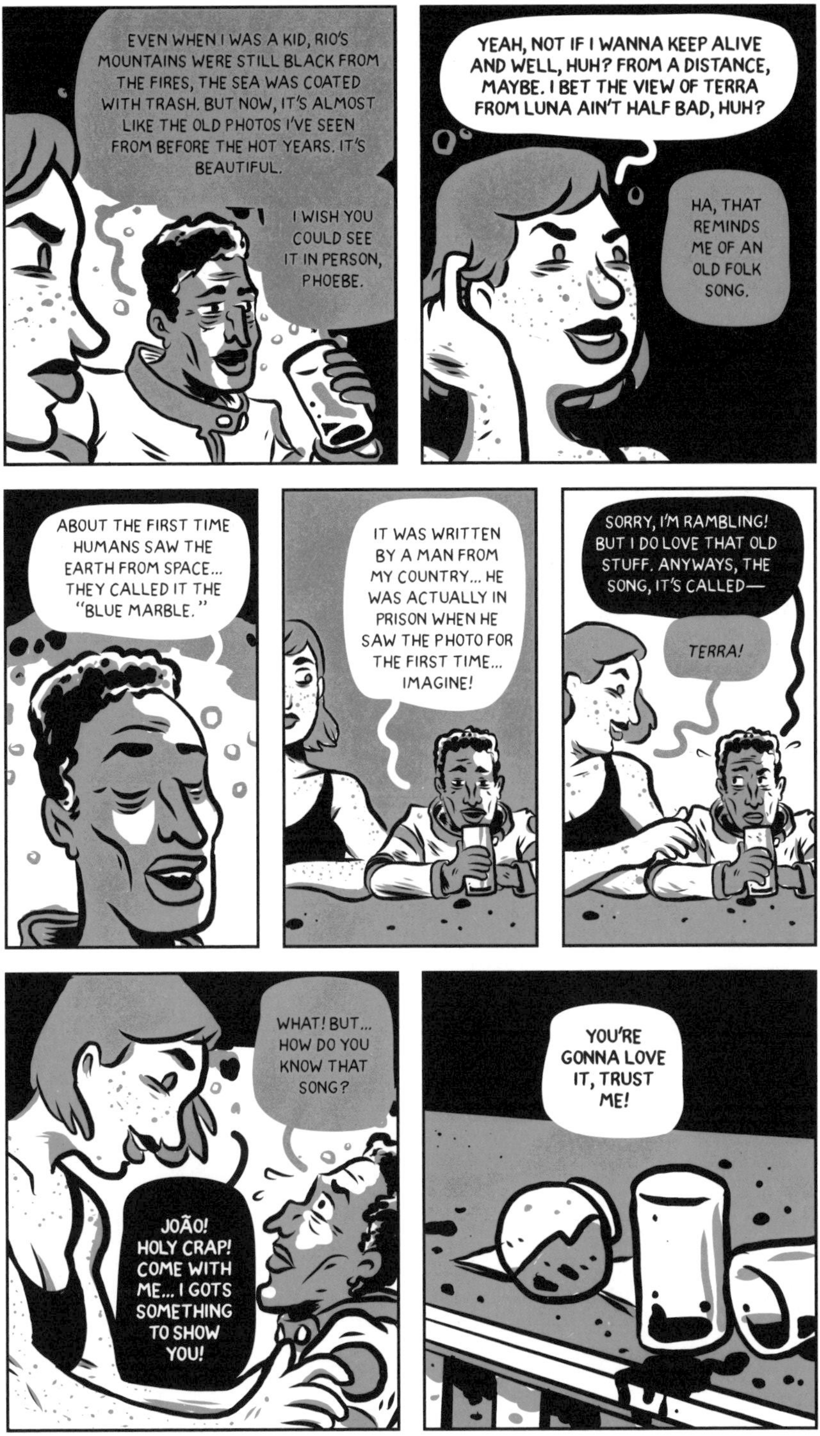
EVEN WHEN I WAS A KID, RIO'S MOUNTAINS WERE STILL BLACK FROM THE FIRES, THE SEA WAS COATED WITH TRASH. BUT NOW, IT'S ALMOST LIKE THE OLD PHOTOS I'VE SEEN FROM BEFORE THE HOT YEARS. IT'S BEAUTIFUL.
I WISH YOU COULD SEE IT IN PERSON, PHOEBE.
YEAH, NOT IF I WANNA KEEP ALIVE AND WELL, HUH? FROM A DISTANCE, MAYBE. I BET THE VIEW OF TERRA FROM LUNA AIN'T HALF BAD, HUH?
HA, THAT REMINDS ME OF AN OLD FOLK SONG.
ABOUT THE FIRST TIME HUMANS SAW THE EARTH FROM SPACE... THEY CALLED IT THE "BLUE MARBLE."
IT WAS WRITTEN BY A MAN FROM MY COUNTRY... HE WAS ACTUALLY IN PRISON WHEN HE SAW THE PHOTO FOR THE FIRST TIME... IMAGINE!
SORRY, I'M RAMBLING! BUT I DO LOVE THAT OLD STUFF. ANYWAYS, THE SONG, IT'S CALLED—
TERRA!
WHAT! BUT... HOW DO YOU KNOW THAT SONG?
JOÃO! HOLY CRAP! COME WITH ME... I GOTS SOMETHING TO SHOW YOU!
YOU'RE GONNA LOVE IT, TRUST ME!

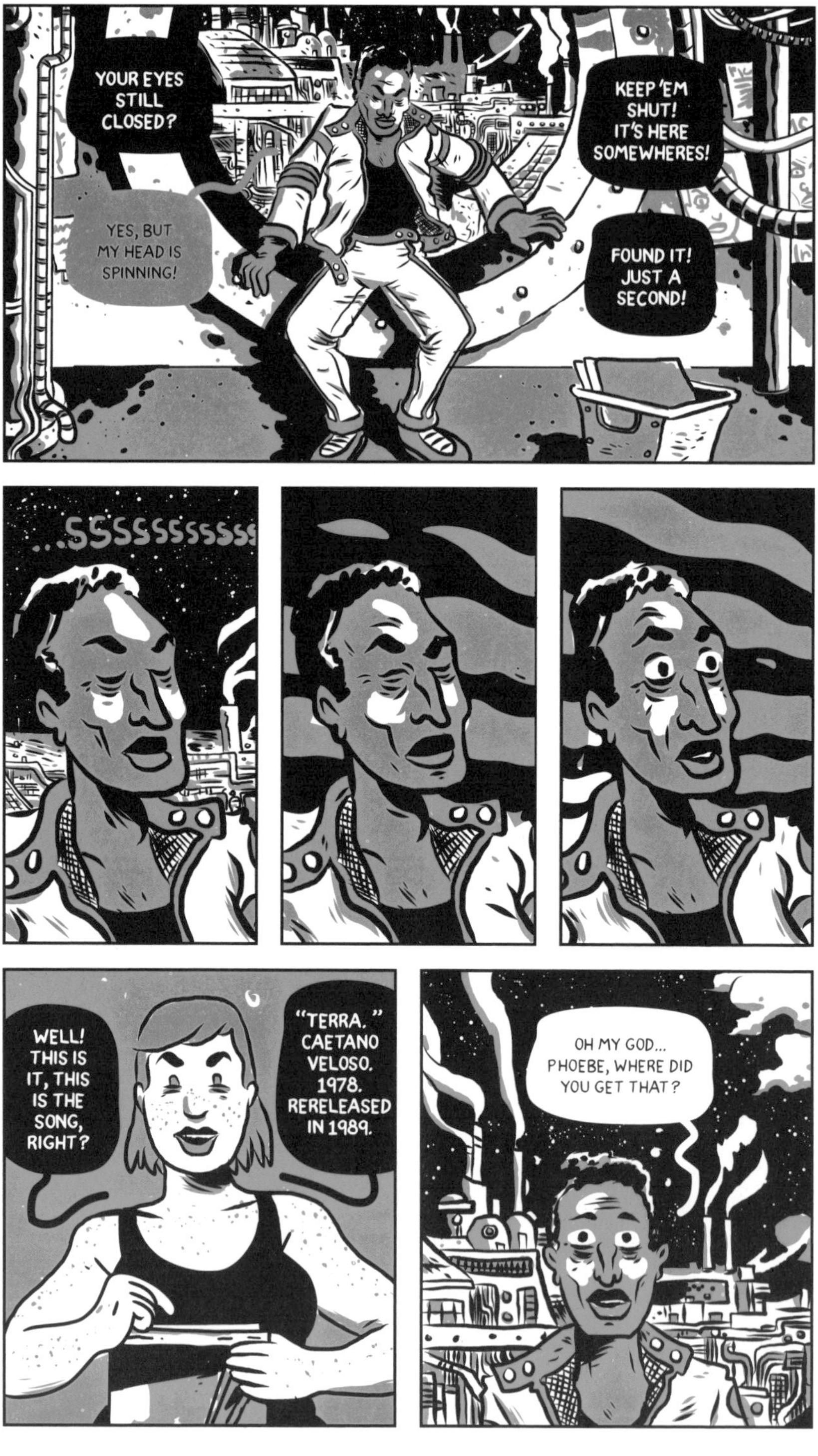
YOUR EYES STILL CLOSED?
KEEP 'EM SHUT! IT'S HERE SOMEWHERES!
YES, BUT MY HEAD IS SPINNING!
FOUND IT! JUST A SECOND!
...SSSSSSSSSS
WELL! THIS IS IT, THIS IS THE SONG, RIGHT?
"TERRA." CAETANO VELOSO. 1978. RERELEASED IN 1989.
OH MY GOD... PHOEBE, WHERE DID YOU GET THAT?

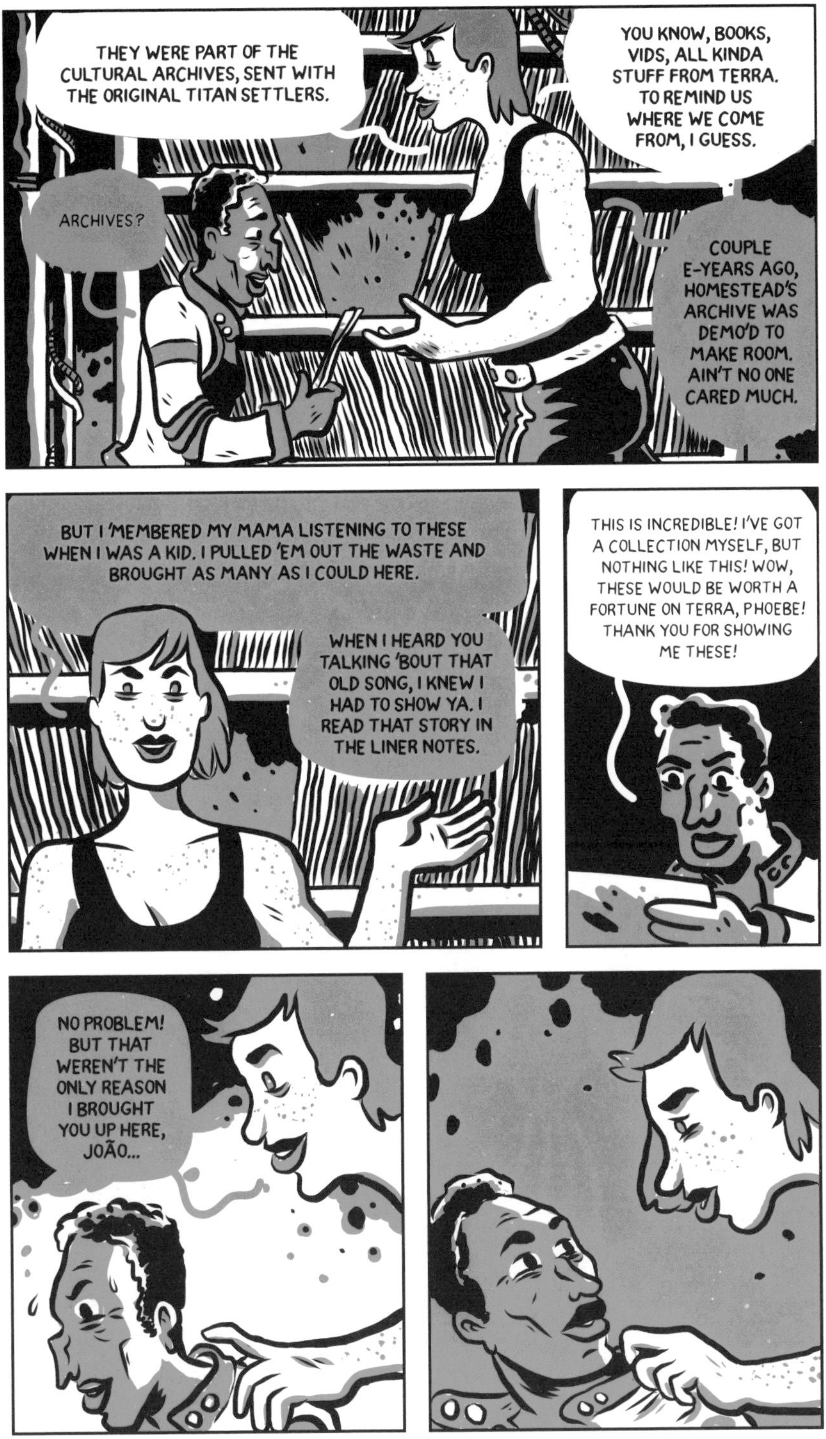
THEY WERE PART OF THE CULTURAL ARCHIVES, SENT WITH THE ORIGINAL TITAN SETTLERS.
YOU KNOW, BOOKS, VIDS, ALL KINDA STUFF FROM TERRA. TO REMIND US WHERE WE COME FROM, I GUESS.
ARCHIVES?
COUPLE E-YEARS AGO, HOMESTEAD'S ARCHIVE WAS DEMO'D TO MAKE ROOM. AIN'T NO ONE CARED MUCH.
BUT I 'MEMBERED MY MAMA LISTENING TO THESE WHEN I WAS A KID. I PULLED 'EM OUT THE WASTE AND BROUGHT AS MANY AS I COULD HERE.
WHEN I HEARD YOU TALKING 'BOUT THAT OLD SONG, I KNEW I HAD TO SHOW YA. I READ THAT STORY IN THE LINER NOTES.
THIS IS INCREDIBLE! I'VE GOT A COLLECTION MYSELF, BUT NOTHING LIKE THIS! WOW, THESE WOULD BE WORTH A FORTUNE ON TERRA, PHOEBE! THANK YOU FOR SHOWING ME THESE!
NO PROBLEM! BUT THAT WEREN'T THE ONLY REASON I BROUGHT YOU UP HERE, JOÃO...

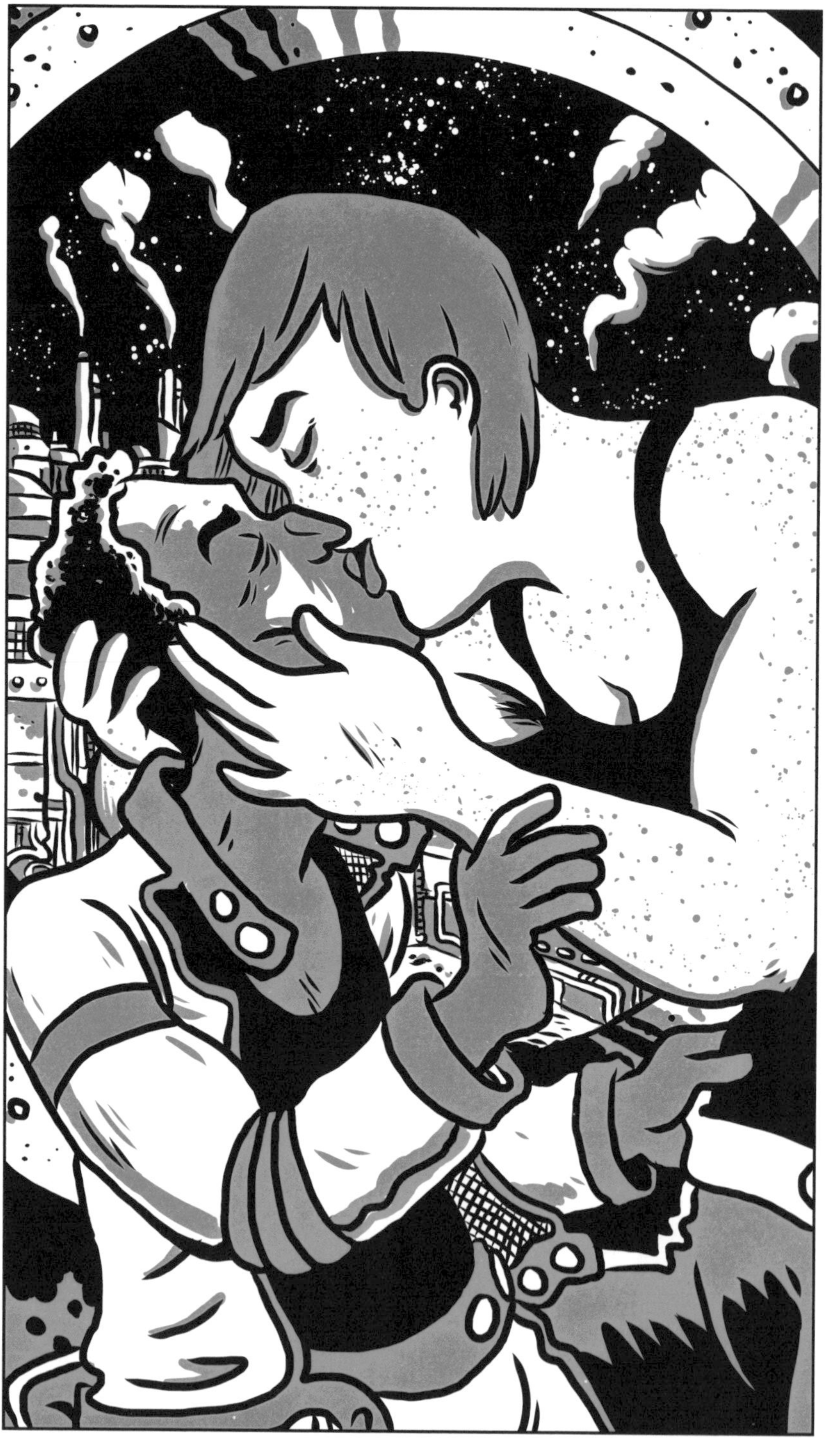

PART 05: JUST LIKE HONEY

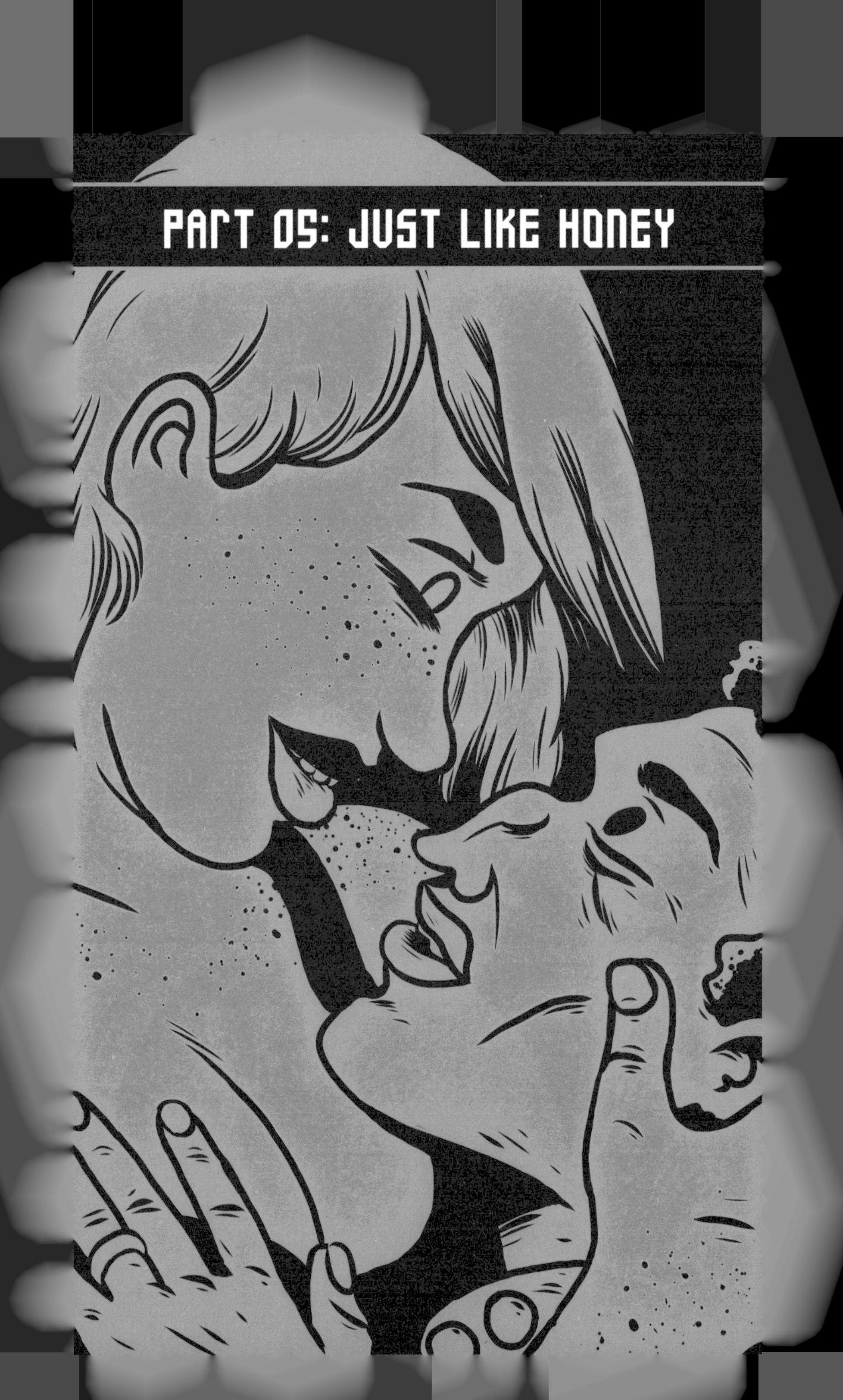

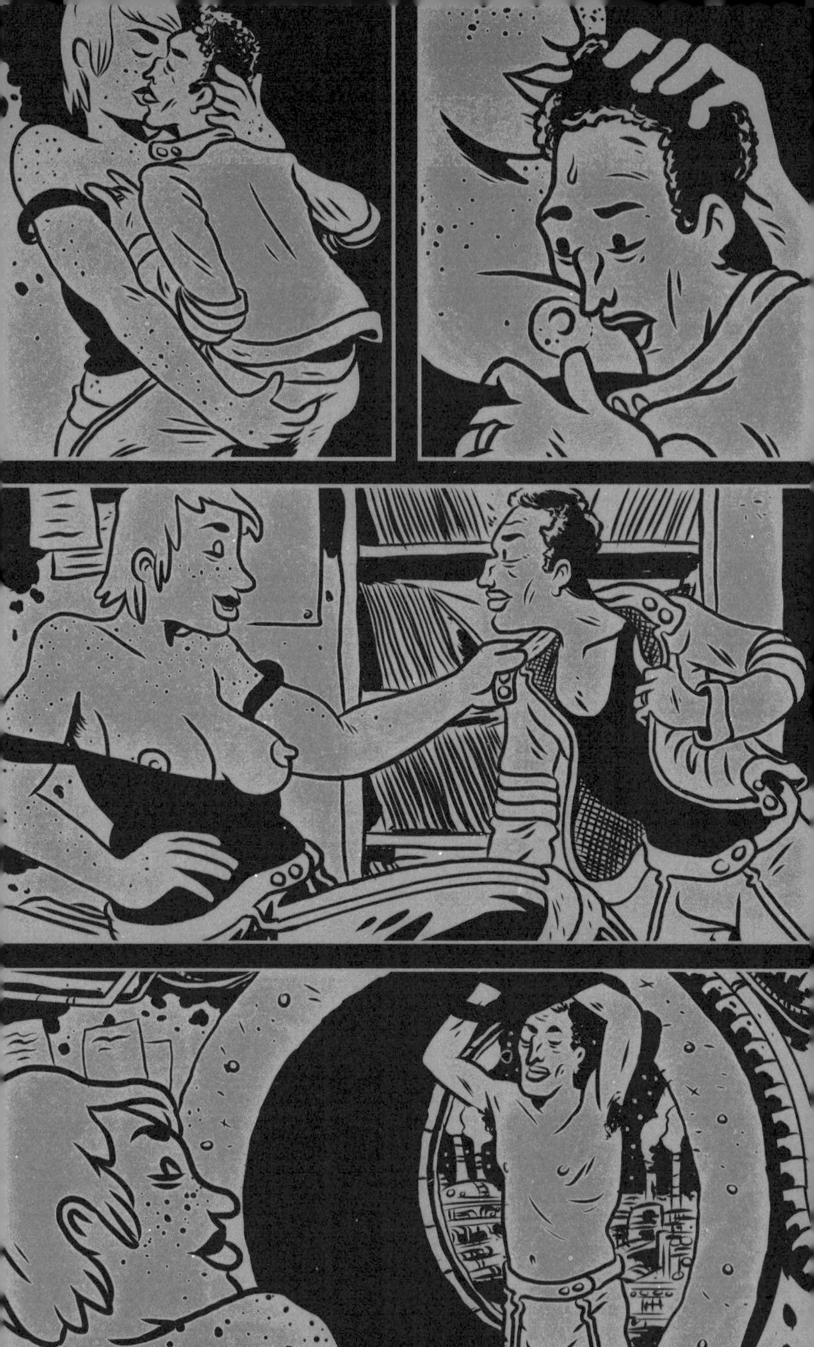

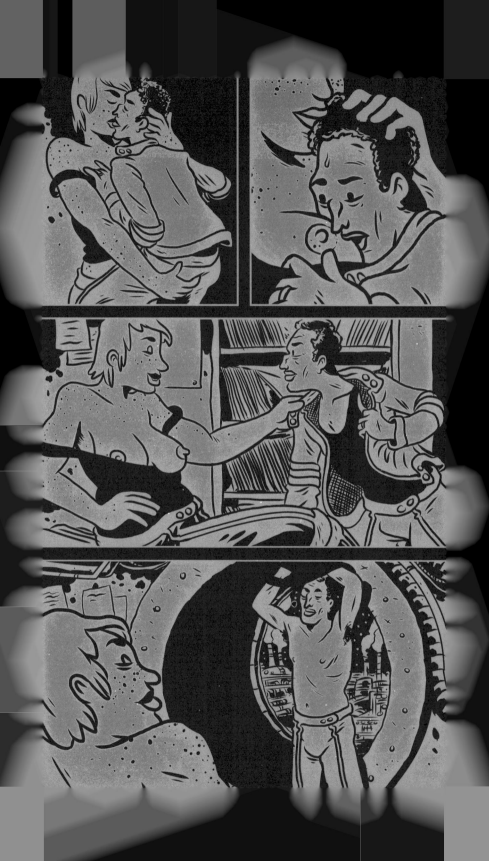

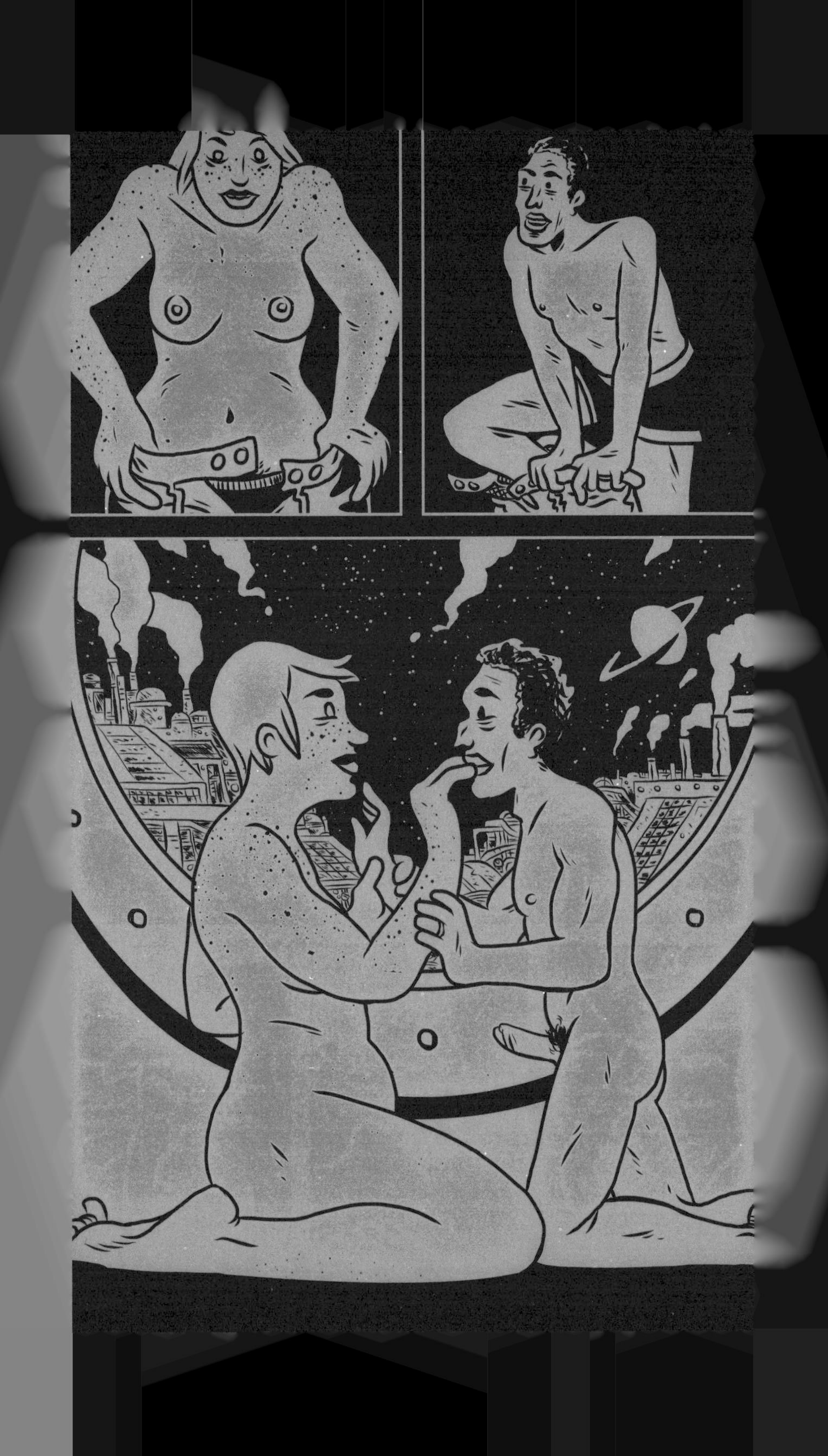

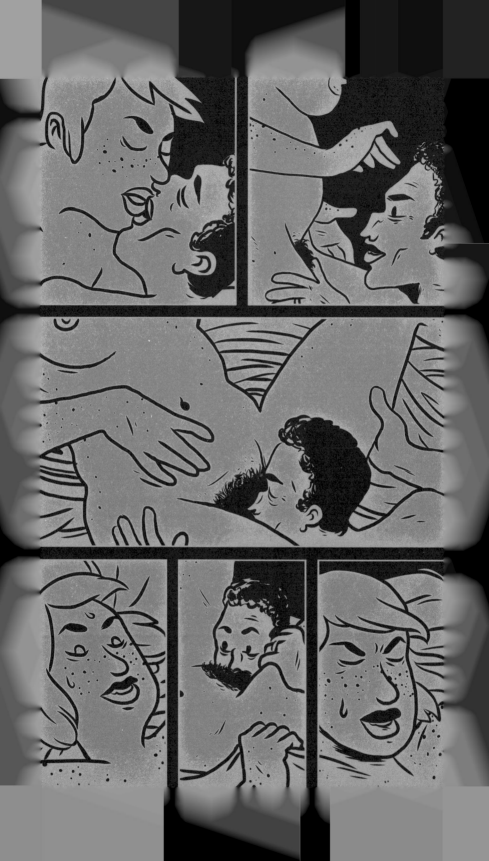

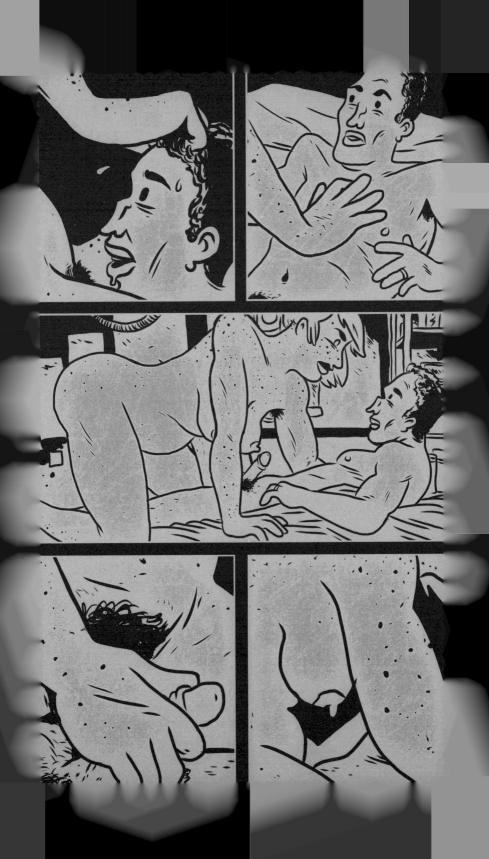

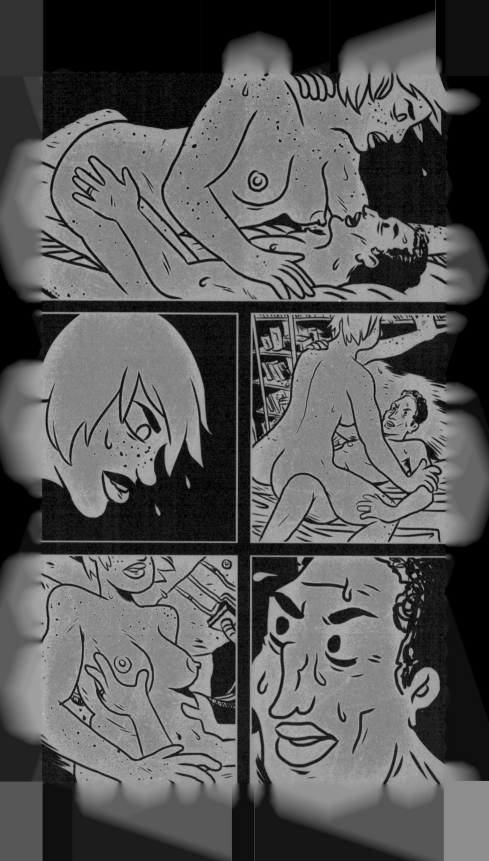

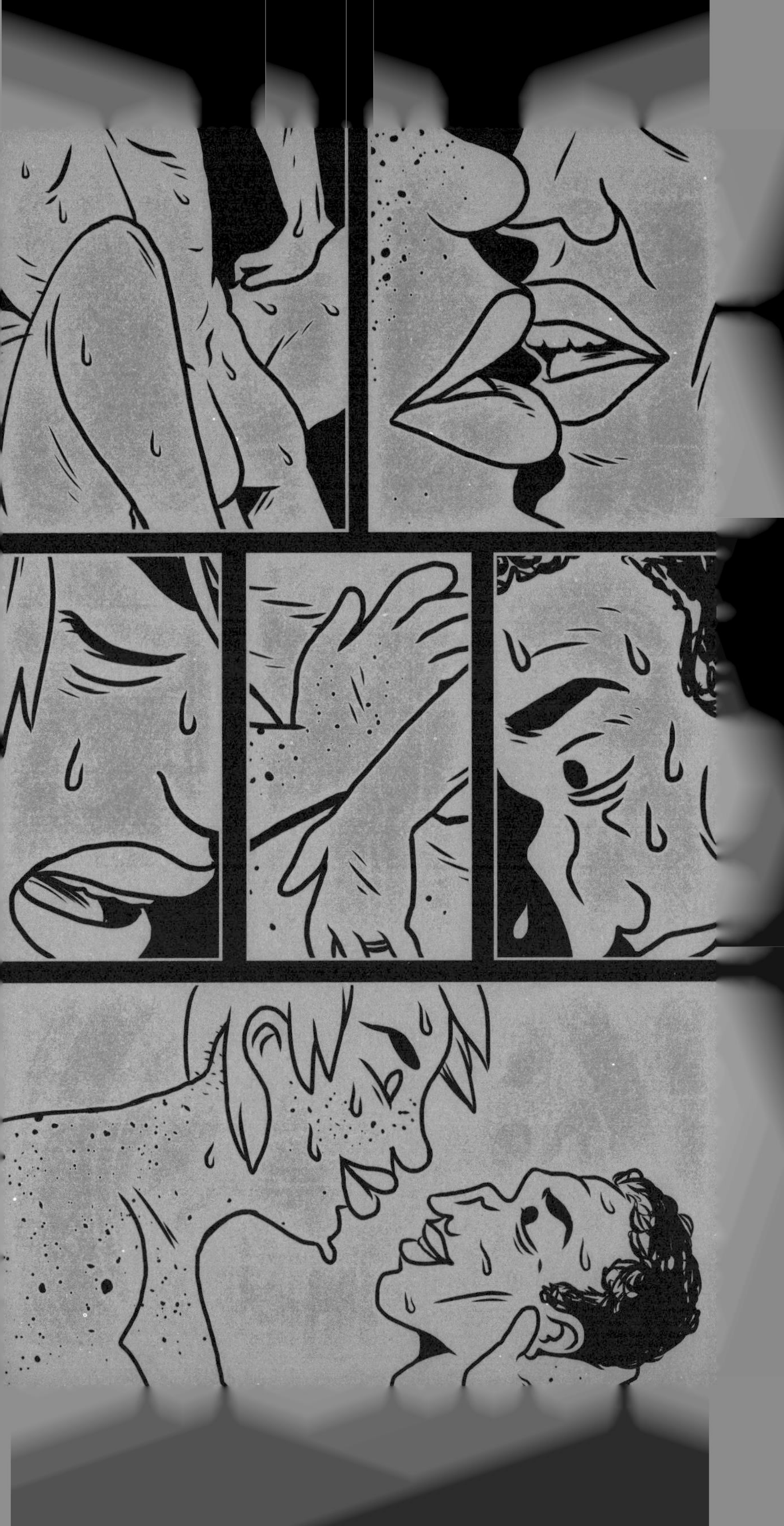

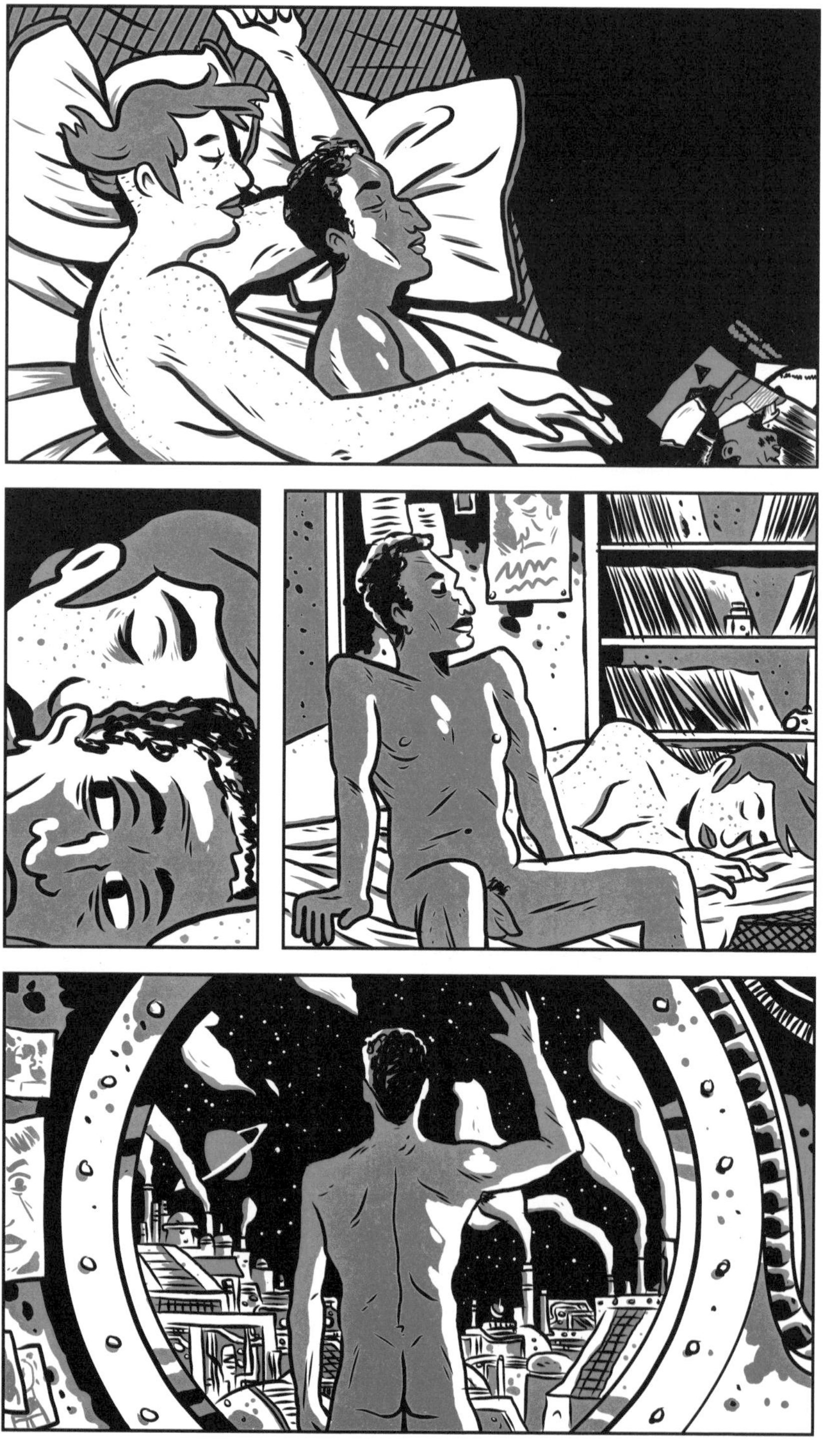

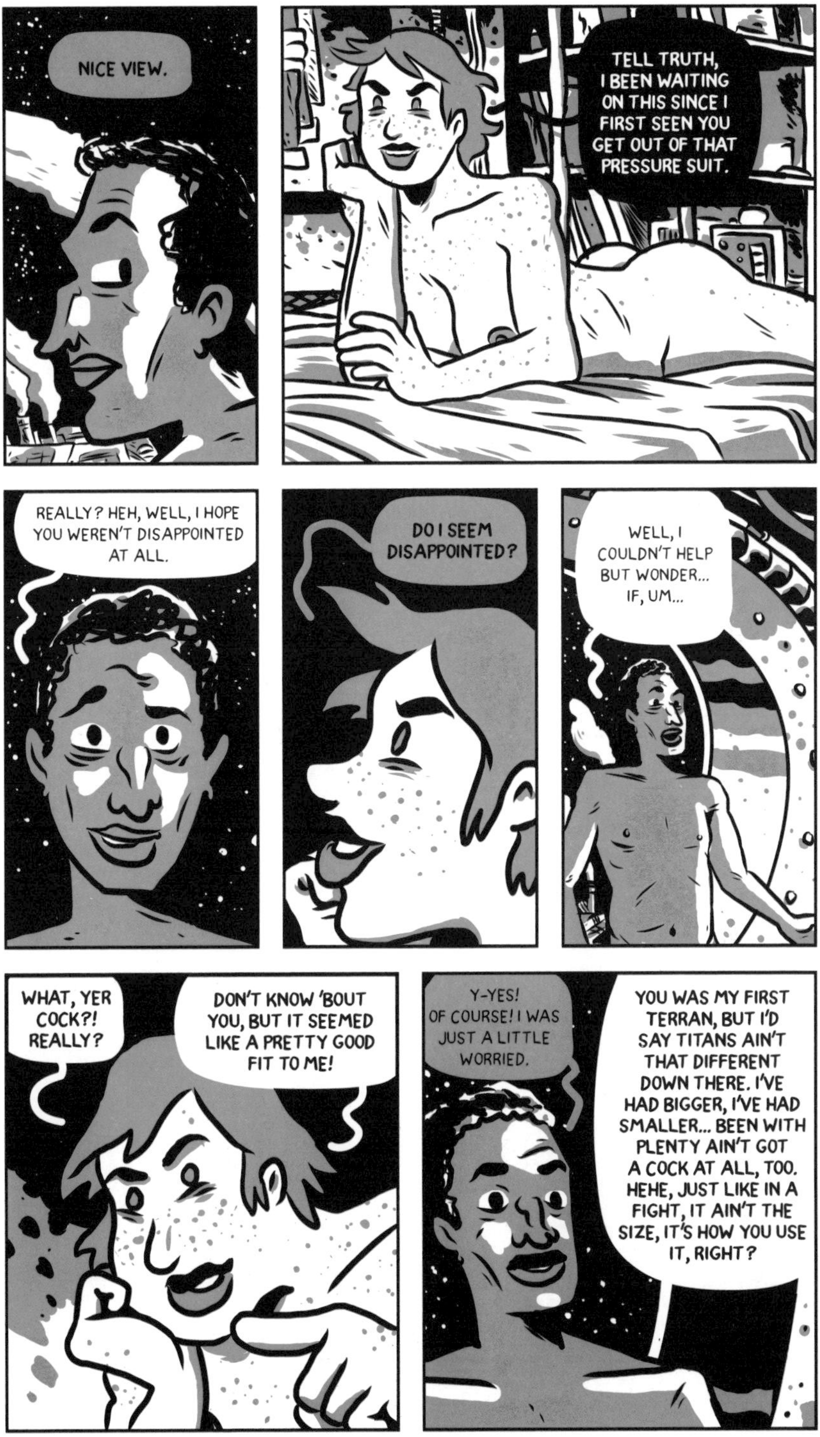
NICE VIEW.
TELL TRUTH, I BEEN WAITING ON THIS SINCE I FIRST SEEN YOU GET OUT OF THAT PRESSURE SUIT.
REALLY? HEH, WELL, I HOPE YOU WEREN'T DISAPPOINTED AT ALL.
DO I SEEM DISAPPOINTED?
WELL, I COULDN'T HELP BUT WONDER... IF, UM...
WHAT, YER COCK?! REALLY?
DON'T KNOW 'BOUT YOU, BUT IT SEEMED LIKE A PRETTY GOOD FIT TO ME!
Y-YES! OF COURSE! I WAS JUST A LITTLE WORRIED.
YOU WAS MY FIRST TERRAN, BUT I'D SAY TITANS AIN'T THAT DIFFERENT DOWN THERE. I'VE HAD BIGGER, I'VE HAD SMALLER... BEEN WITH PLENTY AIN'T GOT A COCK AT ALL, TOO. HEHE, JUST LIKE IN A FIGHT, IT AIN'T THE SIZE, IT'S HOW YOU USE IT, RIGHT?

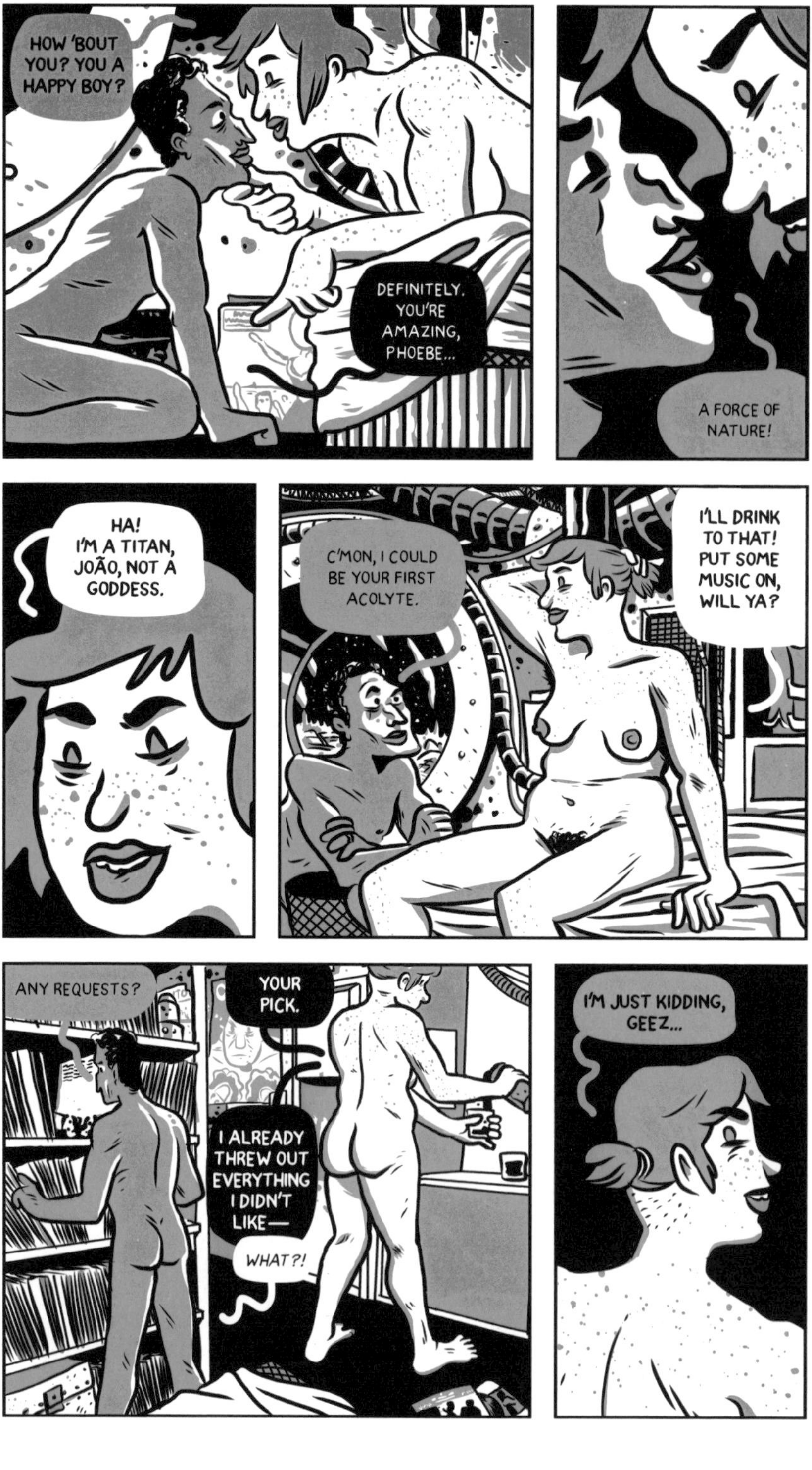
HOW 'BOUT YOU? YOU A HAPPY BOY?
DEFINITELY. YOU'RE AMAZING, PHOEBE...
A FORCE OF NATURE!
HA! I'M A TITAN, JOÃO, NOT A GODDESS.
C'MON, I COULD BE YOUR FIRST ACOLYTE.
I'LL DRINK TO THAT! PUT SOME MUSIC ON, WILL YA?
ANY REQUESTS?
YOUR PICK.
I ALREADY THREW OUT EVERYTHING I DIDN'T LIKE—
WHAT?!
I'M JUST KIDDING, GEEZ...

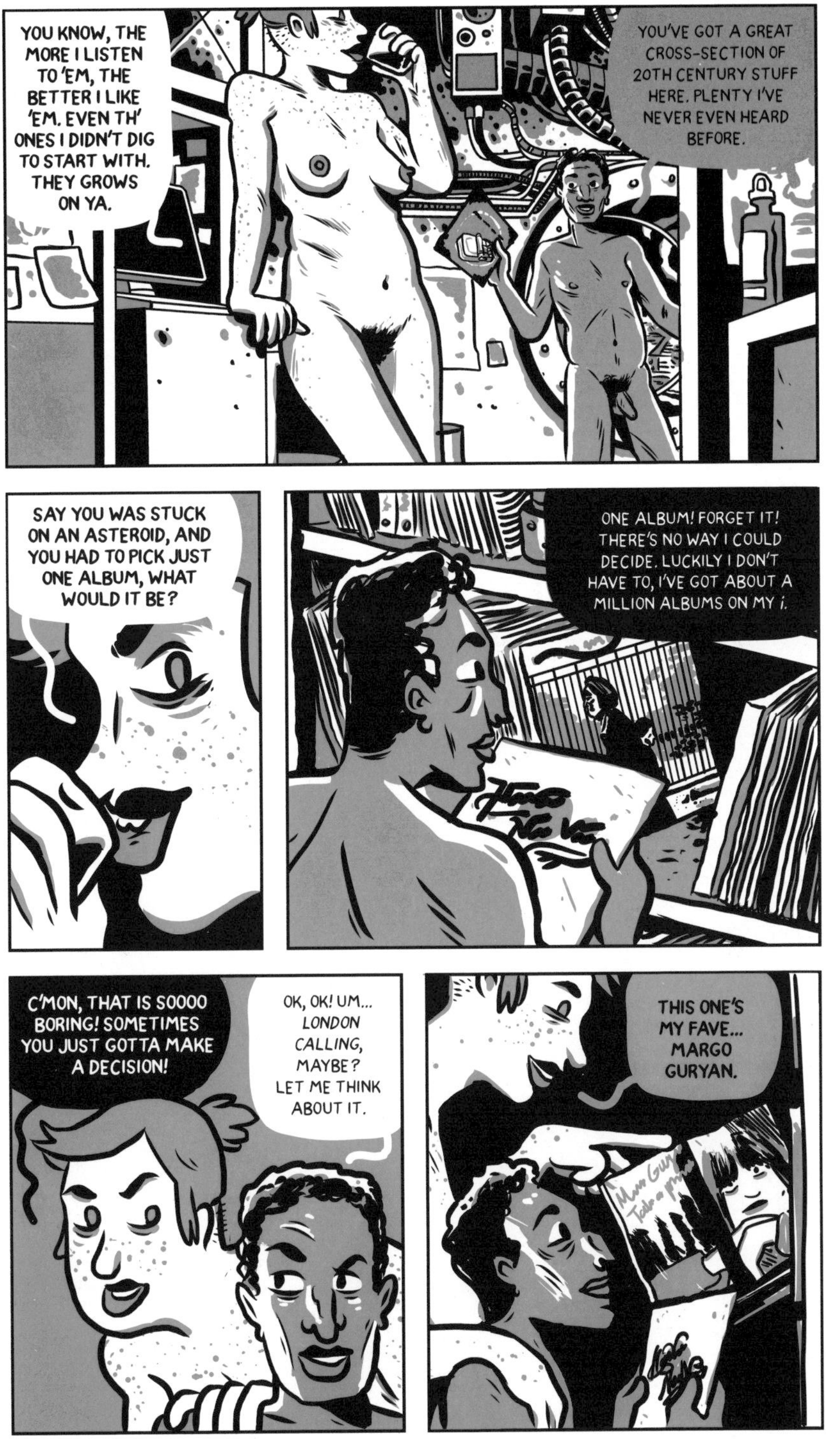
YOU KNOW, THE MORE I LISTEN TO 'EM, THE BETTER I LIKE 'EM. EVEN TH' ONES I DIDN'T DIG TO START WITH. THEY GROWS ON YA.
YOU'VE GOT A GREAT CROSS-SECTION OF 20TH CENTURY STUFF HERE. PLENTY I'VE NEVER EVEN HEARD BEFORE.
SAY YOU WAS STUCK ON AN ASTEROID, AND YOU HAD TO PICK JUST ONE ALBUM, WHAT WOULD IT BE?
ONE ALBUM! FORGET IT! THERE'S NO WAY I COULD DECIDE. LUCKILY I DON'T HAVE TO, I'VE GOT ABOUT A MILLION ALBUMS ON MY *i*.
C'MON, THAT IS SOOOO BORING! SOMETIMES YOU JUST GOTTA MAKE A DECISION!
OK, OK! UM... *LONDON CALLING*, MAYBE? LET ME THINK ABOUT IT.
THIS ONE'S MY FAVE... MARGO GURYAN.

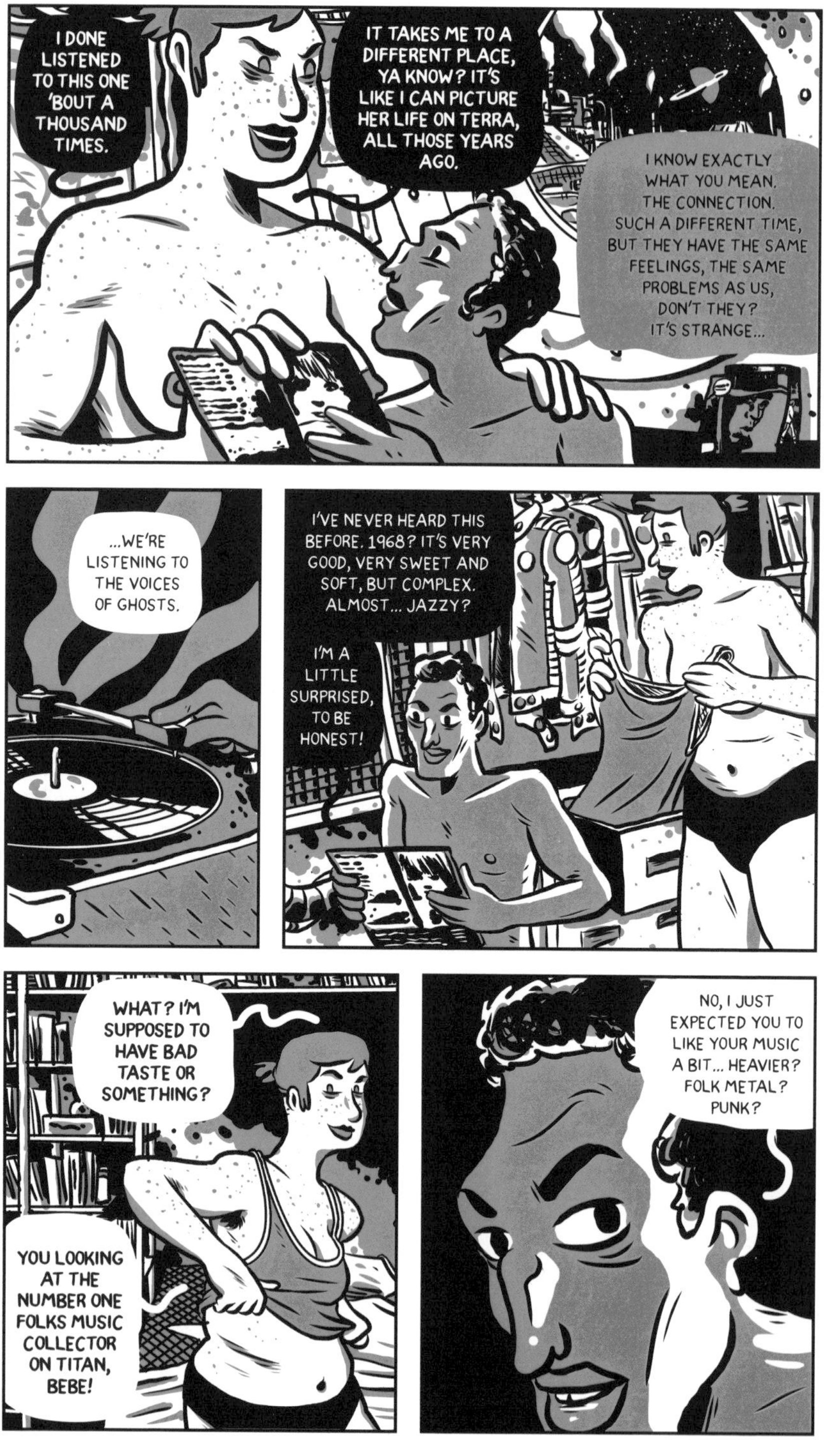
I DONE LISTENED TO THIS ONE 'BOUT A THOUSAND TIMES.
IT TAKES ME TO A DIFFERENT PLACE, YA KNOW? IT'S LIKE I CAN PICTURE HER LIFE ON TERRA, ALL THOSE YEARS AGO.
I KNOW EXACTLY WHAT YOU MEAN. THE CONNECTION. SUCH A DIFFERENT TIME, BUT THEY HAVE THE SAME FEELINGS, THE SAME PROBLEMS AS US, DON'T THEY? IT'S STRANGE...
...WE'RE LISTENING TO THE VOICES OF GHOSTS.
I'VE NEVER HEARD THIS BEFORE. 1968? IT'S VERY GOOD, VERY SWEET AND SOFT, BUT COMPLEX. ALMOST... JAZZY?
I'M A LITTLE SURPRISED, TO BE HONEST!
WHAT? I'M SUPPOSED TO HAVE BAD TASTE OR SOMETHING?
YOU LOOKING AT THE NUMBER ONE FOLKS MUSIC COLLECTOR ON TITAN, BEBE!
NO, I JUST EXPECTED YOU TO LIKE YOUR MUSIC A BIT... HEAVIER? FOLK METAL? PUNK?

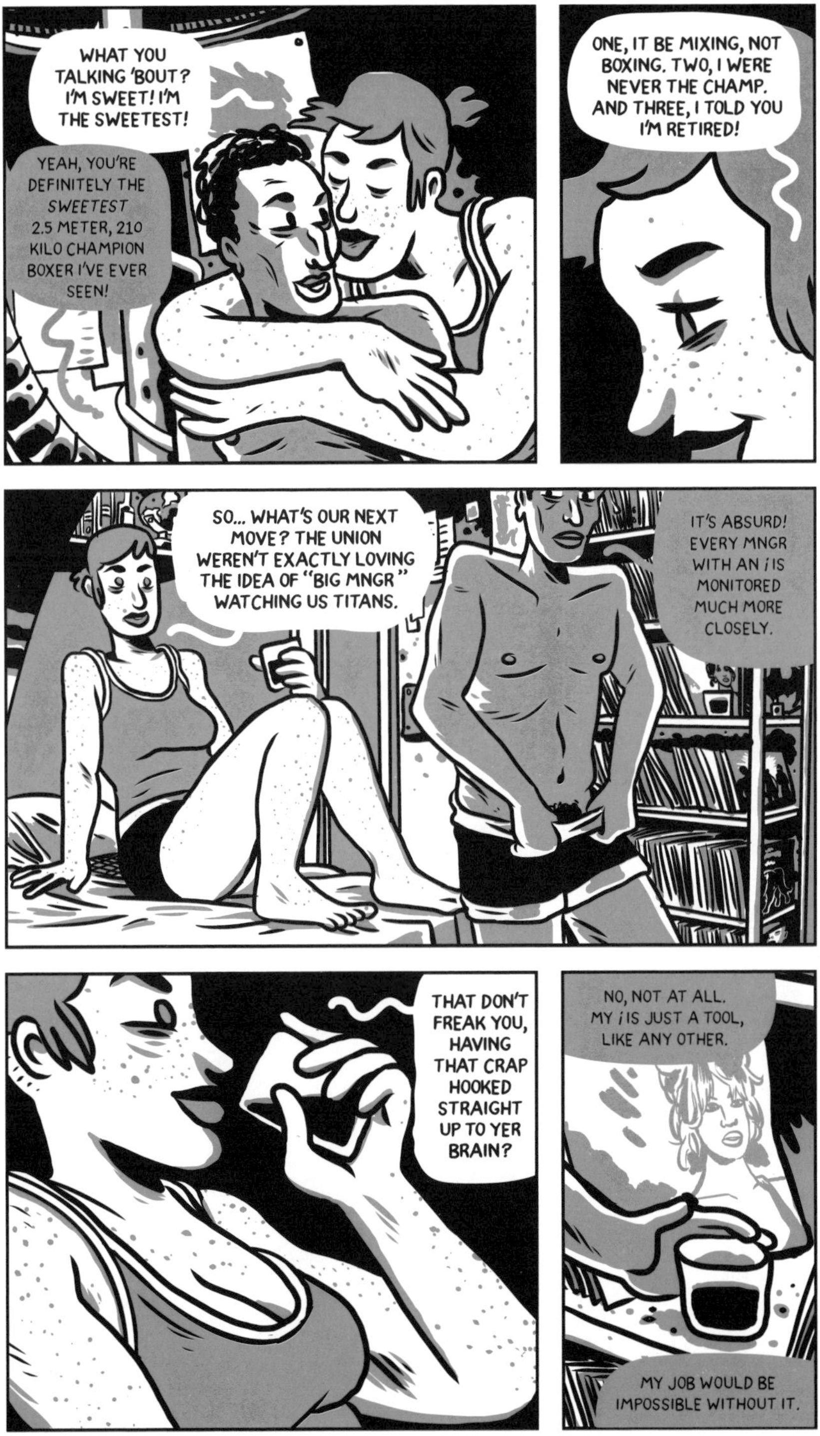

WHAT YOU TALKING 'BOUT? I'M SWEET! I'M THE SWEETEST!
YEAH, YOU'RE DEFINITELY THE *SWEETEST* 2.5 METER, 210 KILO CHAMPION BOXER I'VE EVER SEEN!
ONE, IT BE MIXING, NOT BOXING. TWO, I WERE NEVER THE CHAMP. AND THREE, I TOLD YOU I'M RETIRED!
SO... WHAT'S OUR NEXT MOVE? THE UNION WEREN'T EXACTLY LOVING THE IDEA OF "BIG MNGR" WATCHING US TITANS.
IT'S ABSURD! EVERY MNGR WITH AN ¡ IS MONITORED MUCH MORE CLOSELY.
THAT DON'T FREAK YOU, HAVING THAT CRAP HOOKED STRAIGHT UP TO YER BRAIN?
NO, NOT AT ALL. MY ¡ IS JUST A TOOL, LIKE ANY OTHER.
MY JOB WOULD BE IMPOSSIBLE WITHOUT IT.

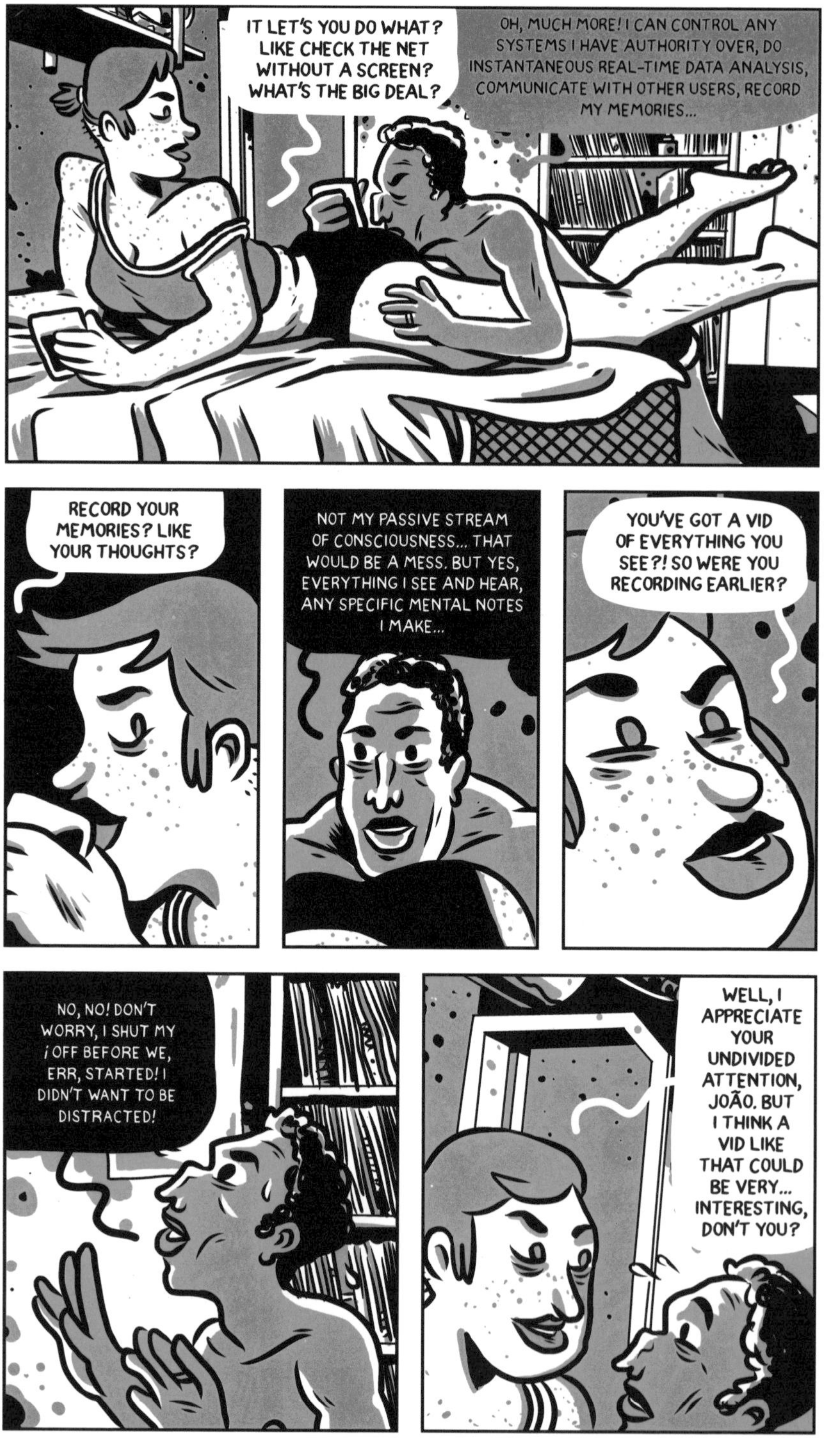
IT LET'S YOU DO WHAT? LIKE CHECK THE NET WITHOUT A SCREEN? WHAT'S THE BIG DEAL?
OH, MUCH MORE! I CAN CONTROL ANY SYSTEMS I HAVE AUTHORITY OVER, DO INSTANTANEOUS REAL-TIME DATA ANALYSIS, COMMUNICATE WITH OTHER USERS, RECORD MY MEMORIES...
RECORD YOUR MEMORIES? LIKE YOUR THOUGHTS?
NOT MY PASSIVE STREAM OF CONSCIOUSNESS... THAT WOULD BE A MESS. BUT YES, EVERYTHING I SEE AND HEAR, ANY SPECIFIC MENTAL NOTES I MAKE...
YOU'VE GOT A VID OF EVERYTHING YOU SEE?! SO WERE YOU RECORDING EARLIER?
NO, NO! DON'T WORRY, I SHUT MY ¡ OFF BEFORE WE, ERR, STARTED! I DIDN'T WANT TO BE DISTRACTED!
WELL, I APPRECIATE YOUR UNDIVIDED ATTENTION, JOÃO. BUT I THINK A VID LIKE THAT COULD BE VERY... INTERESTING, DON'T YOU?

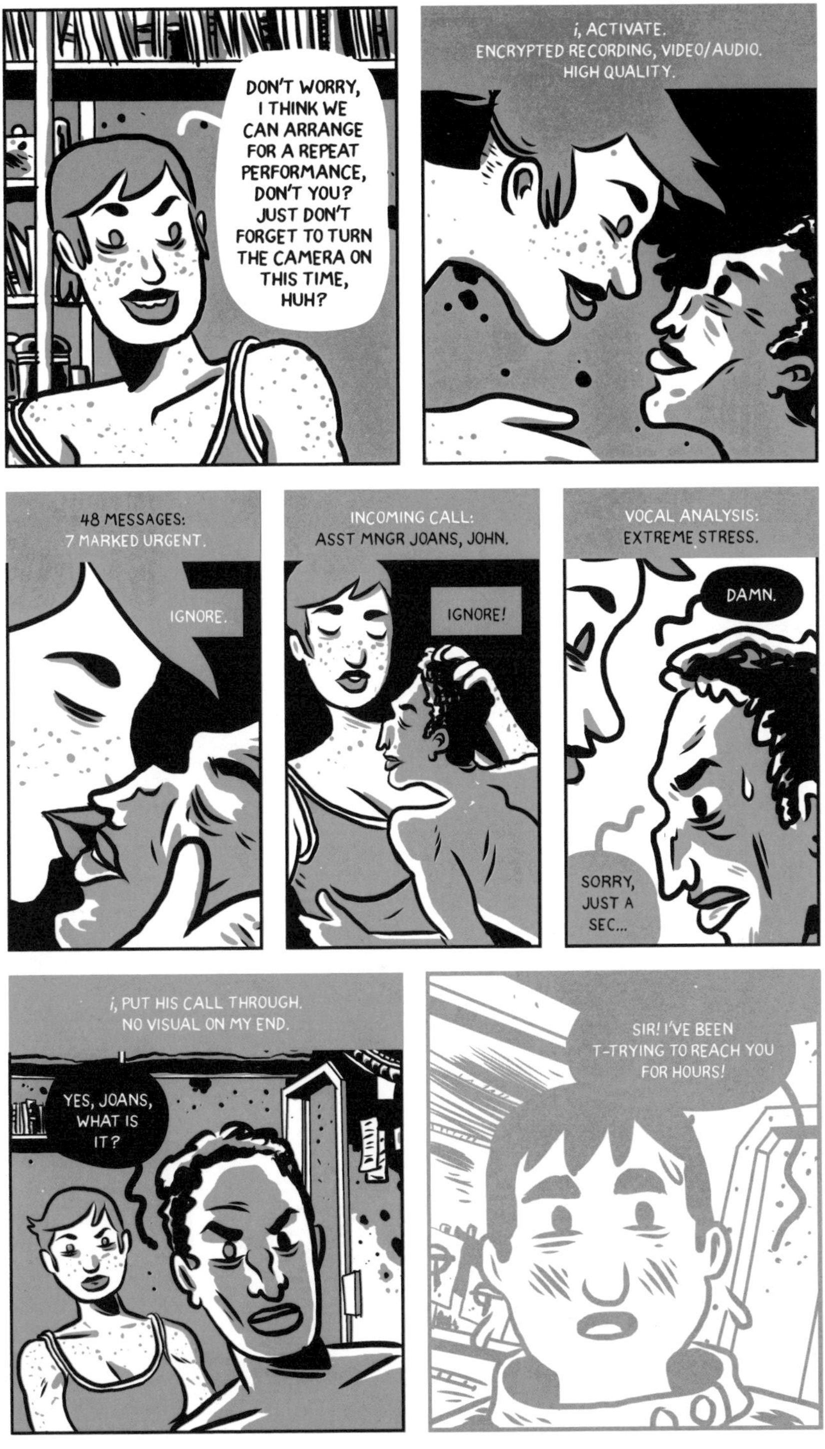
DON'T WORRY, I THINK WE CAN ARRANGE FOR A REPEAT PERFORMANCE, DON'T YOU? JUST DON'T FORGET TO TURN THE CAMERA ON THIS TIME, HUH?
i, ACTIVATE. ENCRYPTED RECORDING, VIDEO/AUDIO. HIGH QUALITY.
48 MESSAGES: 7 MARKED URGENT.
IGNORE.
INCOMING CALL: ASST MNGR JOANS, JOHN.
IGNORE!
VOCAL ANALYSIS: EXTREME STRESS.
DAMN.
SORRY, JUST A SEC...
i, PUT HIS CALL THROUGH. NO VISUAL ON MY END.
YES, JOANS, WHAT IS IT?
SIR! I'VE BEEN T-TRYING TO REACH YOU FOR HOURS!

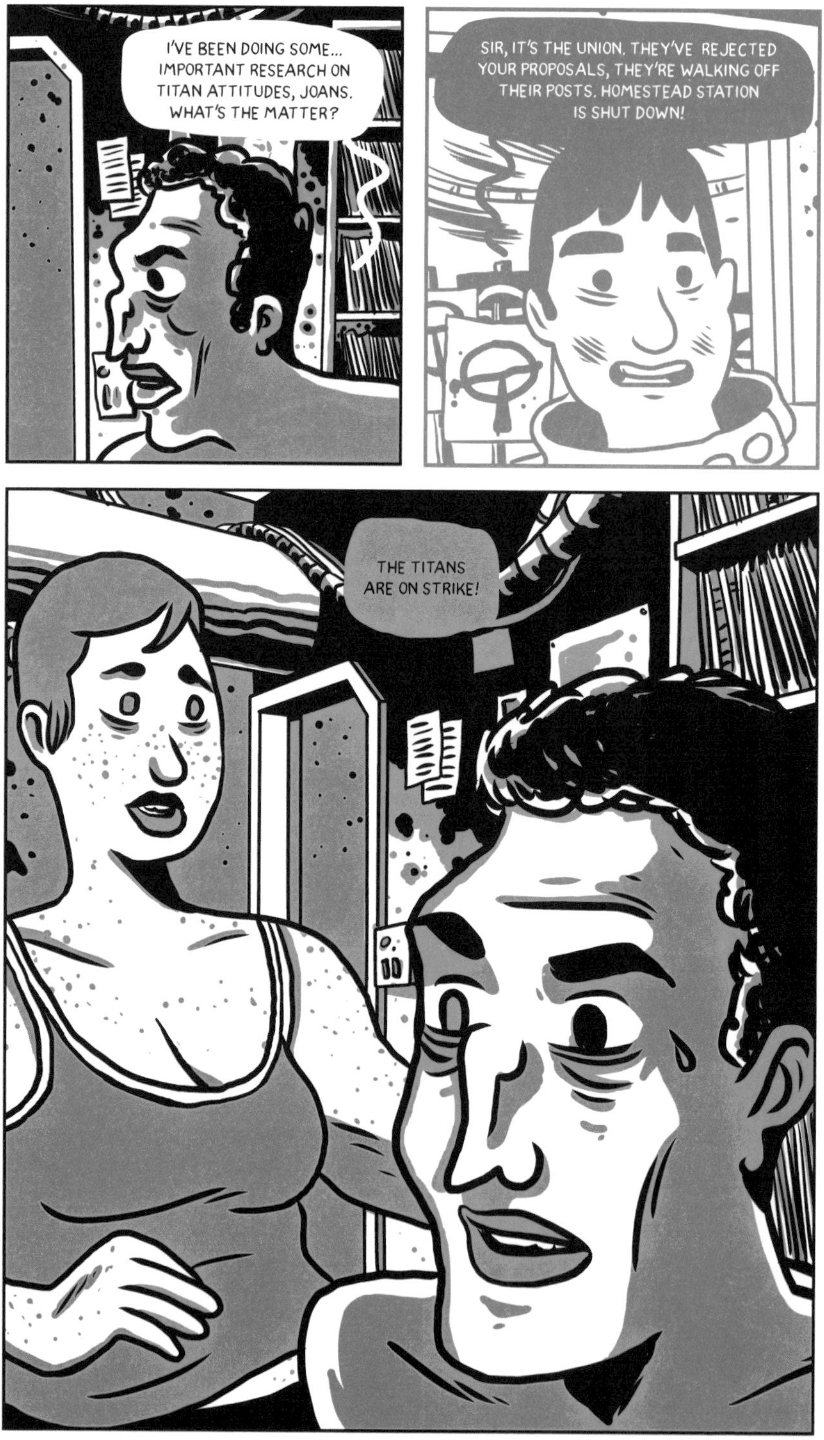
I'VE BEEN DOING SOME... IMPORTANT RESEARCH ON TITAN ATTITUDES, JOANS. WHAT'S THE MATTER?
SIR, IT'S THE UNION. THEY'VE REJECTED YOUR PROPOSALS, THEY'RE WALKING OFF THEIR POSTS. HOMESTEAD STATION IS SHUT DOWN!
THE TITANS ARE ON STRIKE!

PART 06: SERVE THE SERVANTS

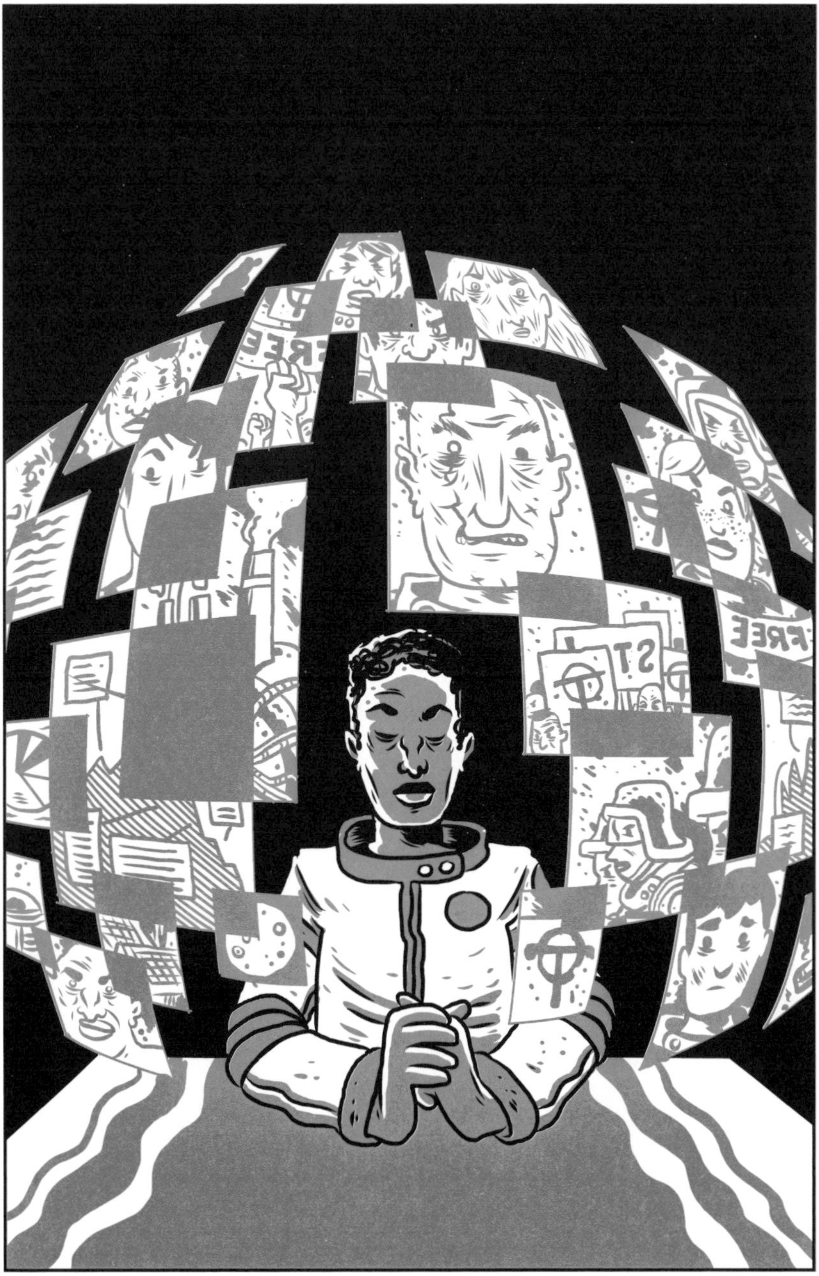

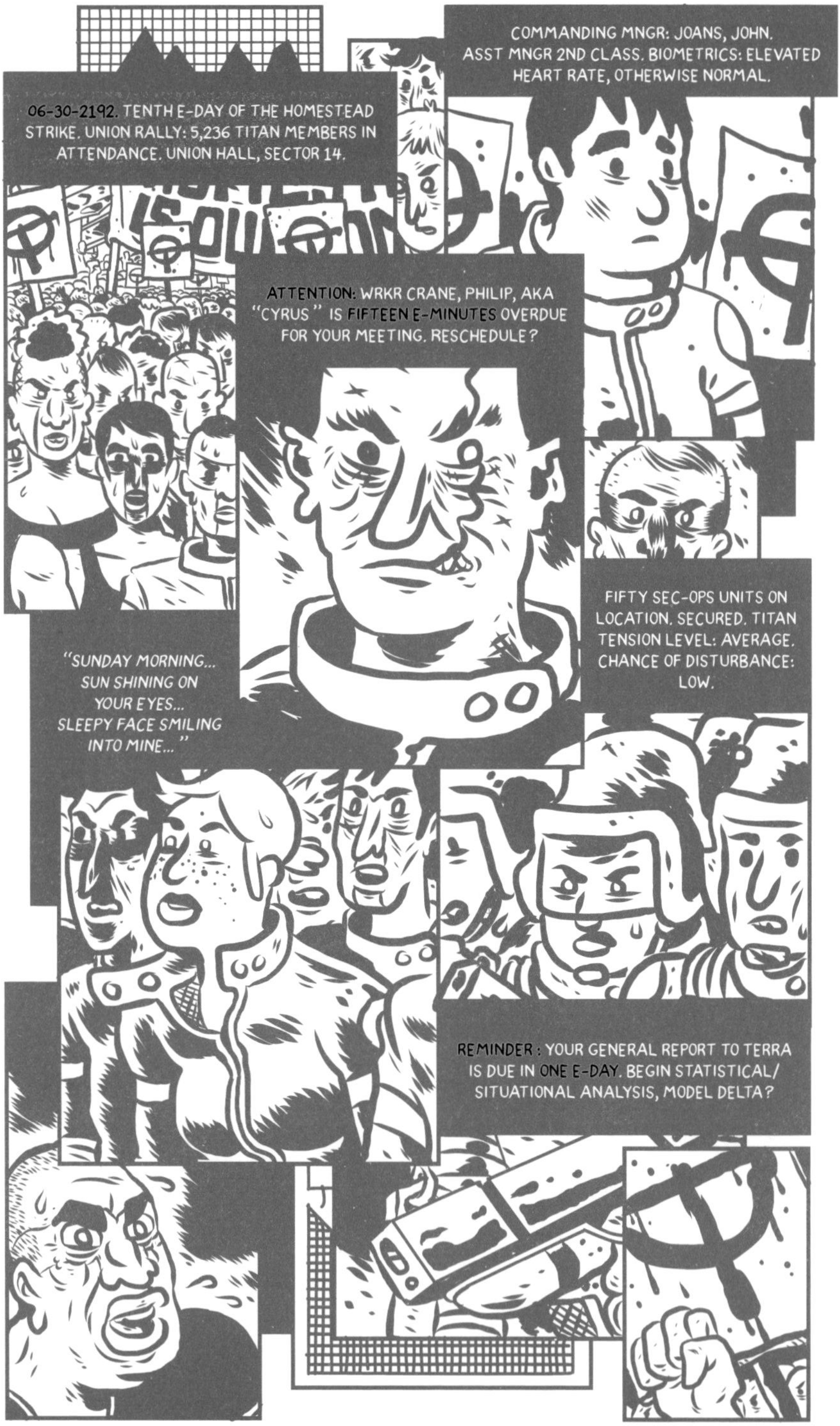

06-30-2192. TENTH E-DAY OF THE HOMESTEAD STRIKE. UNION RALLY: 5,236 TITAN MEMBERS IN ATTENDANCE. UNION HALL, SECTOR 14.
COMMANDING MNGR: JOANS, JOHN. ASST MNGR 2ND CLASS. BIOMETRICS: ELEVATED HEART RATE, OTHERWISE NORMAL.
ATTENTION: WRKR CRANE, PHILIP, AKA "CYRUS" IS FIFTEEN E-MINUTES OVERDUE FOR YOUR MEETING. RESCHEDULE?
FIFTY SEC-OPS UNITS ON LOCATION. SECURED. TITAN TENSION LEVEL: AVERAGE. CHANCE OF DISTURBANCE: LOW.
"SUNDAY MORNING... SUN SHINING ON YOUR EYES... SLEEPY FACE SMILING INTO MINE..."
REMINDER: YOUR GENERAL REPORT TO TERRA IS DUE IN ONE E-DAY. BEGIN STATISTICAL/SITUATIONAL ANALYSIS, MODEL DELTA?

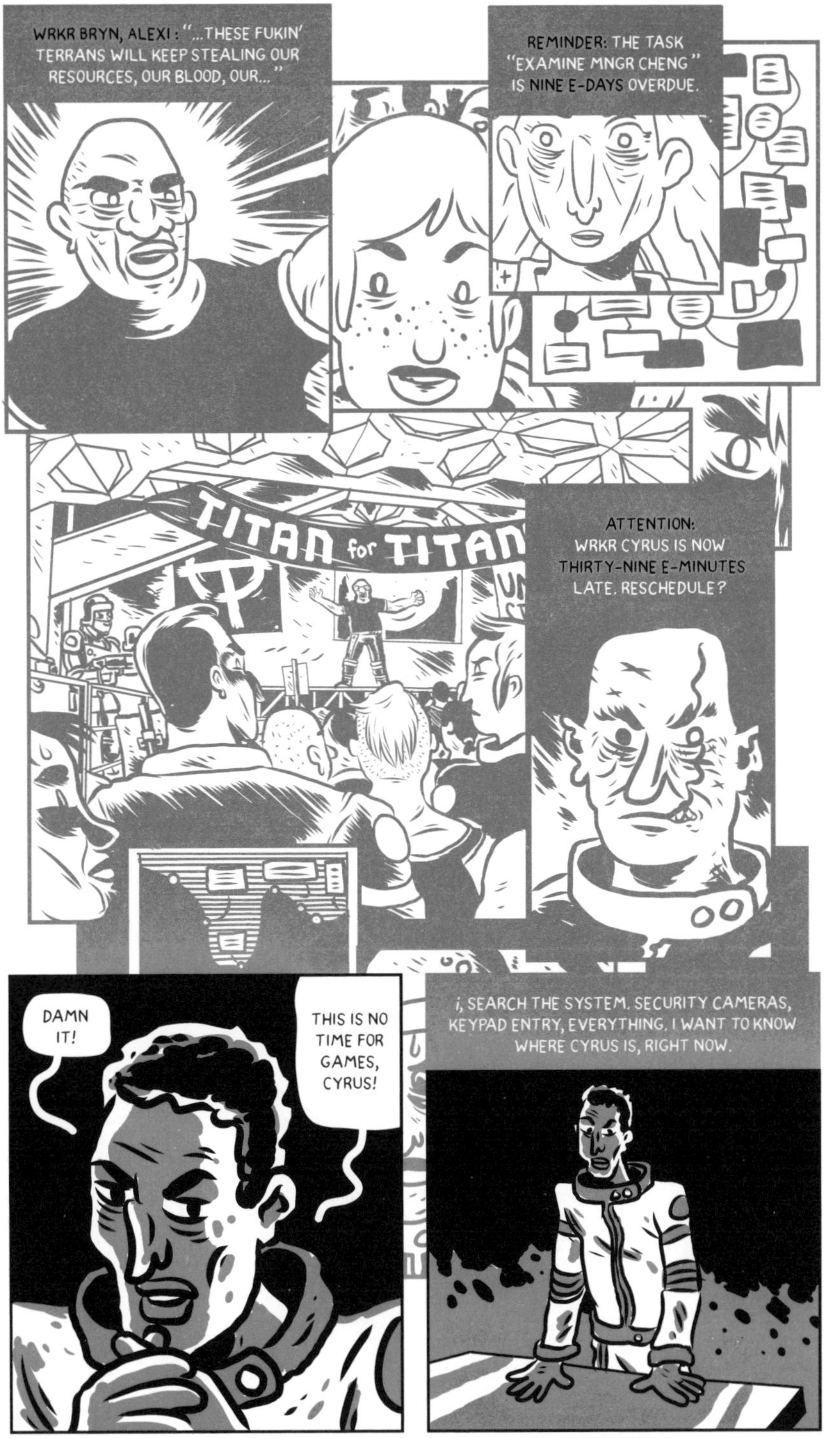
WRKR BRYN, ALEXI : "...THESE FUKIN' TERRANS WILL KEEP STEALING OUR RESOURCES, OUR BLOOD, OUR..."
REMINDER: THE TASK "EXAMINE MNGR CHENG" IS NINE E-DAYS OVERDUE.
TITAN for TITAN
ATTENTION: WRKR CYRUS IS NOW THIRTY-NINE E-MINUTES LATE. RESCHEDULE?
DAMN IT!
THIS IS NO TIME FOR GAMES, CYRUS!
i, SEARCH THE SYSTEM. SECURITY CAMERAS, KEYPAD ENTRY, EVERYTHING. I WANT TO KNOW WHERE CYRUS IS, RIGHT NOW.

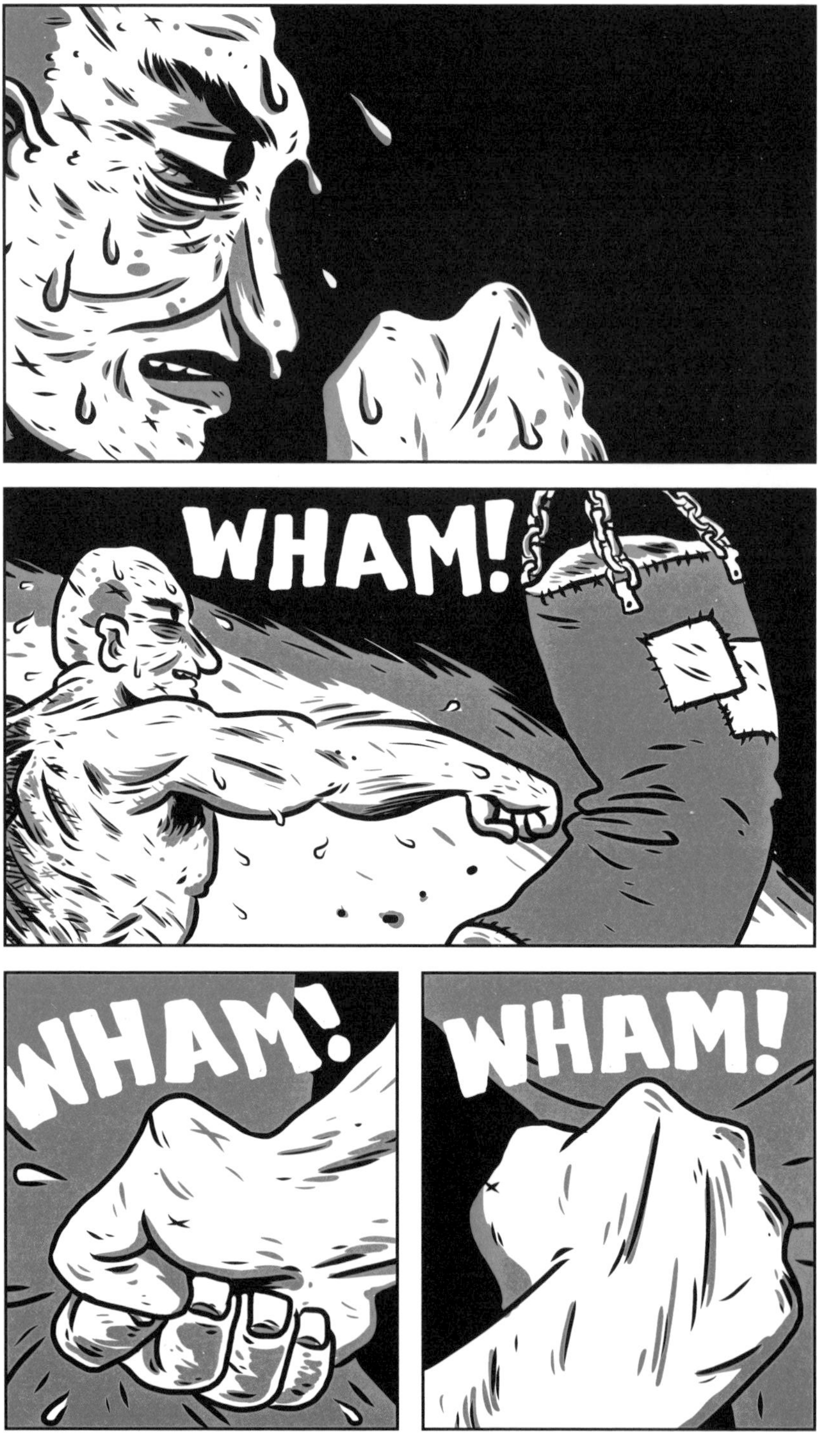
WHAM!
WHAM!
WHAM!

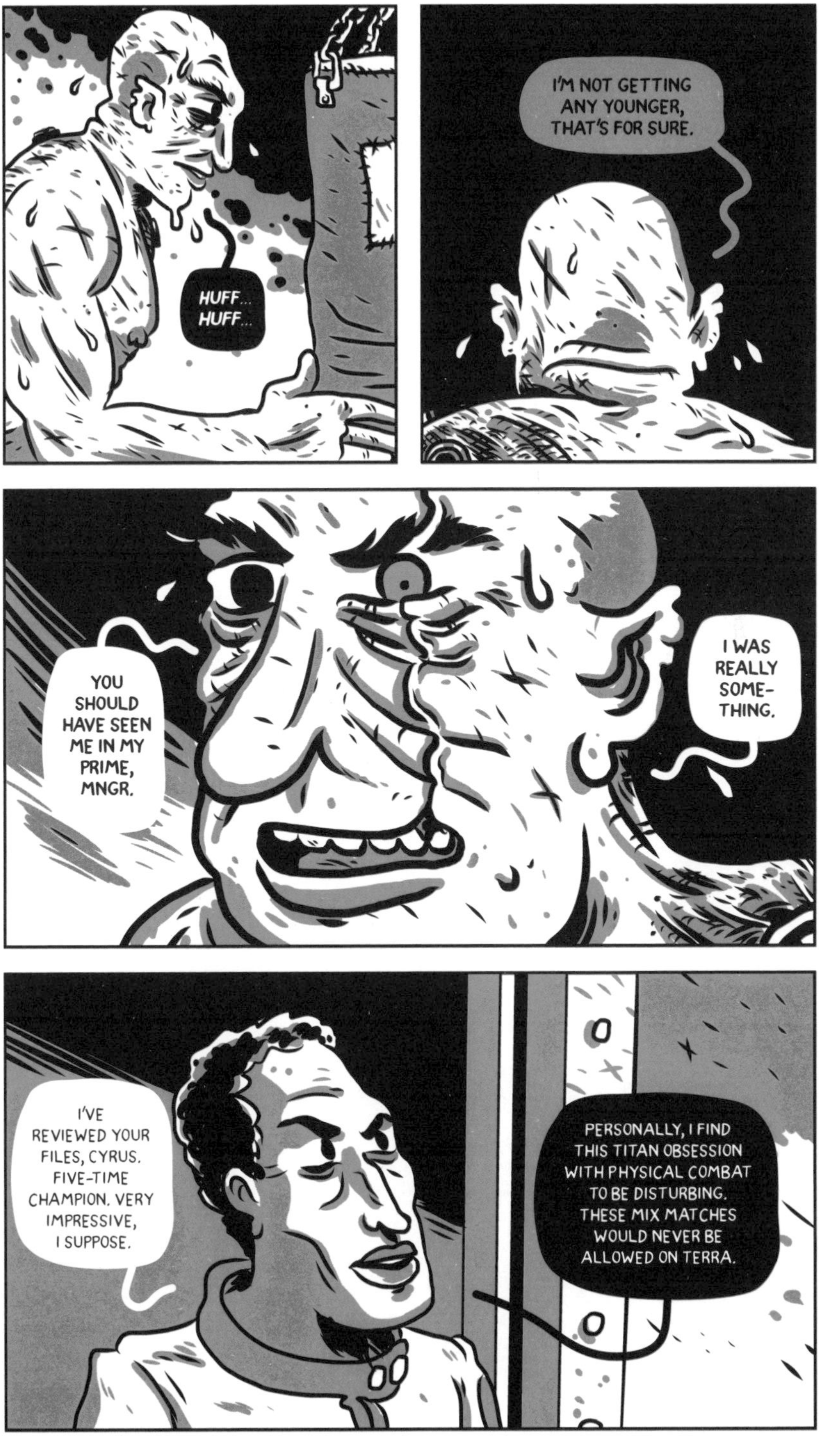
HUFF... HUFF...
I'M NOT GETTING ANY YOUNGER, THAT'S FOR SURE.
YOU SHOULD HAVE SEEN ME IN MY PRIME, MNGR.
I WAS REALLY SOME-THING.
I'VE REVIEWED YOUR FILES, CYRUS. FIVE-TIME CHAMPION. VERY IMPRESSIVE, I SUPPOSE.
PERSONALLY, I FIND THIS TITAN OBSESSION WITH PHYSICAL COMBAT TO BE DISTURBING. THESE MIX MATCHES WOULD NEVER BE ALLOWED ON TERRA.

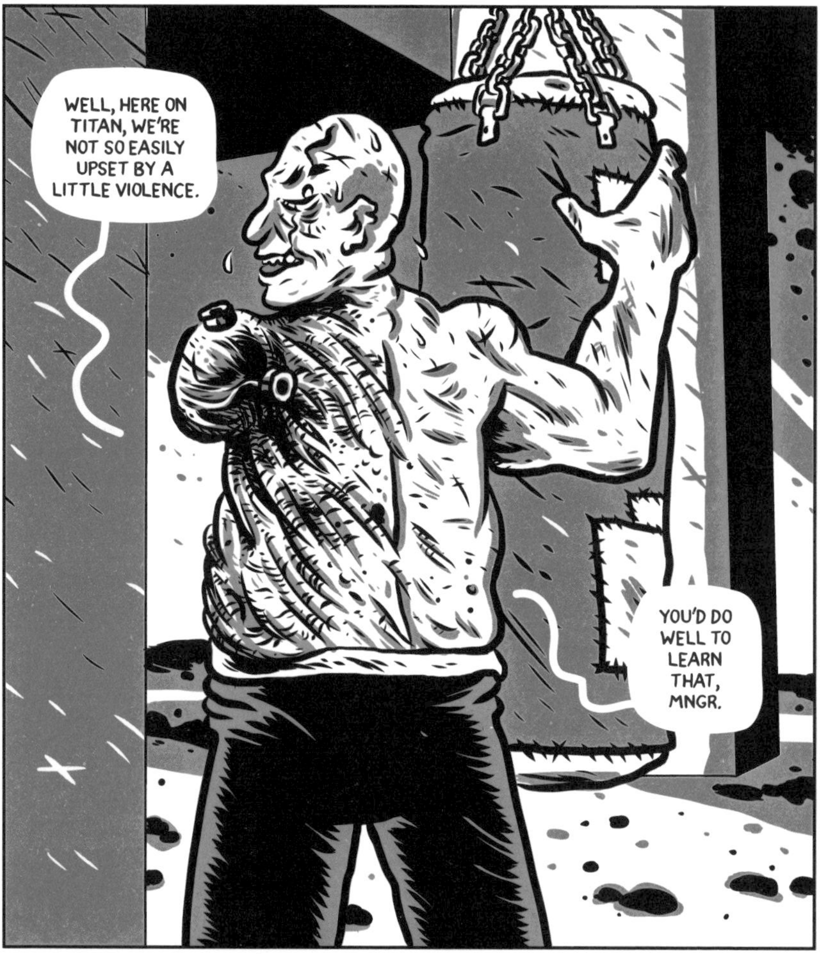
WELL, HERE ON TITAN, WE'RE NOT SO EASILY UPSET BY A LITTLE VIOLENCE.
YOU'D DO WELL TO LEARN THAT, MNGR.

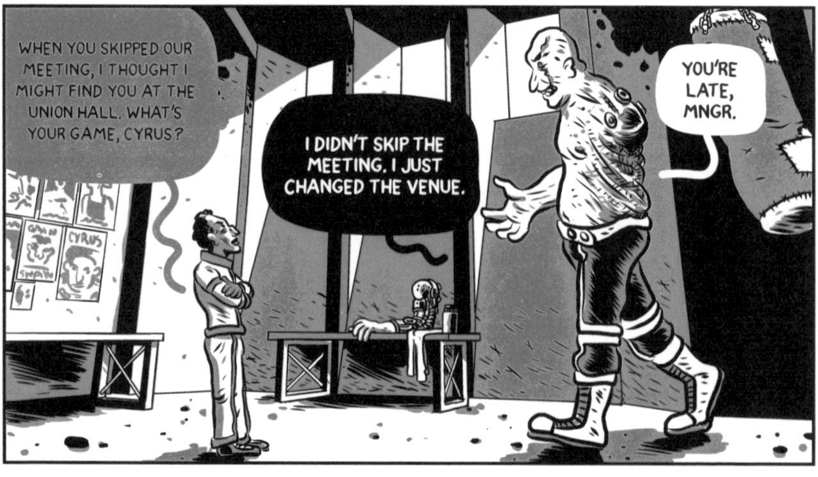
WHEN YOU SKIPPED OUR MEETING, I THOUGHT I MIGHT FIND YOU AT THE UNION HALL. WHAT'S YOUR GAME, CYRUS?
YOU'RE LATE, MNGR.
I DIDN'T SKIP THE MEETING. I JUST CHANGED THE VENUE.

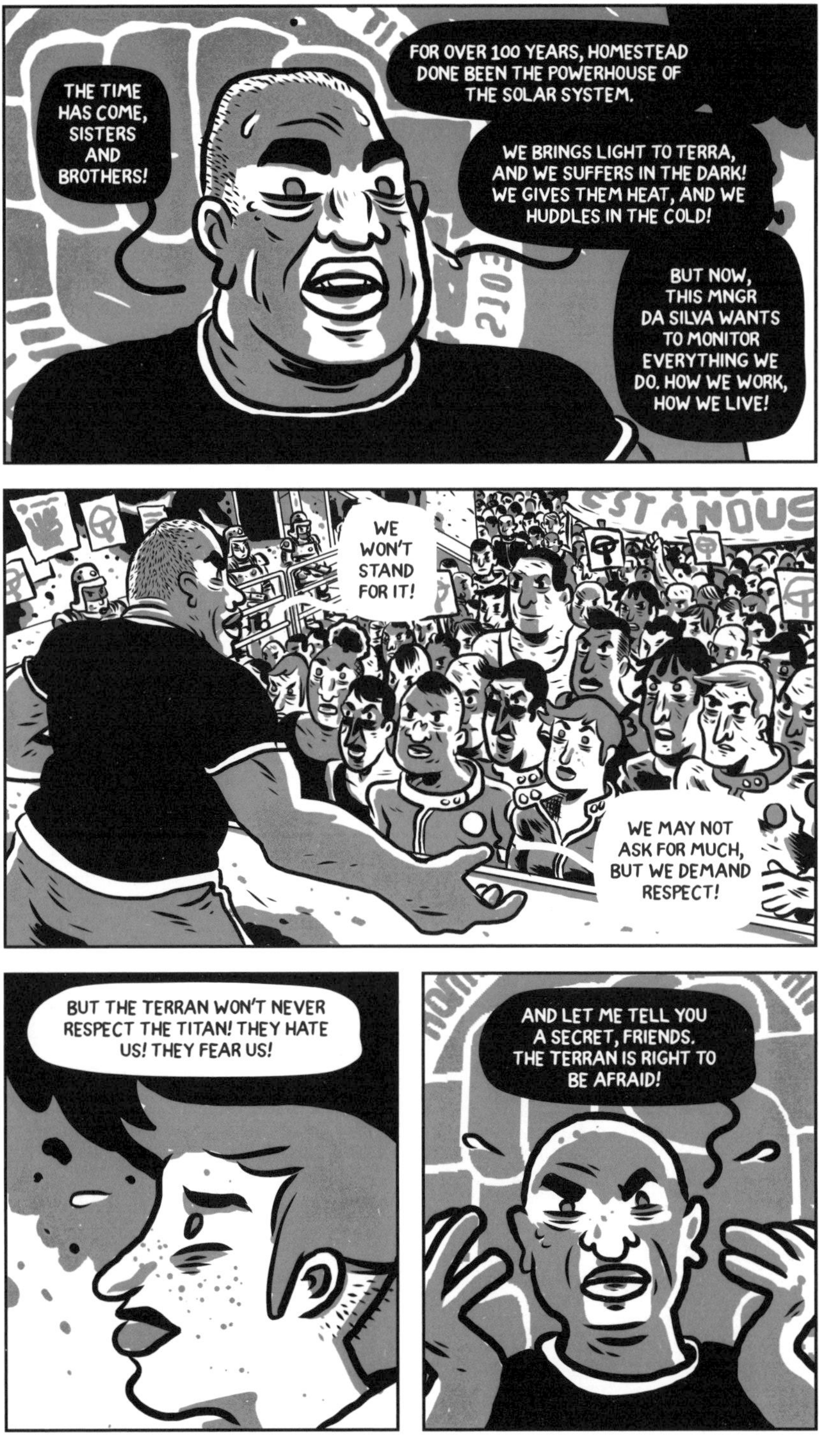

THE TIME HAS COME, SISTERS AND BROTHERS!
FOR OVER 100 YEARS, HOMESTEAD DONE BEEN THE POWERHOUSE OF THE SOLAR SYSTEM.
WE BRINGS LIGHT TO TERRA, AND WE SUFFERS IN THE DARK! WE GIVES THEM HEAT, AND WE HUDDLES IN THE COLD!
BUT NOW, THIS MNGR DA SILVA WANTS TO MONITOR EVERYTHING WE DO. HOW WE WORK, HOW WE LIVE!
WE WON'T STAND FOR IT!
WE MAY NOT ASK FOR MUCH, BUT WE DEMAND RESPECT!
BUT THE TERRAN WON'T NEVER RESPECT THE TITAN! THEY HATE US! THEY FEAR US!
AND LET ME TELL YOU A SECRET, FRIENDS. THE TERRAN IS RIGHT TO BE AFRAID!

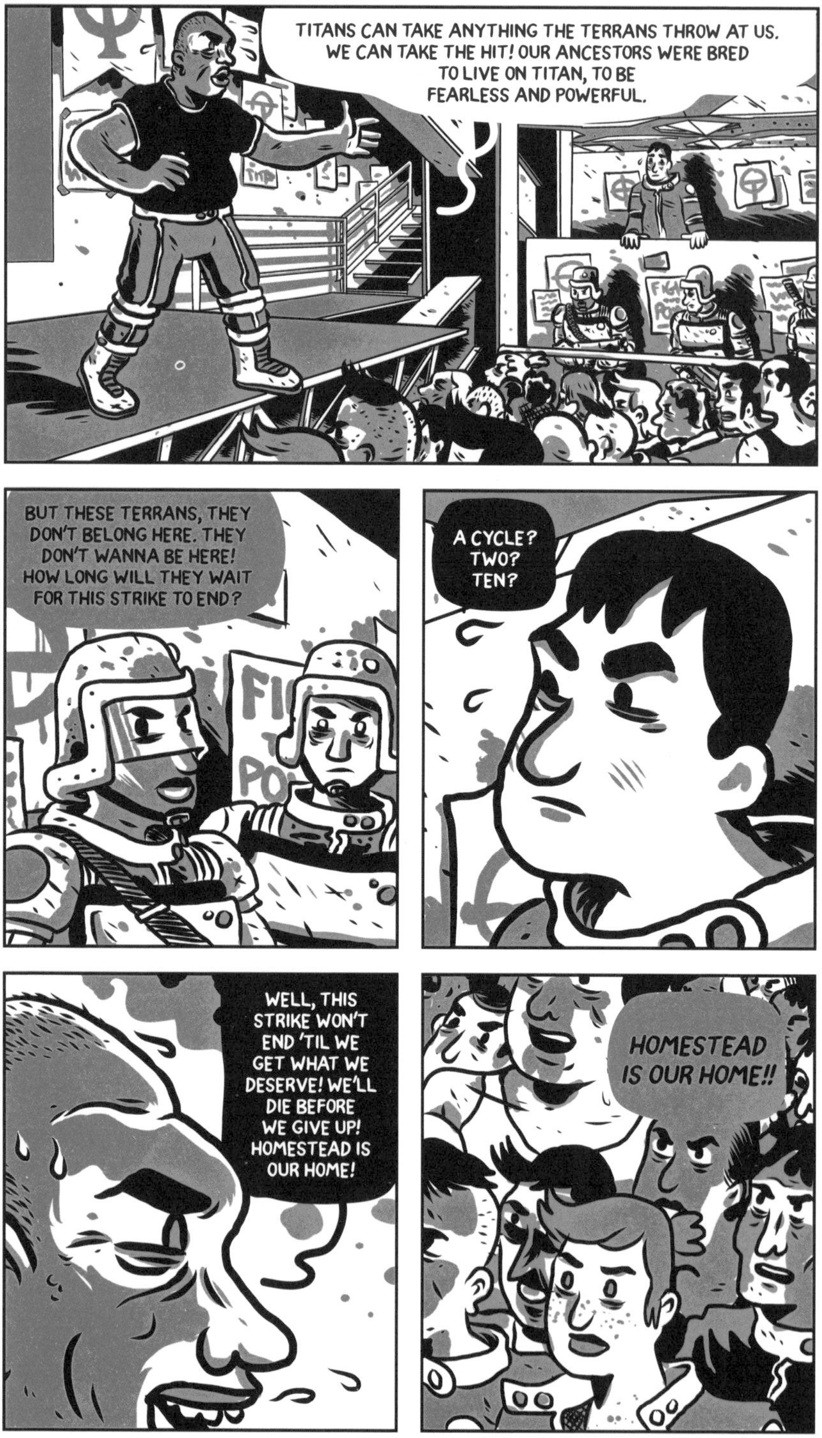
TITANS CAN TAKE ANYTHING THE TERRANS THROW AT US. WE CAN TAKE THE HIT! OUR ANCESTORS WERE BRED TO LIVE ON TITAN, TO BE FEARLESS AND POWERFUL.
BUT THESE TERRANS, THEY DON'T BELONG HERE. THEY DON'T WANNA BE HERE! HOW LONG WILL THEY WAIT FOR THIS STRIKE TO END?
A CYCLE? TWO? TEN?
WELL, THIS STRIKE WON'T END 'TIL WE GET WHAT WE DESERVE! WE'LL DIE BEFORE WE GIVE UP! HOMESTEAD IS OUR HOME!
HOMESTEAD IS OUR HOME!!

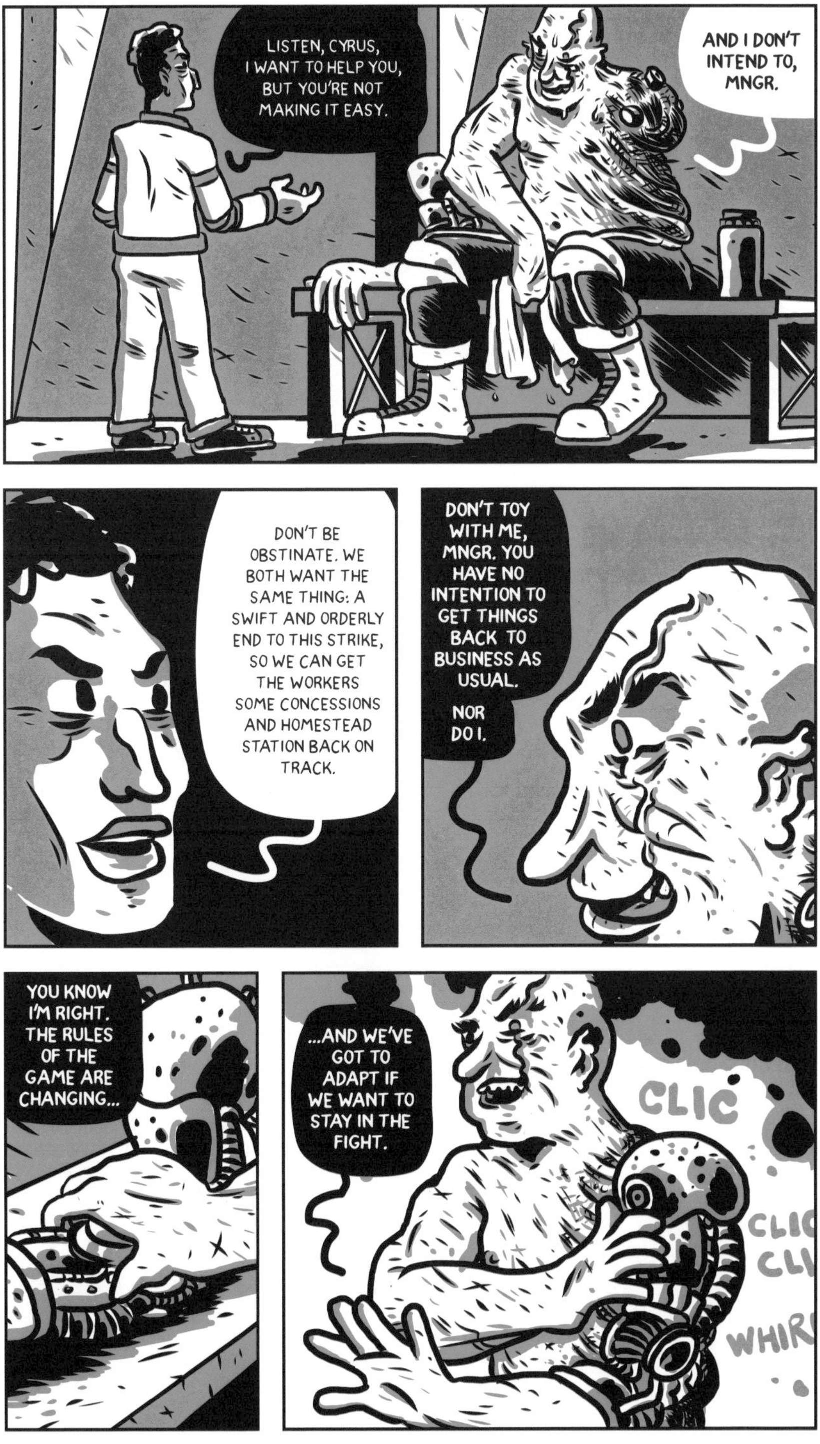

LISTEN, CYRUS, I WANT TO HELP YOU, BUT YOU'RE NOT MAKING IT EASY.
AND I DON'T INTEND TO, MNGR.
DON'T BE OBSTINATE. WE BOTH WANT THE SAME THING: A SWIFT AND ORDERLY END TO THIS STRIKE, SO WE CAN GET THE WORKERS SOME CONCESSIONS AND HOMESTEAD STATION BACK ON TRACK.
DON'T TOY WITH ME, MNGR. YOU HAVE NO INTENTION TO GET THINGS BACK TO BUSINESS AS USUAL.
NOR DO I.
YOU KNOW I'M RIGHT. THE RULES OF THE GAME ARE CHANGING...
...AND WE'VE GOT TO ADAPT IF WE WANT TO STAY IN THE FIGHT.
CLIC

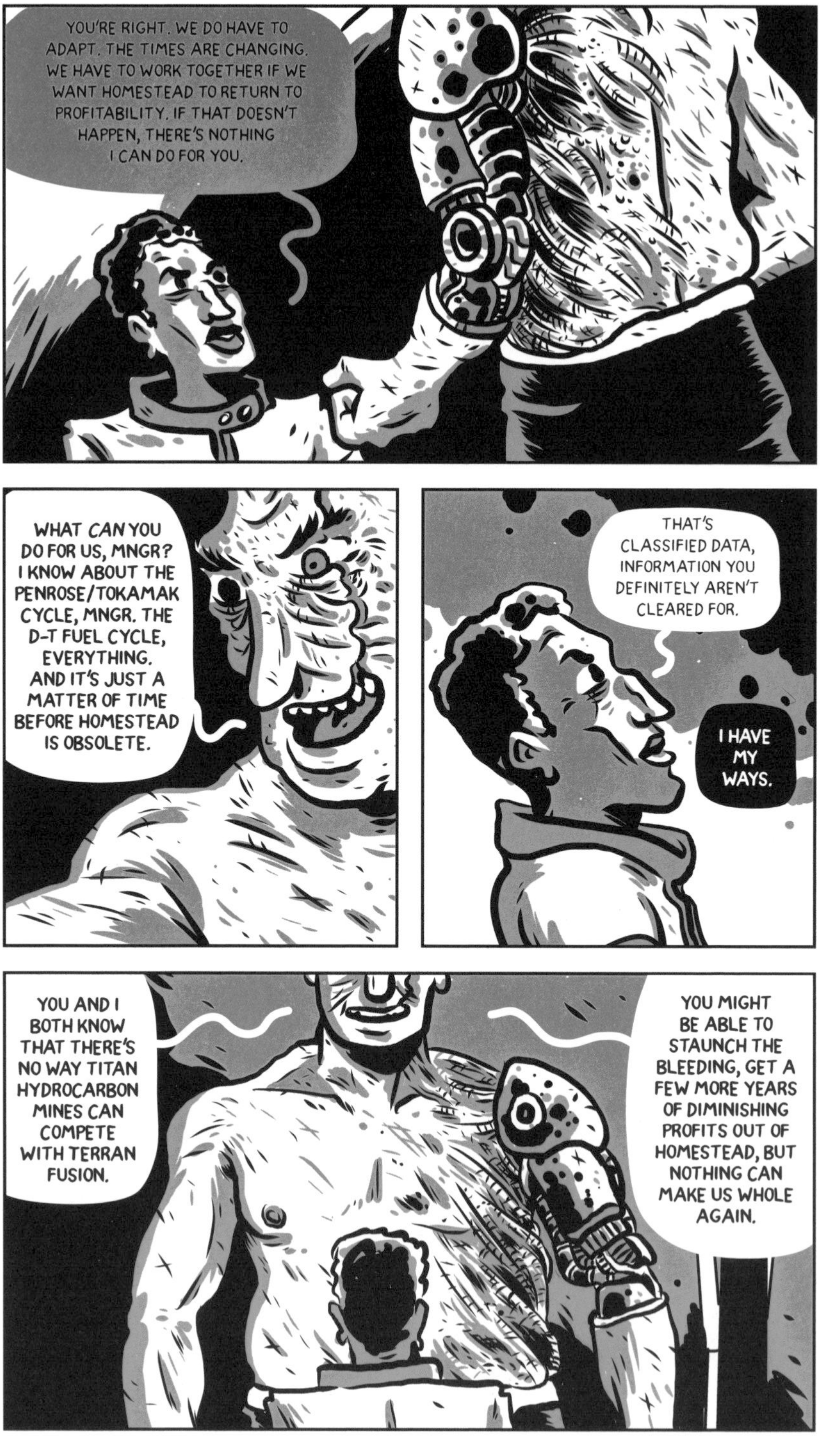
YOU'RE RIGHT. WE DO HAVE TO ADAPT. THE TIMES ARE CHANGING. WE HAVE TO WORK TOGETHER IF WE WANT HOMESTEAD TO RETURN TO PROFITABILITY. IF THAT DOESN'T HAPPEN, THERE'S NOTHING I CAN DO FOR YOU.
WHAT *CAN* YOU DO FOR US, MNGR? I KNOW ABOUT THE PENROSE/TOKAMAK CYCLE, MNGR. THE D-T FUEL CYCLE, EVERYTHING. AND IT'S JUST A MATTER OF TIME BEFORE HOMESTEAD IS OBSOLETE.
THAT'S CLASSIFIED DATA, INFORMATION YOU DEFINITELY AREN'T CLEARED FOR.
I HAVE MY WAYS.
YOU AND I BOTH KNOW THAT THERE'S NO WAY TITAN HYDROCARBON MINES CAN COMPETE WITH TERRAN FUSION.
YOU MIGHT BE ABLE TO STAUNCH THE BLEEDING, GET A FEW MORE YEARS OF DIMINISHING PROFITS OUT OF HOMESTEAD, BUT NOTHING CAN MAKE US WHOLE AGAIN.

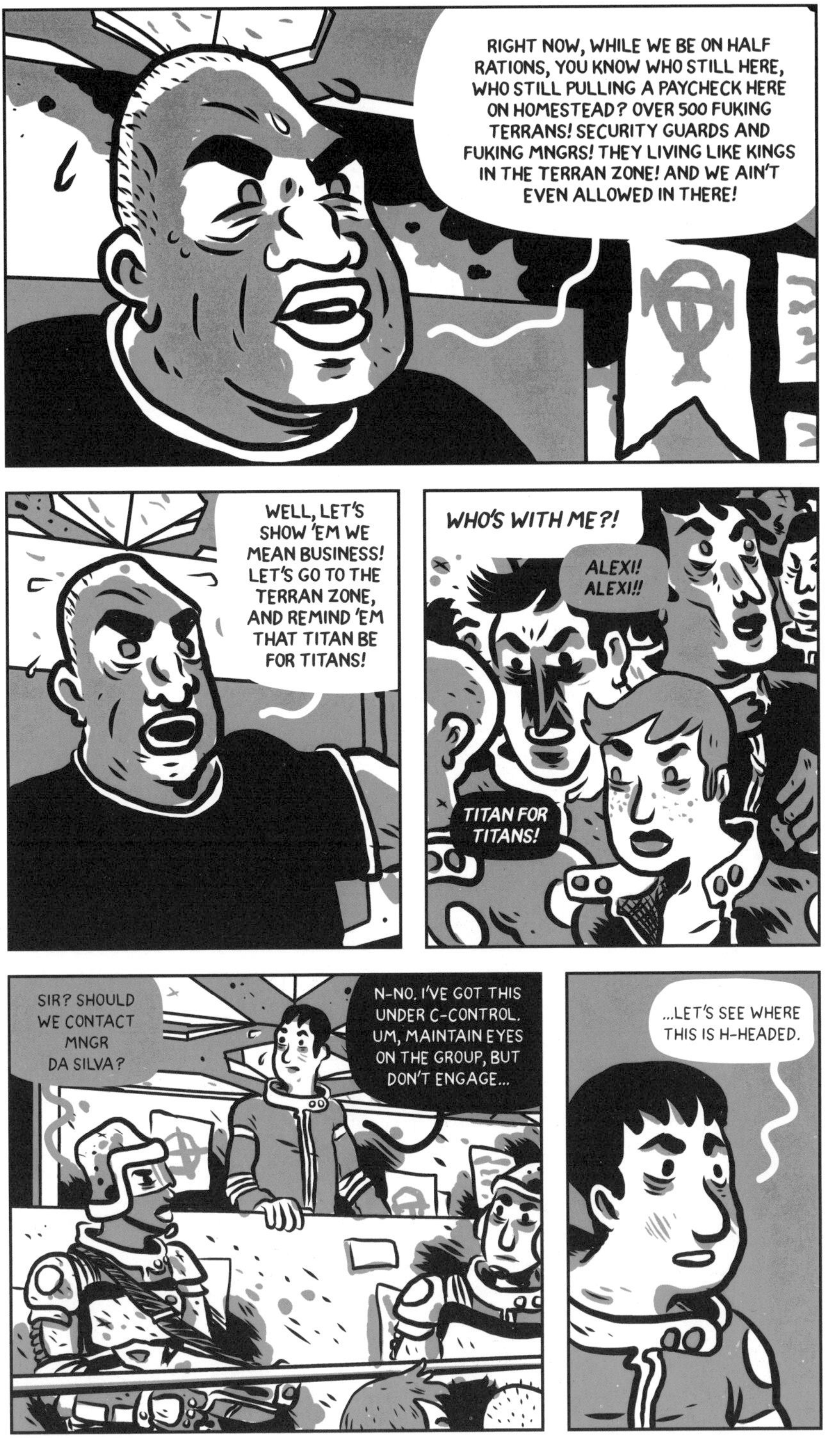
RIGHT NOW, WHILE WE BE ON HALF RATIONS, YOU KNOW WHO STILL HERE, WHO STILL PULLING A PAYCHECK HERE ON HOMESTEAD? OVER 500 FUKING TERRANS! SECURITY GUARDS AND FUKING MNGRS! THEY LIVING LIKE KINGS IN THE TERRAN ZONE! AND WE AIN'T EVEN ALLOWED IN THERE!
WELL, LET'S SHOW 'EM WE MEAN BUSINESS! LET'S GO TO THE TERRAN ZONE, AND REMIND 'EM THAT TITAN BE FOR TITANS!
WHO'S WITH ME?!
ALEXI! ALEXI!!
TITAN FOR TITANS!
SIR? SHOULD WE CONTACT MNGR DA SILVA?
N-NO. I'VE GOT THIS UNDER C-CONTROL. UM, MAINTAIN EYES ON THE GROUP, BUT DON'T ENGAGE...
...LET'S SEE WHERE THIS IS H-HEADED.

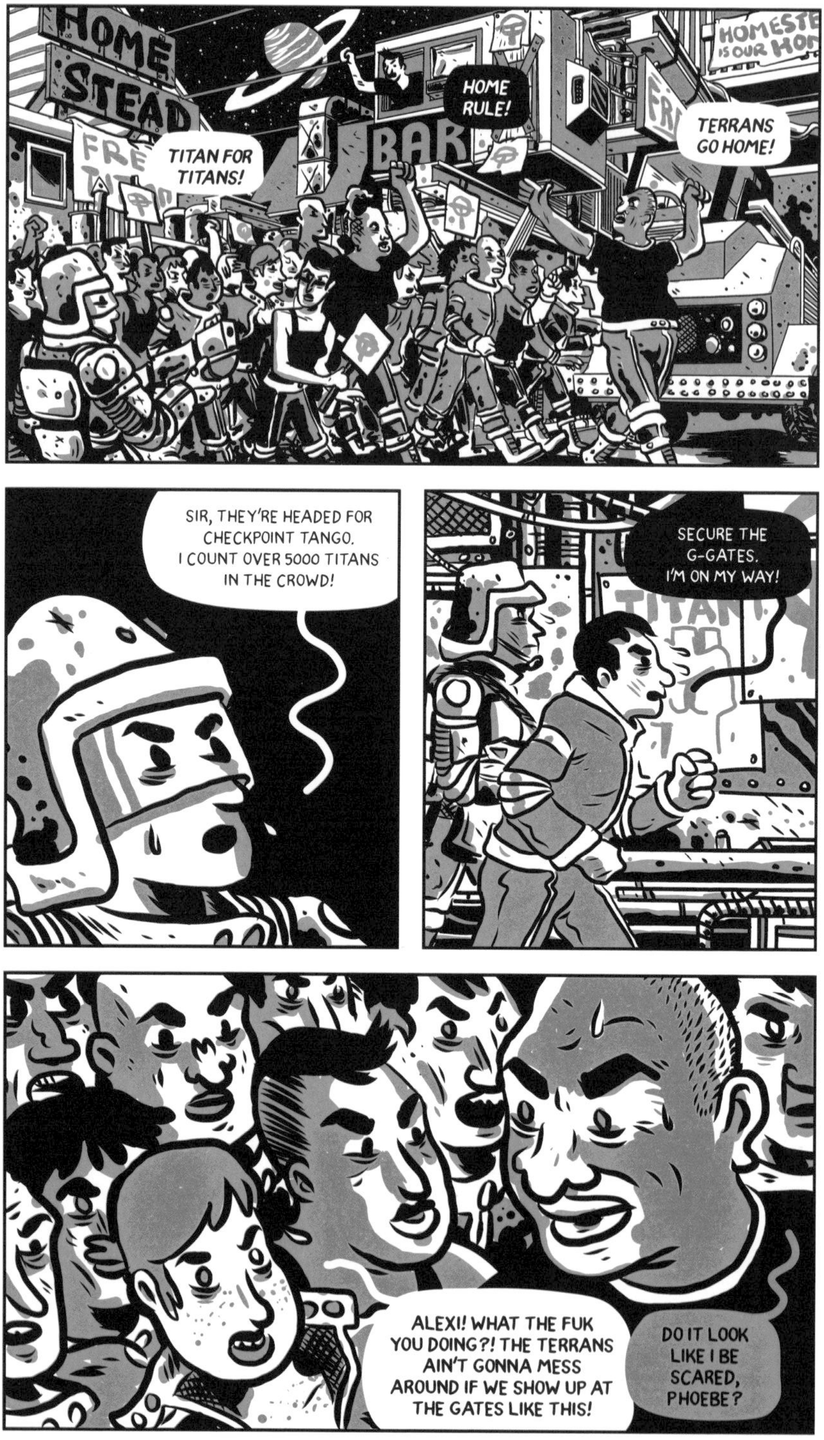
HOME STEAD
BAR
TITAN FOR TITANS!
HOME RULE!
TERRANS GO HOME!
SIR, THEY'RE HEADED FOR CHECKPOINT TANGO. I COUNT OVER 5000 TITANS IN THE CROWD!
SECURE THE G-GATES. I'M ON MY WAY!
ALEXI! WHAT THE FUK YOU DOING?! THE TERRANS AIN'T GONNA MESS AROUND IF WE SHOW UP AT THE GATES LIKE THIS!
DO IT LOOK LIKE I BE SCARED, PHOEBE?

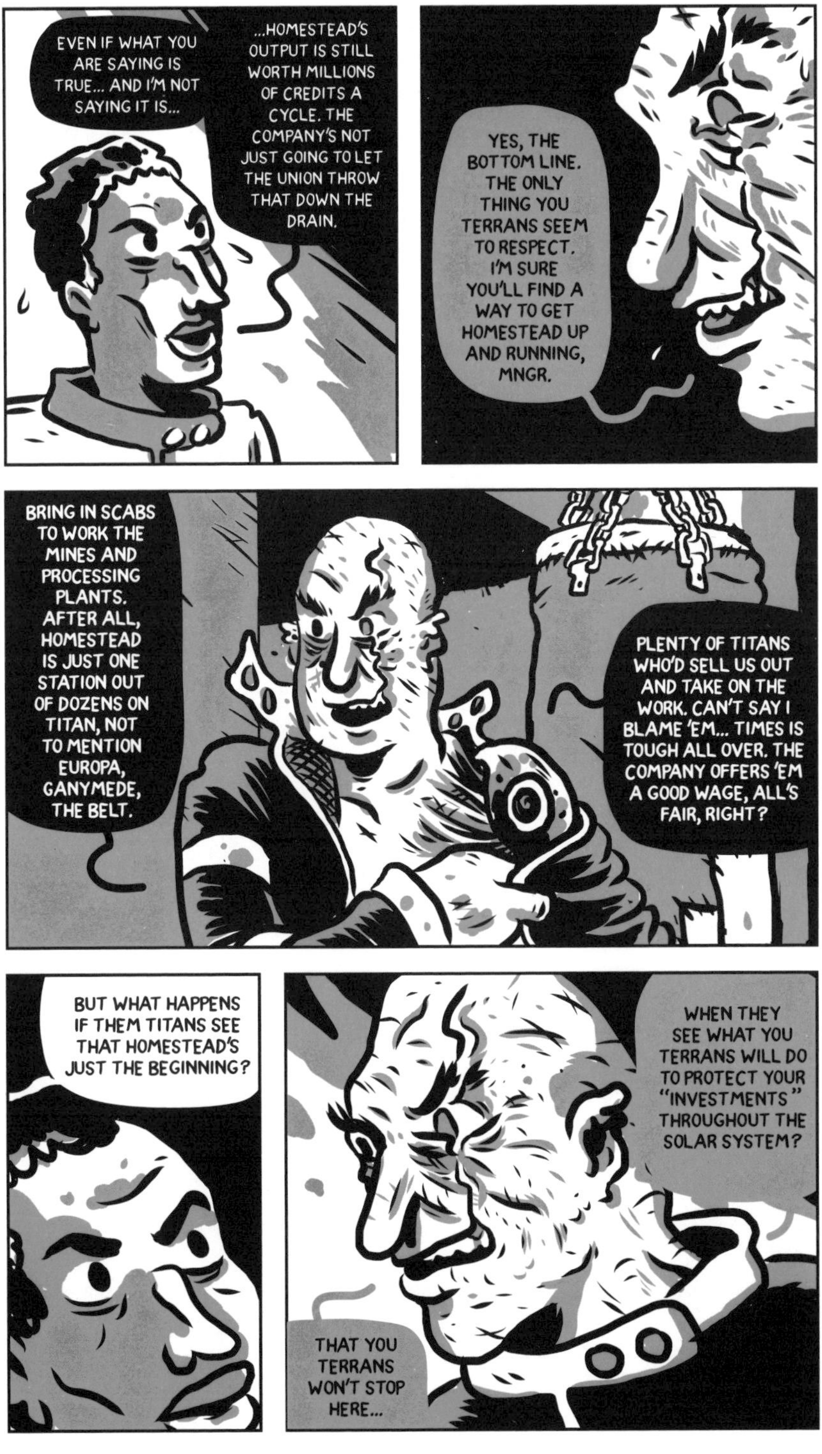
EVEN IF WHAT YOU ARE SAYING IS TRUE... AND I'M NOT SAYING IT IS...
...HOMESTEAD'S OUTPUT IS STILL WORTH MILLIONS OF CREDITS A CYCLE. THE COMPANY'S NOT JUST GOING TO LET THE UNION THROW THAT DOWN THE DRAIN.
YES, THE BOTTOM LINE. THE ONLY THING YOU TERRANS SEEM TO RESPECT. I'M SURE YOU'LL FIND A WAY TO GET HOMESTEAD UP AND RUNNING, MNGR.
BRING IN SCABS TO WORK THE MINES AND PROCESSING PLANTS. AFTER ALL, HOMESTEAD IS JUST ONE STATION OUT OF DOZENS ON TITAN, NOT TO MENTION EUROPA, GANYMEDE, THE BELT.
PLENTY OF TITANS WHO'D SELL US OUT AND TAKE ON THE WORK. CAN'T SAY I BLAME 'EM... TIMES IS TOUGH ALL OVER. THE COMPANY OFFERS 'EM A GOOD WAGE, ALL'S FAIR, RIGHT?
BUT WHAT HAPPENS IF THEM TITANS SEE THAT HOMESTEAD'S JUST THE BEGINNING?
WHEN THEY SEE WHAT YOU TERRANS WILL DO TO PROTECT YOUR "INVESTMENTS" THROUGHOUT THE SOLAR SYSTEM?
THAT YOU TERRANS WON'T STOP HERE...

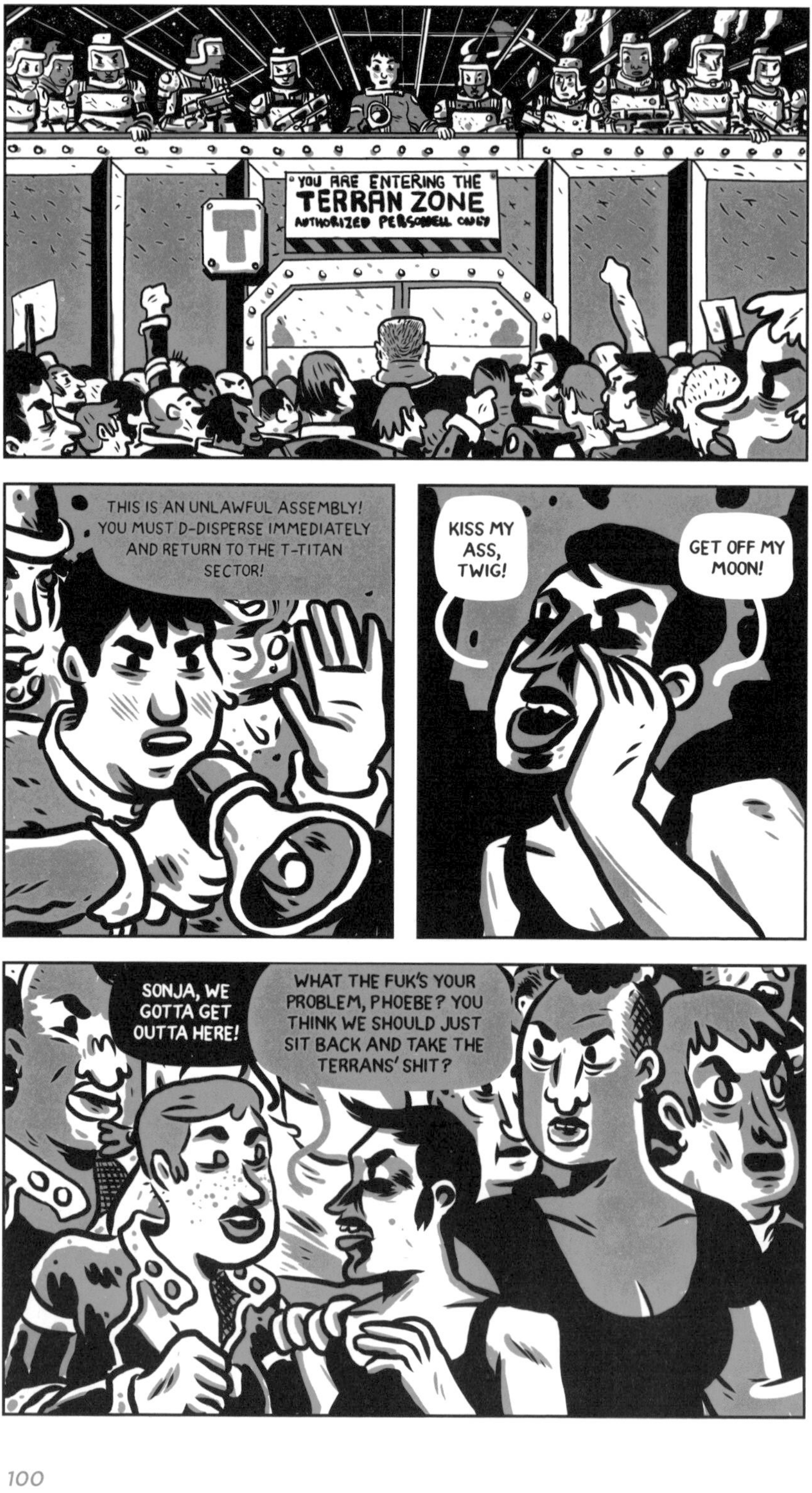

YOU ARE ENTERING THE
TERRAN ZONE
T
THIS IS AN UNLAWFUL ASSEMBLY! YOU MUST D-DISPERSE IMMEDIATELY AND RETURN TO THE T-TITAN SECTOR!
KISS MY ASS, TWIG!
GET OFF MY MOON!
SONJA, WE GOTTA GET OUTTA HERE!
WHAT THE FUK'S YOUR PROBLEM, PHOEBE? YOU THINK WE SHOULD JUST SIT BACK AND TAKE THE TERRANS' SHIT?

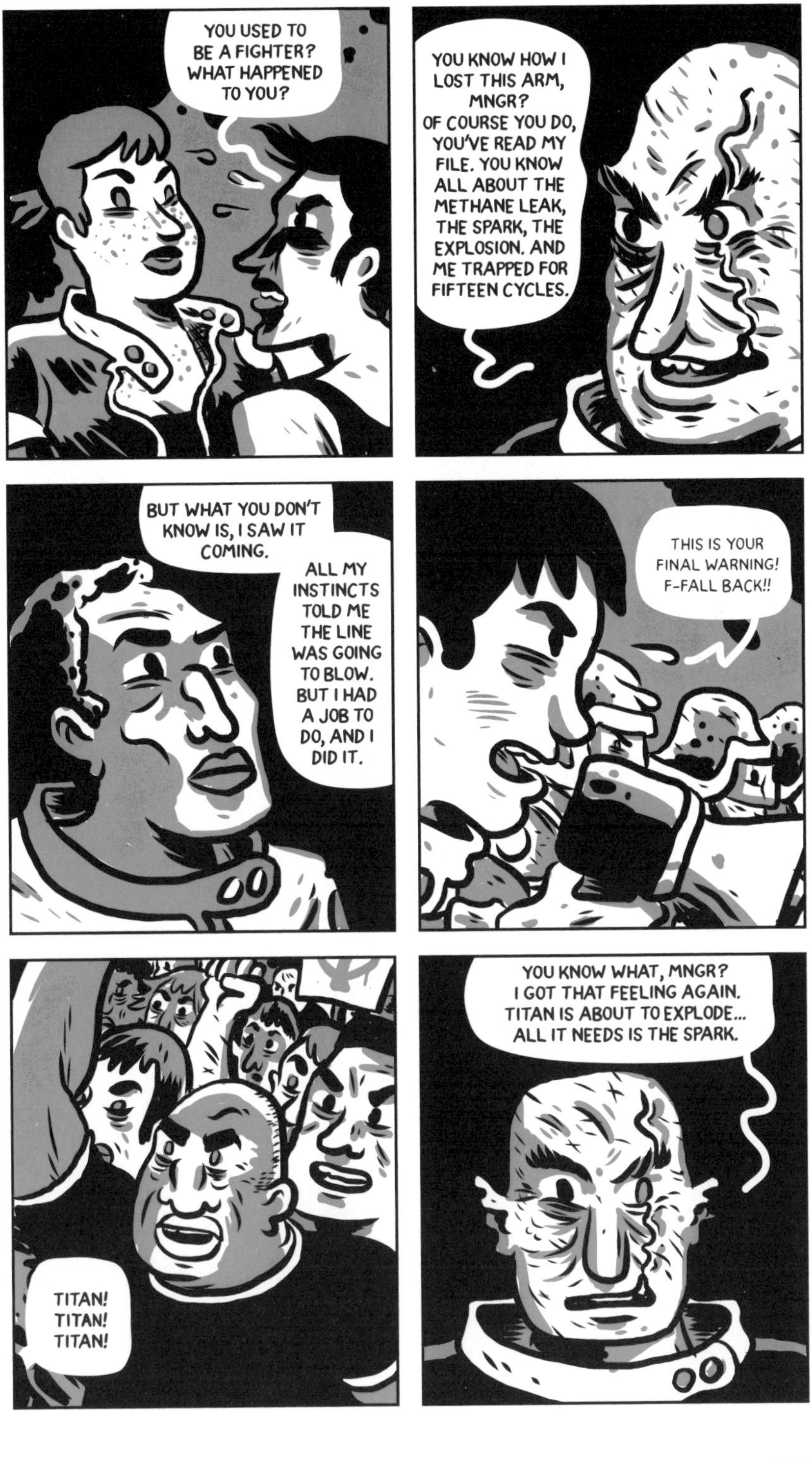

YOU USED TO BE A FIGHTER? WHAT HAPPENED TO YOU?
YOU KNOW HOW I LOST THIS ARM, MNGR? OF COURSE YOU DO, YOU'VE READ MY FILE. YOU KNOW ALL ABOUT THE METHANE LEAK, THE SPARK, THE EXPLOSION. AND ME TRAPPED FOR FIFTEEN CYCLES.
BUT WHAT YOU DON'T KNOW IS, I SAW IT COMING.
ALL MY INSTINCTS TOLD ME THE LINE WAS GOING TO BLOW. BUT I HAD A JOB TO DO, AND I DID IT.
THIS IS YOUR FINAL WARNING! F-FALL BACK!!
TITAN! TITAN! TITAN!
YOU KNOW WHAT, MNGR? I GOT THAT FEELING AGAIN. TITAN IS ABOUT TO EXPLODE... ALL IT NEEDS IS THE SPARK.

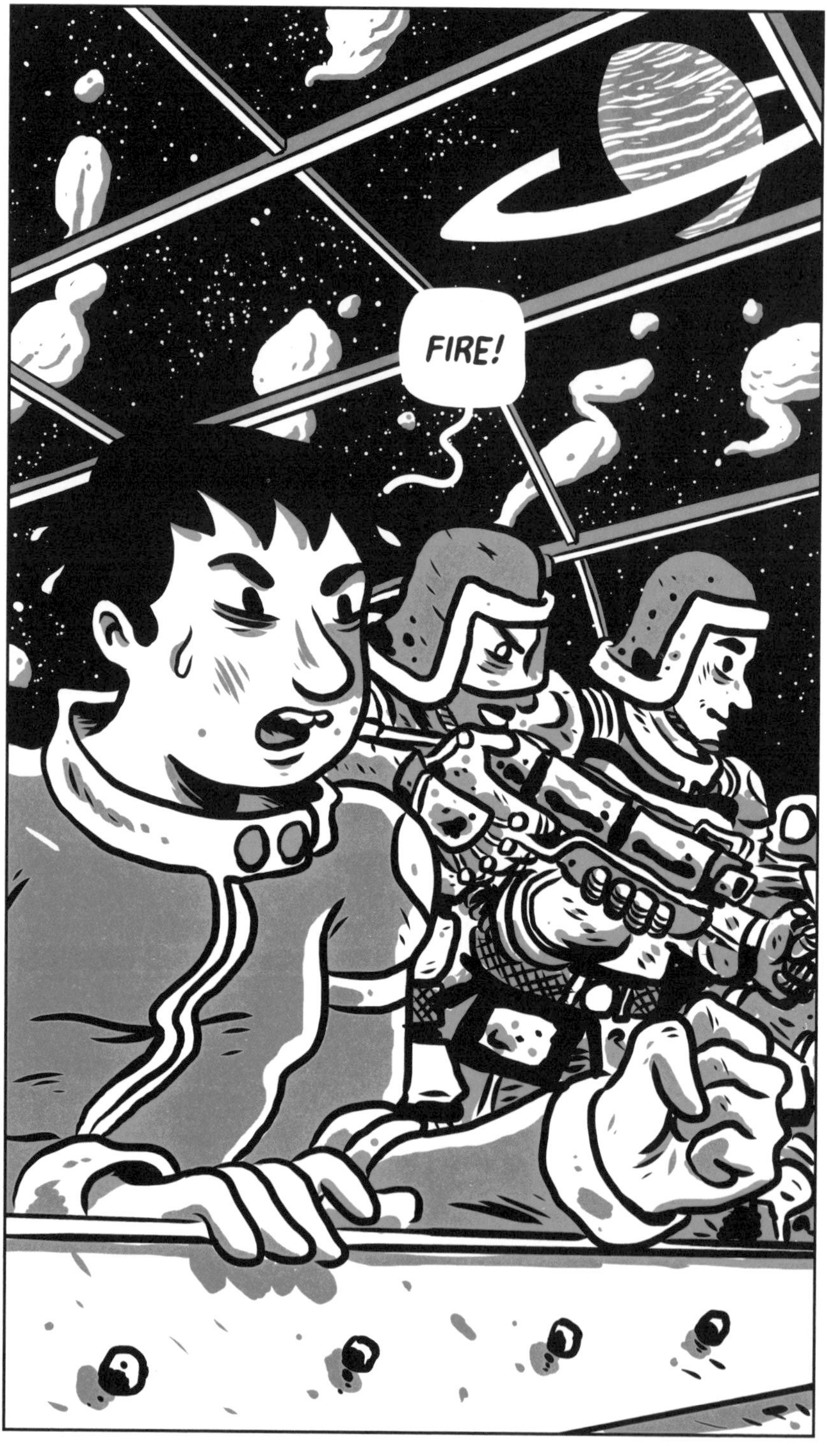
FIRE!

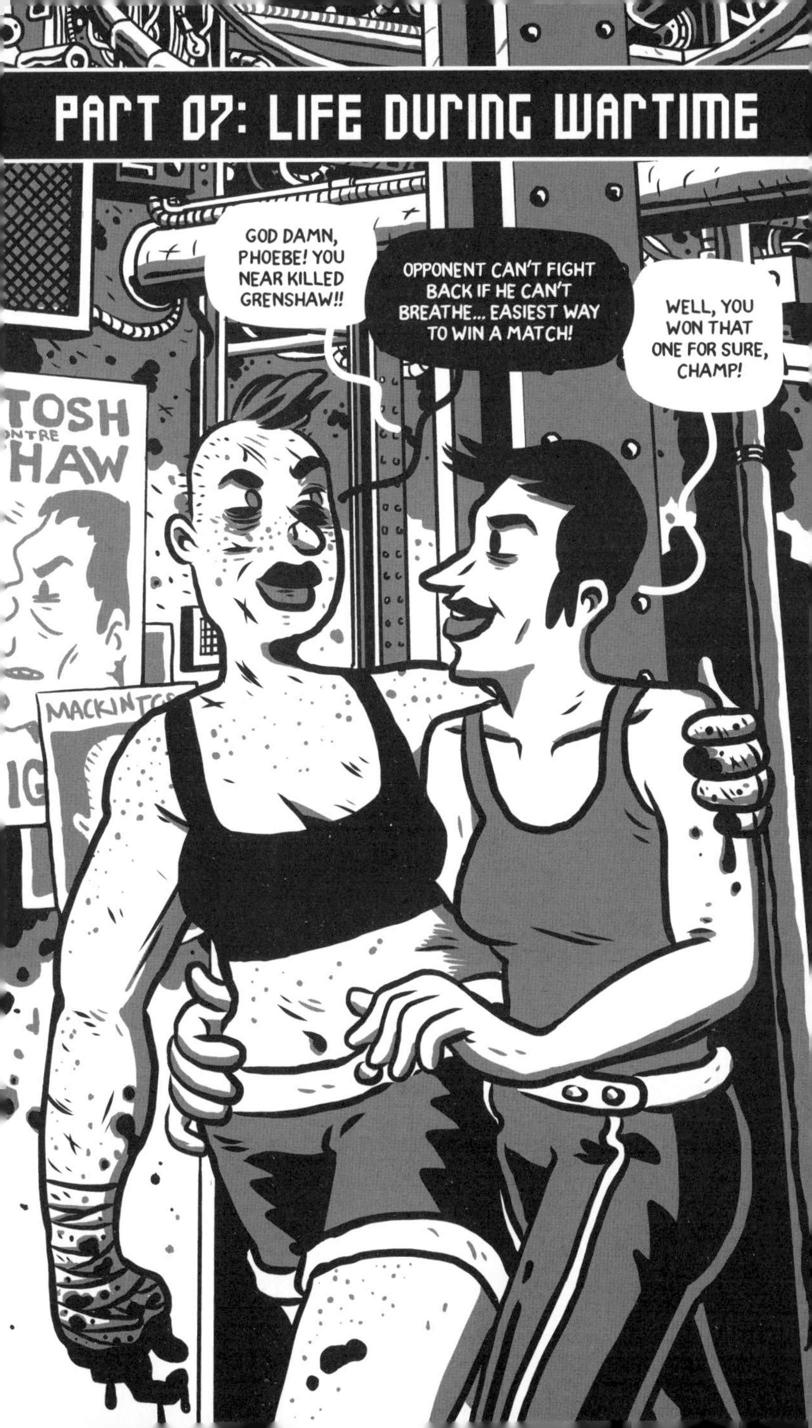
PART 07: LIFE DURING WARTIME
GOD DAMN, PHOEBE! YOU NEAR KILLED GRENSHAW!!
OPPONENT CAN'T FIGHT BACK IF HE CAN'T BREATHE... EASIEST WAY TO WIN A MATCH!
WELL, YOU WON THAT ONE FOR SURE, CHAMP!

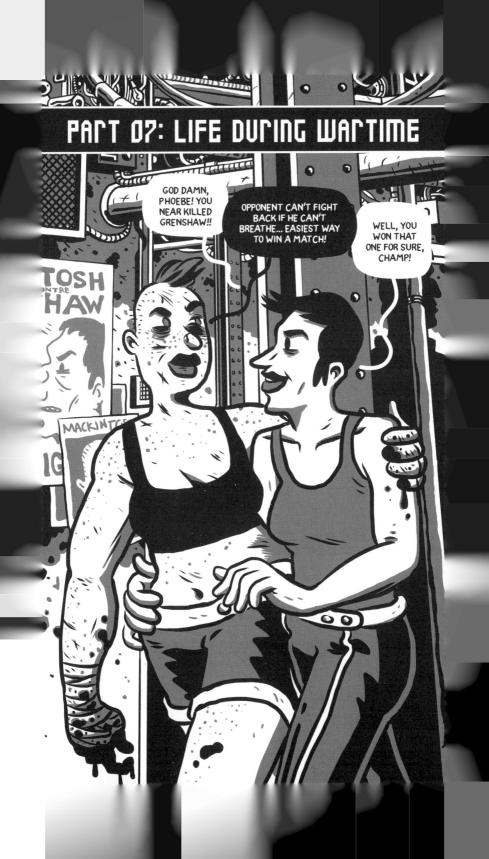

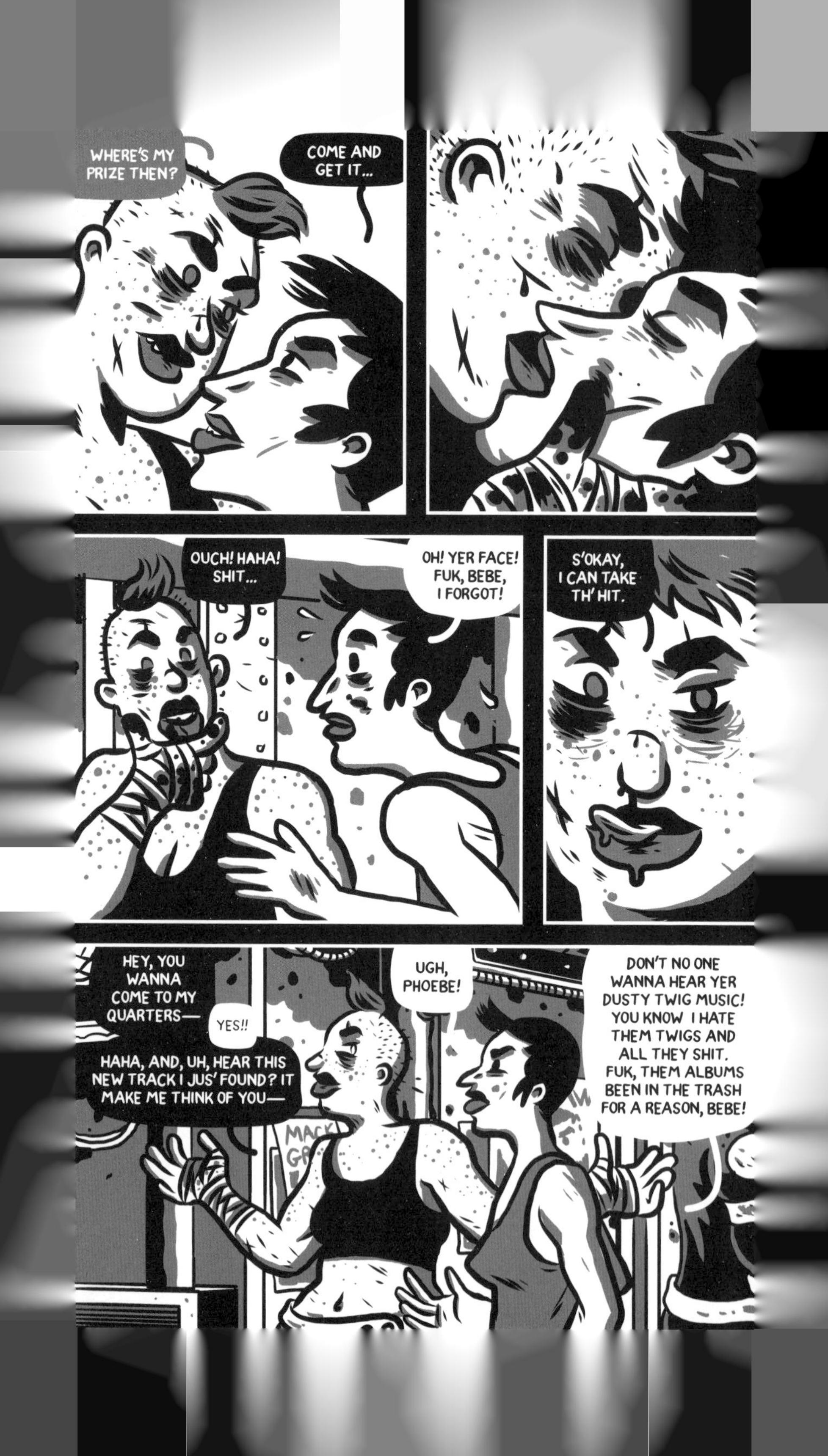
WHERE'S MY PRIZE THEN?
COME AND GET IT...
OUCH! HAHA! SHIT...
OH! YER FACE! FUK, BEBE, I FORGOT!
S'OKAY, I CAN TAKE TH' HIT.
HEY, YOU WANNA COME TO MY QUARTERS—
YES!!
HAHA, AND, UH, HEAR THIS NEW TRACK I JUS' FOUND? IT MAKE ME THINK OF YOU—
UGH, PHOEBE!
DON'T NO ONE WANNA HEAR YER DUSTY TWIG MUSIC! YOU KNOW I HATE THEM TWIGS AND ALL THEY SHIT. FUK, THEM ALBUMS BEEN IN THE TRASH FOR A REASON, BEBE!

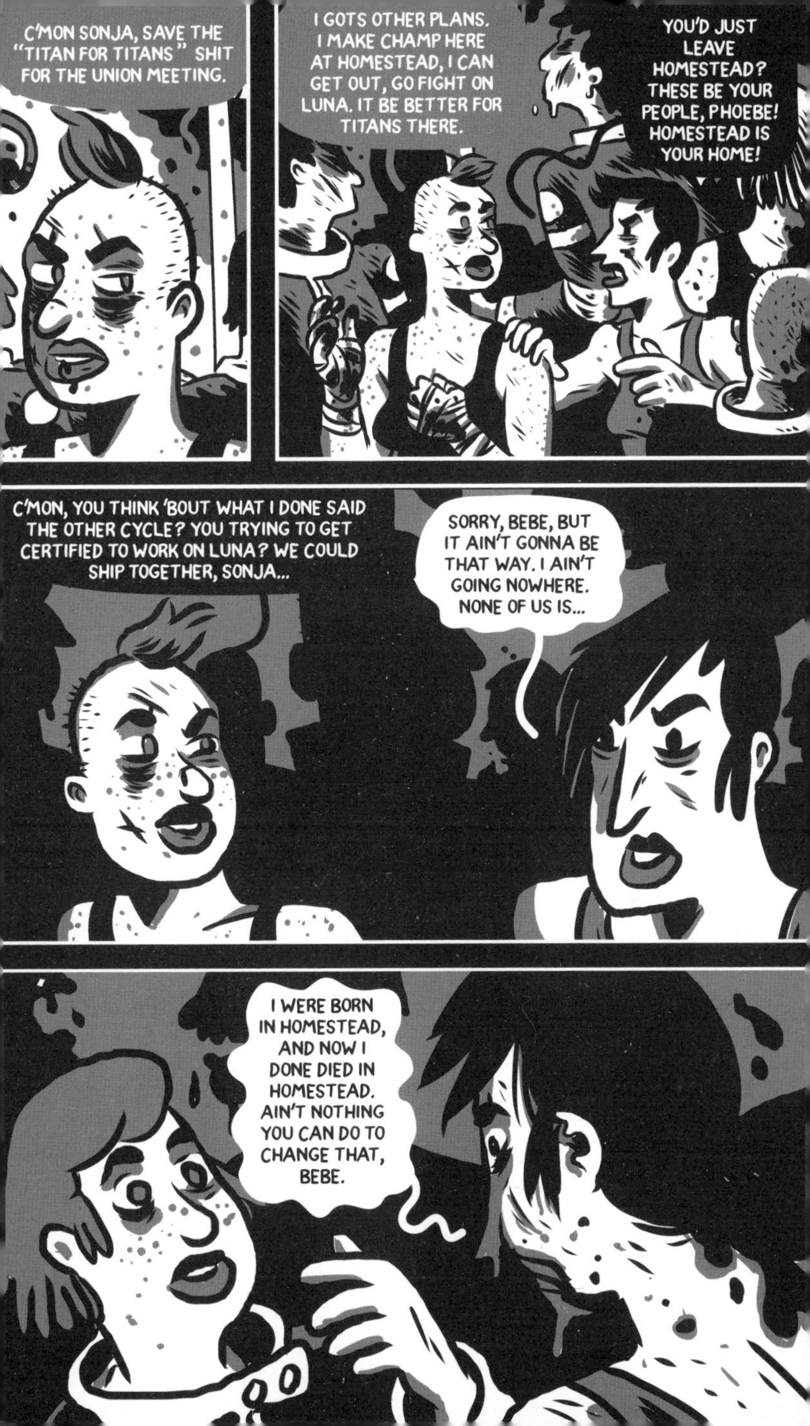
C'MON SONJA, SAVE THE "TITAN FOR TITANS" SHIT FOR THE UNION MEETING.
I GOTS OTHER PLANS. I MAKE CHAMP HERE AT HOMESTEAD, I CAN GET OUT, GO FIGHT ON LUNA. IT BE BETTER FOR TITANS THERE.
YOU'D JUST LEAVE HOMESTEAD? THESE BE YOUR PEOPLE, PHOEBE! HOMESTEAD IS YOUR HOME!
C'MON, YOU THINK 'BOUT WHAT I DONE SAID THE OTHER CYCLE? YOU TRYING TO GET CERTIFIED TO WORK ON LUNA? WE COULD SHIP TOGETHER, SONJA...
SORRY, BEBE, BUT IT AIN'T GONNA BE THAT WAY. I AIN'T GOING NOWHERE. NONE OF US IS...
I WERE BORN IN HOMESTEAD, AND NOW I DONE DIED IN HOMESTEAD. AIN'T NOTHING YOU CAN DO TO CHANGE THAT, BEBE.

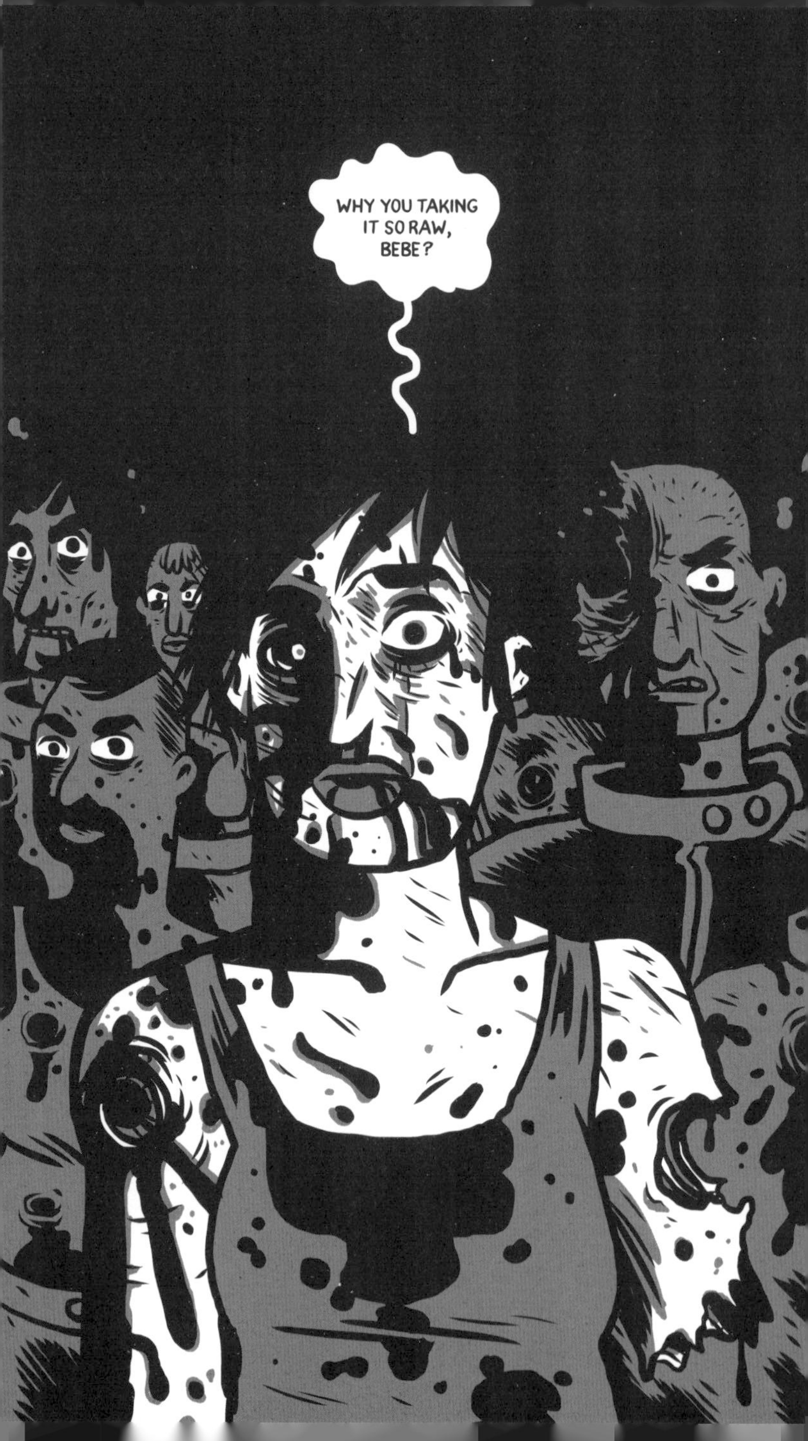
WHY YOU TAKING IT SO RAW, BEBE?

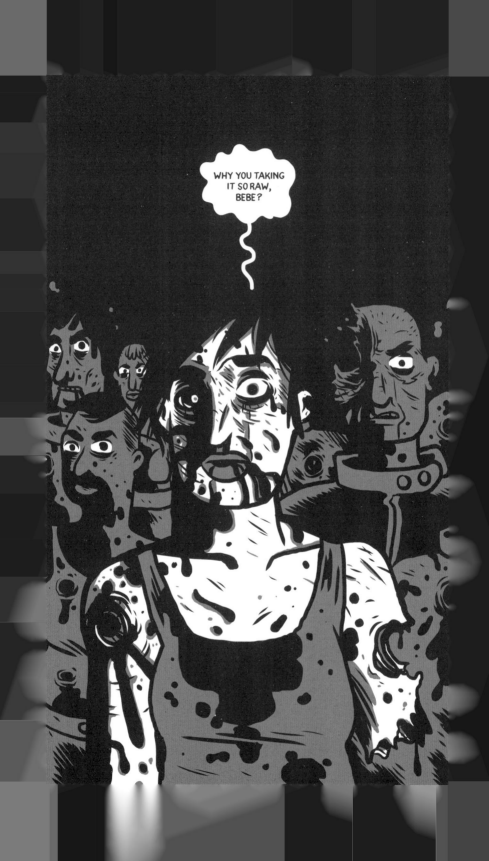

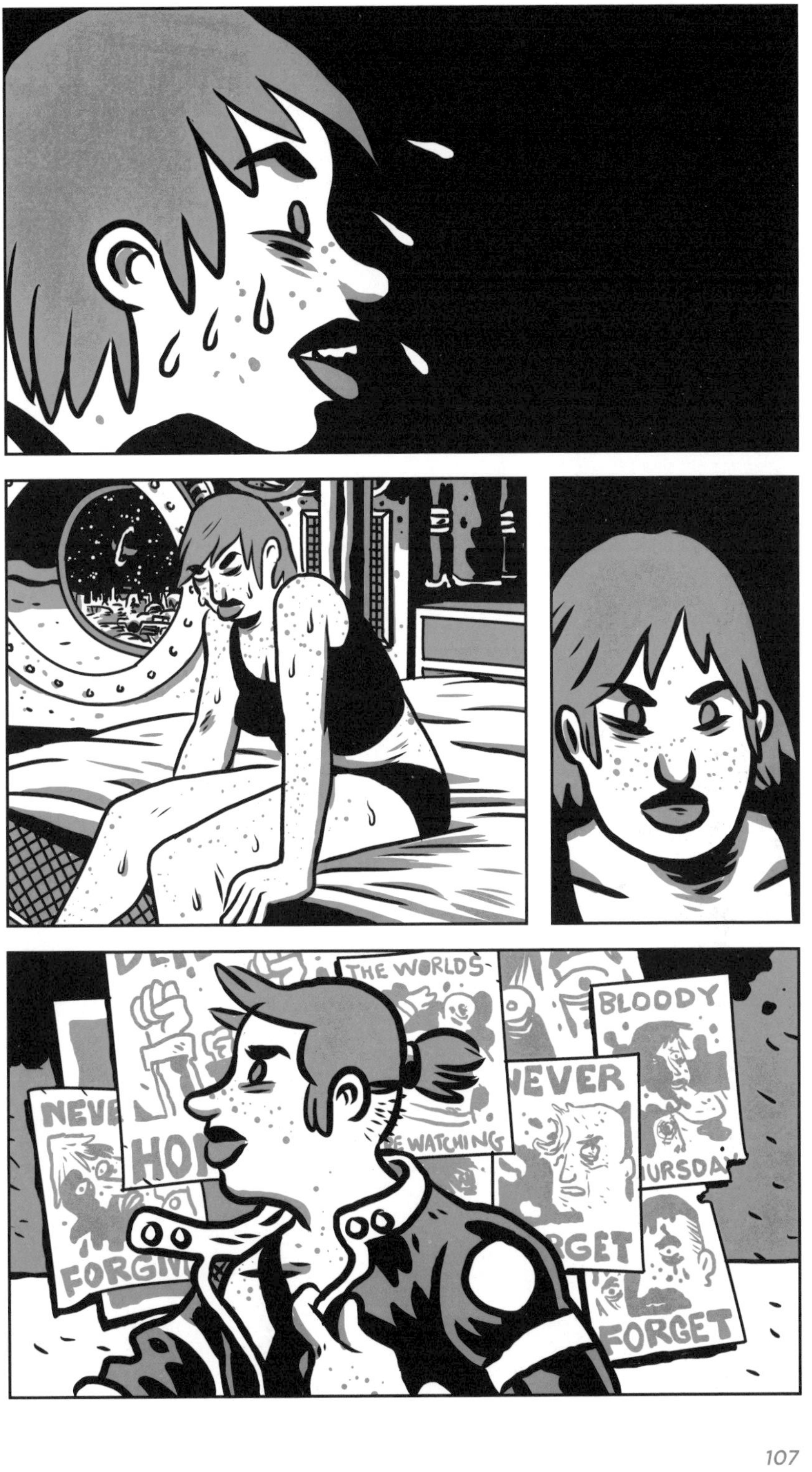
THE WORLDS
BLOODY
FORGET

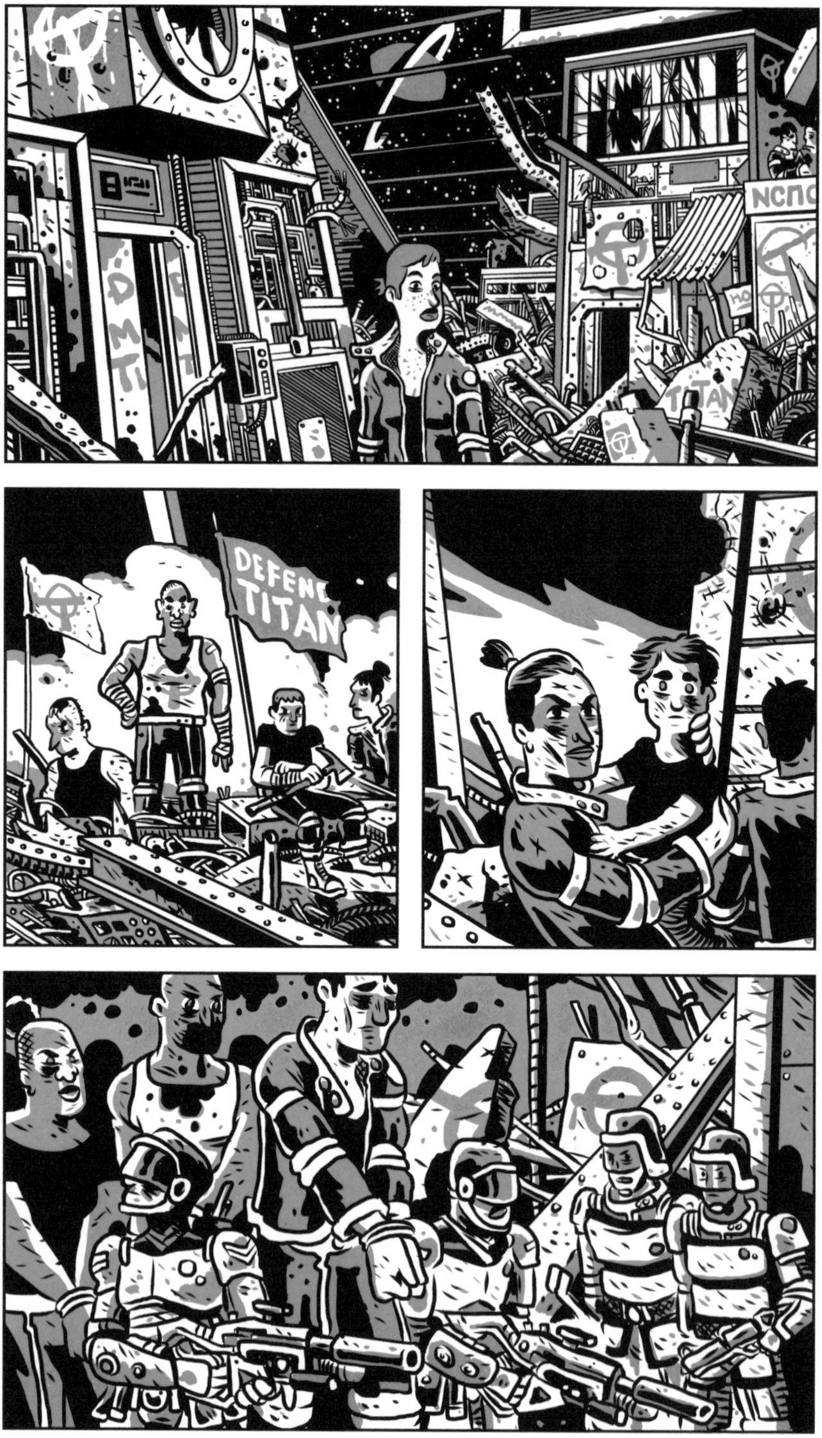
TITAN
TITAN

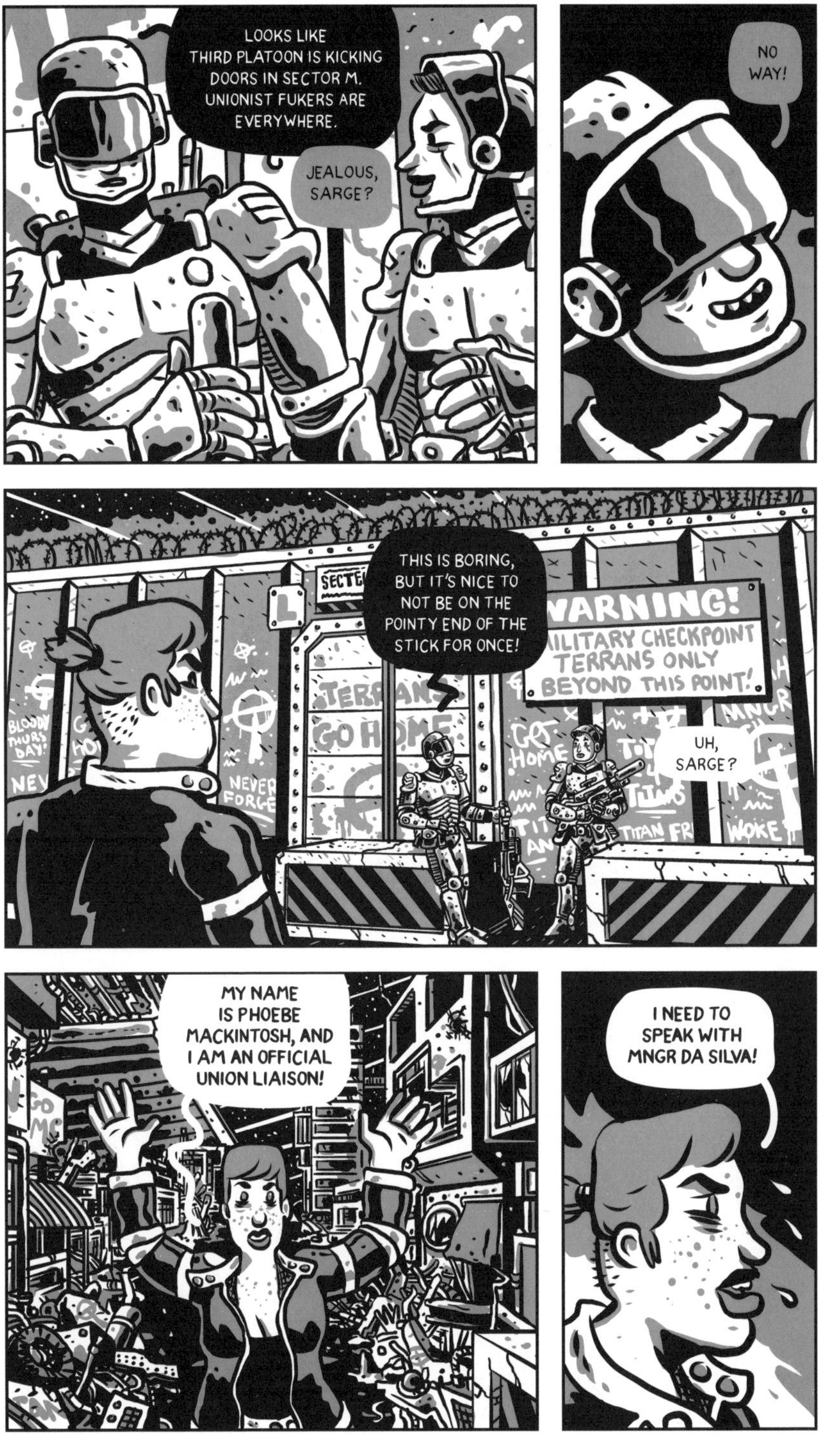
LOOKS LIKE THIRD PLATOON IS KICKING DOORS IN SECTOR M. UNIONIST FUKERS ARE EVERYWHERE.
JEALOUS, SARGE?
NO WAY!
THIS IS BORING, BUT IT'S NICE TO NOT BE ON THE POINTY END OF THE STICK FOR ONCE!
WARNING! MILITARY CHECKPOINT TERRANS ONLY BEYOND THIS POINT!
TERRANS GO HOME
BLOODY THURSDAY!
NEVER FORGET
UH, SARGE?
MY NAME IS PHOEBE MACKINTOSH, AND I AM AN OFFICIAL UNION LIAISON!
I NEED TO SPEAK WITH MNGR DA SILVA!

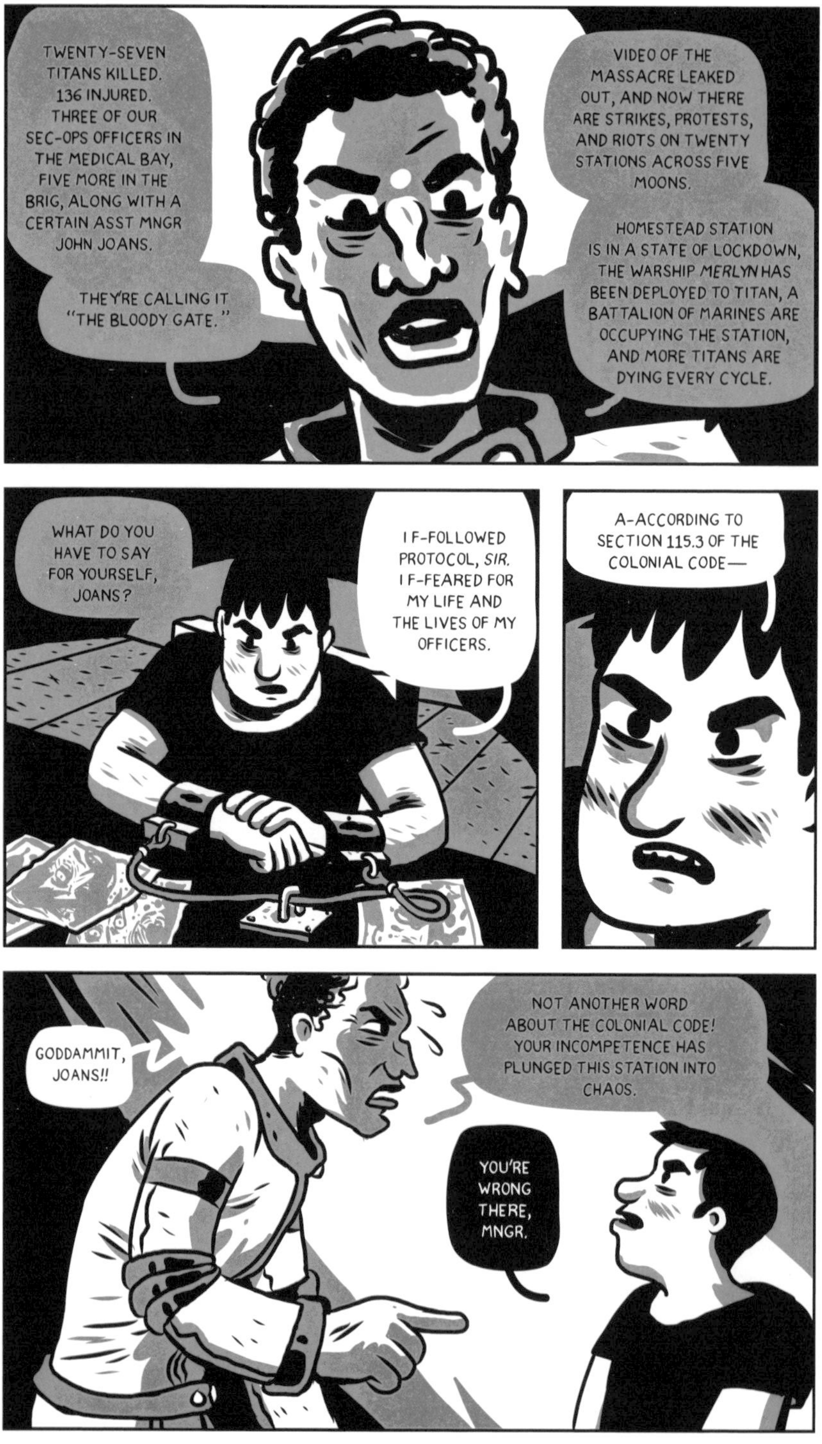
TWENTY-SEVEN TITANS KILLED. 136 INJURED. THREE OF OUR SEC-OPS OFFICERS IN THE MEDICAL BAY, FIVE MORE IN THE BRIG, ALONG WITH A CERTAIN ASST MNGR JOHN JOANS.
THEY'RE CALLING IT "THE BLOODY GATE."
VIDEO OF THE MASSACRE LEAKED OUT, AND NOW THERE ARE STRIKES, PROTESTS, AND RIOTS ON TWENTY STATIONS ACROSS FIVE MOONS.
HOMESTEAD STATION IS IN A STATE OF LOCKDOWN, THE WARSHIP *MERLYN* HAS BEEN DEPLOYED TO TITAN, A BATTALION OF MARINES ARE OCCUPYING THE STATION, AND MORE TITANS ARE DYING EVERY CYCLE.
WHAT DO YOU HAVE TO SAY FOR YOURSELF, JOANS?
I F-FOLLOWED PROTOCOL, *SIR.* I F-FEARED FOR MY LIFE AND THE LIVES OF MY OFFICERS.
A-ACCORDING TO SECTION 115.3 OF THE COLONIAL CODE—
GODDAMMIT, JOANS!!
NOT ANOTHER WORD ABOUT THE COLONIAL CODE! YOUR INCOMPETENCE HAS PLUNGED THIS STATION INTO CHAOS.
YOU'RE WRONG THERE, MNGR.

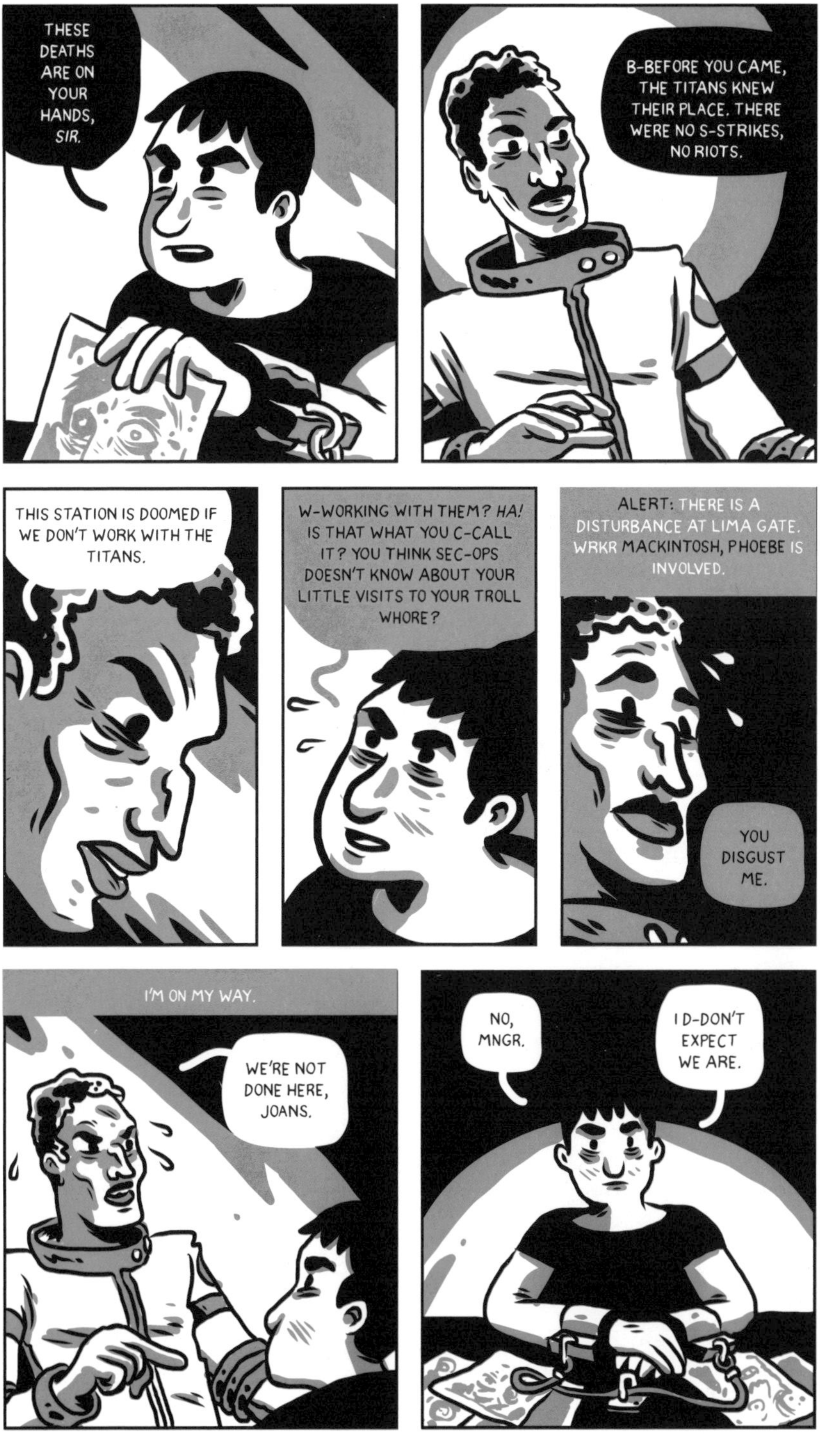
THESE DEATHS ARE ON YOUR HANDS, *SIR.*
B-BEFORE YOU CAME, THE TITANS KNEW THEIR PLACE. THERE WERE NO S-STRIKES, NO RIOTS.
THIS STATION IS DOOMED IF WE DON'T WORK WITH THE TITANS.
W-WORKING WITH THEM? *HA!* IS THAT WHAT YOU C-CALL IT? YOU THINK SEC-OPS DOESN'T KNOW ABOUT YOUR LITTLE VISITS TO YOUR TROLL WHORE?
ALERT: THERE IS A DISTURBANCE AT LIMA GATE. WRKR MACKINTOSH, PHOEBE IS INVOLVED.
YOU DISGUST ME.
I'M ON MY WAY.
WE'RE NOT DONE HERE, JOANS.
NO, MNGR.
I D-DON'T EXPECT WE ARE.

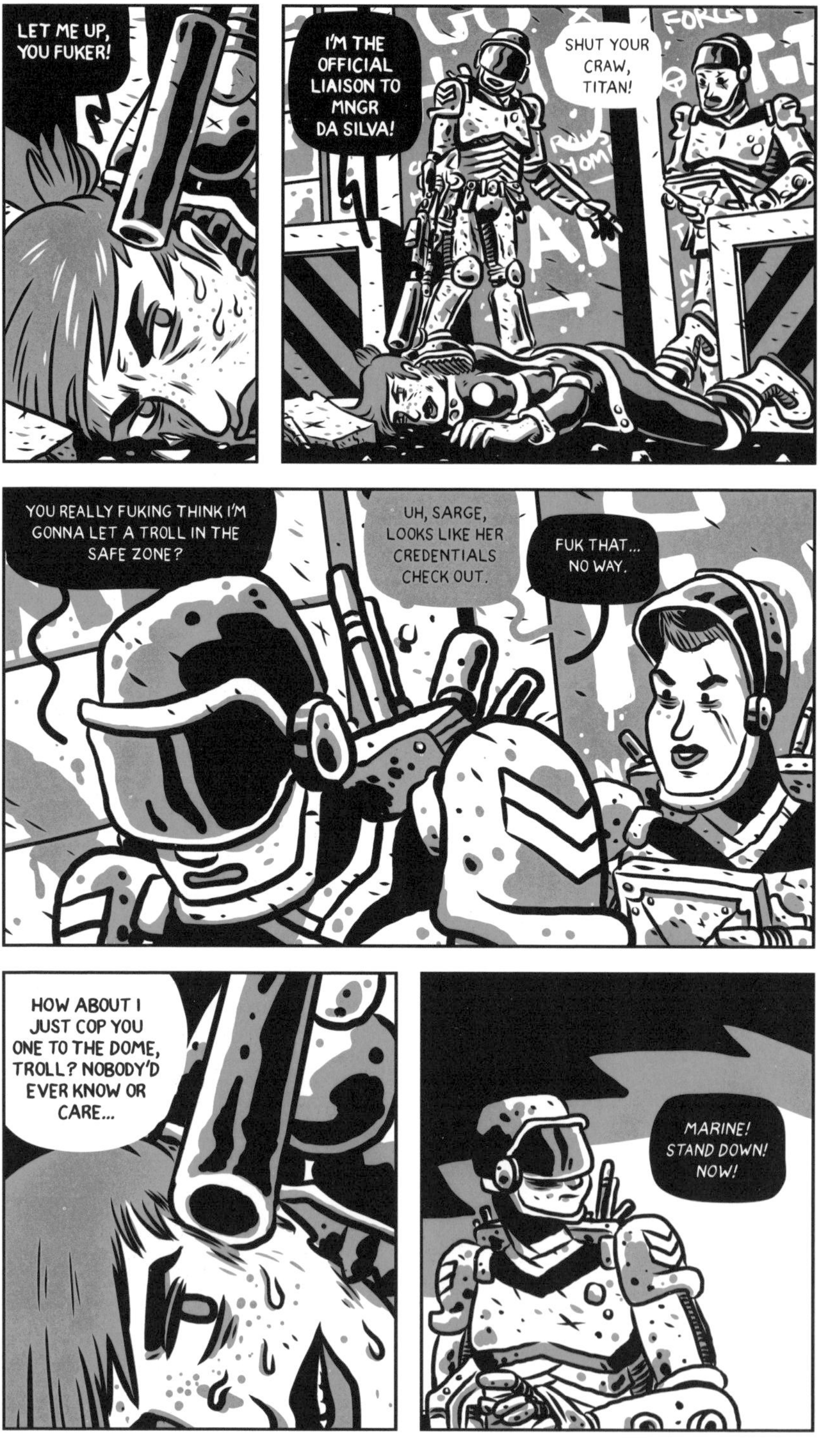
LET ME UP, YOU FUKER!
I'M THE OFFICIAL LIAISON TO MNGR DA SILVA!
SHUT YOUR CRAW, TITAN!
YOU REALLY FUKING THINK I'M GONNA LET A TROLL IN THE SAFE ZONE?
UH, SARGE, LOOKS LIKE HER CREDENTIALS CHECK OUT.
FUK THAT... NO WAY.
HOW ABOUT I JUST COP YOU ONE TO THE DOME, TROLL? NOBODY'D EVER KNOW OR CARE...
MARINE! STAND DOWN! NOW!

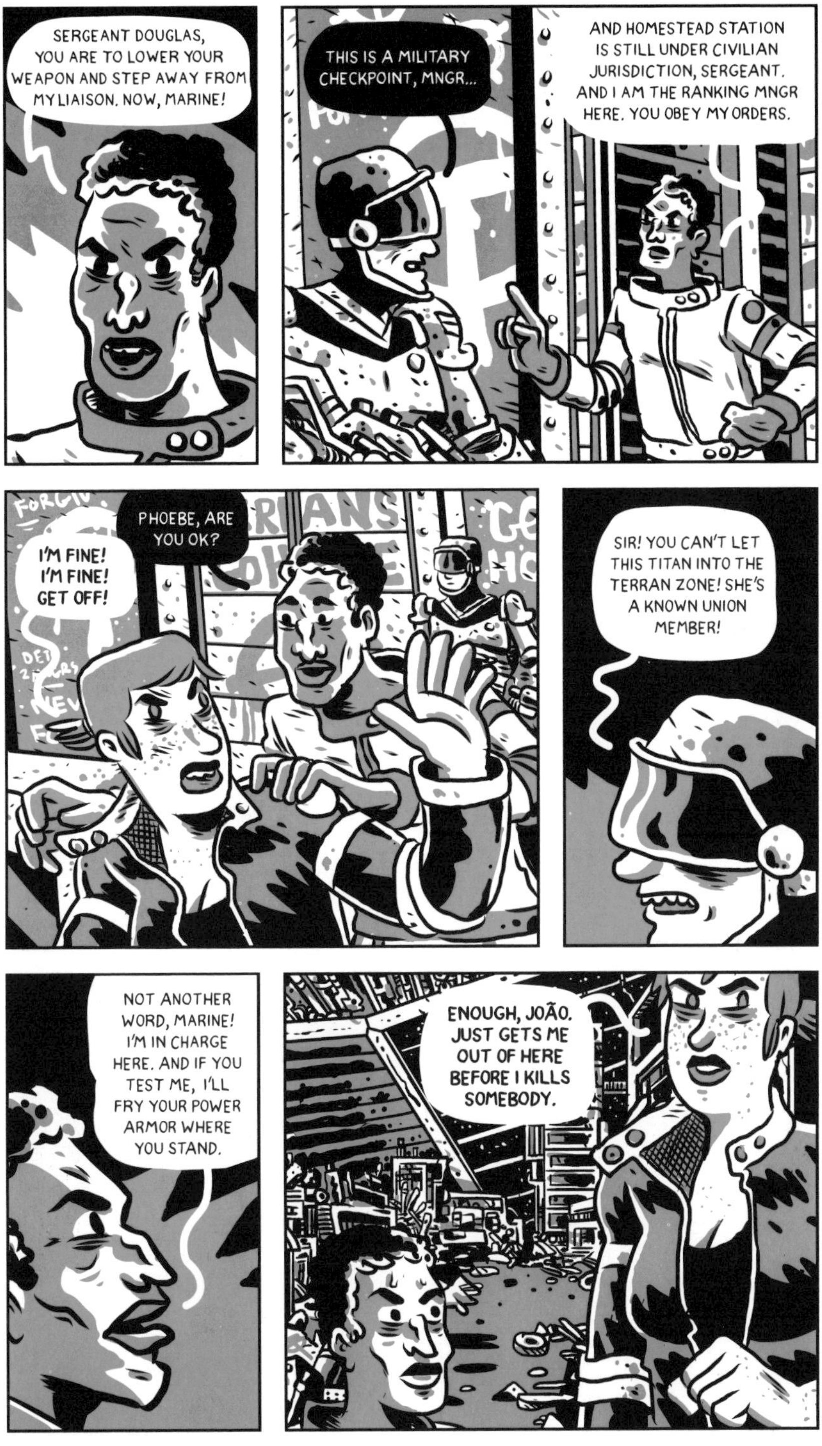

SERGEANT DOUGLAS, YOU ARE TO LOWER YOUR WEAPON AND STEP AWAY FROM MY LIAISON. NOW, MARINE!
THIS IS A MILITARY CHECKPOINT, MNGR...
AND HOMESTEAD STATION IS STILL UNDER CIVILIAN JURISDICTION, SERGEANT. AND I AM THE RANKING MNGR HERE. YOU OBEY MY ORDERS.
PHOEBE, ARE YOU OK?
I'M FINE! I'M FINE! GET OFF!
SIR! YOU CAN'T LET THIS TITAN INTO THE TERRAN ZONE! SHE'S A KNOWN UNION MEMBER!
NOT ANOTHER WORD, MARINE! I'M IN CHARGE HERE. AND IF YOU TEST ME, I'LL FRY YOUR POWER ARMOR WHERE YOU STAND.
ENOUGH, JOÃO. JUST GETS ME OUT OF HERE BEFORE I KILLS SOMEBODY.

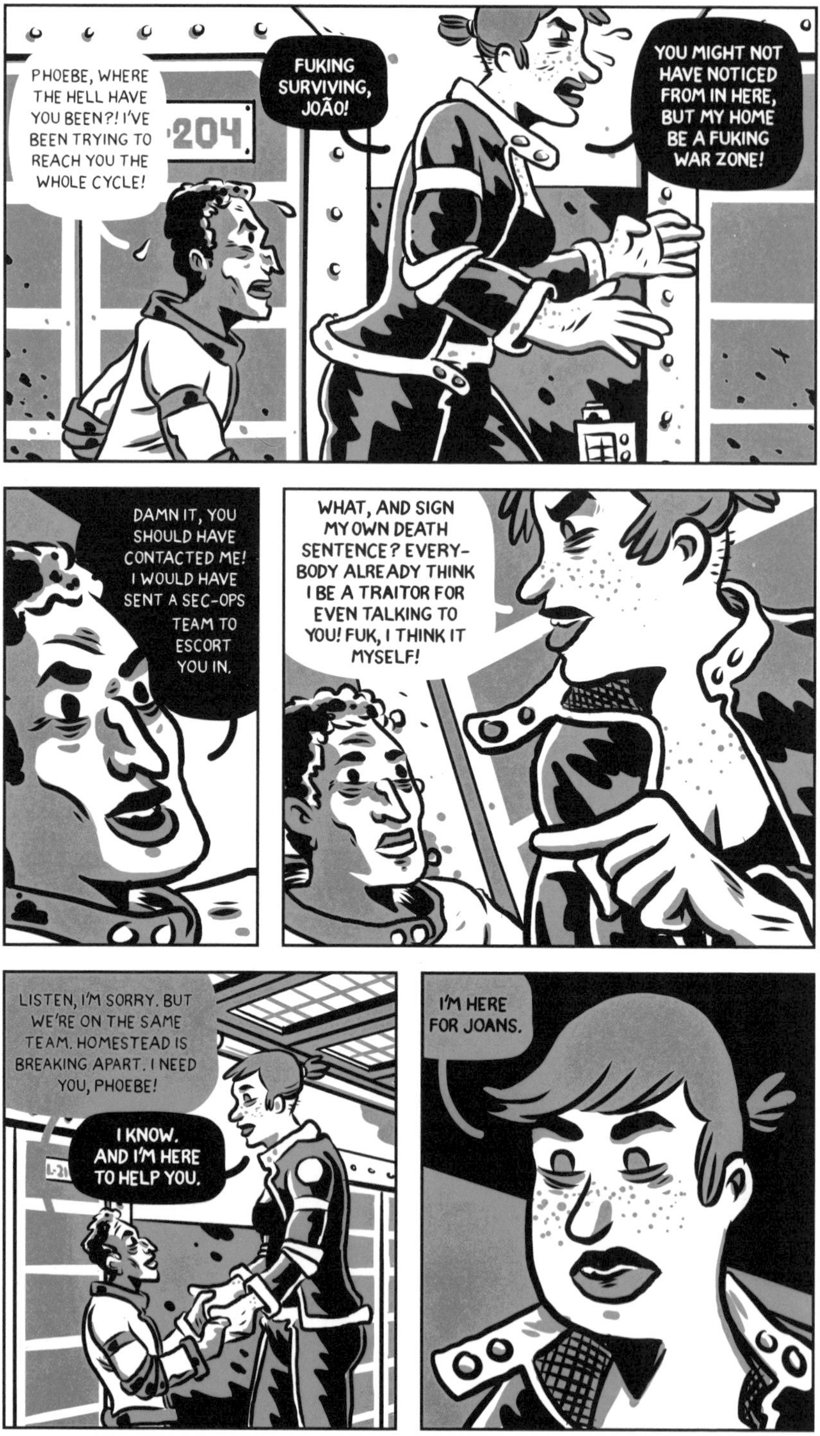
PHOEBE, WHERE THE HELL HAVE YOU BEEN?! I'VE BEEN TRYING TO REACH YOU THE WHOLE CYCLE!
204
FUKING SURVIVING, JOÃO!
YOU MIGHT NOT HAVE NOTICED FROM IN HERE, BUT MY HOME BE A FUKING WAR ZONE!
DAMN IT, YOU SHOULD HAVE CONTACTED ME! I WOULD HAVE SENT A SEC-OPS TEAM TO ESCORT YOU IN.
WHAT, AND SIGN MY OWN DEATH SENTENCE? EVERY-BODY ALREADY THINK I BE A TRAITOR FOR EVEN TALKING TO YOU! FUK, I THINK IT MYSELF!
LISTEN, I'M SORRY. BUT WE'RE ON THE SAME TEAM. HOMESTEAD IS BREAKING APART. I NEED YOU, PHOEBE!
I KNOW. AND I'M HERE TO HELP YOU.
I'M HERE FOR JOANS.

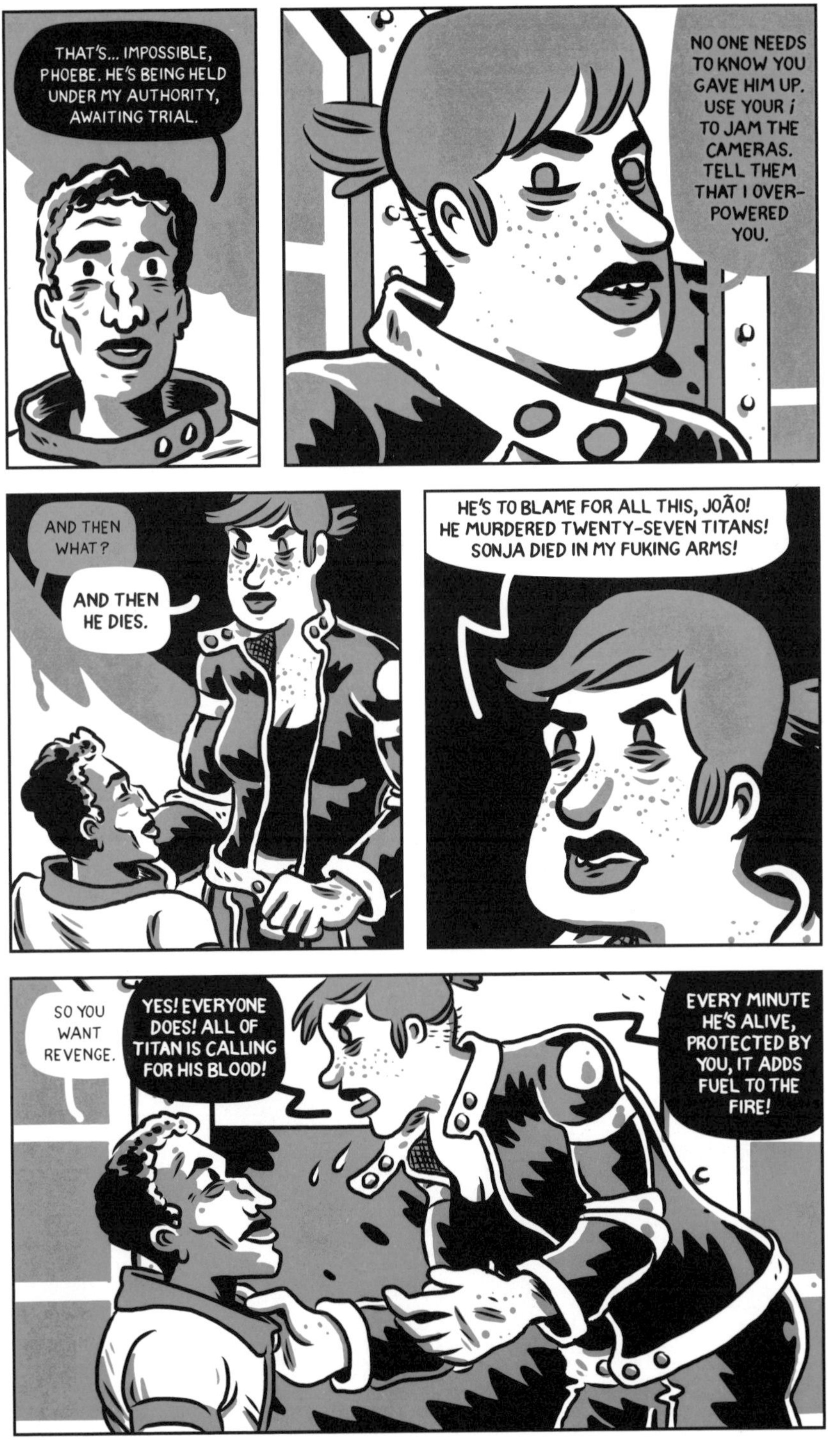
THAT'S... IMPOSSIBLE, PHOEBE. HE'S BEING HELD UNDER MY AUTHORITY, AWAITING TRIAL.
NO ONE NEEDS TO KNOW YOU GAVE HIM UP. USE YOUR *i* TO JAM THE CAMERAS. TELL THEM THAT I OVER-POWERED YOU.
AND THEN WHAT?
AND THEN HE DIES.
HE'S TO BLAME FOR ALL THIS, JOÃO! HE MURDERED TWENTY-SEVEN TITANS! SONJA DIED IN MY FUKING ARMS!
SO YOU WANT REVENGE.
YES! EVERYONE DOES! ALL OF TITAN IS CALLING FOR HIS BLOOD!
EVERY MINUTE HE'S ALIVE, PROTECTED BY YOU, IT ADDS FUEL TO THE FIRE!

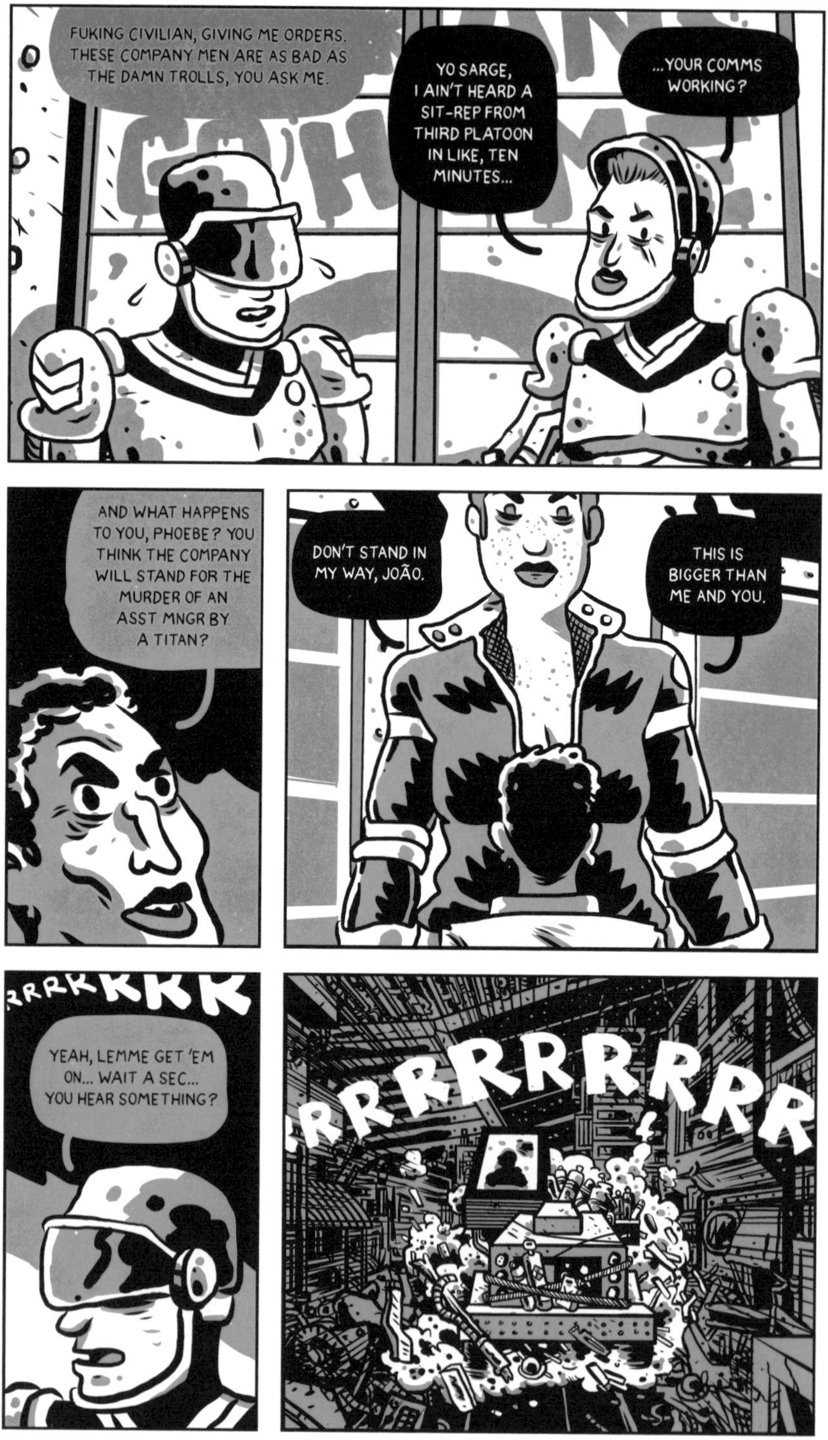
FUKING CIVILIAN, GIVING ME ORDERS. THESE COMPANY MEN ARE AS BAD AS THE DAMN TROLLS, YOU ASK ME.
YO SARGE, I AIN'T HEARD A SIT-REP FROM THIRD PLATOON IN LIKE, TEN MINUTES...
...YOUR COMMS WORKING?
AND WHAT HAPPENS TO YOU, PHOEBE? YOU THINK THE COMPANY WILL STAND FOR THE MURDER OF AN ASST MNGR BY A TITAN?
DON'T STAND IN MY WAY, JOÃO.
THIS IS BIGGER THAN ME AND YOU.
RRRKKKK
YEAH, LEMME GET 'EM ON... WAIT A SEC... YOU HEAR SOMETHING?
RRRRRRRRRR

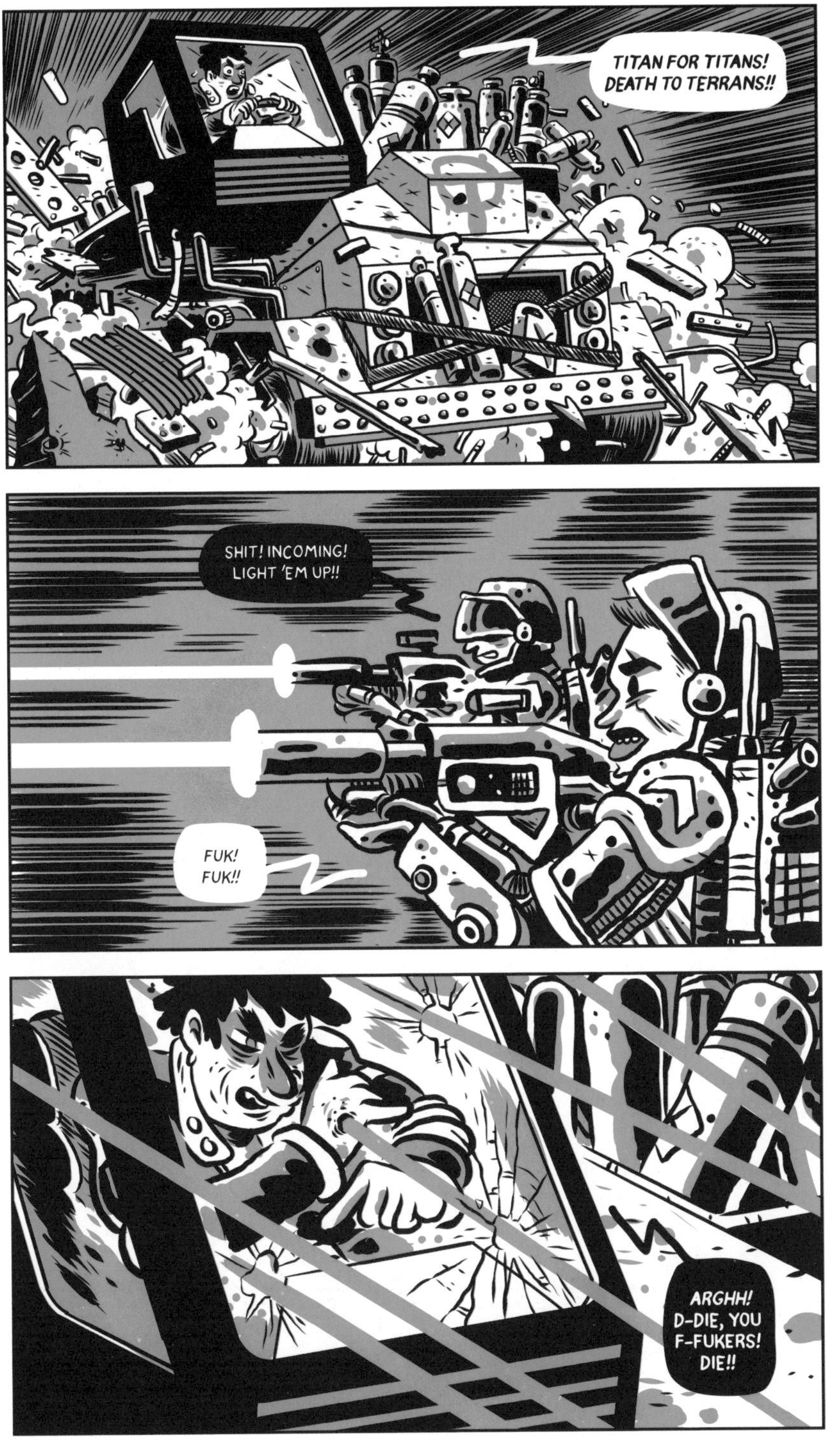
TITAN FOR TITANS! DEATH TO TERRANS!!
SHIT! INCOMING! LIGHT 'EM UP!!
FUK! FUK!!
ARGHH! D-DIE, YOU F-FUKERS! DIE!!

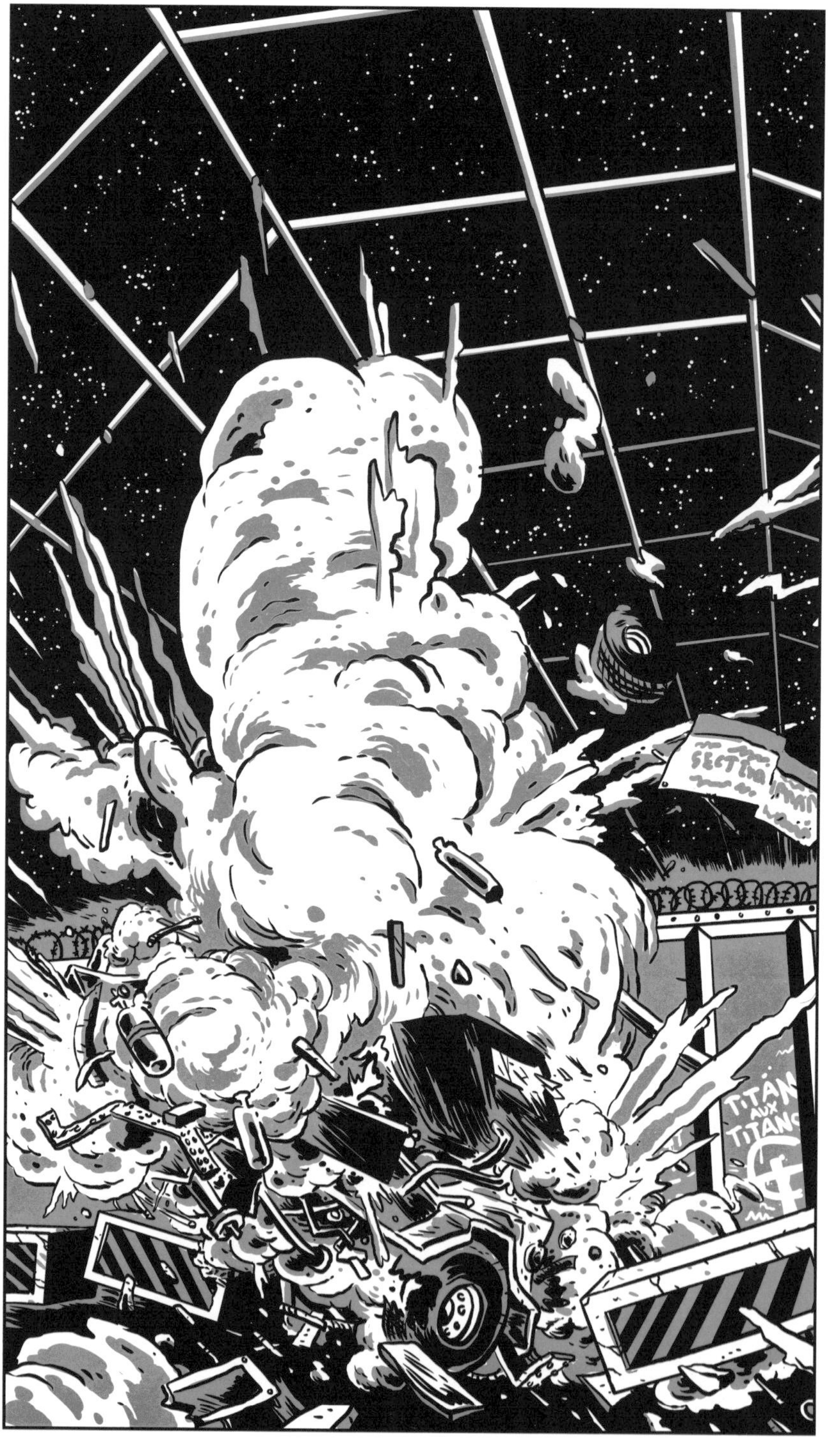
TITAN
AUX
TITANS

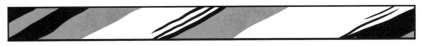

PART 08: MY MOON MY MAN

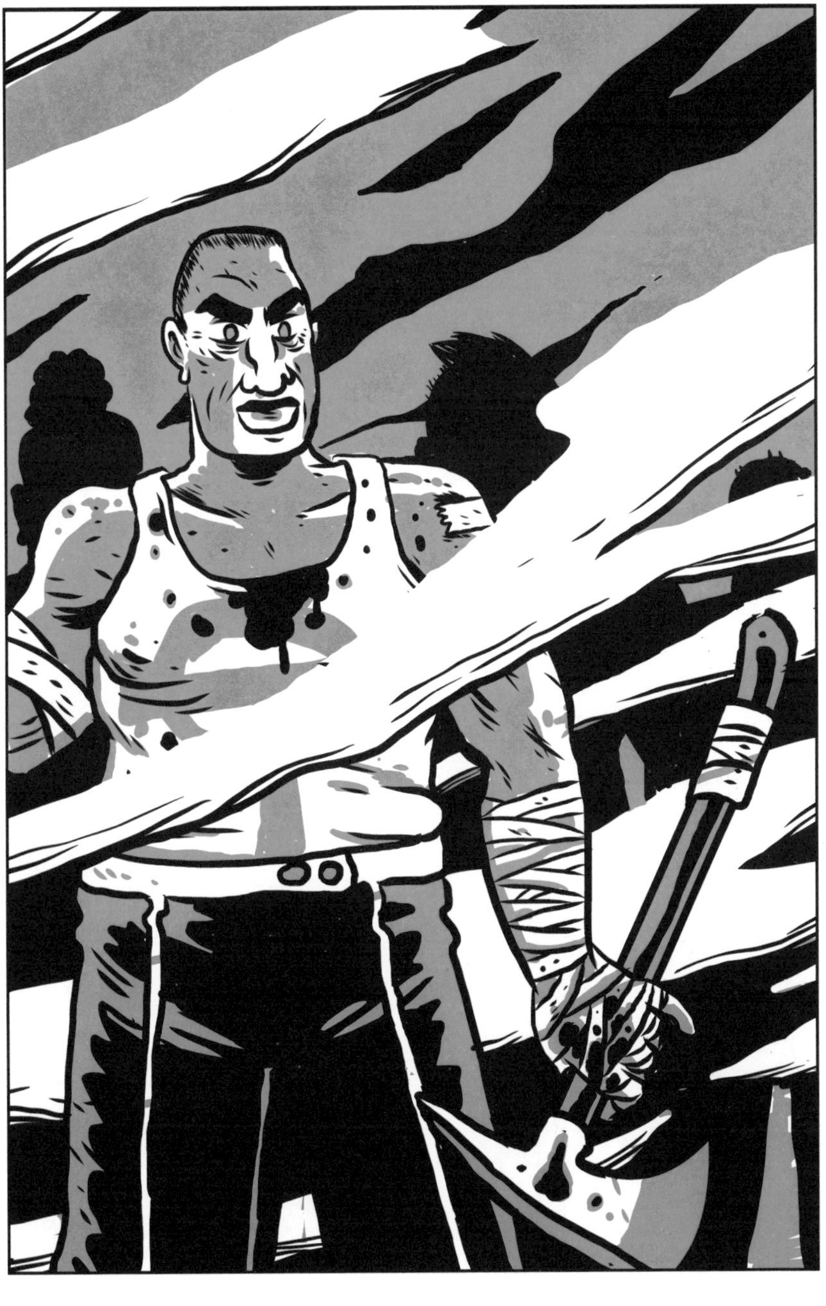

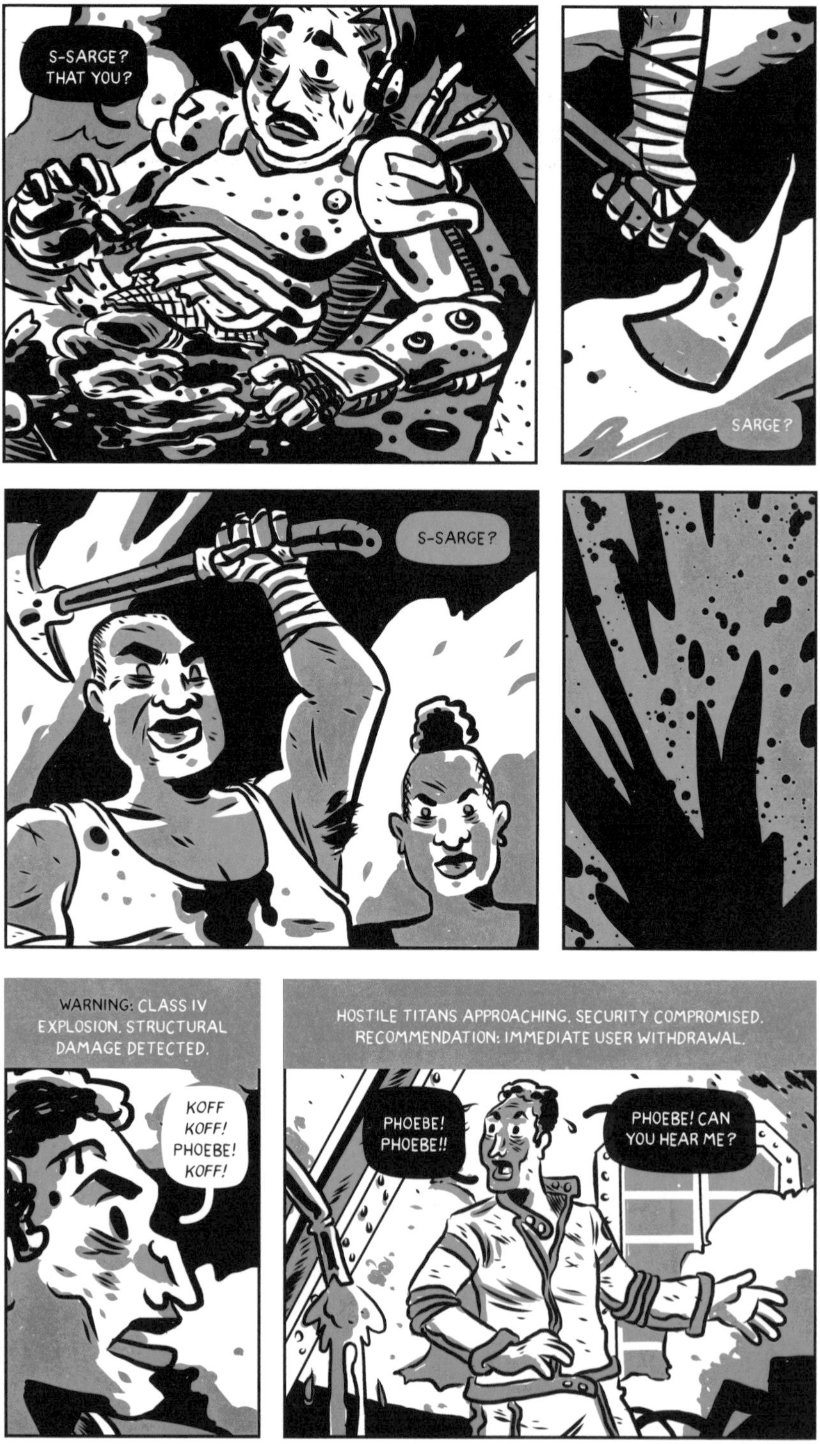

S-SARGE? THAT YOU?
SARGE?
S-SARGE?
WARNING: CLASS IV EXPLOSION. STRUCTURAL DAMAGE DETECTED.
KOFF KOFF! PHOEBE! KOFF!
HOSTILE TITANS APPROACHING. SECURITY COMPROMISED. RECOMMENDATION: IMMEDIATE USER WITHDRAWAL.
PHOEBE! PHOEBE!!
PHOEBE! CAN YOU HEAR ME?

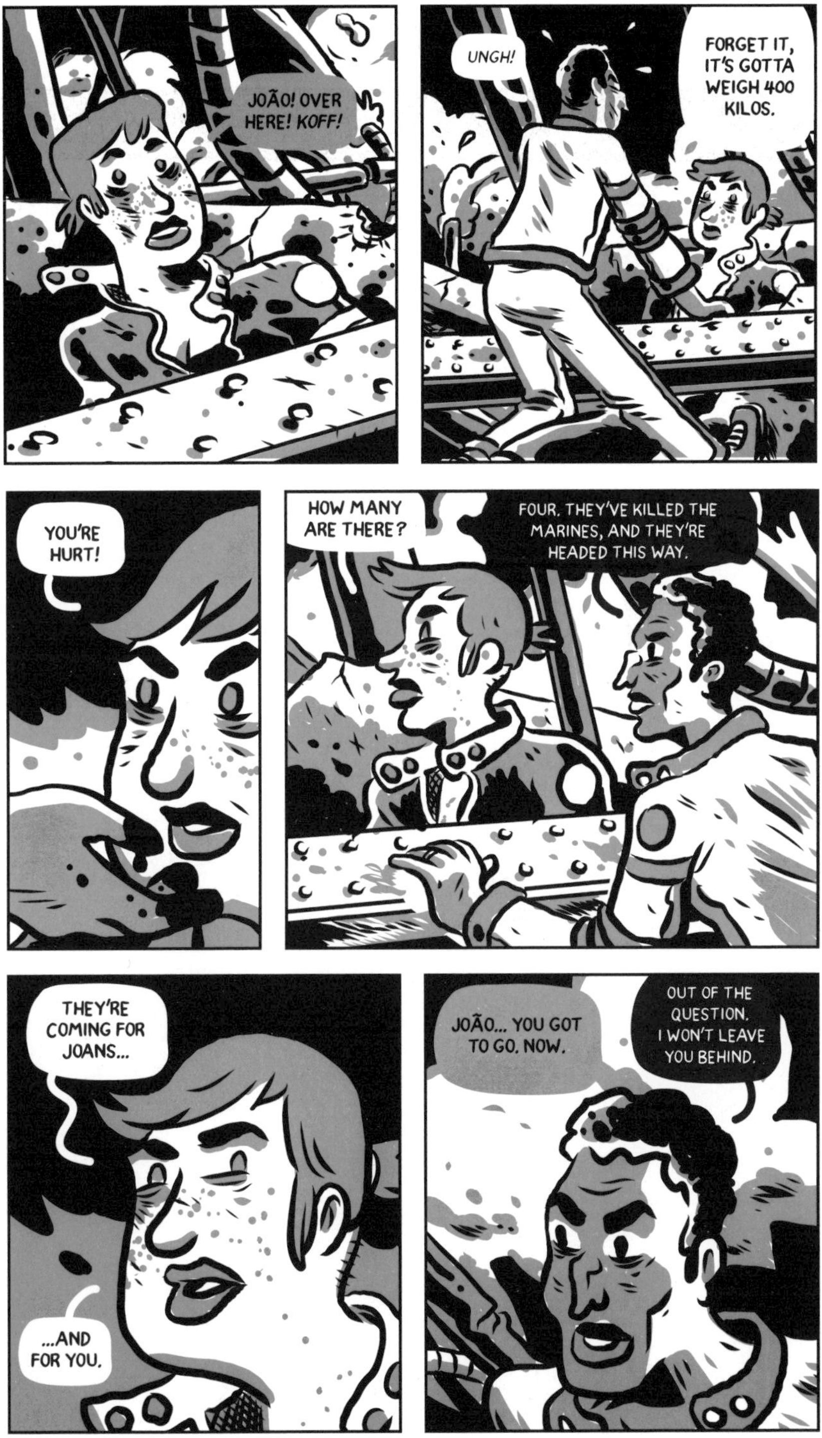
JOÃO! OVER HERE! KOFF!
UNGH!
FORGET IT, IT'S GOTTA WEIGH 400 KILOS.
YOU'RE HURT!
HOW MANY ARE THERE?
FOUR. THEY'VE KILLED THE MARINES, AND THEY'RE HEADED THIS WAY.
THEY'RE COMING FOR JOANS...
...AND FOR YOU.
JOÃO... YOU GOT TO GO. NOW.
OUT OF THE QUESTION. I WON'T LEAVE YOU BEHIND.

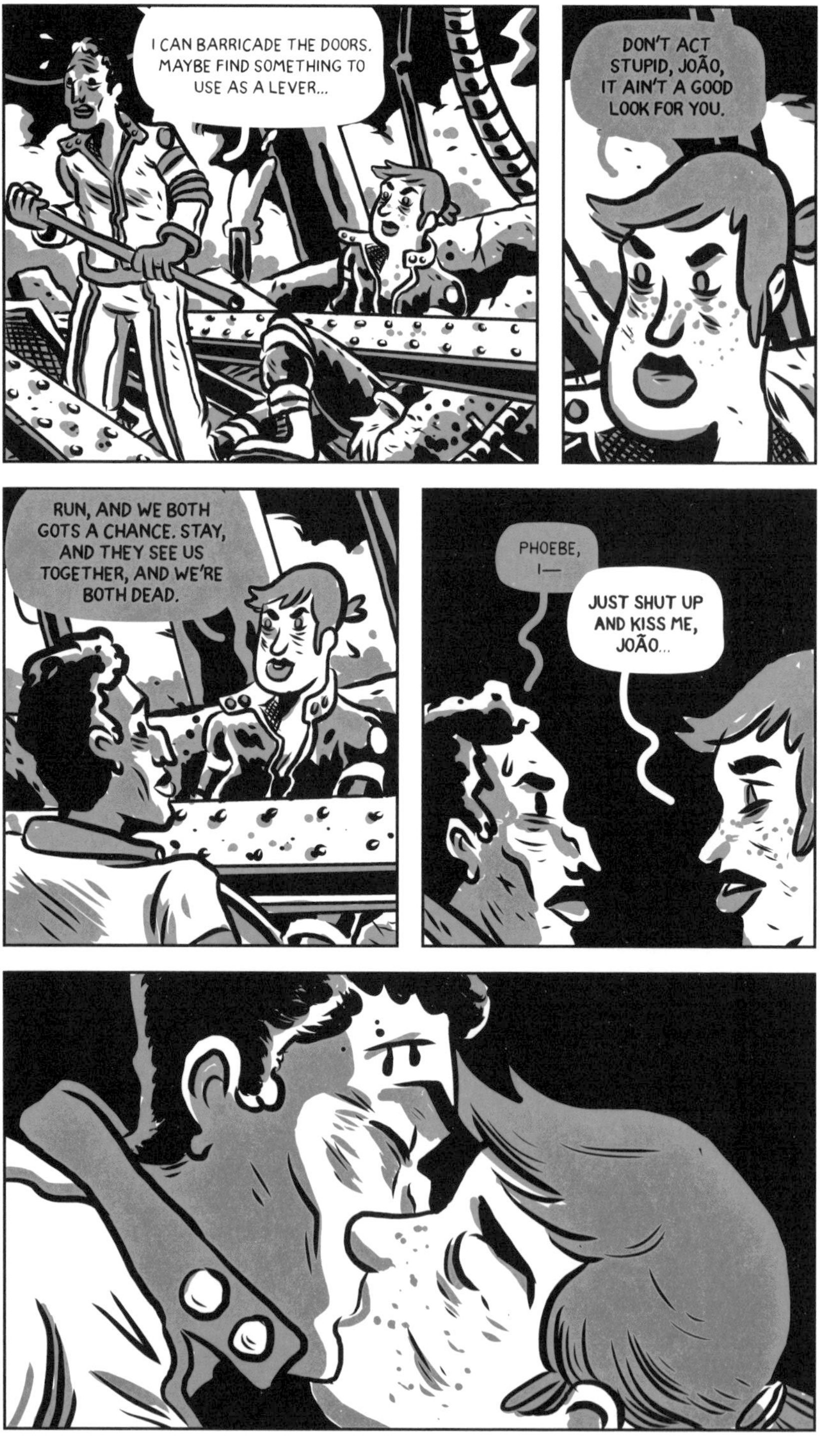
I CAN BARRICADE THE DOORS. MAYBE FIND SOMETHING TO USE AS A LEVER...
DON'T ACT STUPID, JOÃO, IT AIN'T A GOOD LOOK FOR YOU.
RUN, AND WE BOTH GOTS A CHANCE. STAY, AND THEY SEE US TOGETHER, AND WE'RE BOTH DEAD.
PHOEBE, I—
JUST SHUT UP AND KISS ME, JOÃO...

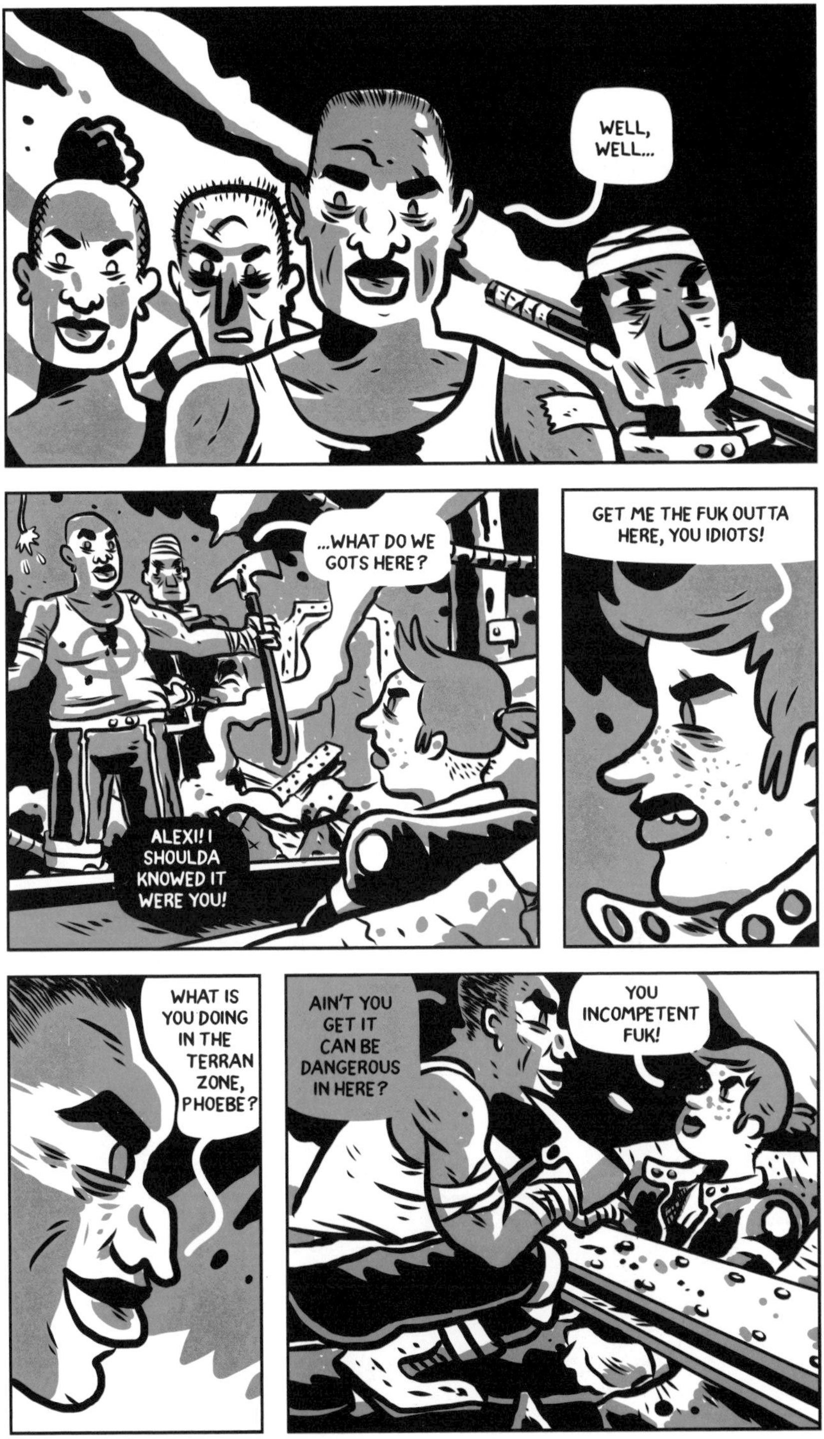
WELL, WELL...
...WHAT DO WE GOTS HERE?
ALEXI! I SHOULDA KNOWED IT WERE YOU!
GET ME THE FUK OUTTA HERE, YOU IDIOTS!
WHAT IS YOU DOING IN THE TERRAN ZONE, PHOEBE?
AIN'T YOU GET IT CAN BE DANGEROUS IN HERE?
YOU INCOMPETENT FUK!

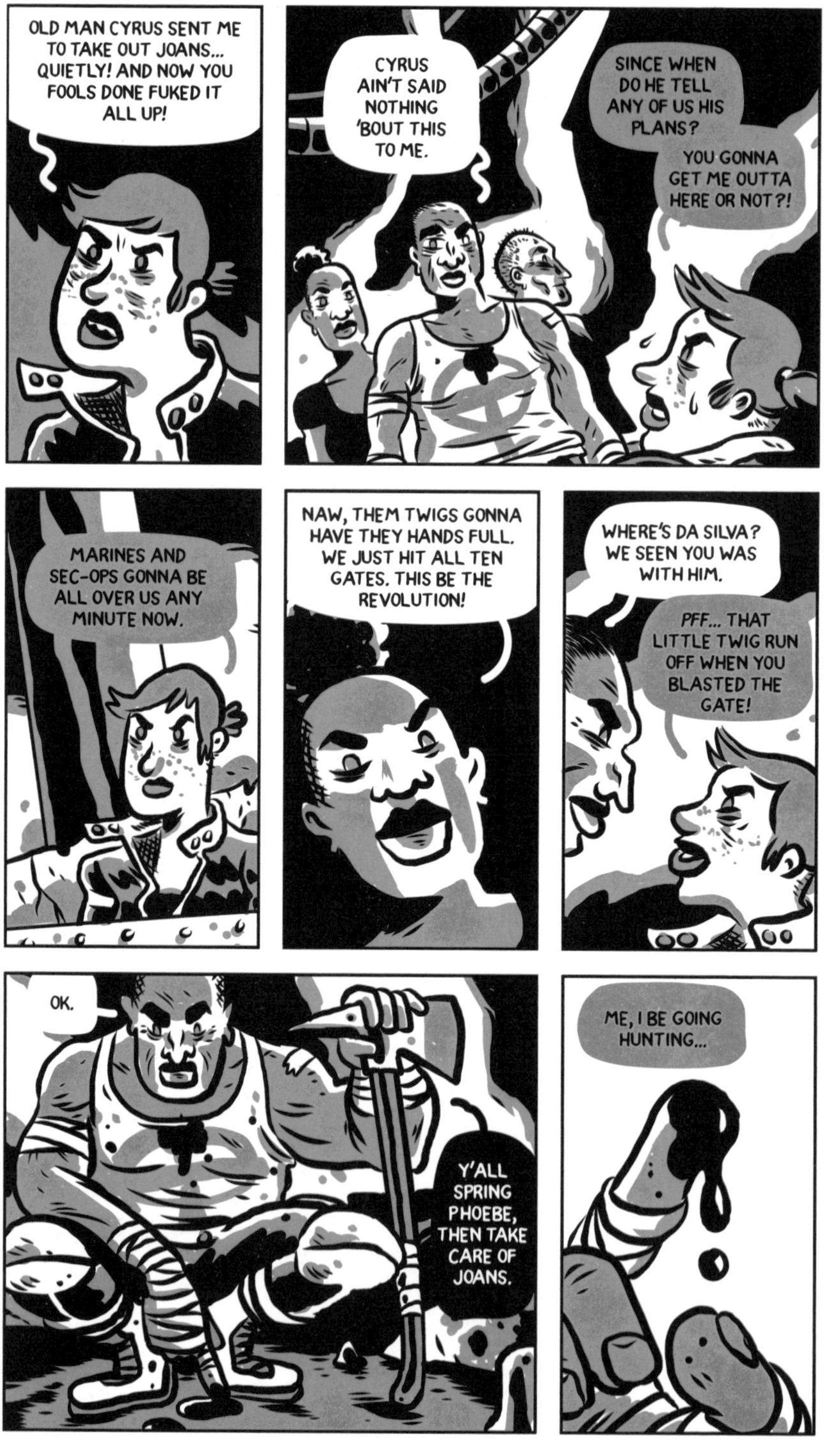
OLD MAN CYRUS SENT ME TO TAKE OUT JOANS... QUIETLY! AND NOW YOU FOOLS DONE FUKED IT ALL UP!
CYRUS AIN'T SAID NOTHING 'BOUT THIS TO ME.
SINCE WHEN DO HE TELL ANY OF US HIS PLANS?
YOU GONNA GET ME OUTTA HERE OR NOT?!
MARINES AND SEC-OPS GONNA BE ALL OVER US ANY MINUTE NOW.
NAW, THEM TWIGS GONNA HAVE THEY HANDS FULL. WE JUST HIT ALL TEN GATES. THIS BE THE REVOLUTION!
WHERE'S DA SILVA? WE SEEN YOU WAS WITH HIM.
PFF... THAT LITTLE TWIG RUN OFF WHEN YOU BLASTED THE GATE!
OK.
Y'ALL SPRING PHOEBE, THEN TAKE CARE OF JOANS.
ME, I BE GOING HUNTING...

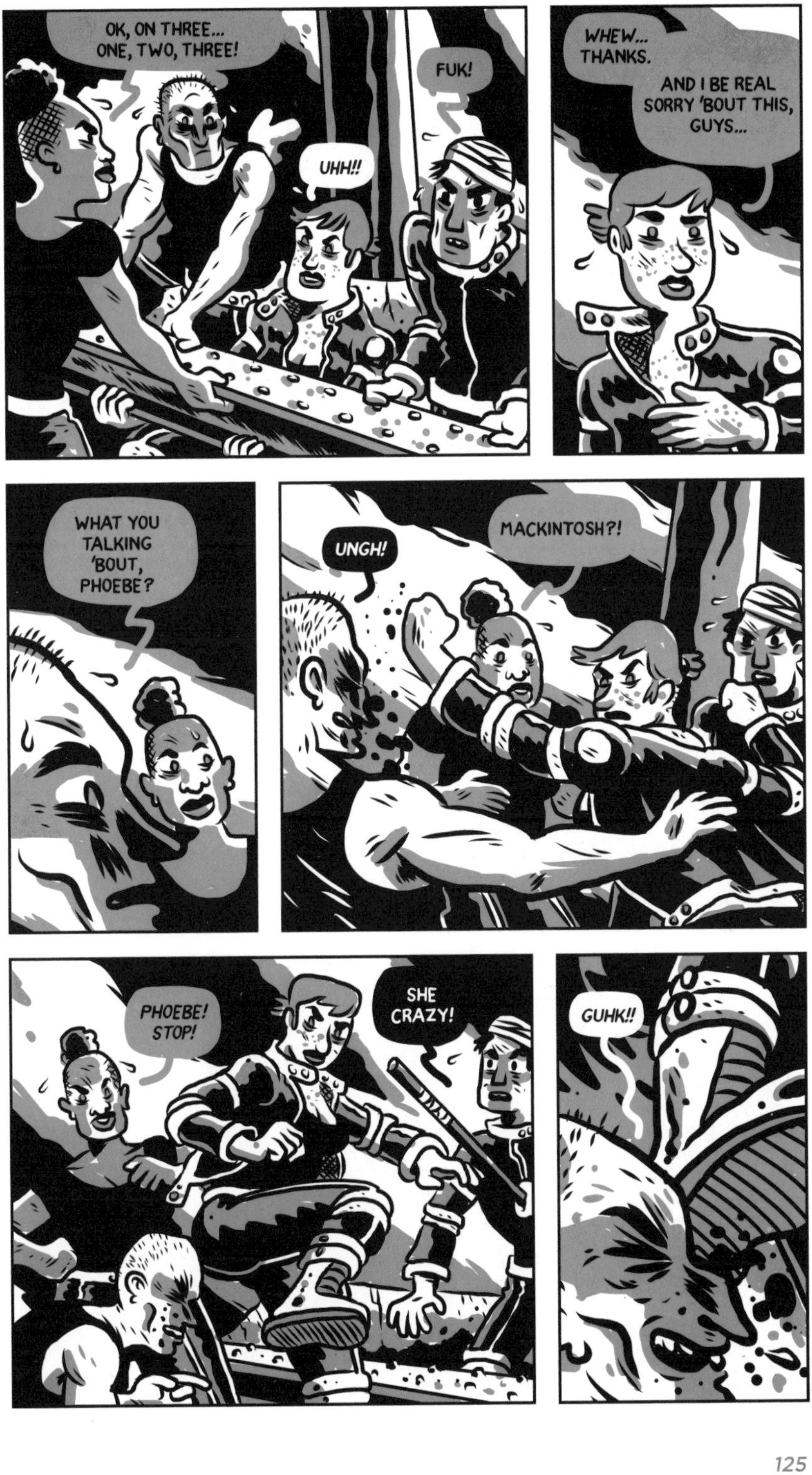
OK, ON THREE... ONE, TWO, THREE!
FUK!
UHH!!
WHEW... THANKS.
AND I BE REAL SORRY 'BOUT THIS, GUYS...
WHAT YOU TALKING 'BOUT, PHOEBE?
UNGH!
MACKINTOSH?!
PHOEBE! STOP!
SHE CRAZY!
GUHK!!

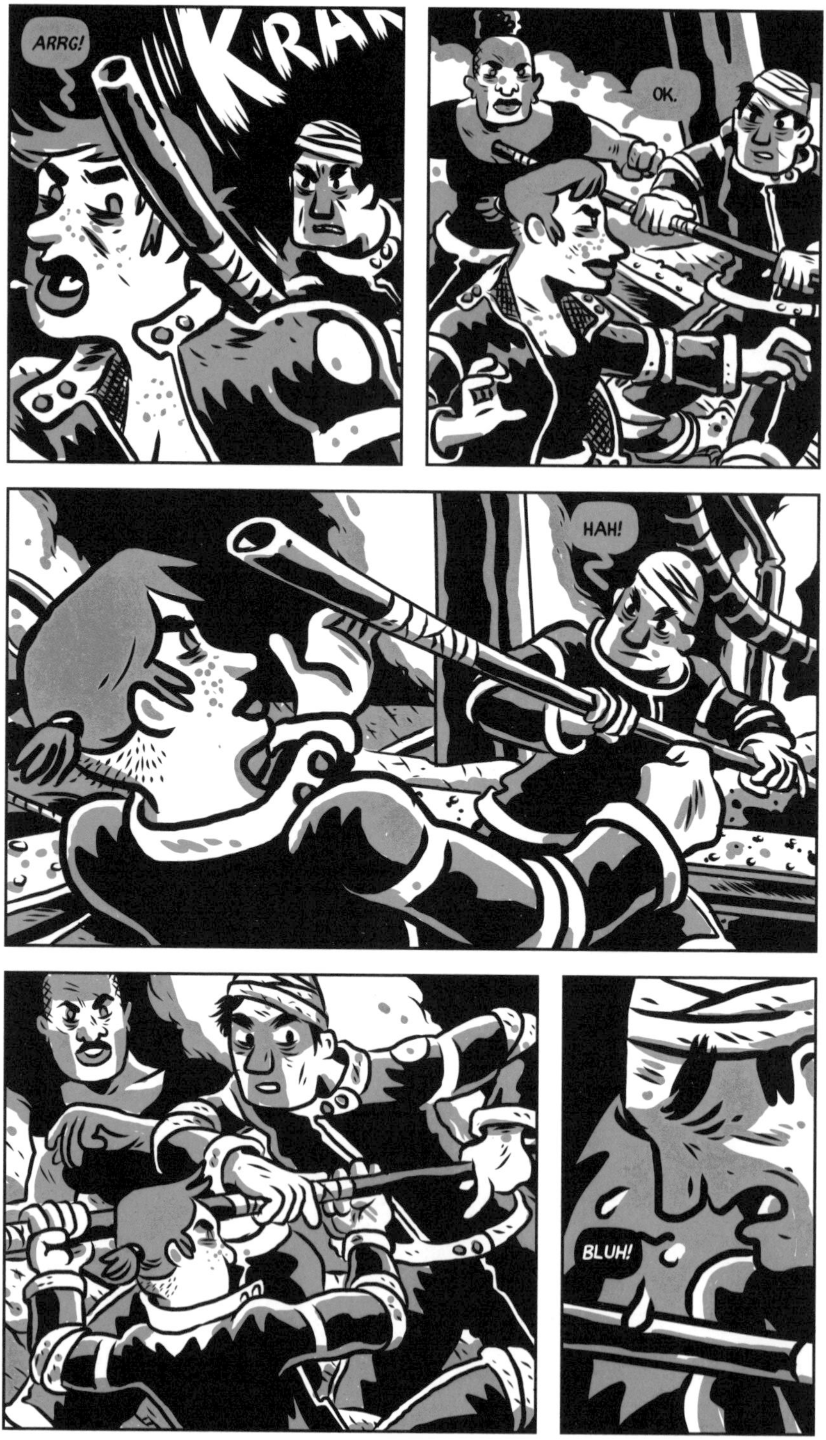
ARRG!
KRA
OK.
HAH!
BLUH!

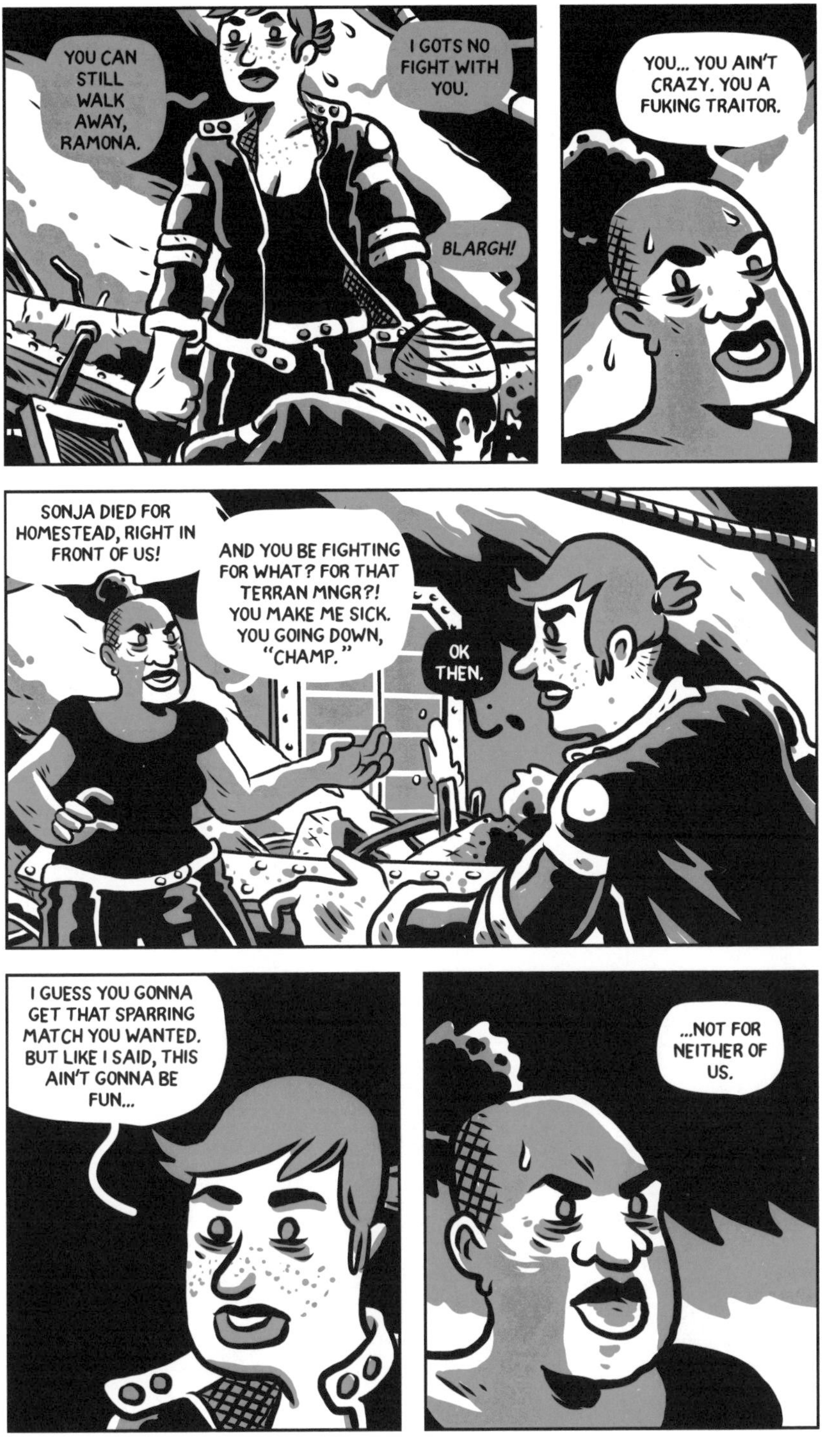
YOU CAN STILL WALK AWAY, RAMONA.
I GOTS NO FIGHT WITH YOU.
BLARGH!
YOU... YOU AIN'T CRAZY. YOU A FUKING TRAITOR.
SONJA DIED FOR HOMESTEAD, RIGHT IN FRONT OF US!
AND YOU BE FIGHTING FOR WHAT? FOR THAT TERRAN MNGR?! YOU MAKE ME SICK. YOU GOING DOWN, "CHAMP."
OK THEN.
I GUESS YOU GONNA GET THAT SPARRING MATCH YOU WANTED. BUT LIKE I SAID, THIS AIN'T GONNA BE FUN...
...NOT FOR NEITHER OF US.

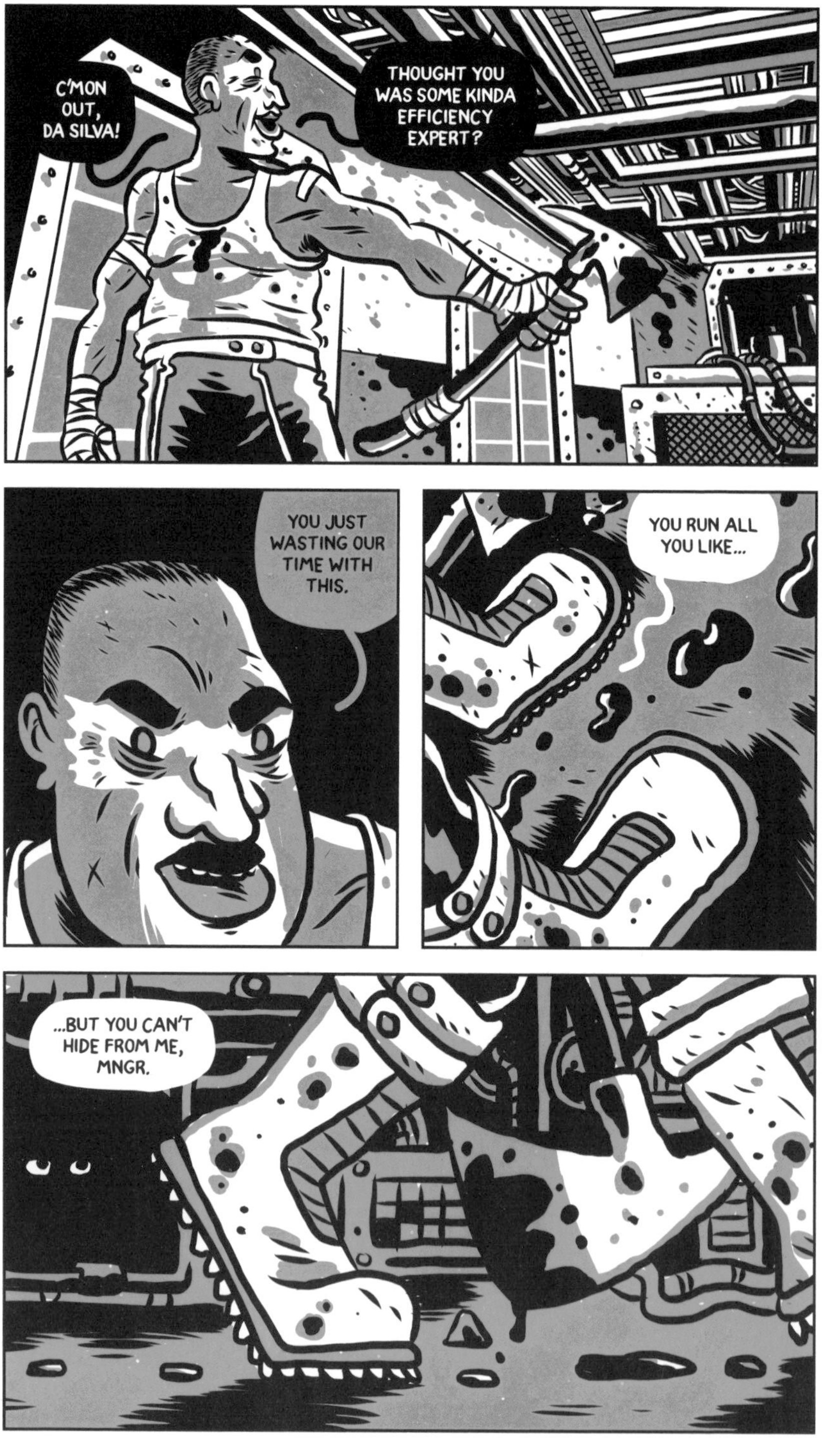
C'MON OUT, DA SILVA!
THOUGHT YOU WAS SOME KINDA EFFICIENCY EXPERT?
YOU JUST WASTING OUR TIME WITH THIS.
YOU RUN ALL YOU LIKE...
...BUT YOU CAN'T HIDE FROM ME, MNGR.

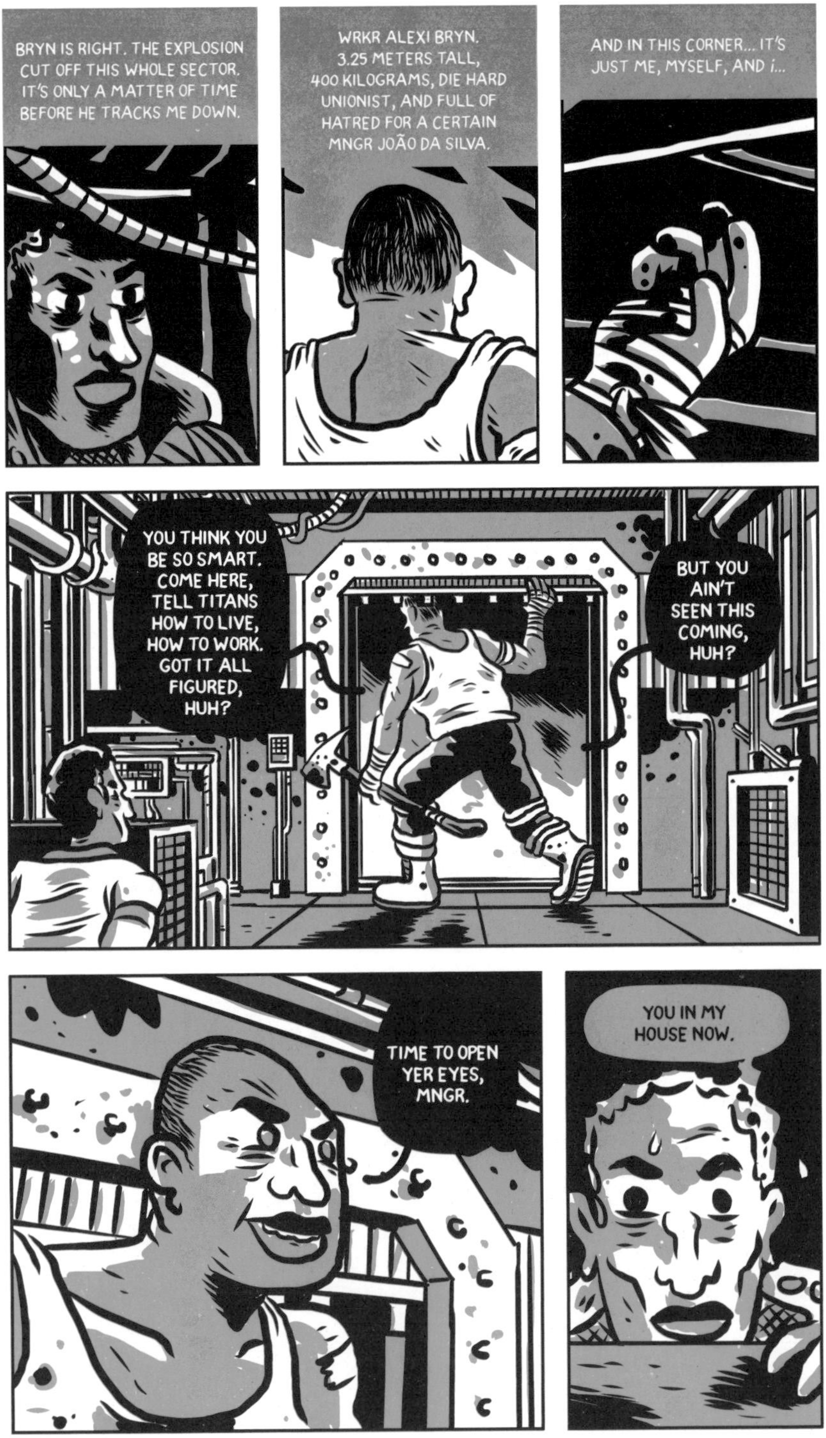
BRYN IS RIGHT. THE EXPLOSION CUT OFF THIS WHOLE SECTOR. IT'S ONLY A MATTER OF TIME BEFORE HE TRACKS ME DOWN.
WRKR ALEXI BRYN. 3.25 METERS TALL, 400 KILOGRAMS, DIE HARD UNIONIST, AND FULL OF HATRED FOR A CERTAIN MNGR JOÃO DA SILVA.
AND IN THIS CORNER... IT'S JUST ME, MYSELF, AND I...
YOU THINK YOU BE SO SMART. COME HERE, TELL TITANS HOW TO LIVE, HOW TO WORK. GOT IT ALL FIGURED, HUH?
BUT YOU AIN'T SEEN THIS COMING, HUH?
TIME TO OPEN YER EYES, MNGR.
YOU IN MY HOUSE NOW.

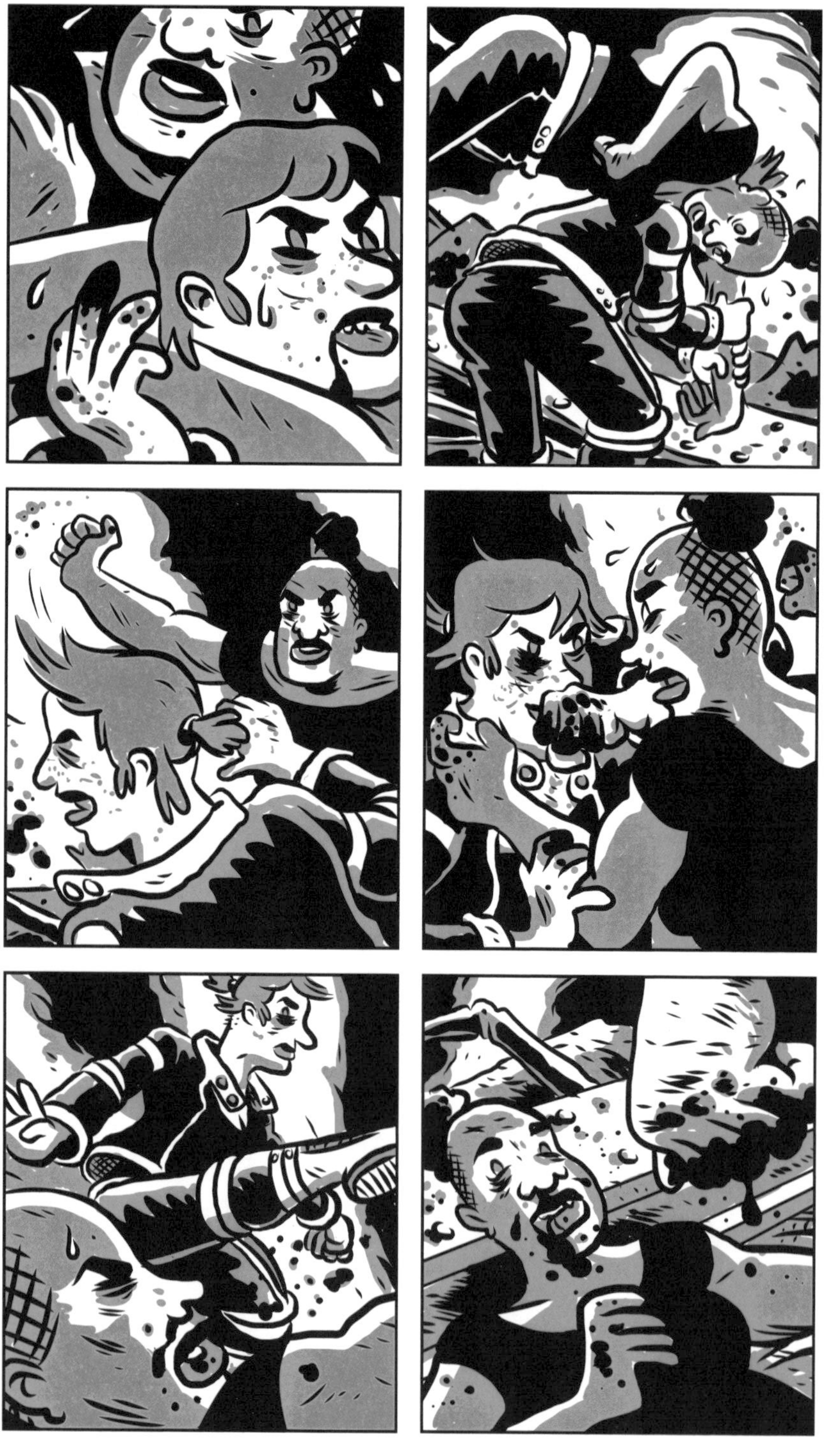

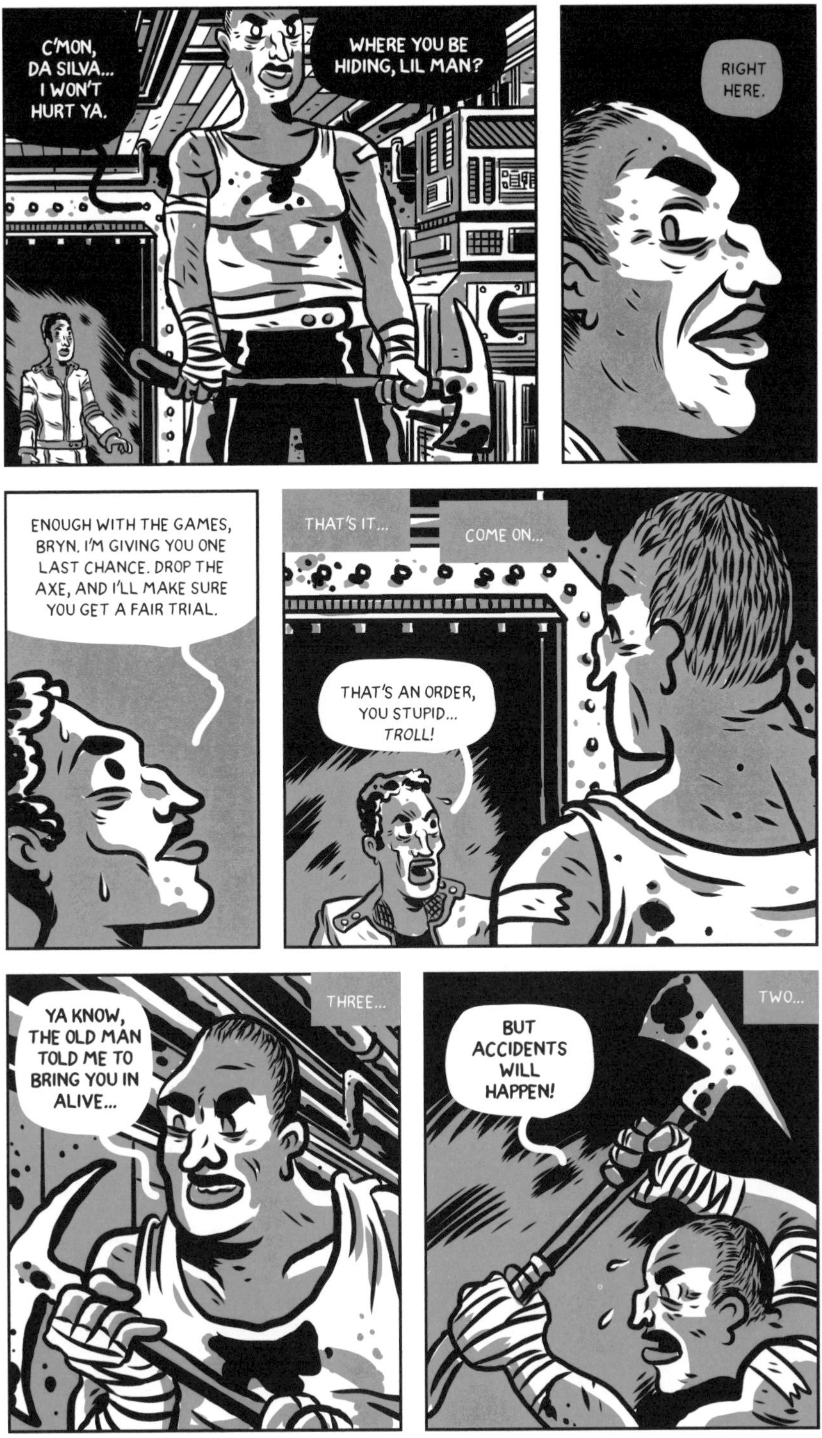
C'MON, DA SILVA... I WON'T HURT YA.
WHERE YOU BE HIDING, LIL MAN?
RIGHT HERE.
ENOUGH WITH THE GAMES, BRYN. I'M GIVING YOU ONE LAST CHANCE. DROP THE AXE, AND I'LL MAKE SURE YOU GET A FAIR TRIAL.
THAT'S IT...
COME ON...
THAT'S AN ORDER, YOU STUPID... *TROLL!*
YA KNOW, THE OLD MAN TOLD ME TO BRING YOU IN ALIVE...
THREE...
BUT ACCIDENTS WILL HAPPEN!
TWO...

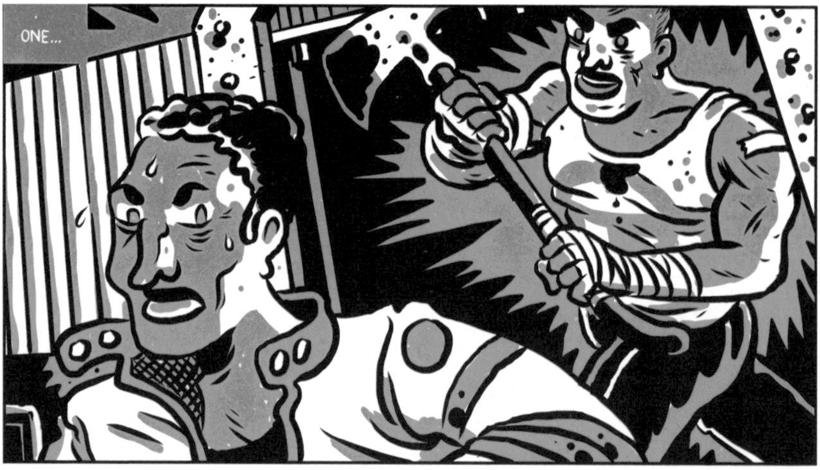
ONE...

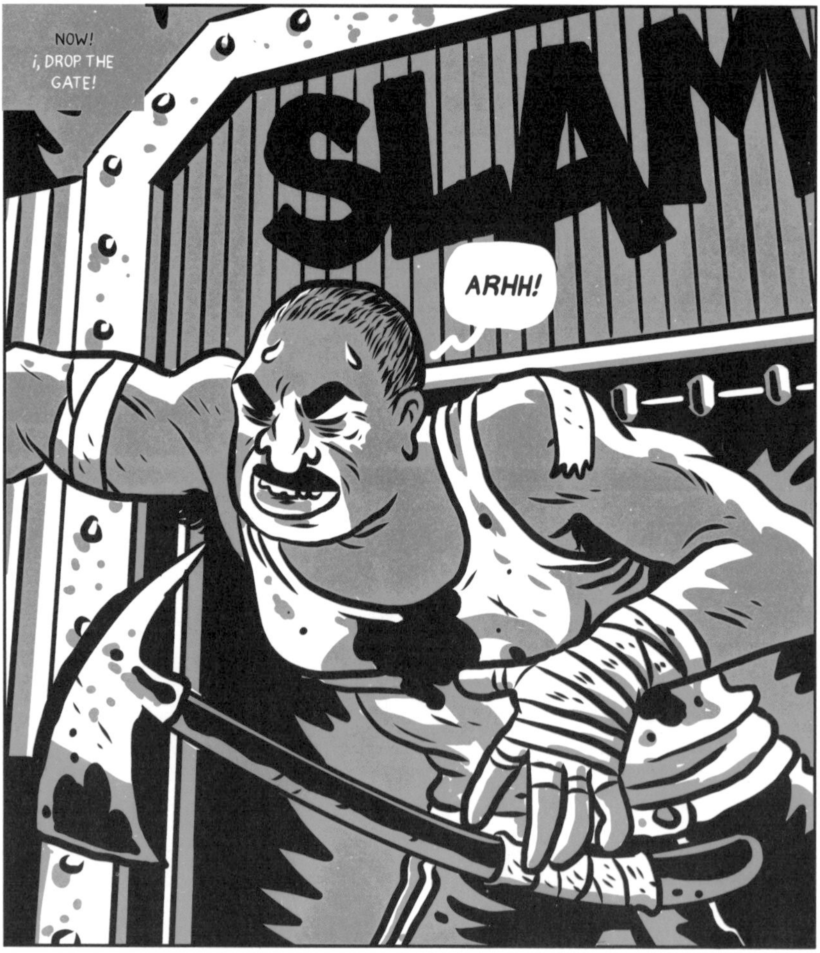
NOW!
¡, DROP THE GATE!
SLAM
ARHH!

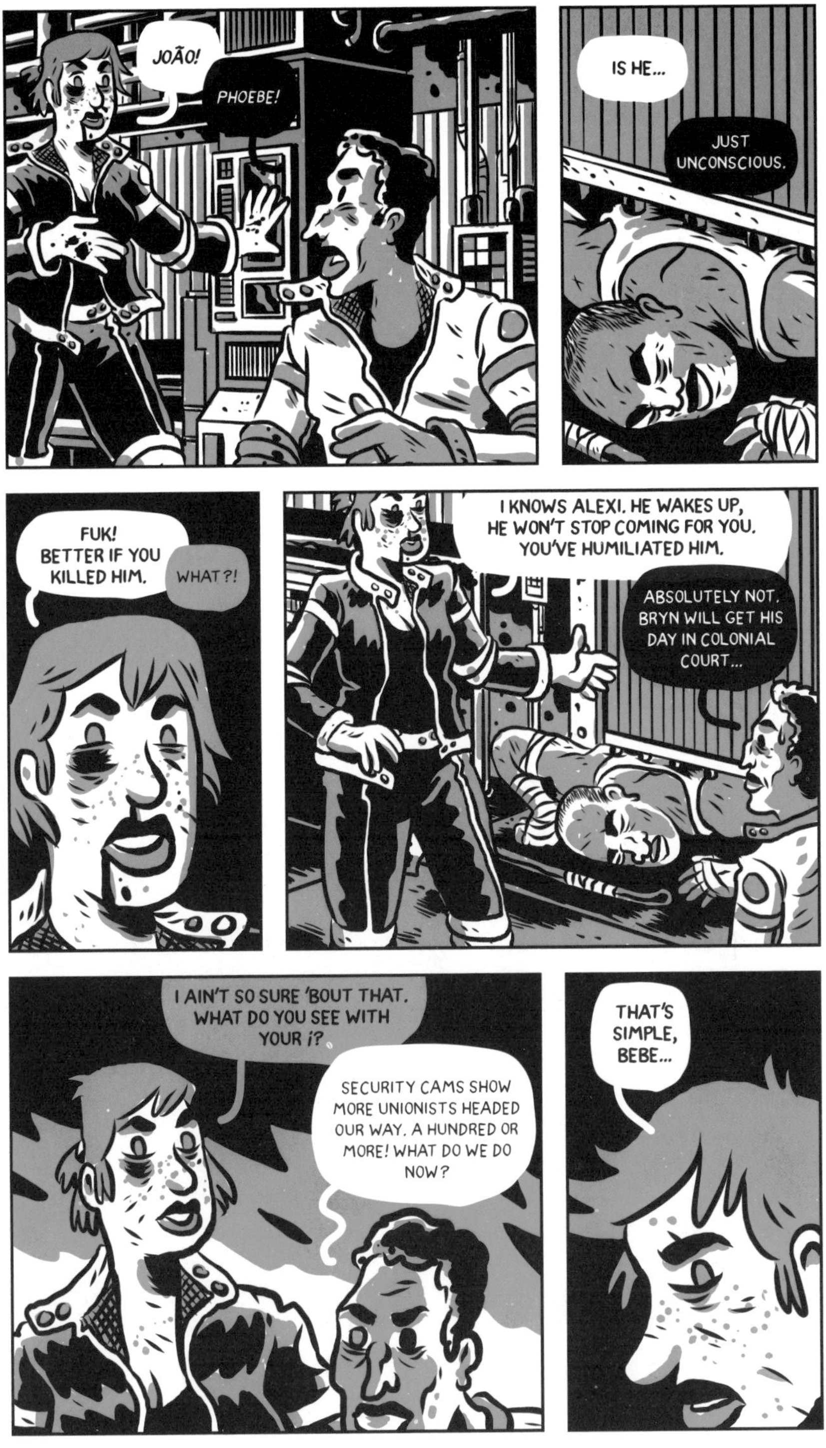
JOÃO!
PHOEBE!
IS HE...
JUST UNCONSCIOUS.
FUK! BETTER IF YOU KILLED HIM.
WHAT?!
I KNOWS ALEXI. HE WAKES UP, HE WON'T STOP COMING FOR YOU. YOU'VE HUMILIATED HIM.
ABSOLUTELY NOT. BRYN WILL GET HIS DAY IN COLONIAL COURT...
I AIN'T SO SURE 'BOUT THAT. WHAT DO YOU SEE WITH YOUR *i*?
SECURITY CAMS SHOW MORE UNIONISTS HEADED OUR WAY. A HUNDRED OR MORE! WHAT DO WE DO NOW?
THAT'S SIMPLE, BEBE...

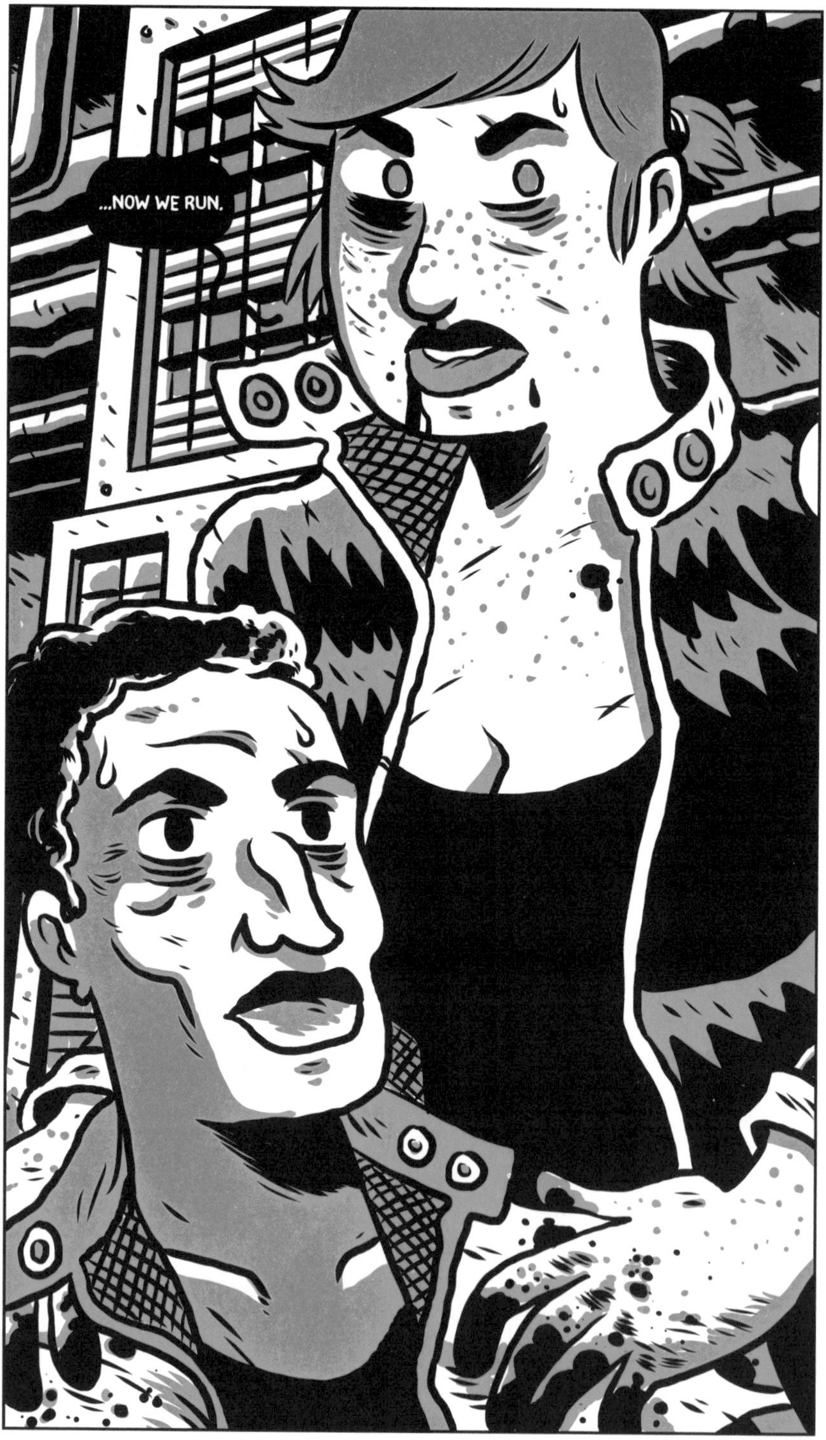
...NOW WE RUN.

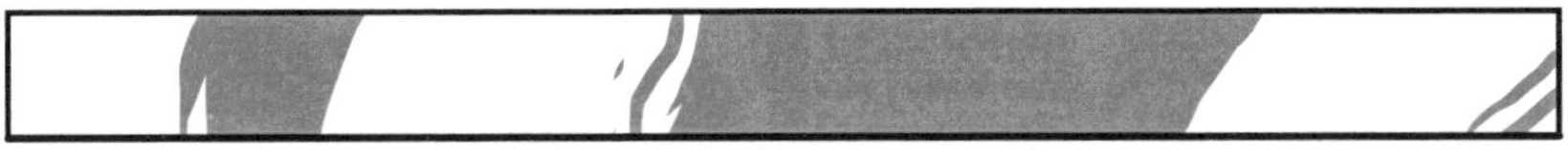

PART 09: STAND BY ME

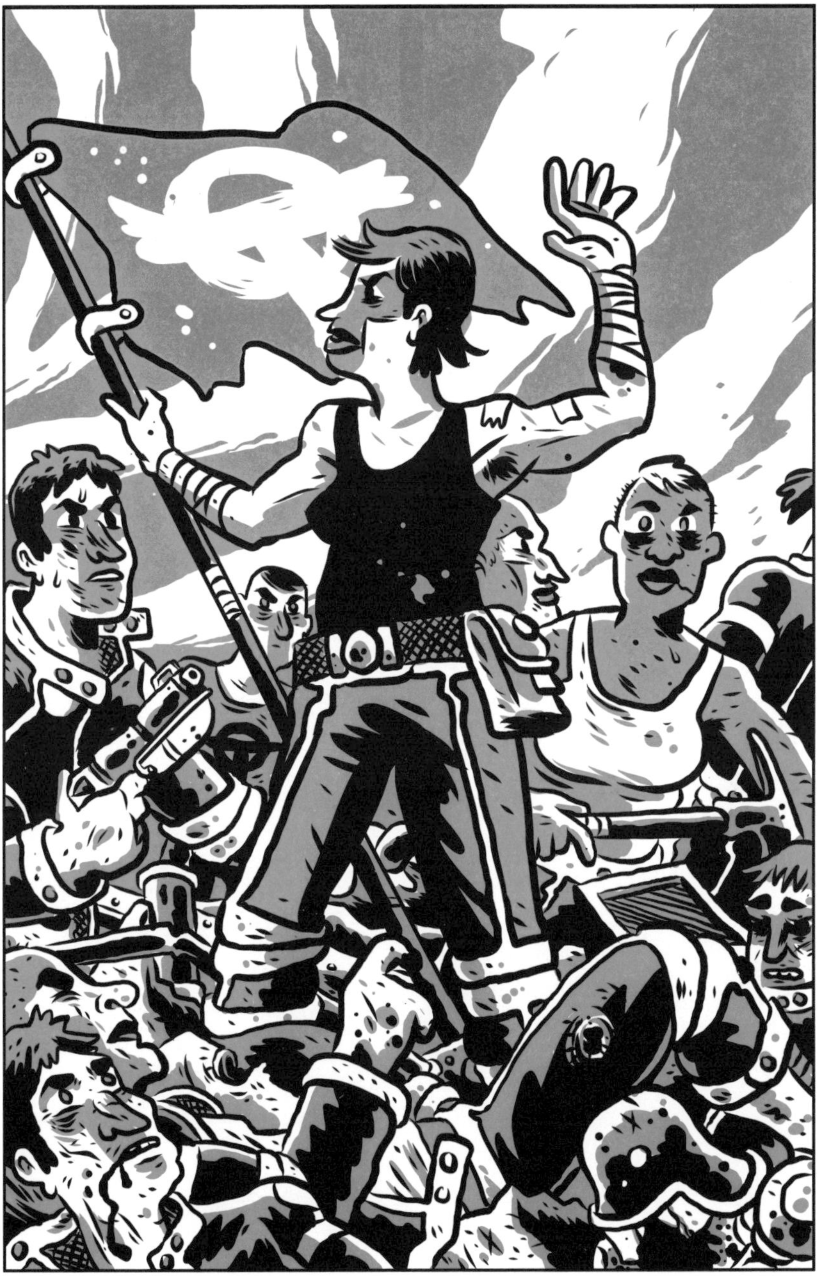

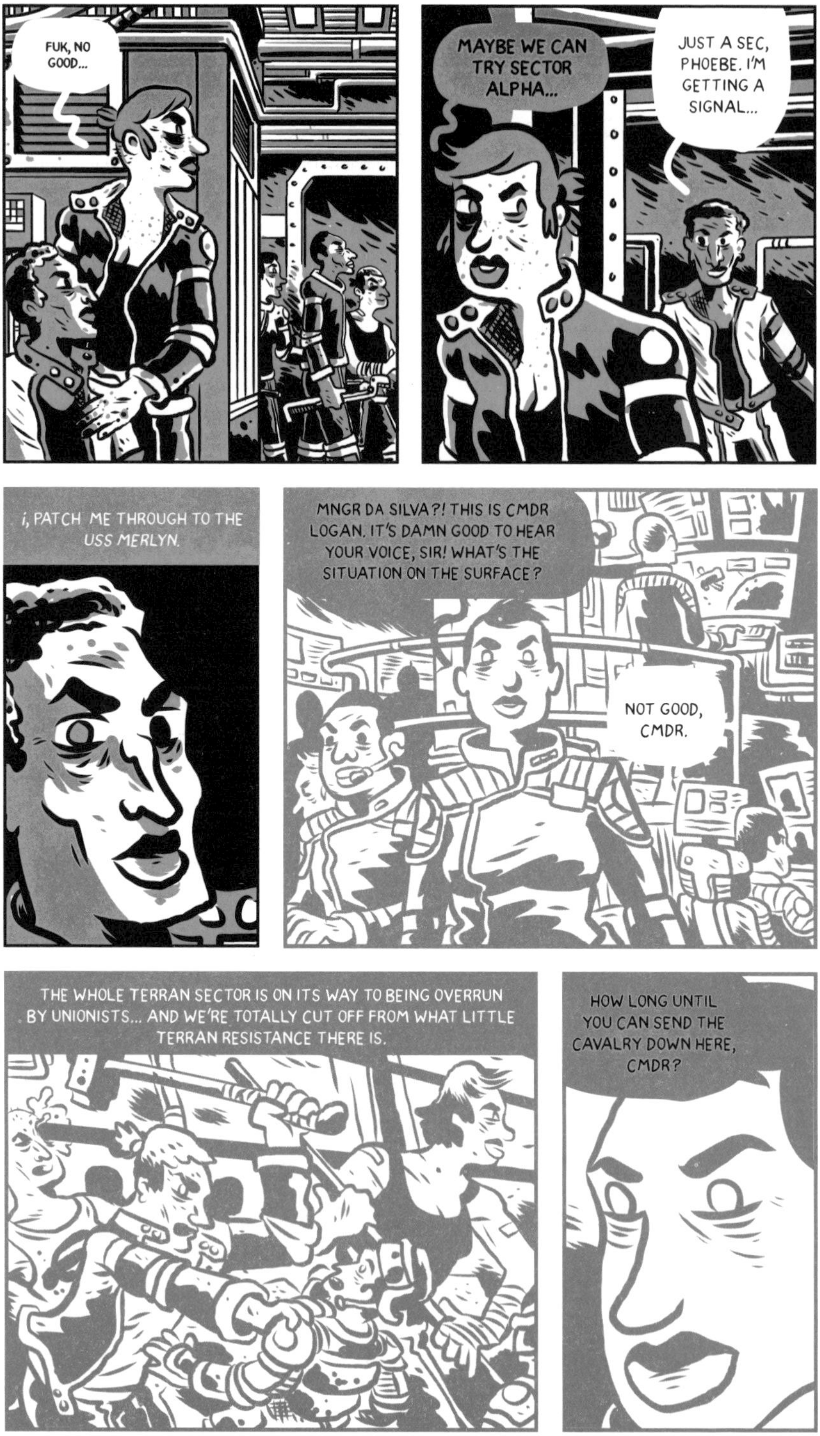
FUK, NO GOOD...
MAYBE WE CAN TRY SECTOR ALPHA...
JUST A SEC, PHOEBE. I'M GETTING A SIGNAL...
i, PATCH ME THROUGH TO THE USS MERLYN.
MNGR DA SILVA?! THIS IS CMDR LOGAN. IT'S DAMN GOOD TO HEAR YOUR VOICE, SIR! WHAT'S THE SITUATION ON THE SURFACE?
NOT GOOD, CMDR.
THE WHOLE TERRAN SECTOR IS ON ITS WAY TO BEING OVERRUN BY UNIONISTS... AND WE'RE TOTALLY CUT OFF FROM WHAT LITTLE TERRAN RESISTANCE THERE IS.
HOW LONG UNTIL YOU CAN SEND THE CAVALRY DOWN HERE, CMDR?

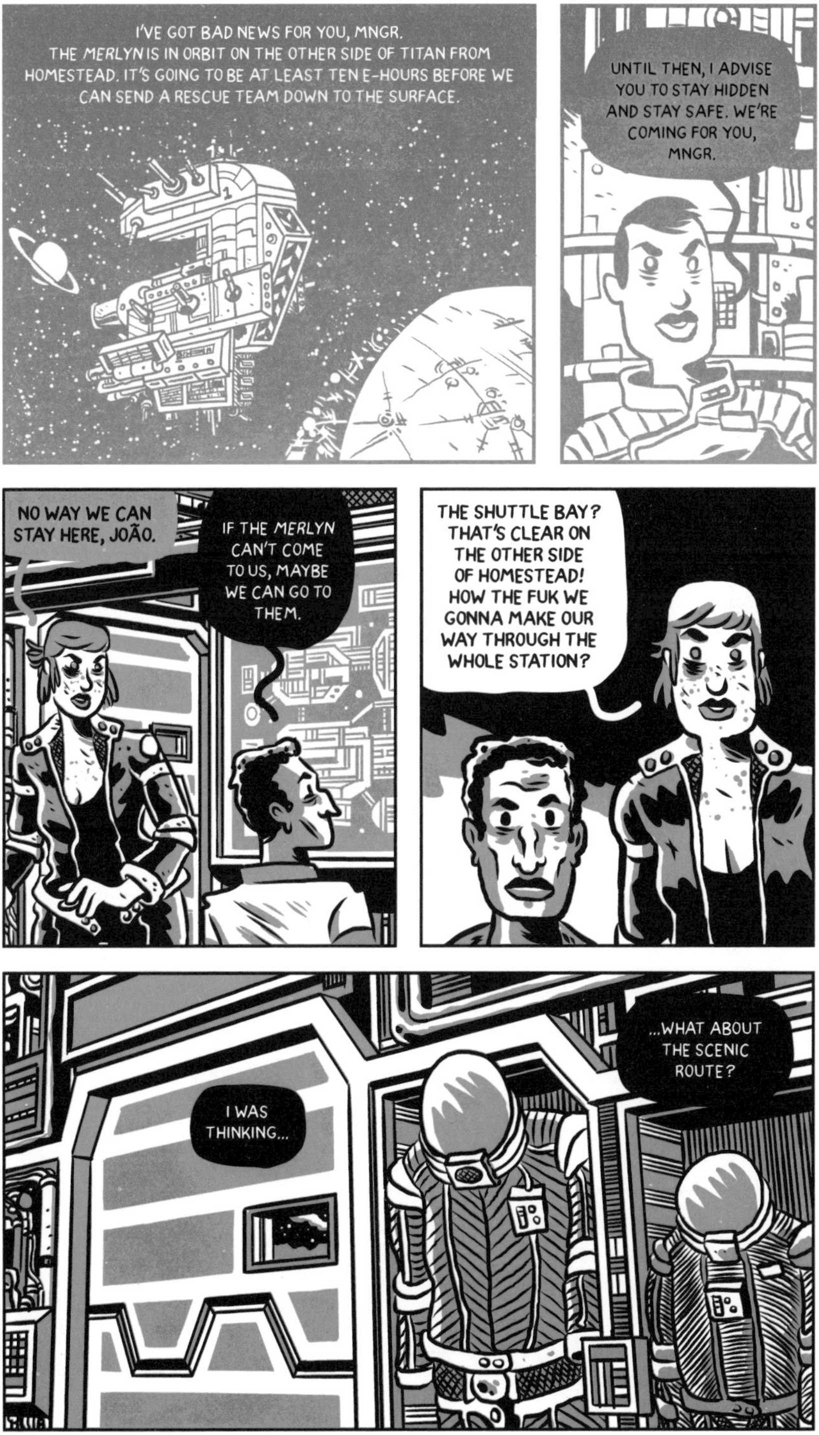
I'VE GOT BAD NEWS FOR YOU, MNGR. THE MERLYN IS IN ORBIT ON THE OTHER SIDE OF TITAN FROM HOMESTEAD. IT'S GOING TO BE AT LEAST TEN E-HOURS BEFORE WE CAN SEND A RESCUE TEAM DOWN TO THE SURFACE.
UNTIL THEN, I ADVISE YOU TO STAY HIDDEN AND STAY SAFE. WE'RE COMING FOR YOU, MNGR.
NO WAY WE CAN STAY HERE, JOÃO.
IF THE MERLYN CAN'T COME TO US, MAYBE WE CAN GO TO THEM.
THE SHUTTLE BAY? THAT'S CLEAR ON THE OTHER SIDE OF HOMESTEAD! HOW THE FUK WE GONNA MAKE OUR WAY THROUGH THE WHOLE STATION?
I WAS THINKING...
...WHAT ABOUT THE SCENIC ROUTE?

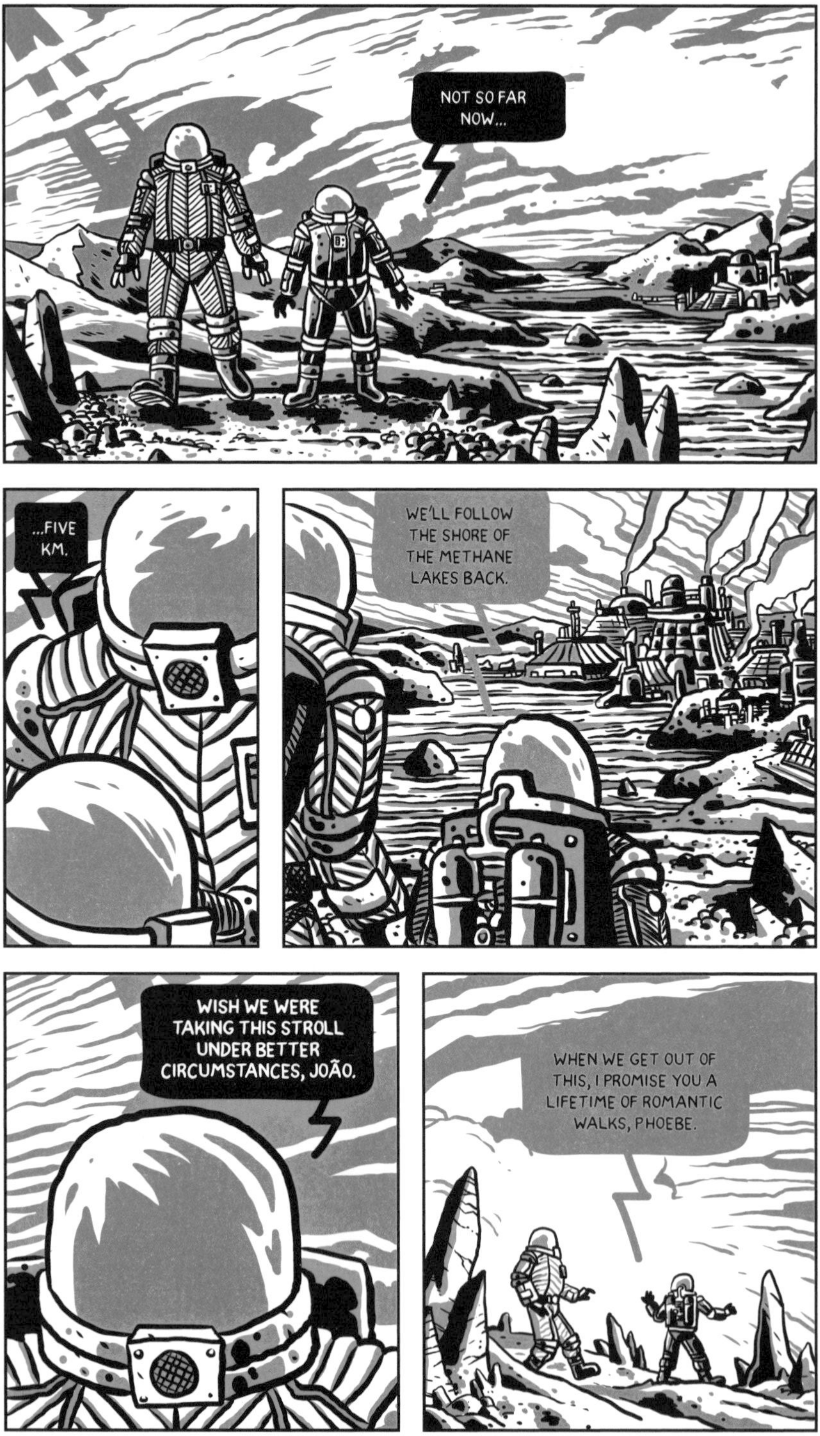
NOT SO FAR NOW...
...FIVE KM.
WE'LL FOLLOW THE SHORE OF THE METHANE LAKES BACK.
WISH WE WERE TAKING THIS STROLL UNDER BETTER CIRCUMSTANCES, JOÃO.
WHEN WE GET OUT OF THIS, I PROMISE YOU A LIFETIME OF ROMANTIC WALKS, PHOEBE.

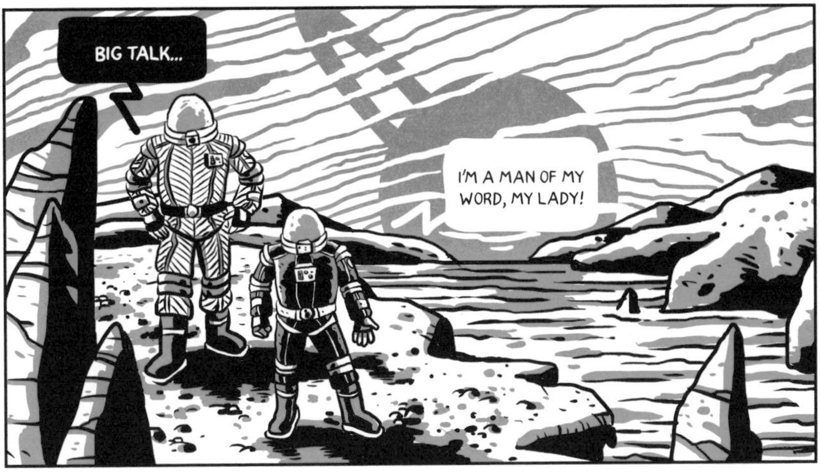
BIG TALK...
I'M A MAN OF MY WORD, MY LADY!

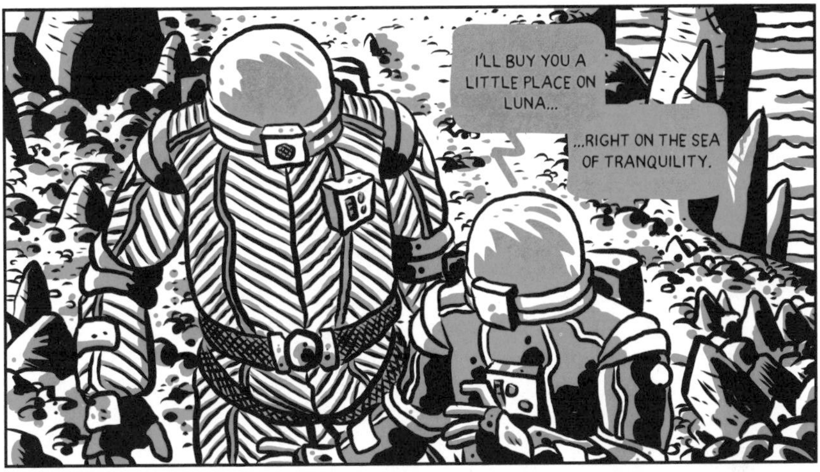
I'LL BUY YOU A LITTLE PLACE ON LUNA...
...RIGHT ON THE SEA OF TRANQUILITY.

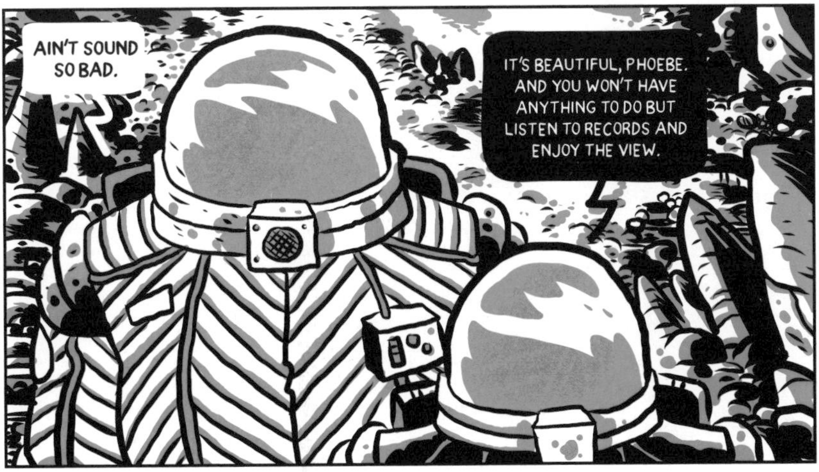
AIN'T SOUND SO BAD.
IT'S BEAUTIFUL, PHOEBE. AND YOU WON'T HAVE ANYTHING TO DO BUT LISTEN TO RECORDS AND ENJOY THE VIEW.

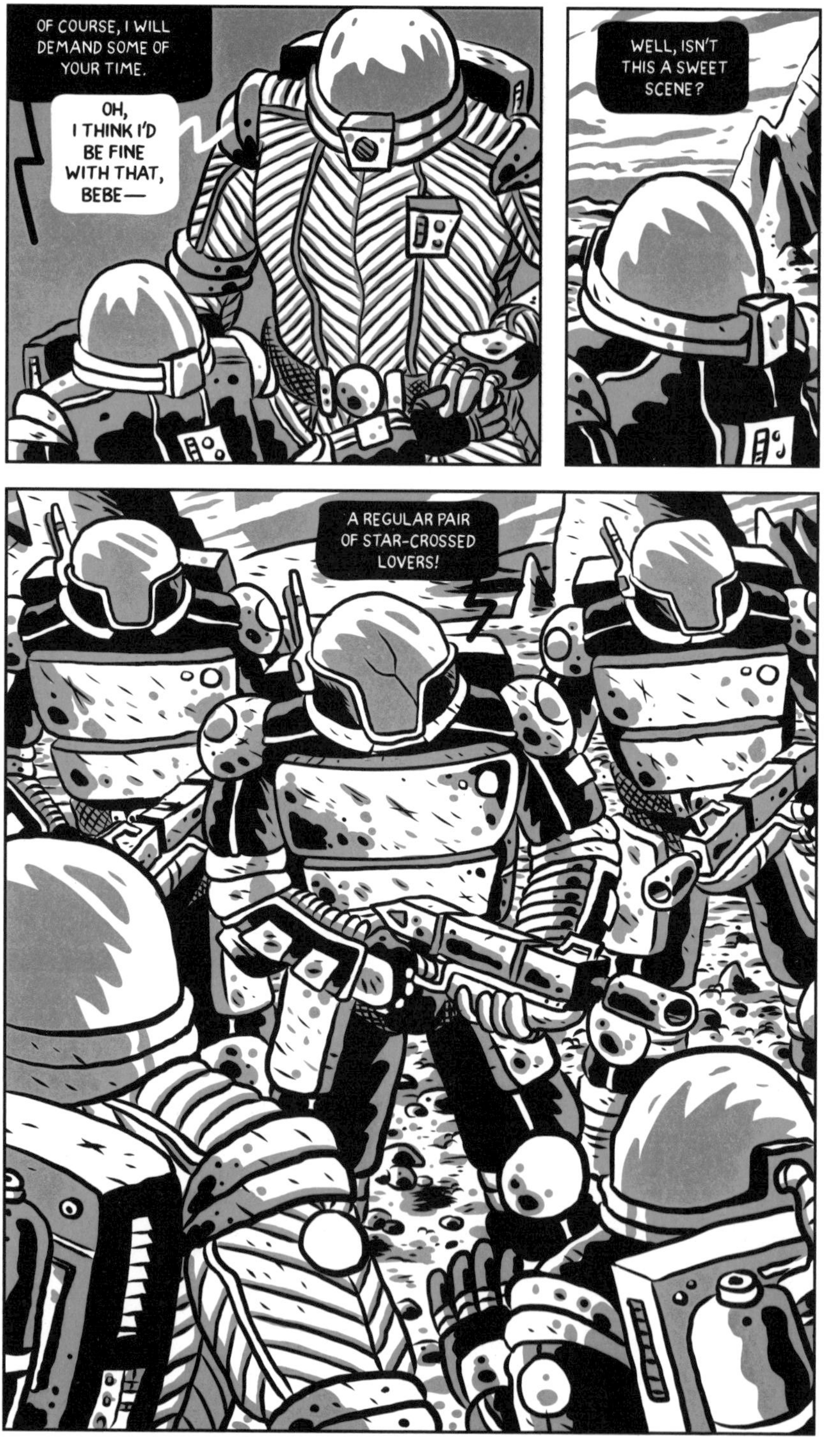
OF COURSE, I WILL DEMAND SOME OF YOUR TIME.
OH, I THINK I'D BE FINE WITH THAT, BEBE—
WELL, ISN'T THIS A SWEET SCENE?
A REGULAR PAIR OF STAR-CROSSED LOVERS!

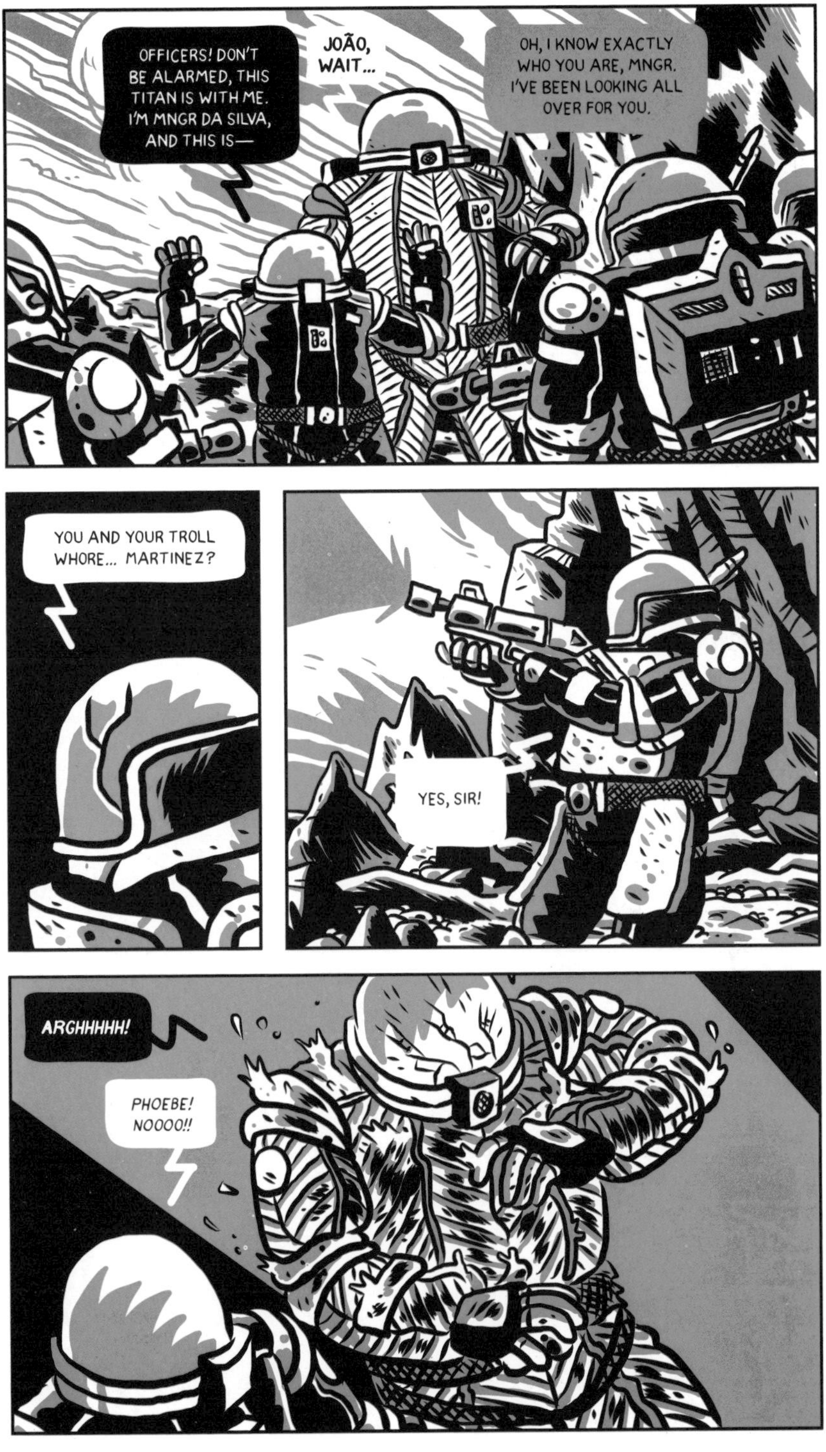
OFFICERS! DON'T BE ALARMED, THIS TITAN IS WITH ME. I'M MNGR DA SILVA, AND THIS IS—
JOÃO, WAIT...
OH, I KNOW EXACTLY WHO YOU ARE, MNGR. I'VE BEEN LOOKING ALL OVER FOR YOU.
YOU AND YOUR TROLL WHORE... MARTINEZ?
YES, SIR!
ARGHHHHH!
PHOEBE! NOOOO!!

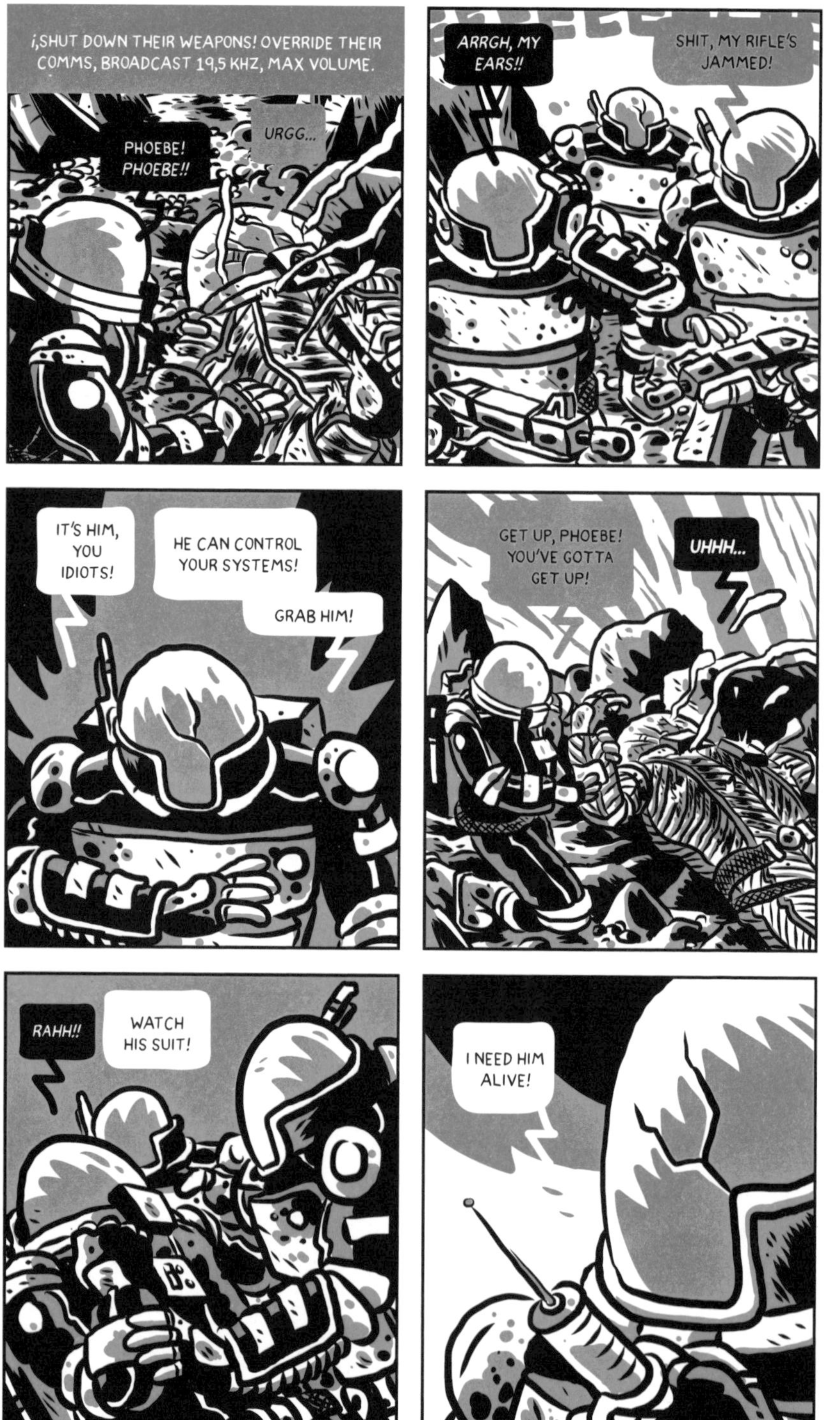
¡SHUT DOWN THEIR WEAPONS! OVERRIDE THEIR COMMS, BROADCAST 19,5 KHZ, MAX VOLUME.
PHOEBE! PHOEBE!!
URGG...
ARRGH, MY EARS!!
SHIT, MY RIFLE'S JAMMED!
IT'S HIM, YOU IDIOTS!
HE CAN CONTROL YOUR SYSTEMS!
GRAB HIM!
GET UP, PHOEBE! YOU'VE GOTTA GET UP!
UHHH...
RAHH!!
WATCH HIS SUIT!
I NEED HIM ALIVE!

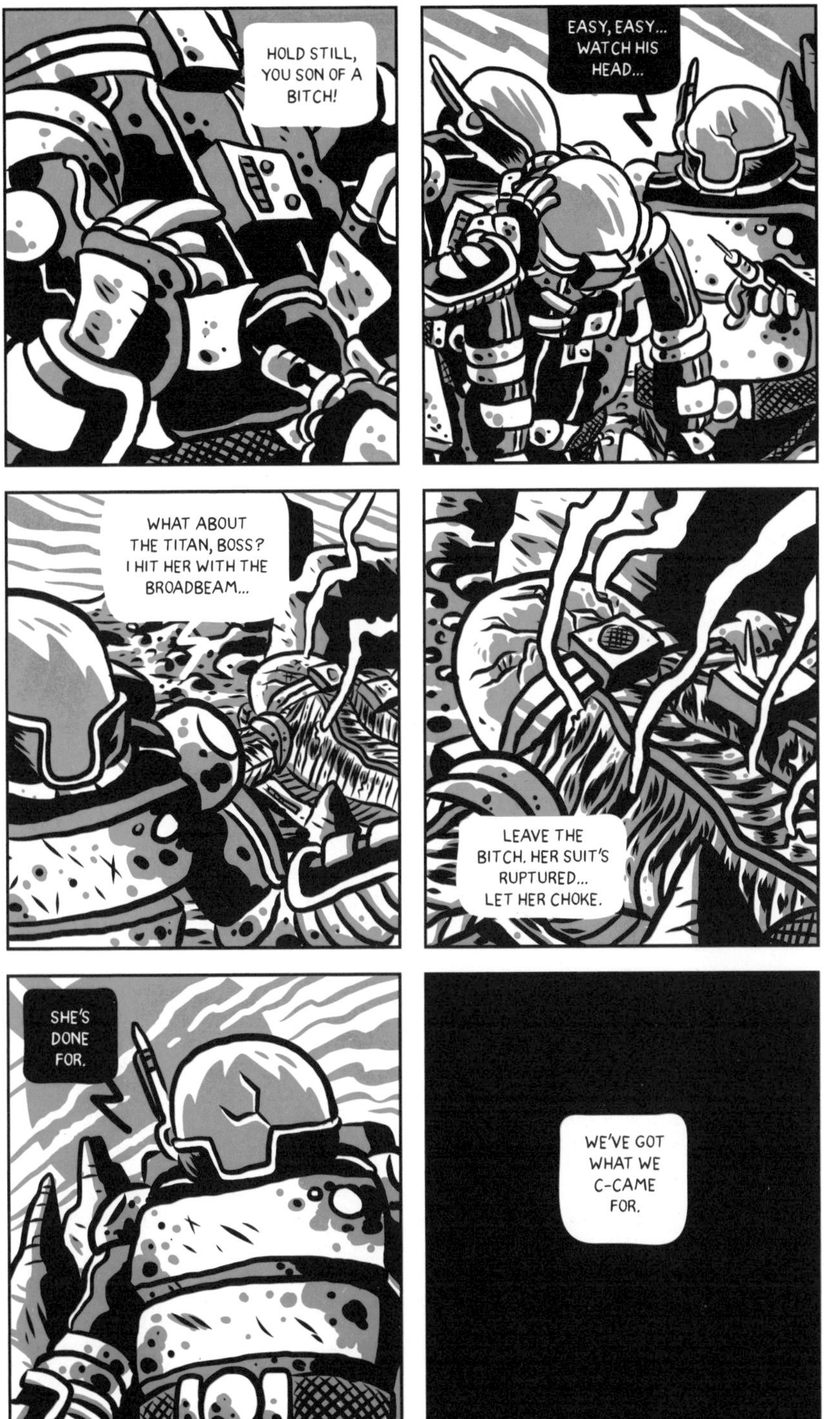
HOLD STILL, YOU SON OF A BITCH!
EASY, EASY... WATCH HIS HEAD...
WHAT ABOUT THE TITAN, BOSS? I HIT HER WITH THE BROADBEAM...
LEAVE THE BITCH. HER SUIT'S RUPTURED... LET HER CHOKE.
SHE'S DONE FOR.
WE'VE GOT WHAT WE C-CAME FOR.

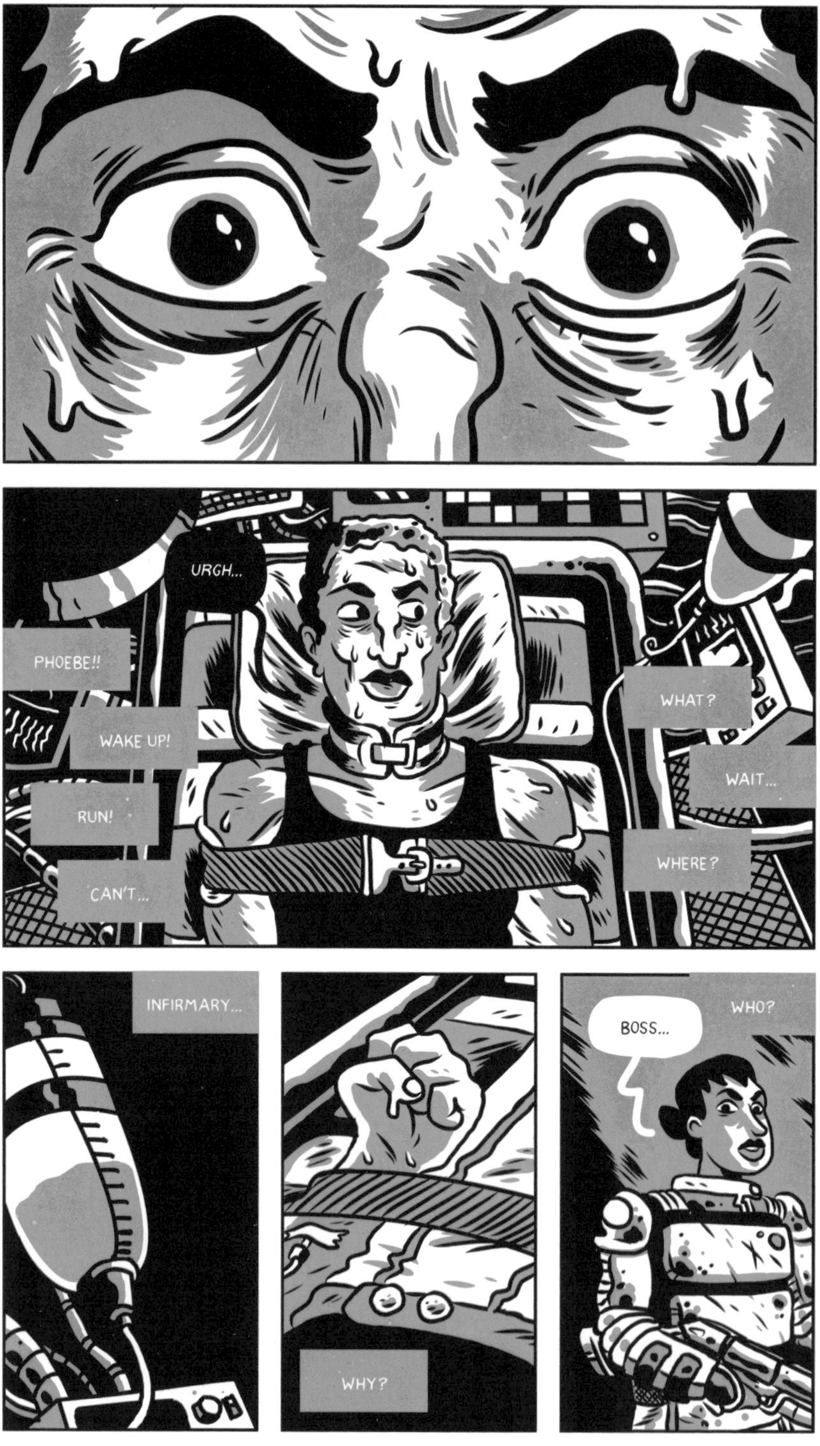
URGH...
PHOEBE!!
WAKE UP!
RUN!
CAN'T...
WHAT?
WAIT...
WHERE?
INFIRMARY...
WHY?
WHO?
BOSS...

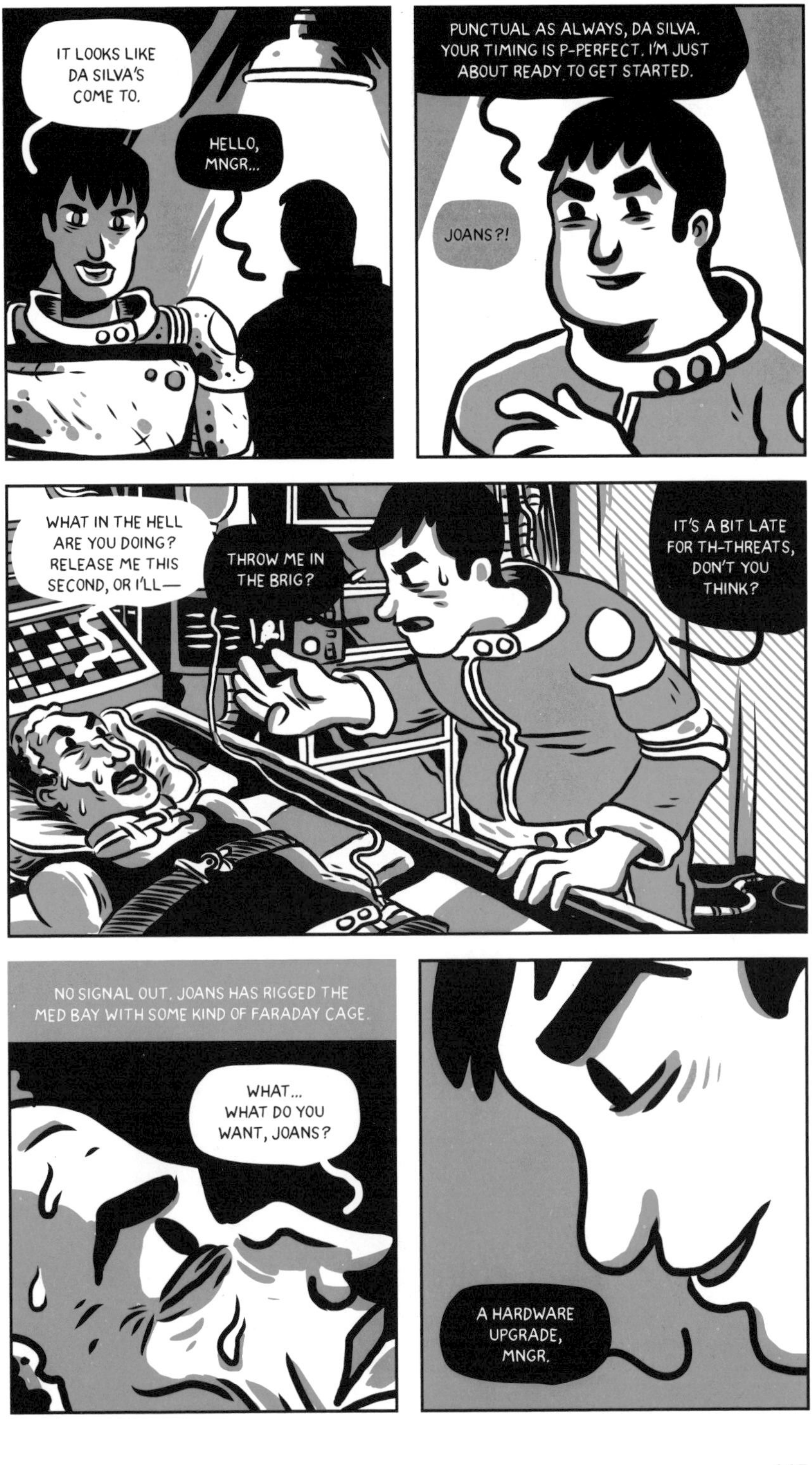
IT LOOKS LIKE DA SILVA'S COME TO.
HELLO, MNGR...
PUNCTUAL AS ALWAYS, DA SILVA. YOUR TIMING IS P-PERFECT. I'M JUST ABOUT READY TO GET STARTED.
JOANS?!
WHAT IN THE HELL ARE YOU DOING? RELEASE ME THIS SECOND, OR I'LL—
THROW ME IN THE BRIG?
IT'S A BIT LATE FOR TH-THREATS, DON'T YOU THINK?
NO SIGNAL OUT. JOANS HAS RIGGED THE MED BAY WITH SOME KIND OF FARADAY CAGE.
WHAT... WHAT DO YOU WANT, JOANS?
A HARDWARE UPGRADE, MNGR.

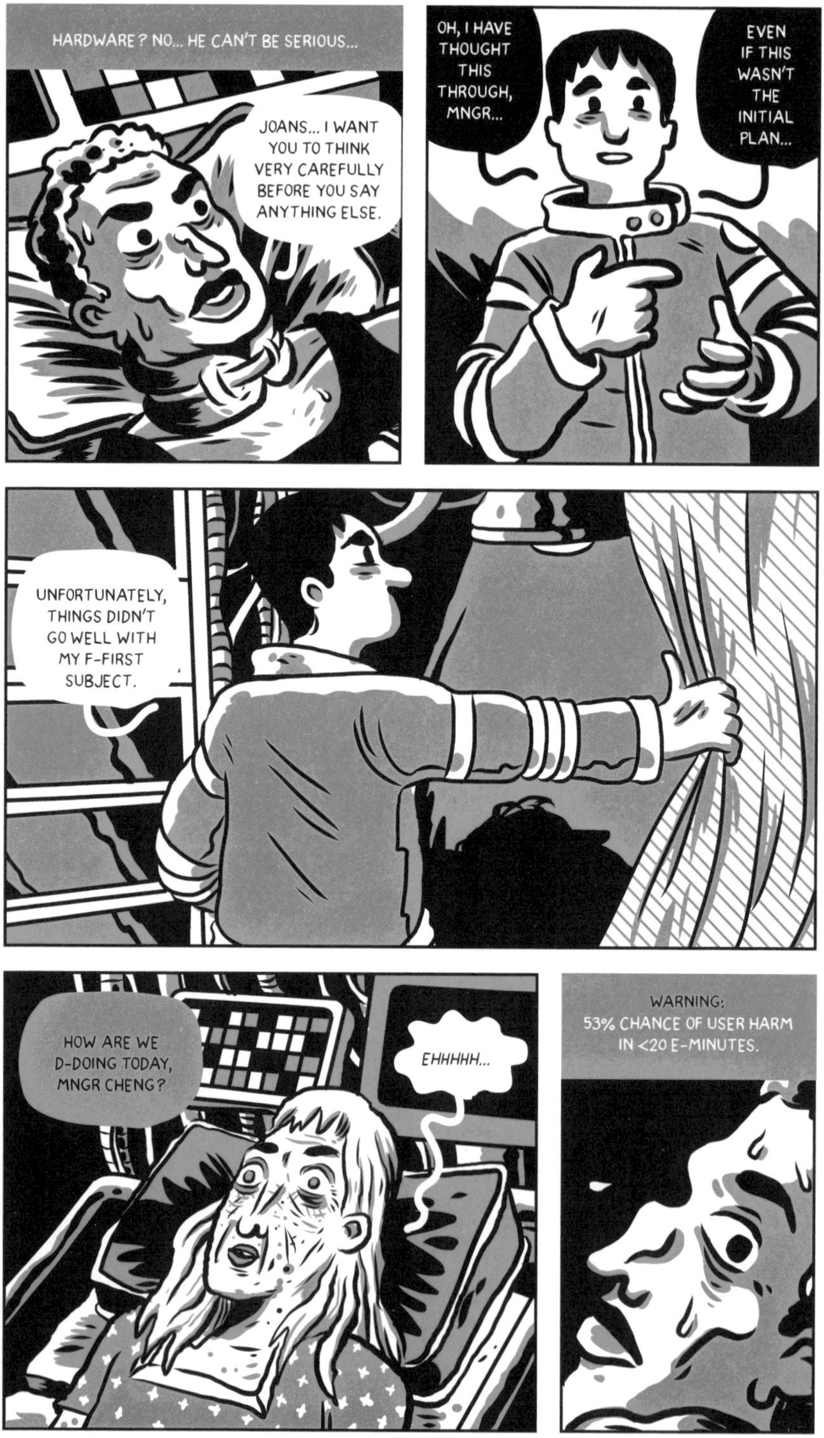
HARDWARE? NO... HE CAN'T BE SERIOUS...
JOANS... I WANT YOU TO THINK VERY CAREFULLY BEFORE YOU SAY ANYTHING ELSE.
OH, I HAVE THOUGHT THIS THROUGH, MNGR...
EVEN IF THIS WASN'T THE INITIAL PLAN...
UNFORTUNATELY, THINGS DIDN'T GO WELL WITH MY F-FIRST SUBJECT.
HOW ARE WE D-DOING TODAY, MNGR CHENG?
EHHHHH...
WARNING: 53% CHANCE OF USER HARM IN <20 E-MINUTES.

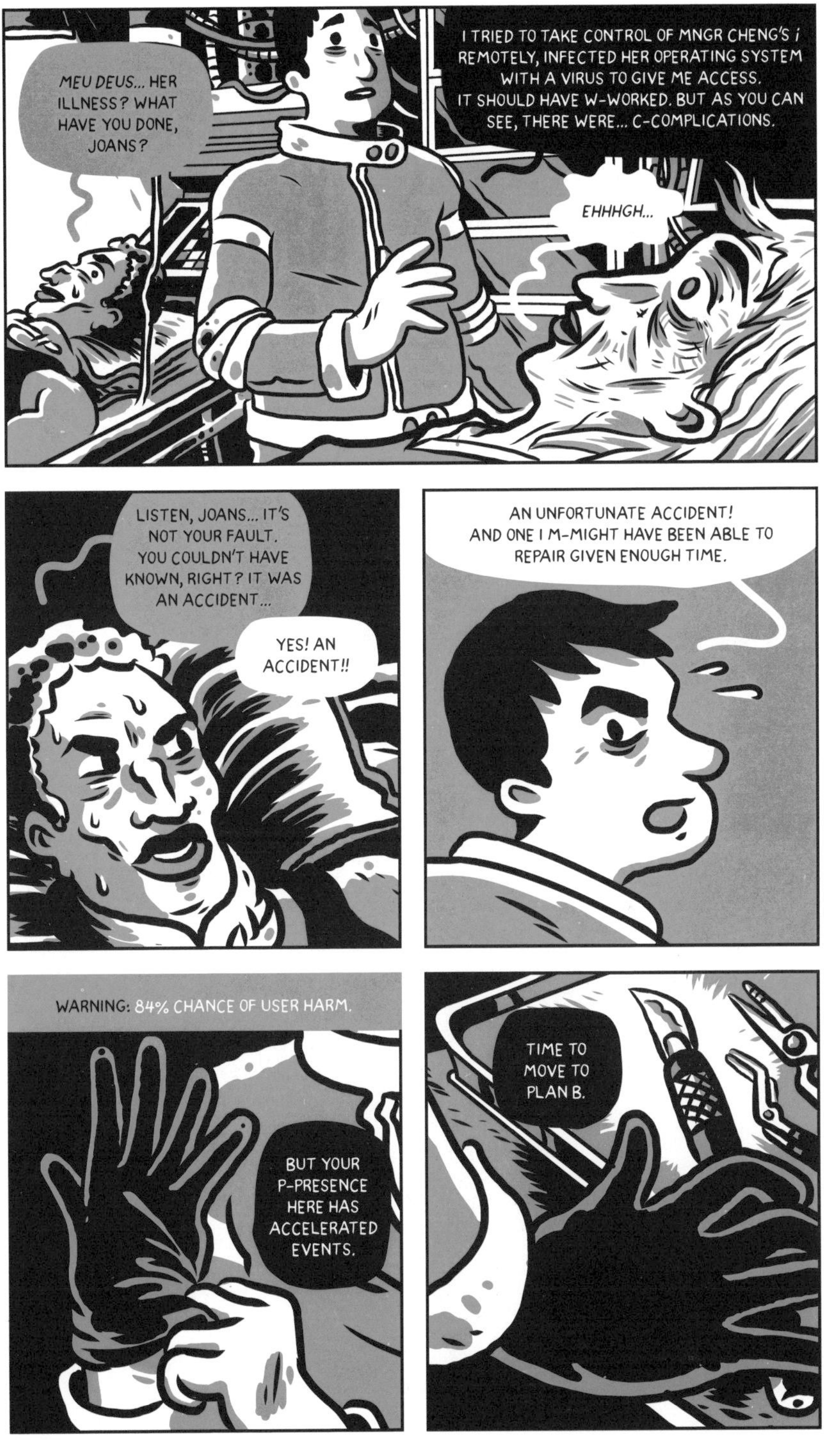
MEU DEUS... HER ILLNESS? WHAT HAVE YOU DONE, JOANS?
I TRIED TO TAKE CONTROL OF MNGR CHENG'S i REMOTELY, INFECTED HER OPERATING SYSTEM WITH A VIRUS TO GIVE ME ACCESS. IT SHOULD HAVE W-WORKED. BUT AS YOU CAN SEE, THERE WERE... C-COMPLICATIONS.
EHHHGH...
LISTEN, JOANS... IT'S NOT YOUR FAULT. YOU COULDN'T HAVE KNOWN, RIGHT? IT WAS AN ACCIDENT...
YES! AN ACCIDENT!!
AN UNFORTUNATE ACCIDENT! AND ONE I M-MIGHT HAVE BEEN ABLE TO REPAIR GIVEN ENOUGH TIME.
WARNING: 84% CHANCE OF USER HARM.
BUT YOUR P-PRESENCE HERE HAS ACCELERATED EVENTS.
TIME TO MOVE TO PLAN B.

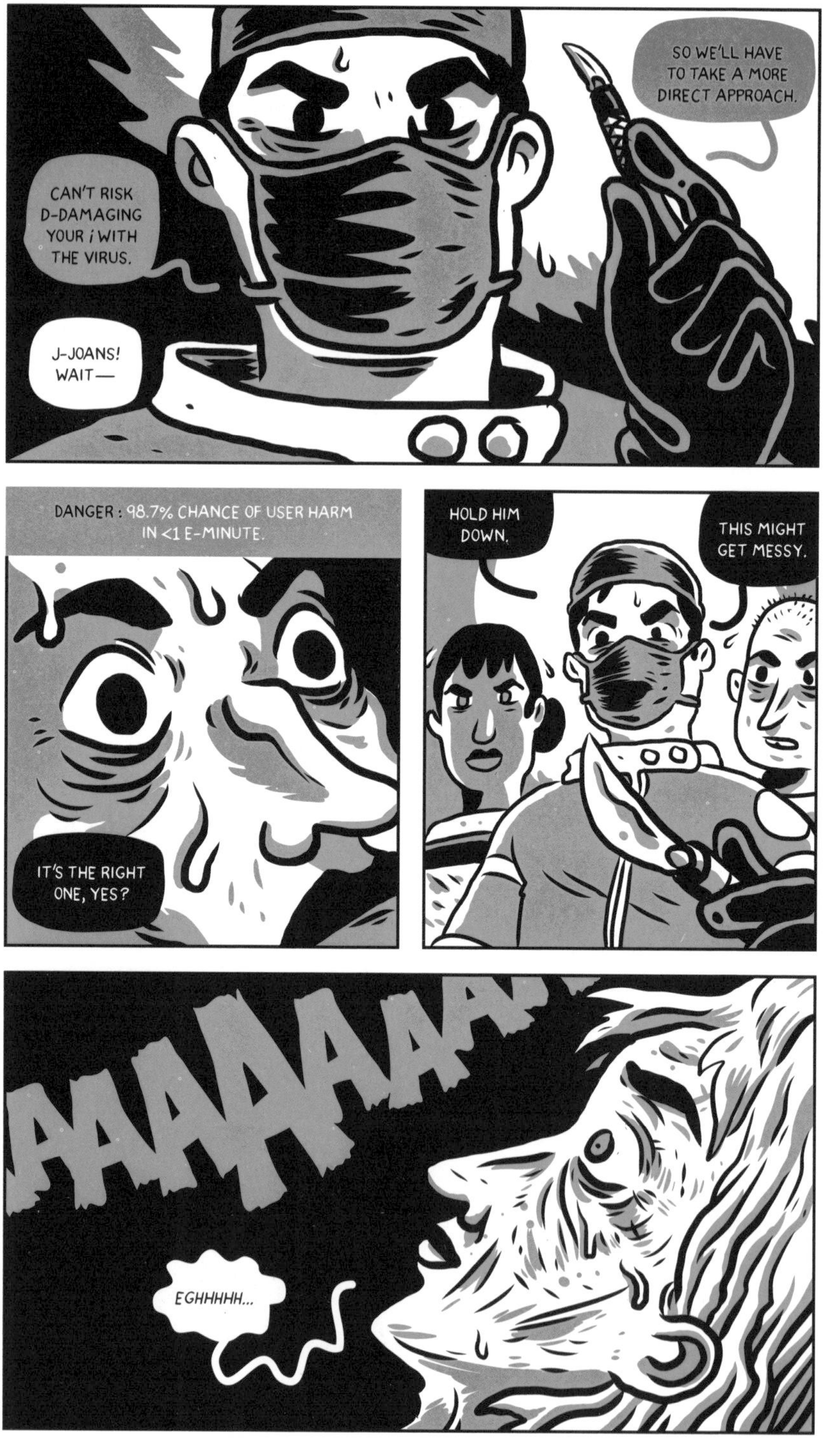
SO WE'LL HAVE TO TAKE A MORE DIRECT APPROACH.
CAN'T RISK D-DAMAGING YOUR *i* WITH THE VIRUS.
J-JOANS! WAIT—
DANGER : 98.7% CHANCE OF USER HARM IN <1 E-MINUTE.
IT'S THE RIGHT ONE, YES?
HOLD HIM DOWN.
THIS MIGHT GET MESSY.
AAAAAAAA
EGHHHHH...

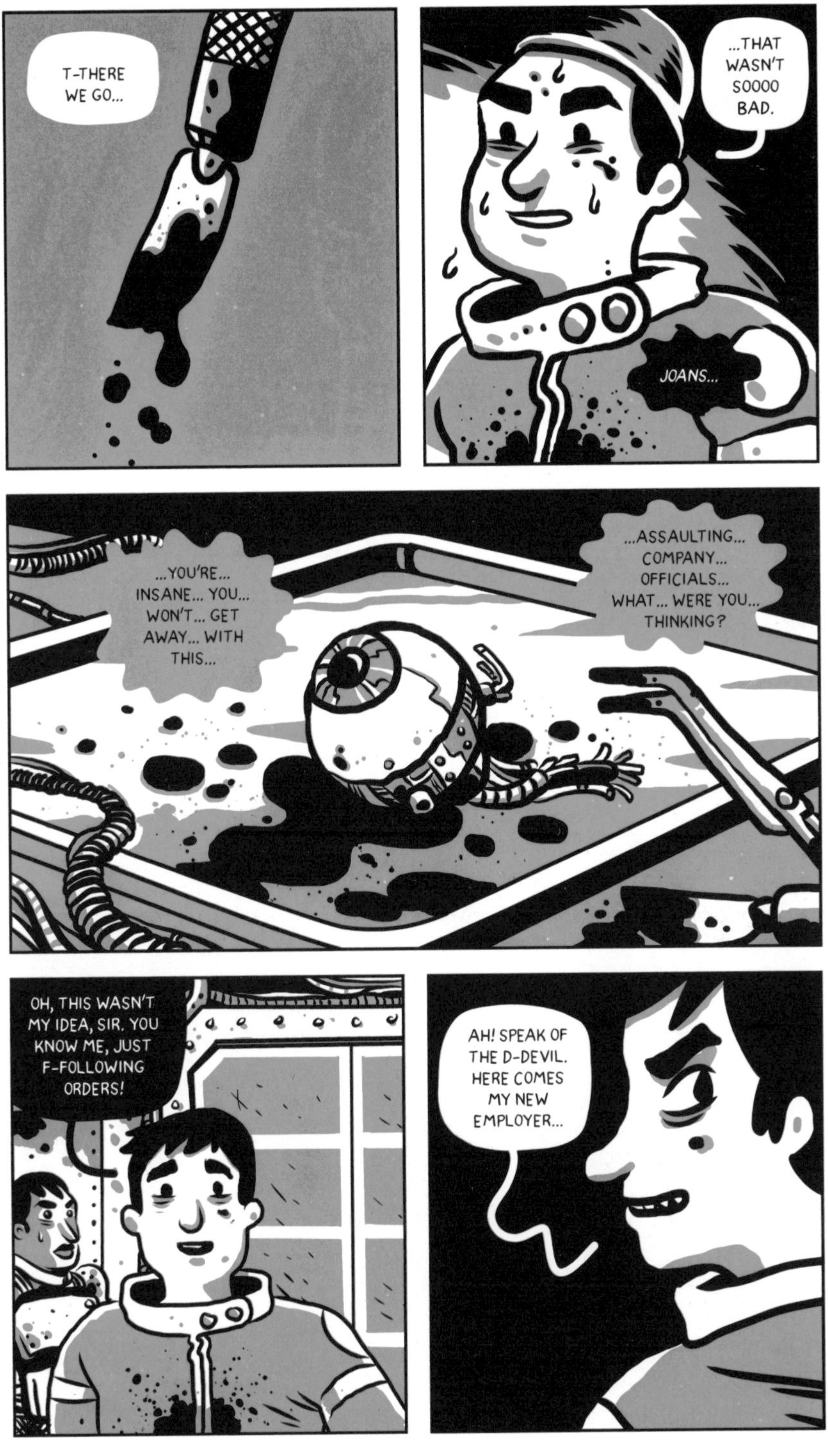
T-THERE WE GO...
...THAT WASN'T SOOOO BAD.
JOANS...
...YOU'RE... INSANE... YOU... WON'T... GET AWAY... WITH THIS...
...ASSAULTING... COMPANY... OFFICIALS... WHAT... WERE YOU... THINKING?
OH, THIS WASN'T MY IDEA, SIR. YOU KNOW ME, JUST F-FOLLOWING ORDERS!
AH! SPEAK OF THE D-DEVIL. HERE COMES MY NEW EMPLOYER...

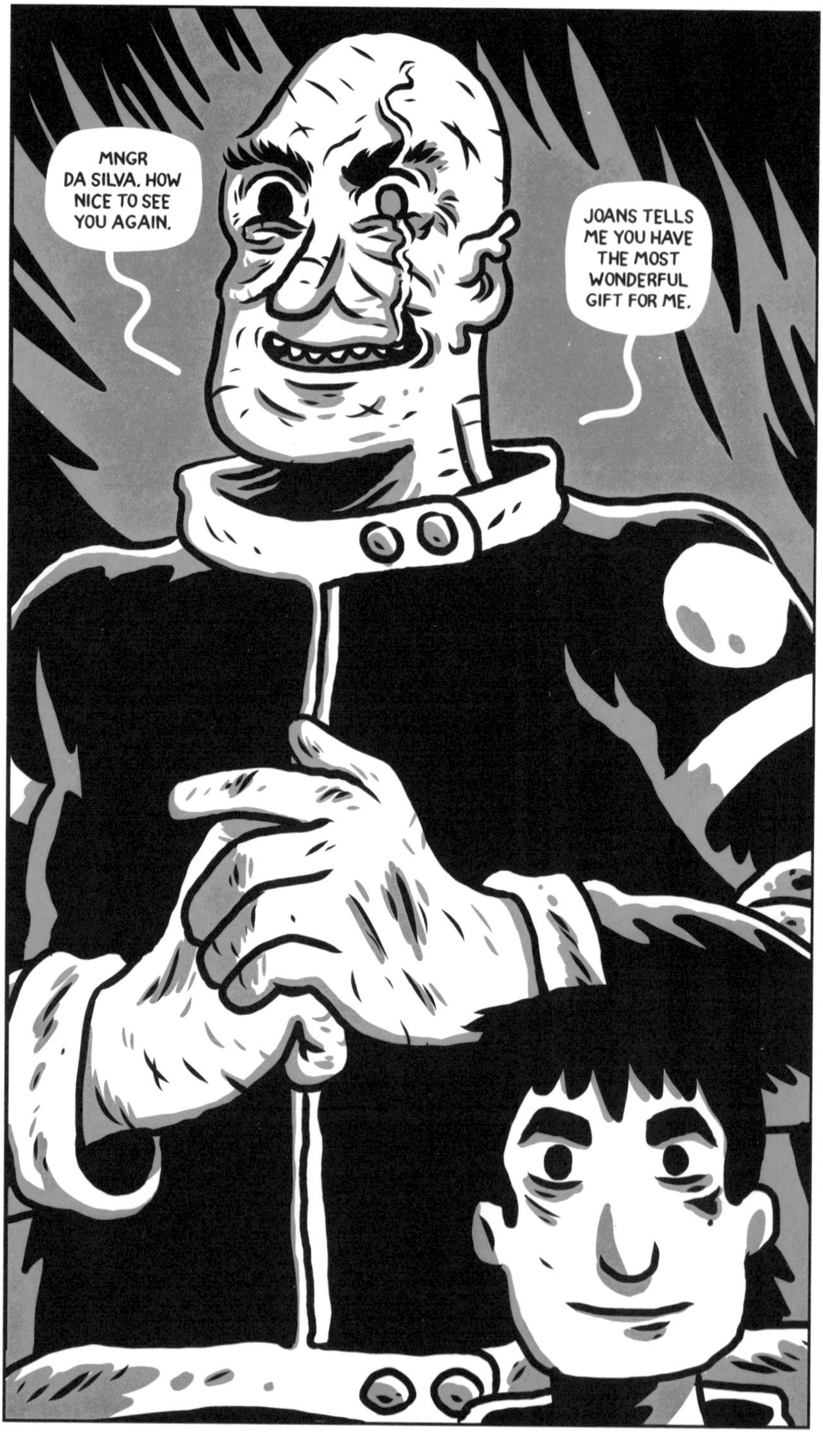
MNGR DA SILVA. HOW NICE TO SEE YOU AGAIN.
JOANS TELLS ME YOU HAVE THE MOST WONDERFUL GIFT FOR ME.

PART 10: OH! YOU PRETTY THINGS

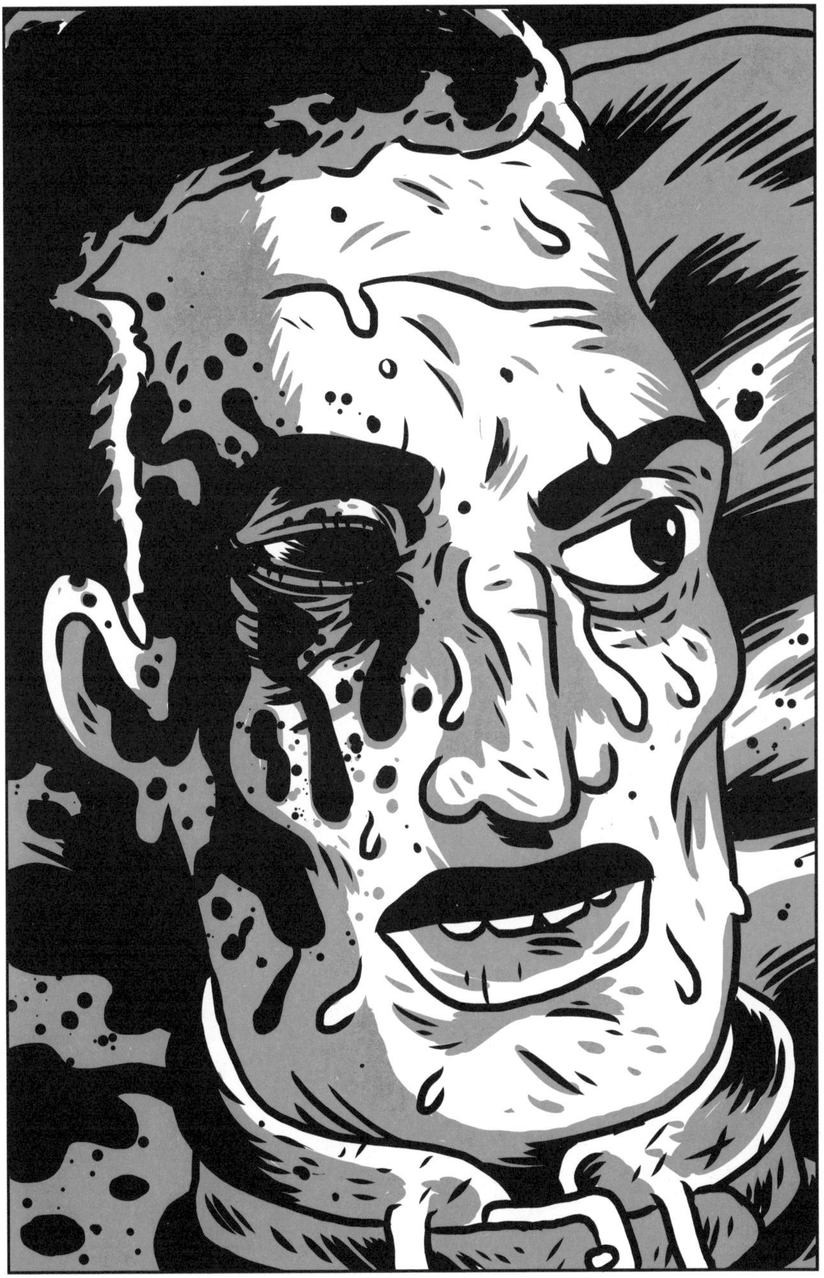

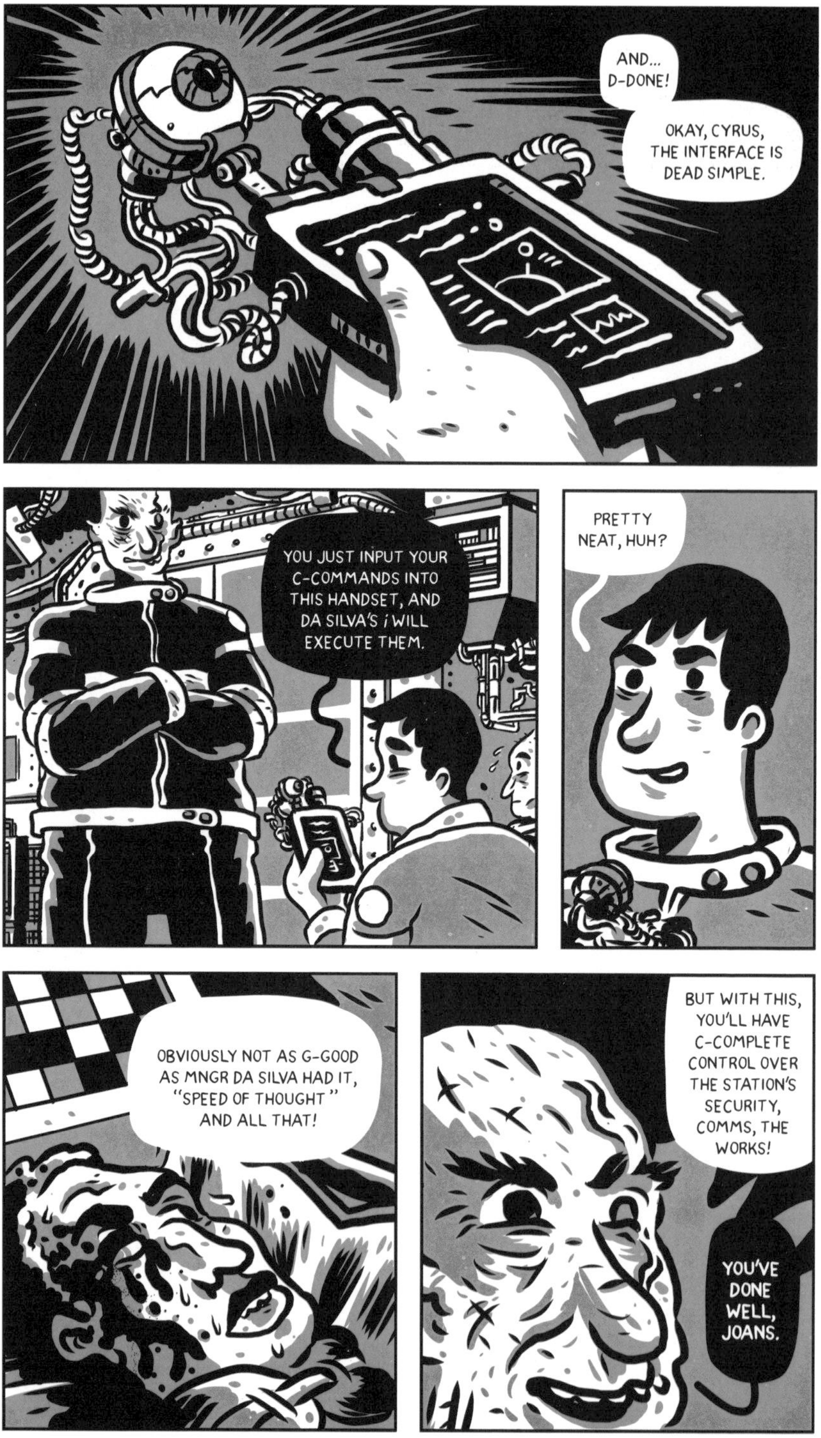
AND... D-DONE!
OKAY, CYRUS, THE INTERFACE IS DEAD SIMPLE.
YOU JUST INPUT YOUR C-COMMANDS INTO THIS HANDSET, AND DA SILVA'S *i* WILL EXECUTE THEM.
PRETTY NEAT, HUH?
OBVIOUSLY NOT AS G-GOOD AS MNGR DA SILVA HAD IT, "SPEED OF THOUGHT" AND ALL THAT!
BUT WITH THIS, YOU'LL HAVE C-COMPLETE CONTROL OVER THE STATION'S SECURITY, COMMS, THE WORKS!
YOU'VE DONE WELL, JOANS.

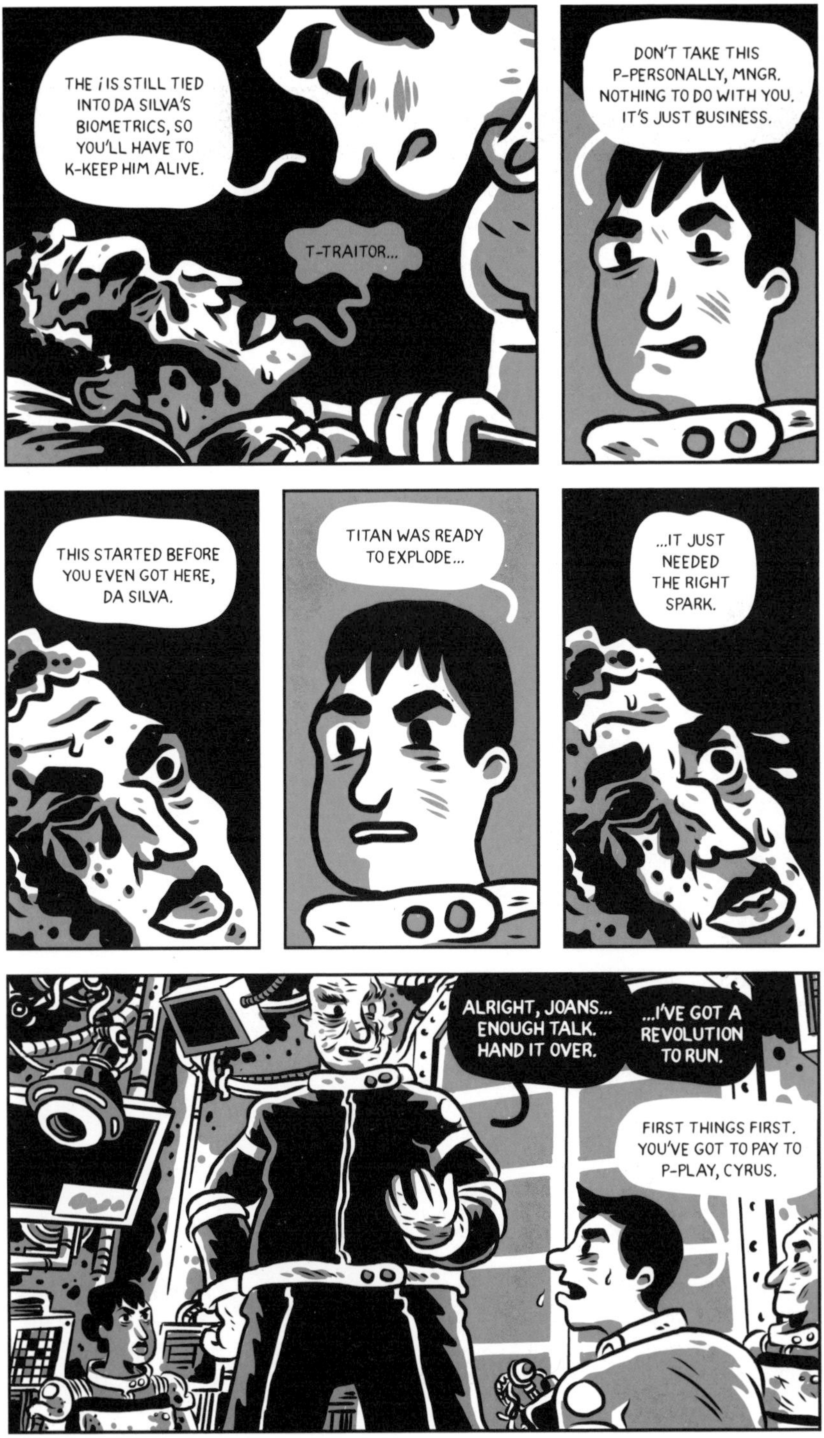

THE i IS STILL TIED INTO DA SILVA'S BIOMETRICS, SO YOU'LL HAVE TO K-KEEP HIM ALIVE.
T-TRAITOR...
DON'T TAKE THIS P-PERSONALLY, MNGR. NOTHING TO DO WITH YOU. IT'S JUST BUSINESS.
THIS STARTED BEFORE YOU EVEN GOT HERE, DA SILVA.
TITAN WAS READY TO EXPLODE...
...IT JUST NEEDED THE RIGHT SPARK.
ALRIGHT, JOANS... ENOUGH TALK. HAND IT OVER.
...I'VE GOT A REVOLUTION TO RUN.
FIRST THINGS FIRST. YOU'VE GOT TO PAY TO P-PLAY, CYRUS.

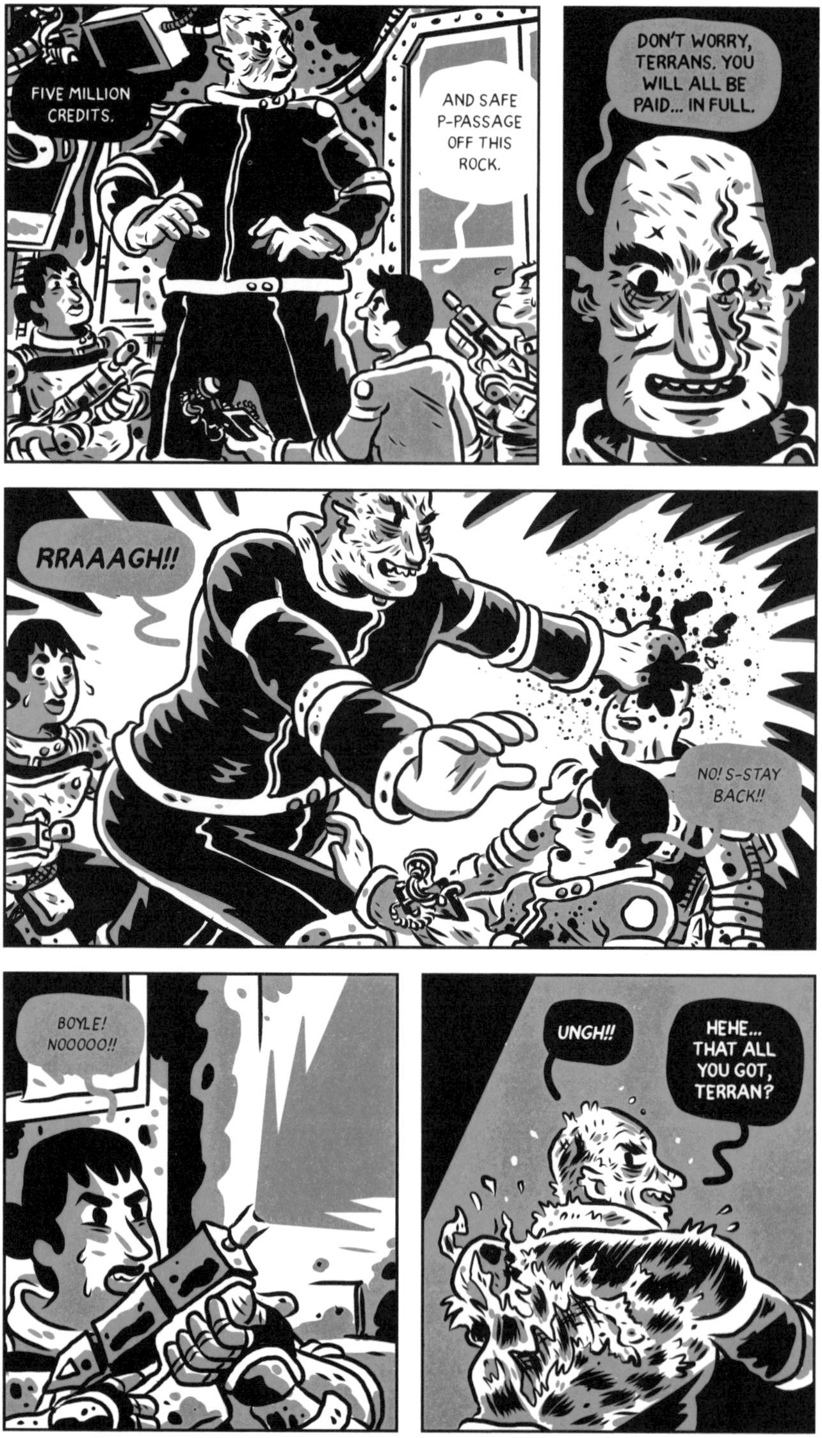
FIVE MILLION CREDITS.
AND SAFE P-PASSAGE OFF THIS ROCK.
DON'T WORRY, TERRANS. YOU WILL ALL BE PAID... IN FULL.
RRAAAGH!!
NO! S-STAY BACK!!
BOYLE! NOOOOO!!
UNGH!!
HEHE... THAT ALL YOU GOT, TERRAN?

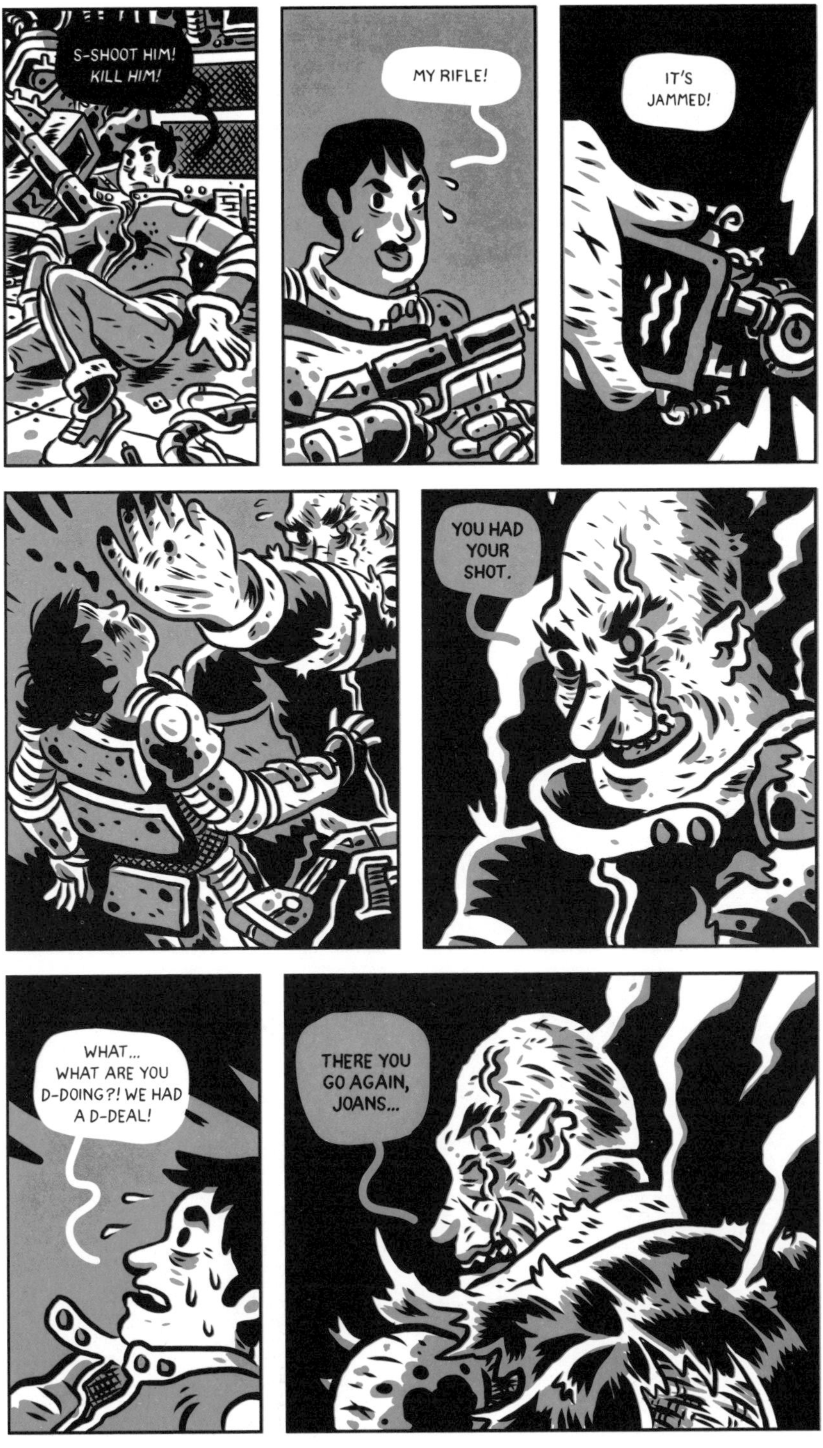
S-SHOOT HIM! KILL HIM!
MY RIFLE!
IT'S JAMMED!
YOU HAD YOUR SHOT.
WHAT... WHAT ARE YOU D-DOING?! WE HAD A D-DEAL!
THERE YOU GO AGAIN, JOANS...

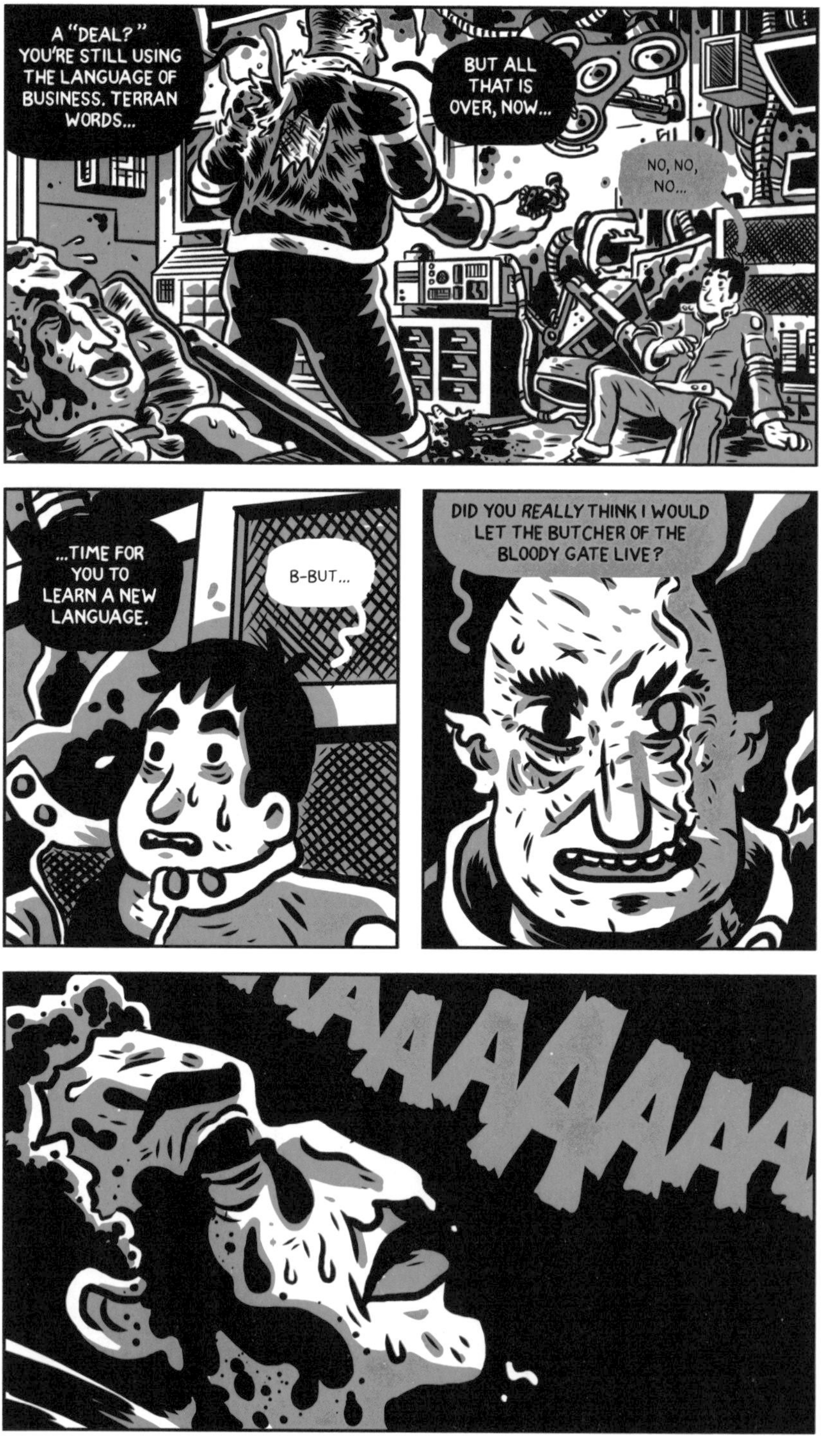
A "DEAL?" YOU'RE STILL USING THE LANGUAGE OF BUSINESS. TERRAN WORDS...
BUT ALL THAT IS OVER, NOW...
NO, NO, NO...
...TIME FOR YOU TO LEARN A NEW LANGUAGE.
B-BUT...
DID YOU *REALLY* THINK I WOULD LET THE BUTCHER OF THE BLOODY GATE LIVE?
AAAAAAAAA

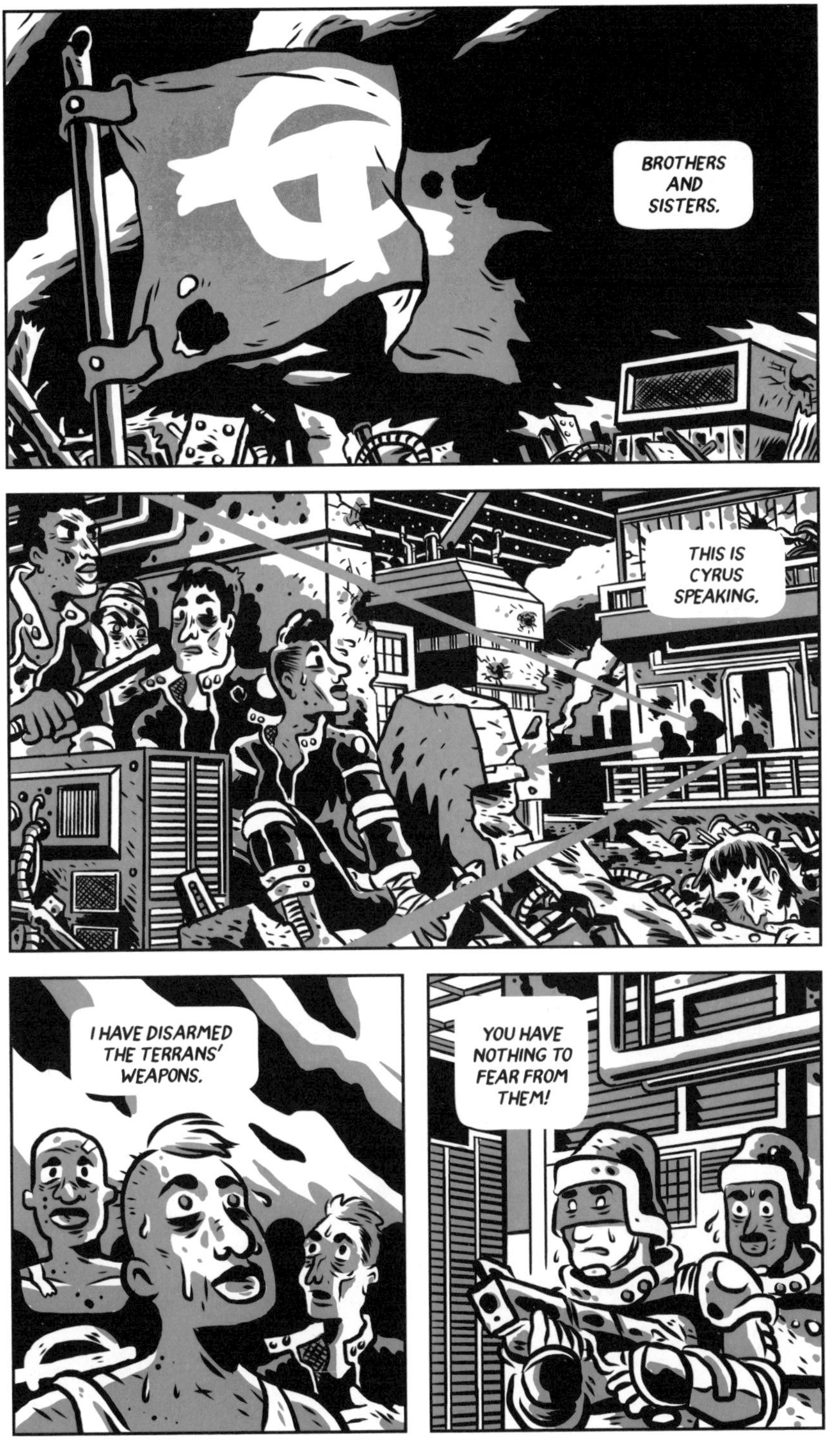
BROTHERS AND SISTERS.
THIS IS CYRUS SPEAKING.
I HAVE DISARMED THE TERRANS' WEAPONS.
YOU HAVE NOTHING TO FEAR FROM THEM!

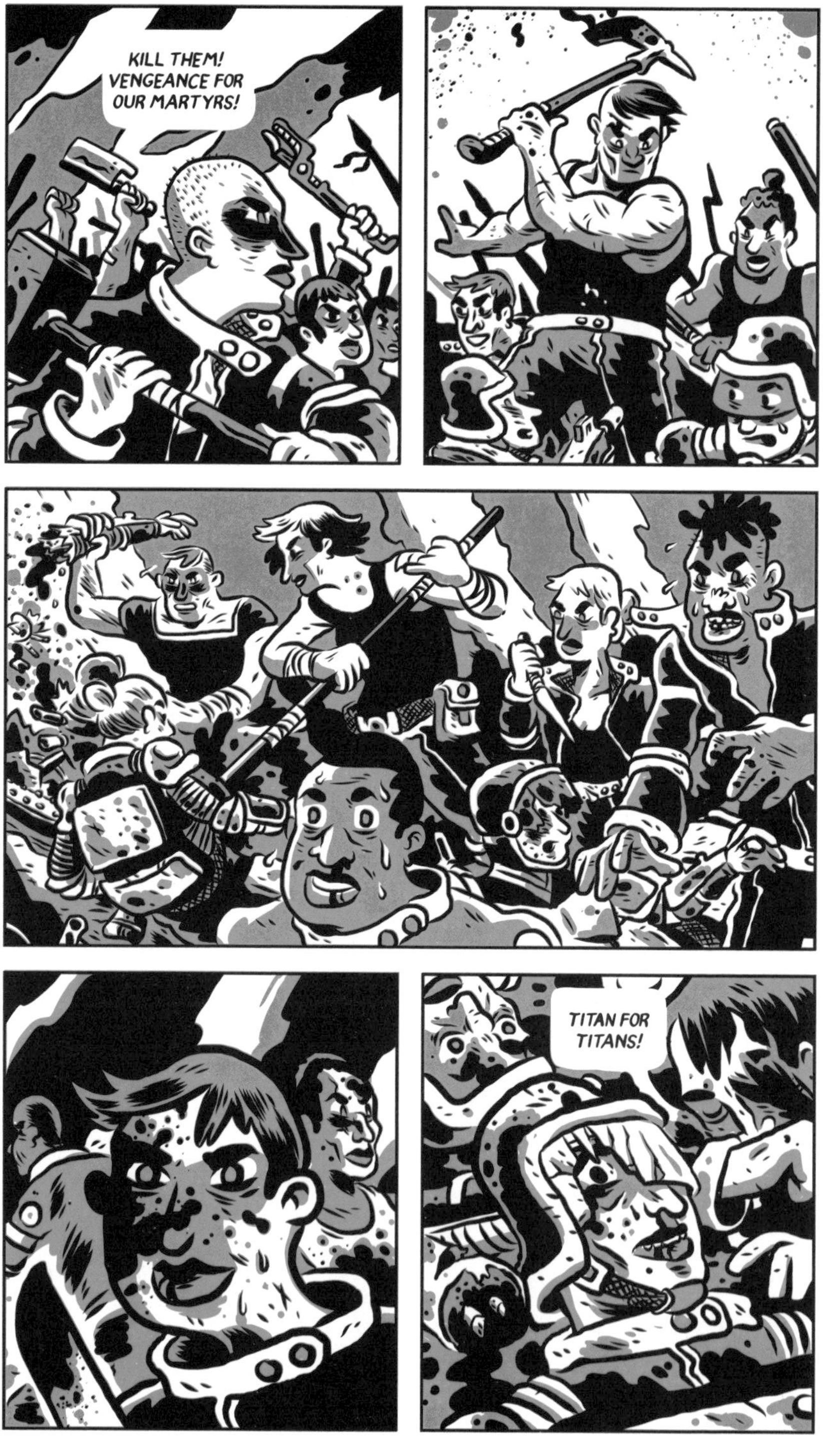
KILL THEM! VENGEANCE FOR OUR MARTYRS!
TITAN FOR TITANS!

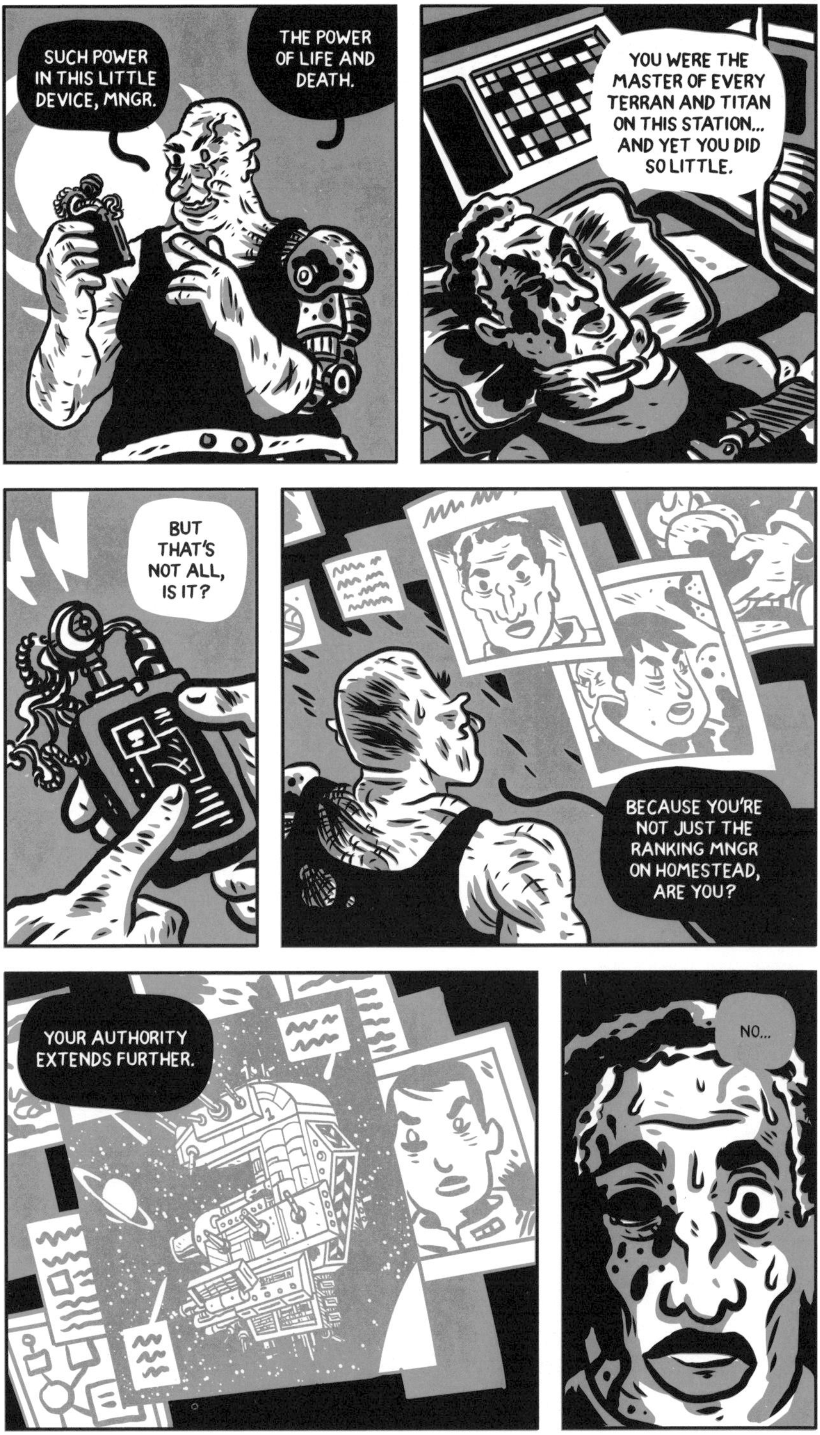
SUCH POWER IN THIS LITTLE DEVICE, MNGR.
THE POWER OF LIFE AND DEATH.
YOU WERE THE MASTER OF EVERY TERRAN AND TITAN ON THIS STATION... AND YET YOU DID SO LITTLE.
BUT THAT'S NOT ALL, IS IT?
BECAUSE YOU'RE NOT JUST THE RANKING MNGR ON HOMESTEAD, ARE YOU?
YOUR AUTHORITY EXTENDS FURTHER.
NO...

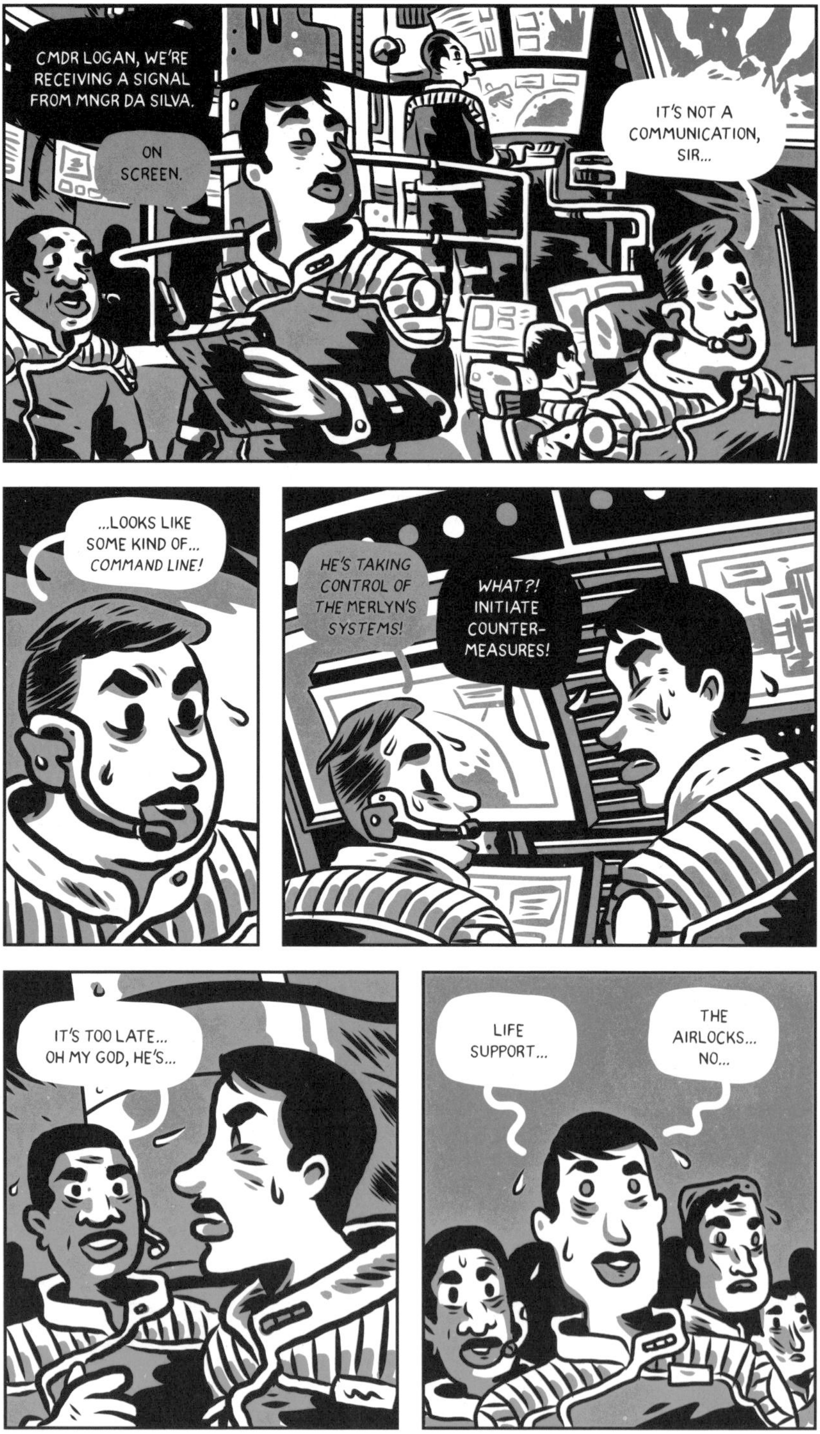
CMDR LOGAN, WE'RE RECEIVING A SIGNAL FROM MNGR DA SILVA.
ON SCREEN.
IT'S NOT A COMMUNICATION, SIR...
...LOOKS LIKE SOME KIND OF... COMMAND LINE!
HE'S TAKING CONTROL OF THE MERLYN'S SYSTEMS!
WHAT?! INITIATE COUNTER-MEASURES!
IT'S TOO LATE... OH MY GOD, HE'S...
LIFE SUPPORT...
THE AIRLOCKS... NO...

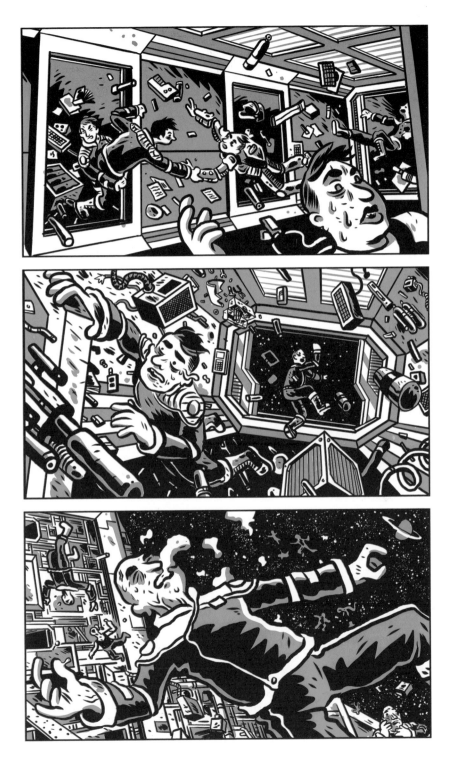

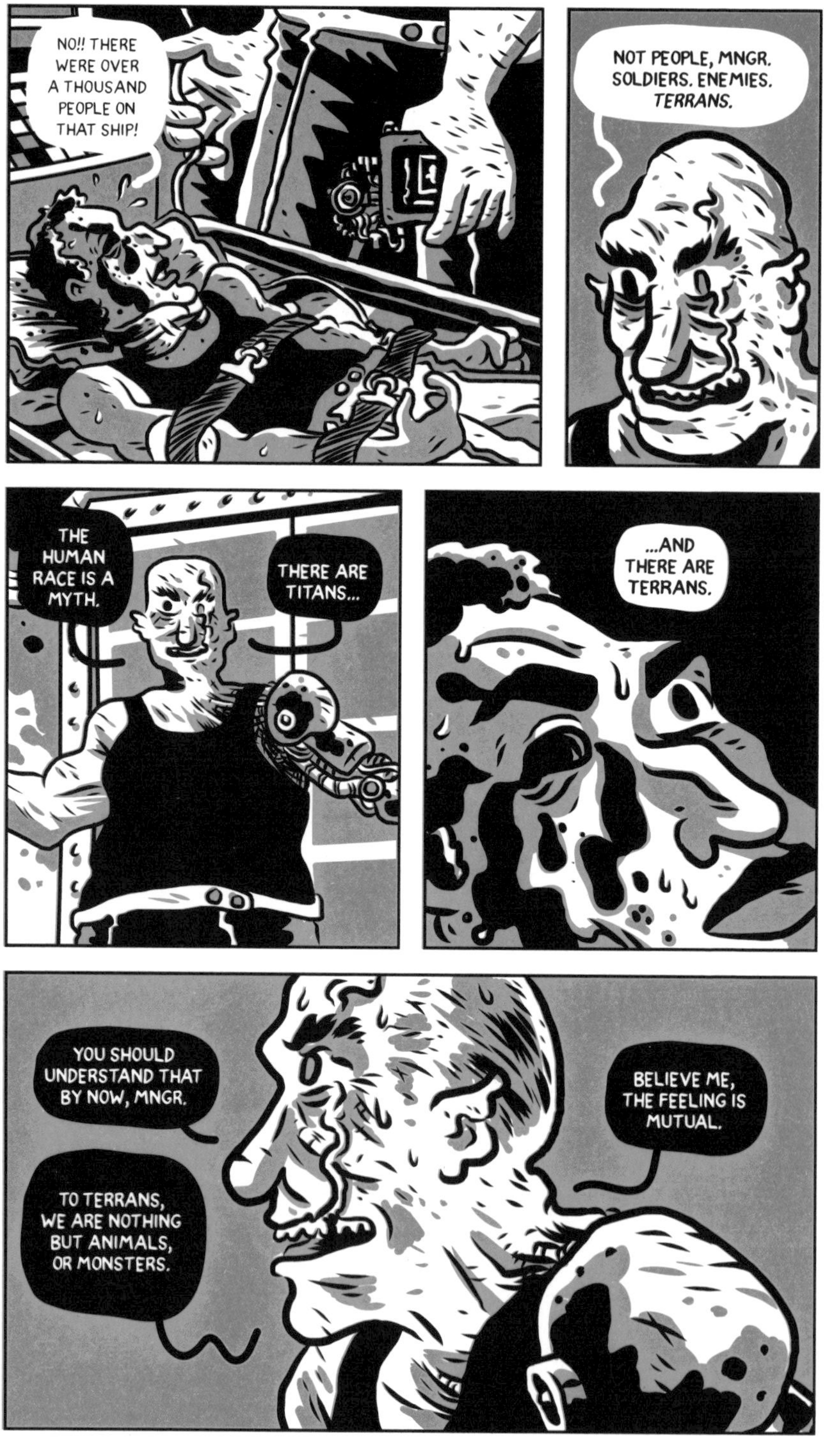
NO!! THERE WERE OVER A THOUSAND PEOPLE ON THAT SHIP!
NOT PEOPLE, MNGR. SOLDIERS. ENEMIES. *TERRANS.*
THE HUMAN RACE IS A MYTH.
THERE ARE TITANS...
...AND THERE ARE TERRANS.
YOU SHOULD UNDERSTAND THAT BY NOW, MNGR.
TO TERRANS, WE ARE NOTHING BUT ANIMALS, OR MONSTERS.
BELIEVE ME, THE FEELING IS MUTUAL.

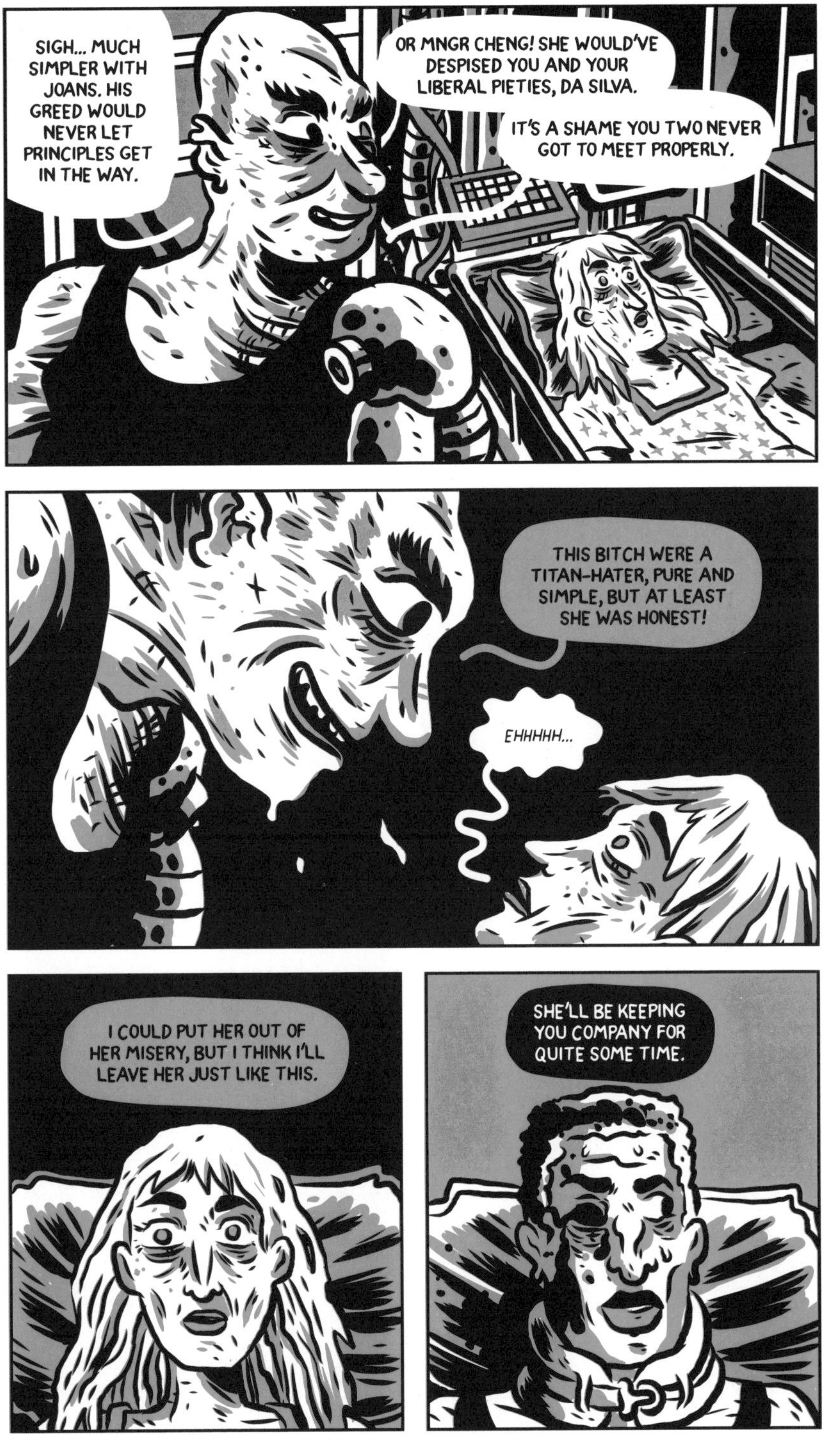
SIGH... MUCH SIMPLER WITH JOANS. HIS GREED WOULD NEVER LET PRINCIPLES GET IN THE WAY.
OR MNGR CHENG! SHE WOULD'VE DESPISED YOU AND YOUR LIBERAL PIETIES, DA SILVA.
IT'S A SHAME YOU TWO NEVER GOT TO MEET PROPERLY.
THIS BITCH WERE A TITAN-HATER, PURE AND SIMPLE, BUT AT LEAST SHE WAS HONEST!
EHHHHH...
I COULD PUT HER OUT OF HER MISERY, BUT I THINK I'LL LEAVE HER JUST LIKE THIS.
SHE'LL BE KEEPING YOU COMPANY FOR QUITE SOME TIME.

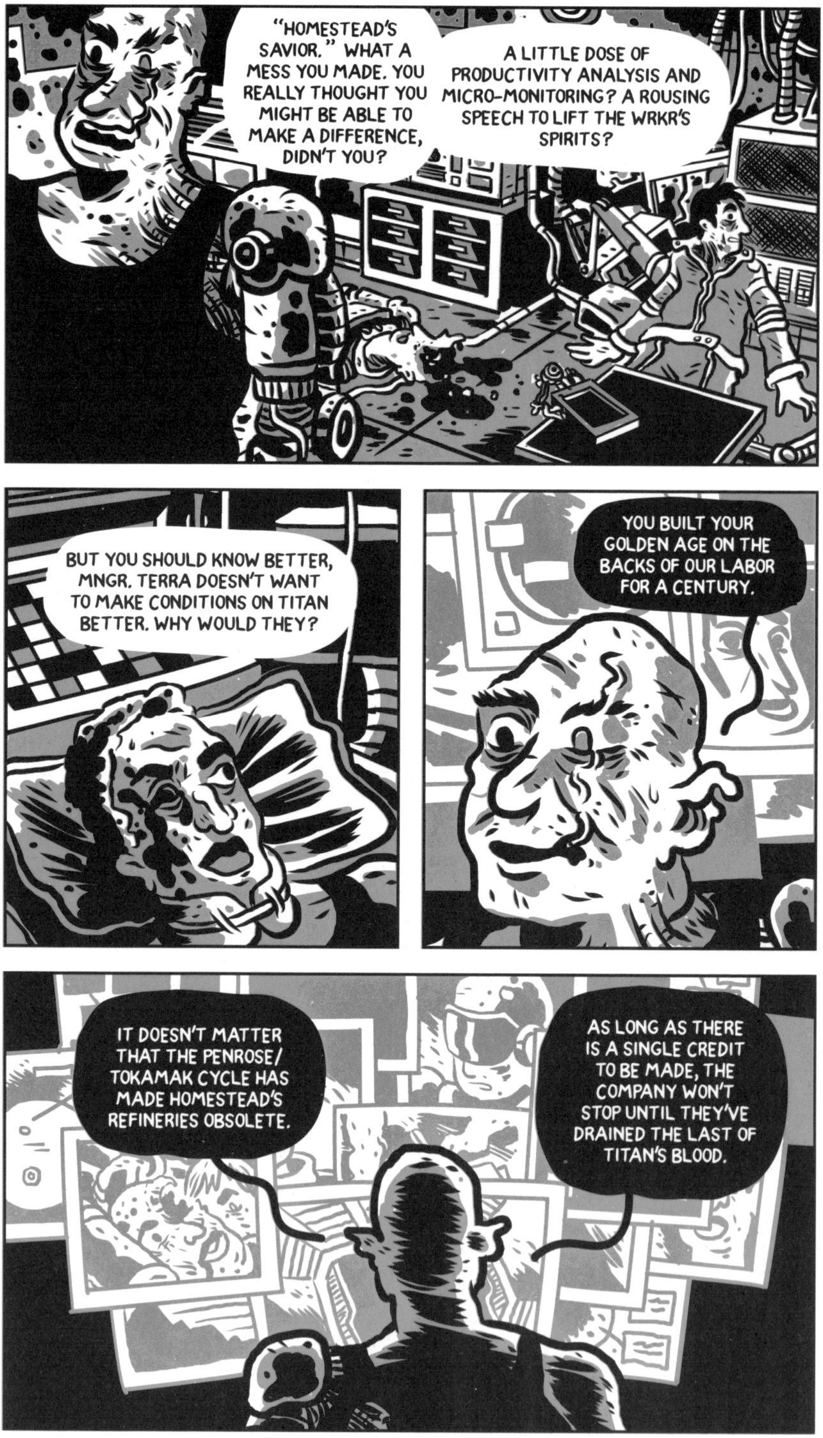
"HOMESTEAD'S SAVIOR." WHAT A MESS YOU MADE. YOU REALLY THOUGHT YOU MIGHT BE ABLE TO MAKE A DIFFERENCE, DIDN'T YOU?
A LITTLE DOSE OF PRODUCTIVITY ANALYSIS AND MICRO-MONITORING? A ROUSING SPEECH TO LIFT THE WRKR'S SPIRITS?
BUT YOU SHOULD KNOW BETTER, MNGR. TERRA DOESN'T WANT TO MAKE CONDITIONS ON TITAN BETTER. WHY WOULD THEY?
YOU BUILT YOUR GOLDEN AGE ON THE BACKS OF OUR LABOR FOR A CENTURY.
IT DOESN'T MATTER THAT THE PENROSE/ TOKAMAK CYCLE HAS MADE HOMESTEAD'S REFINERIES OBSOLETE.
AS LONG AS THERE IS A SINGLE CREDIT TO BE MADE, THE COMPANY WON'T STOP UNTIL THEY'VE DRAINED THE LAST OF TITAN'S BLOOD.

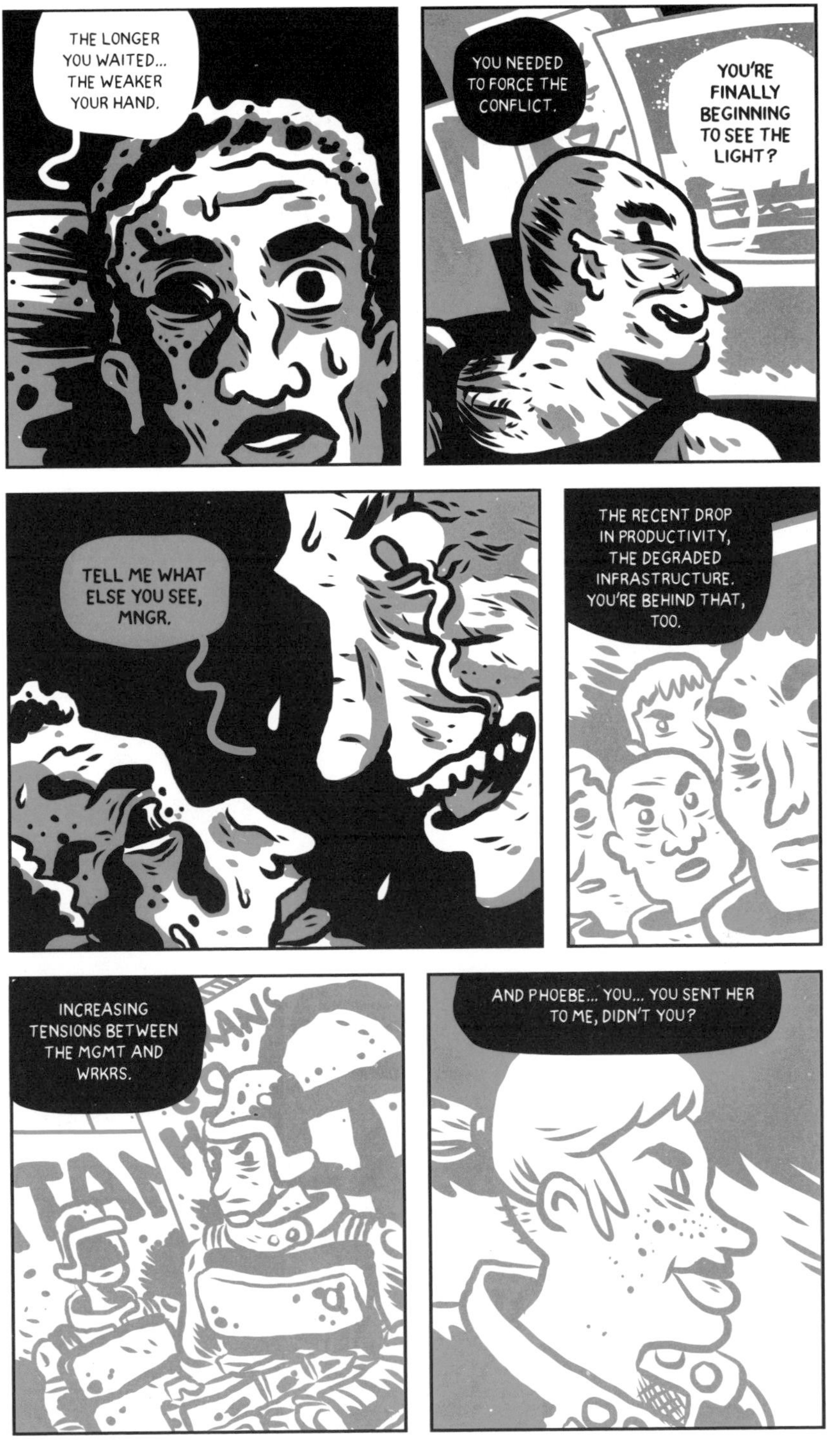
THE LONGER YOU WAITED... THE WEAKER YOUR HAND.
YOU NEEDED TO FORCE THE CONFLICT.
YOU'RE FINALLY BEGINNING TO SEE THE LIGHT?
TELL ME WHAT ELSE YOU SEE, MNGR.
THE RECENT DROP IN PRODUCTIVITY, THE DEGRADED INFRASTRUCTURE. YOU'RE BEHIND THAT, TOO.
INCREASING TENSIONS BETWEEN THE MGMT AND WRKRS.
AND PHOEBE... YOU... YOU SENT HER TO ME, DIDN'T YOU?

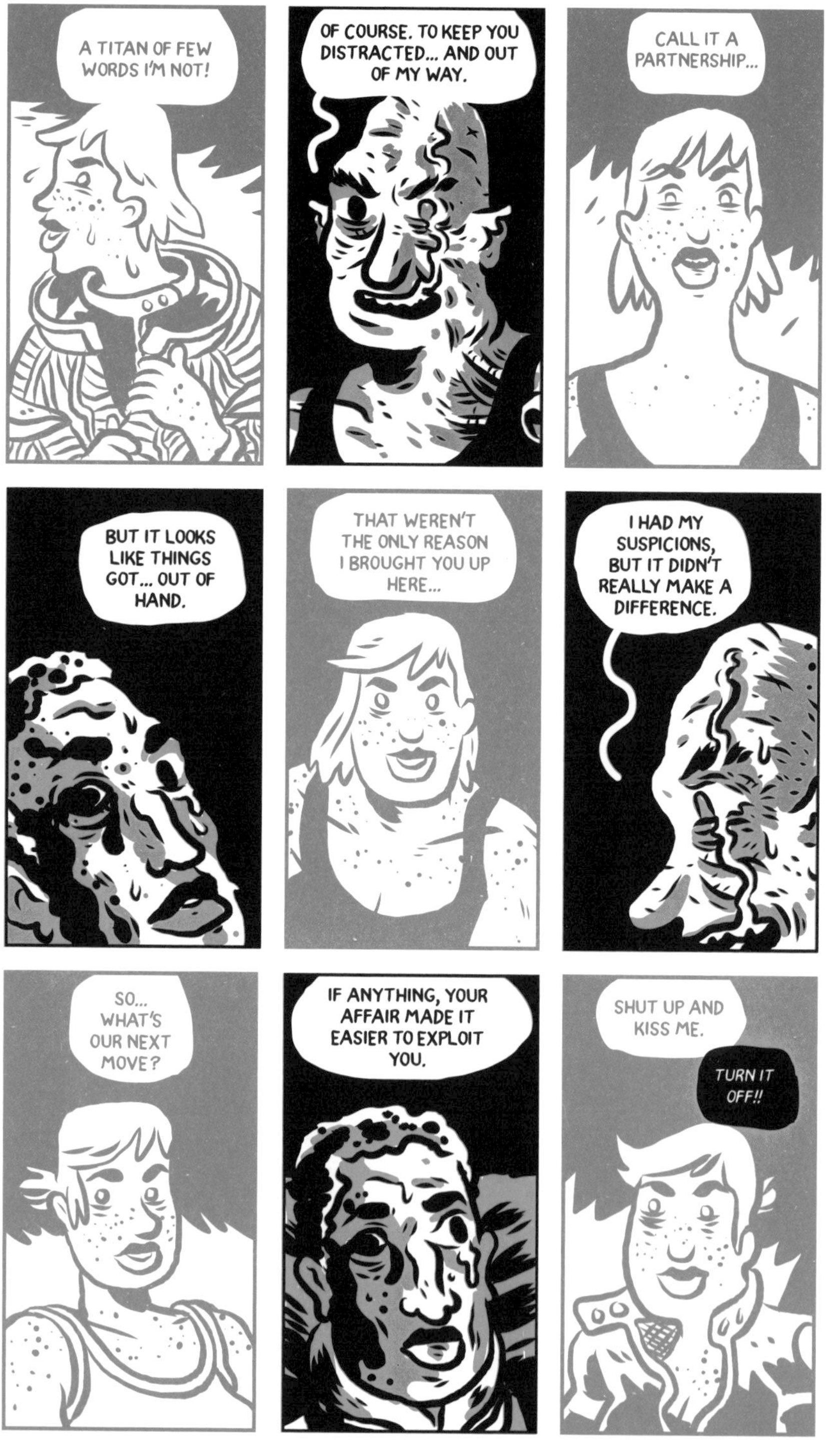
A TITAN OF FEW WORDS I'M NOT!
OF COURSE. TO KEEP YOU DISTRACTED... AND OUT OF MY WAY.
CALL IT A PARTNERSHIP...
BUT IT LOOKS LIKE THINGS GOT... OUT OF HAND.
THAT WEREN'T THE ONLY REASON I BROUGHT YOU UP HERE...
I HAD MY SUSPICIONS, BUT IT DIDN'T REALLY MAKE A DIFFERENCE.
SO... WHAT'S OUR NEXT MOVE?
IF ANYTHING, YOUR AFFAIR MADE IT EASIER TO EXPLOIT YOU.
SHUT UP AND KISS ME.
TURN IT OFF!!

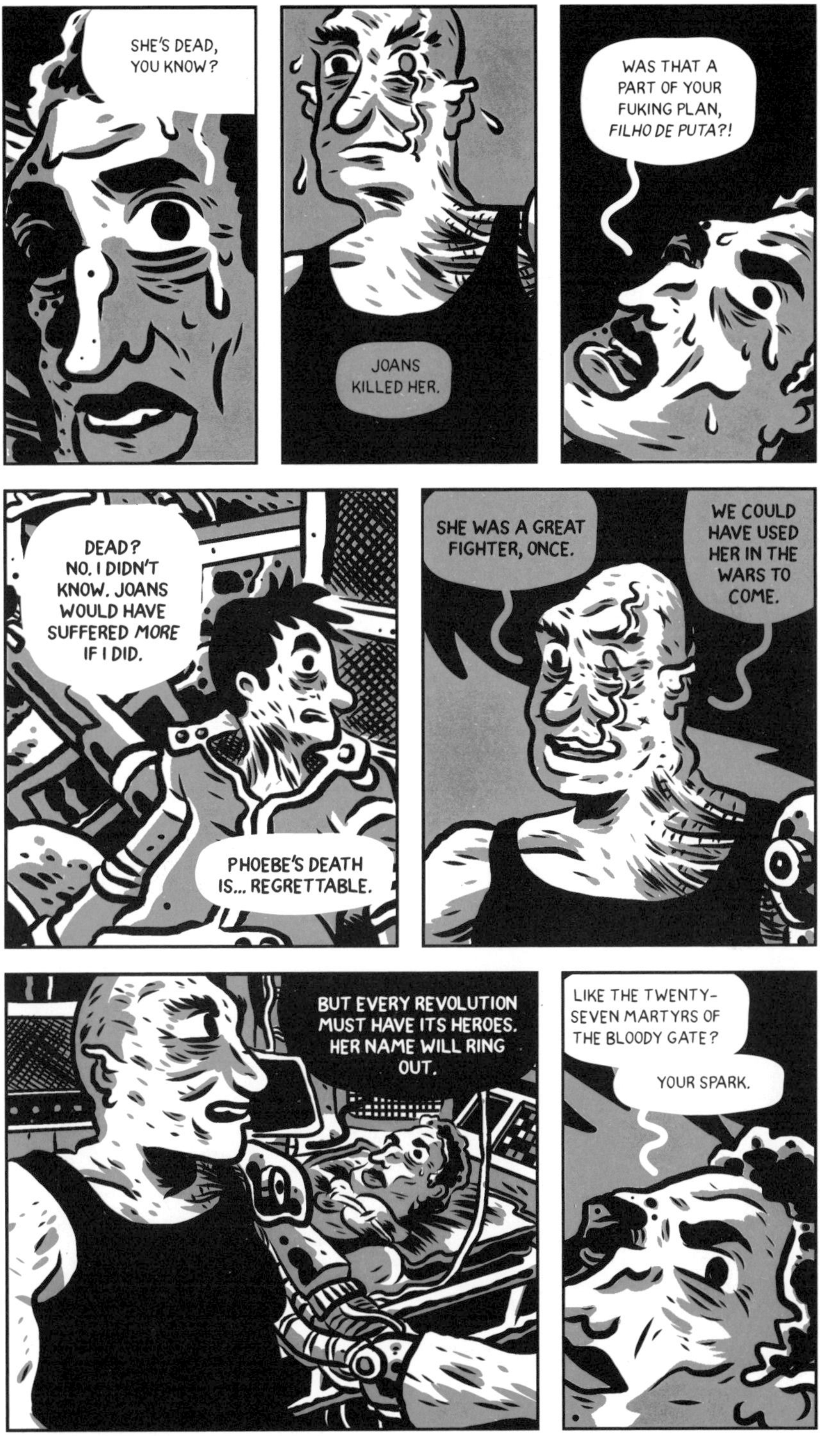

SHE'S DEAD, YOU KNOW?
JOANS KILLED HER.
WAS THAT A PART OF YOUR FUKING PLAN, *FILHO DE PUTA?!*
DEAD? NO. I DIDN'T KNOW. JOANS WOULD HAVE SUFFERED *MORE* IF I DID.
PHOEBE'S DEATH IS... REGRETTABLE.
SHE WAS A GREAT FIGHTER, ONCE.
WE COULD HAVE USED HER IN THE WARS TO COME.
BUT EVERY REVOLUTION MUST HAVE ITS HEROES. HER NAME WILL RING OUT.
LIKE THE TWENTY-SEVEN MARTYRS OF THE BLOODY GATE?
YOUR SPARK.

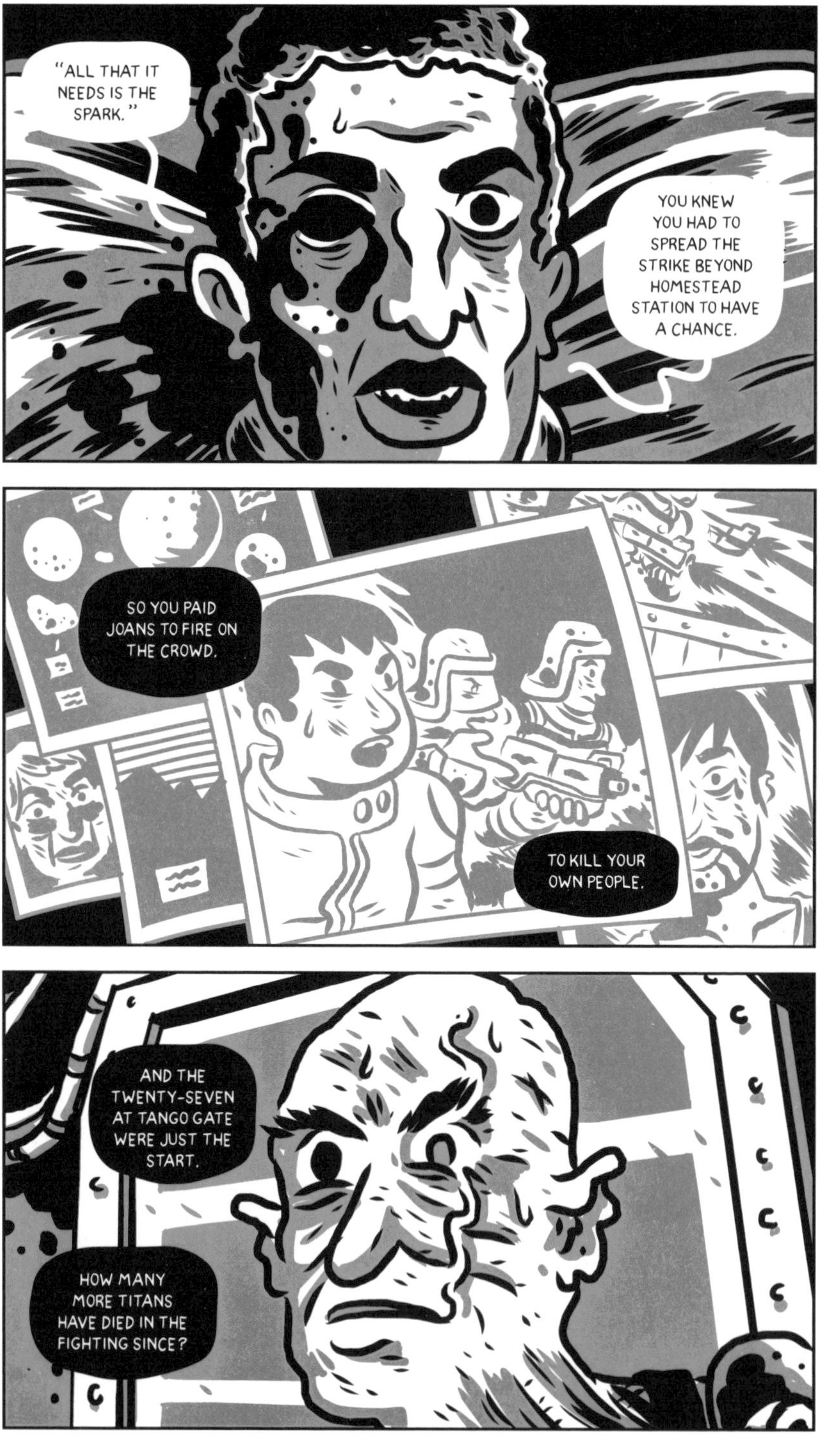
"ALL THAT IT NEEDS IS THE SPARK."
YOU KNEW YOU HAD TO SPREAD THE STRIKE BEYOND HOMESTEAD STATION TO HAVE A CHANCE.
SO YOU PAID JOANS TO FIRE ON THE CROWD.
TO KILL YOUR OWN PEOPLE.
AND THE TWENTY-SEVEN AT TANGO GATE WERE JUST THE START.
HOW MANY MORE TITANS HAVE DIED IN THE FIGHTING SINCE?

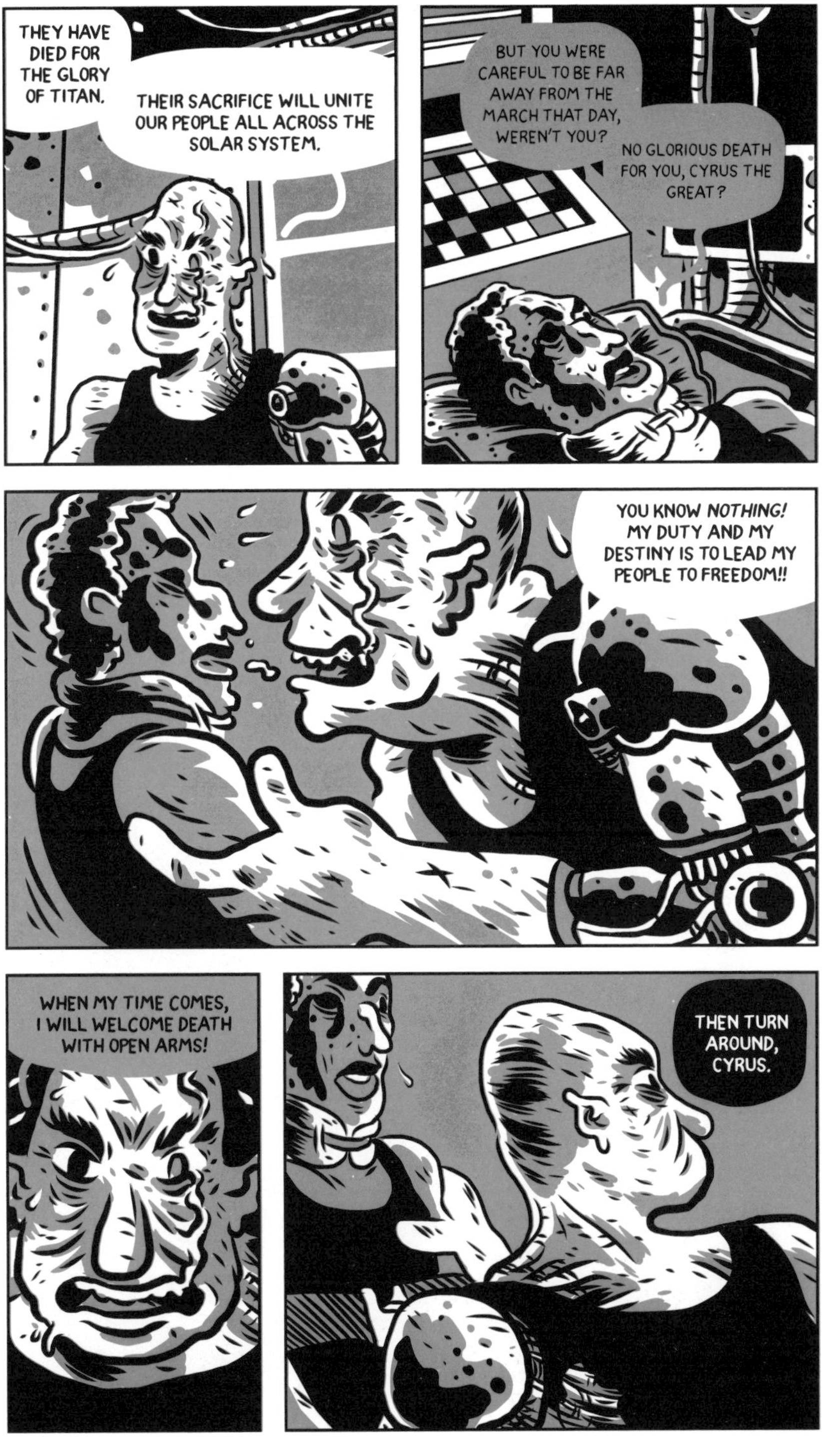
THEY HAVE DIED FOR THE GLORY OF TITAN.
THEIR SACRIFICE WILL UNITE OUR PEOPLE ALL ACROSS THE SOLAR SYSTEM.
BUT YOU WERE CAREFUL TO BE FAR AWAY FROM THE MARCH THAT DAY, WEREN'T YOU?
NO GLORIOUS DEATH FOR YOU, CYRUS THE GREAT?
YOU KNOW *NOTHING!* MY DUTY AND MY DESTINY IS TO LEAD MY PEOPLE TO FREEDOM!!
WHEN MY TIME COMES, I WILL WELCOME DEATH WITH OPEN ARMS!
THEN TURN AROUND, CYRUS.

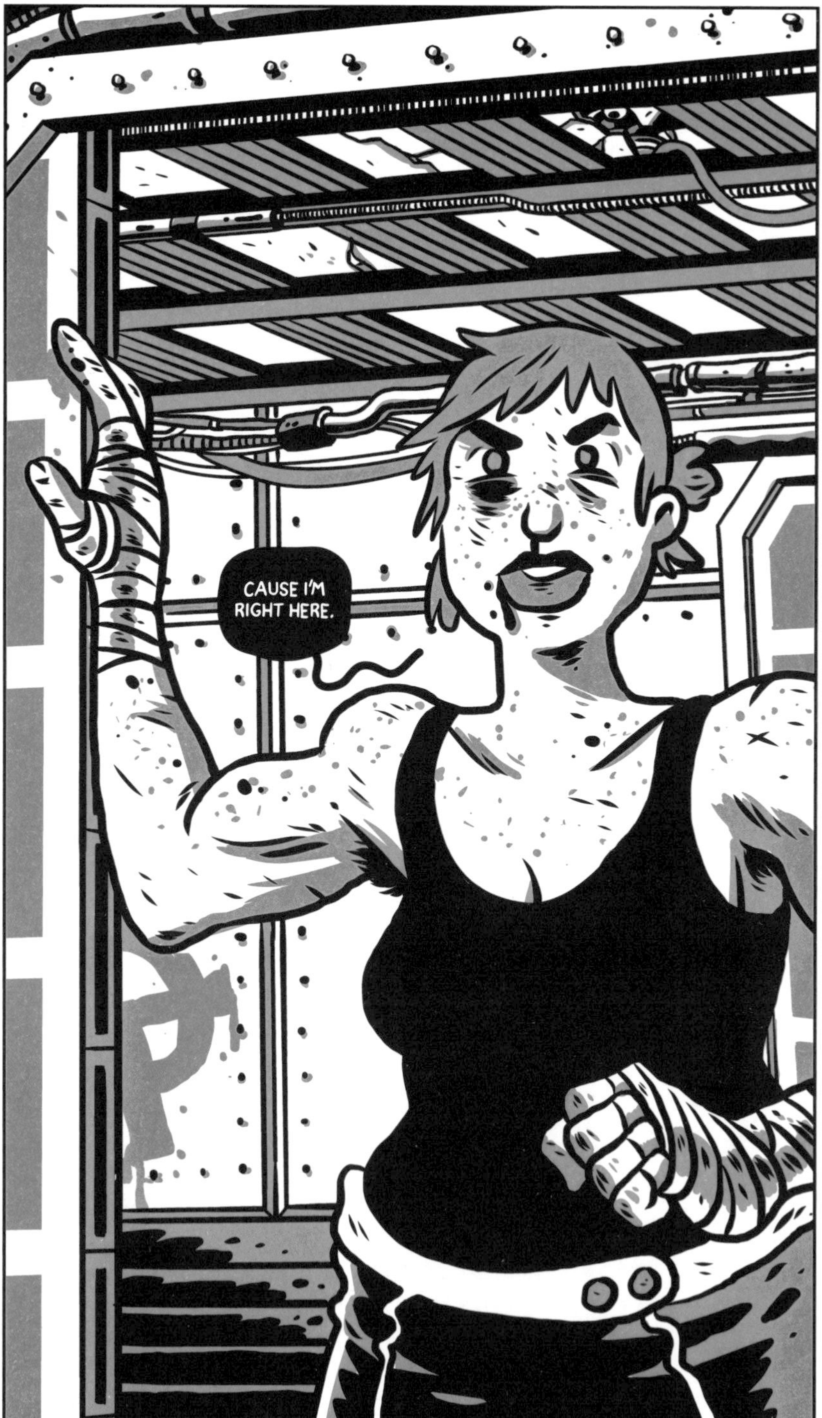
CAUSE I'M
RIGHT HERE.

PART 11: THE GREATEST

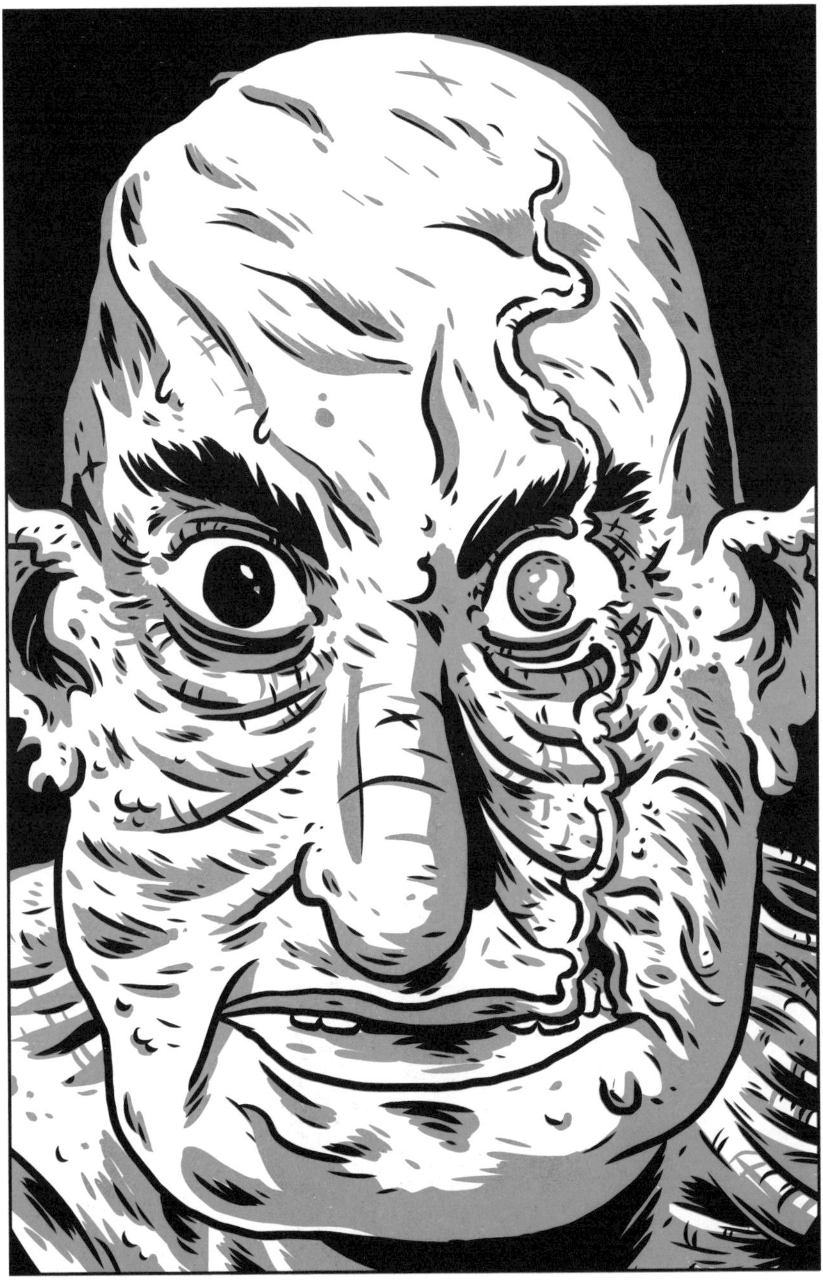

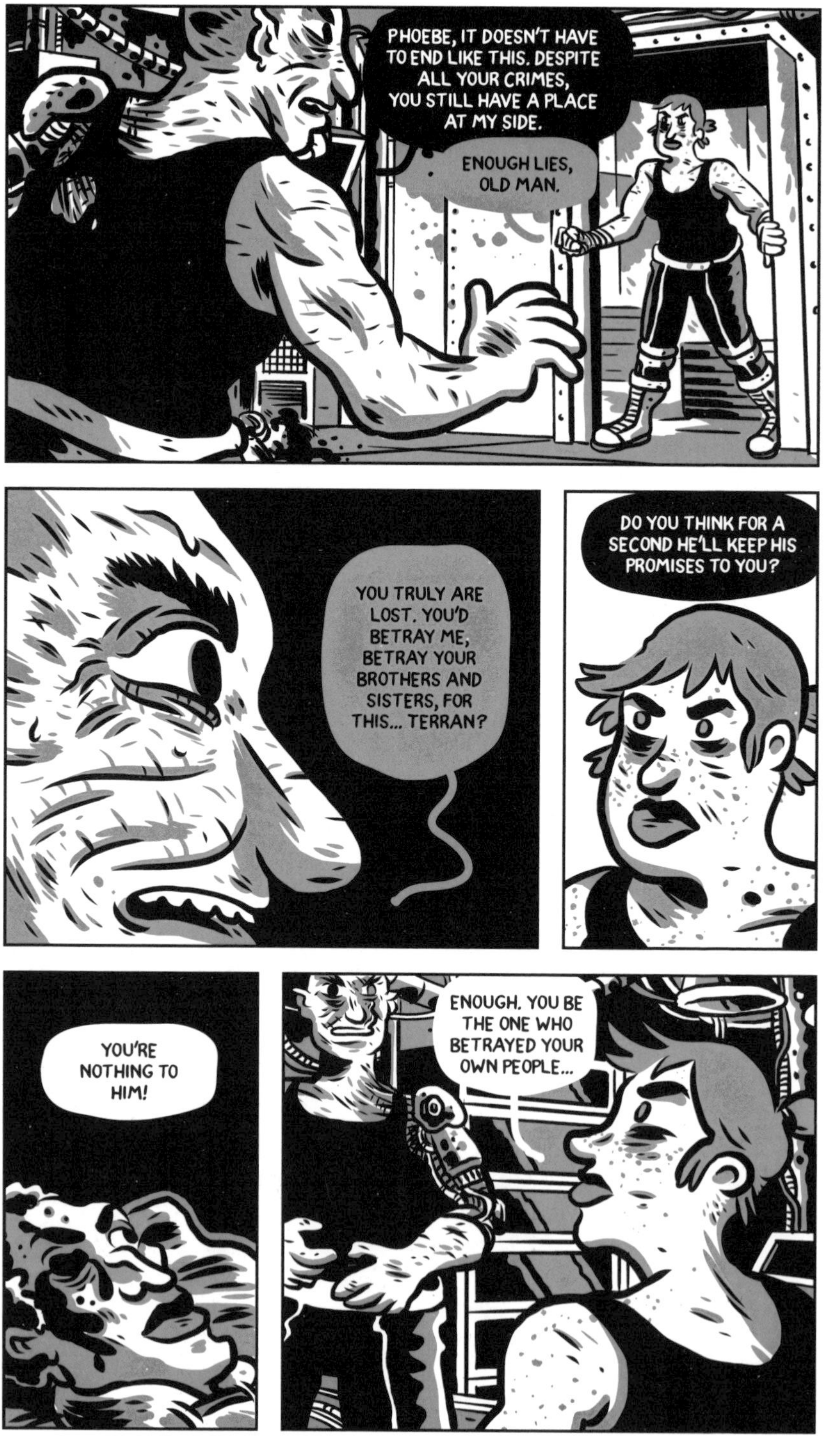
PHOEBE, IT DOESN'T HAVE TO END LIKE THIS. DESPITE ALL YOUR CRIMES, YOU STILL HAVE A PLACE AT MY SIDE.
ENOUGH LIES, OLD MAN.
YOU TRULY ARE LOST. YOU'D BETRAY ME, BETRAY YOUR BROTHERS AND SISTERS, FOR THIS... TERRAN?
DO YOU THINK FOR A SECOND HE'LL KEEP HIS PROMISES TO YOU?
YOU'RE NOTHING TO HIM!
ENOUGH. YOU BE THE ONE WHO BETRAYED YOUR OWN PEOPLE...

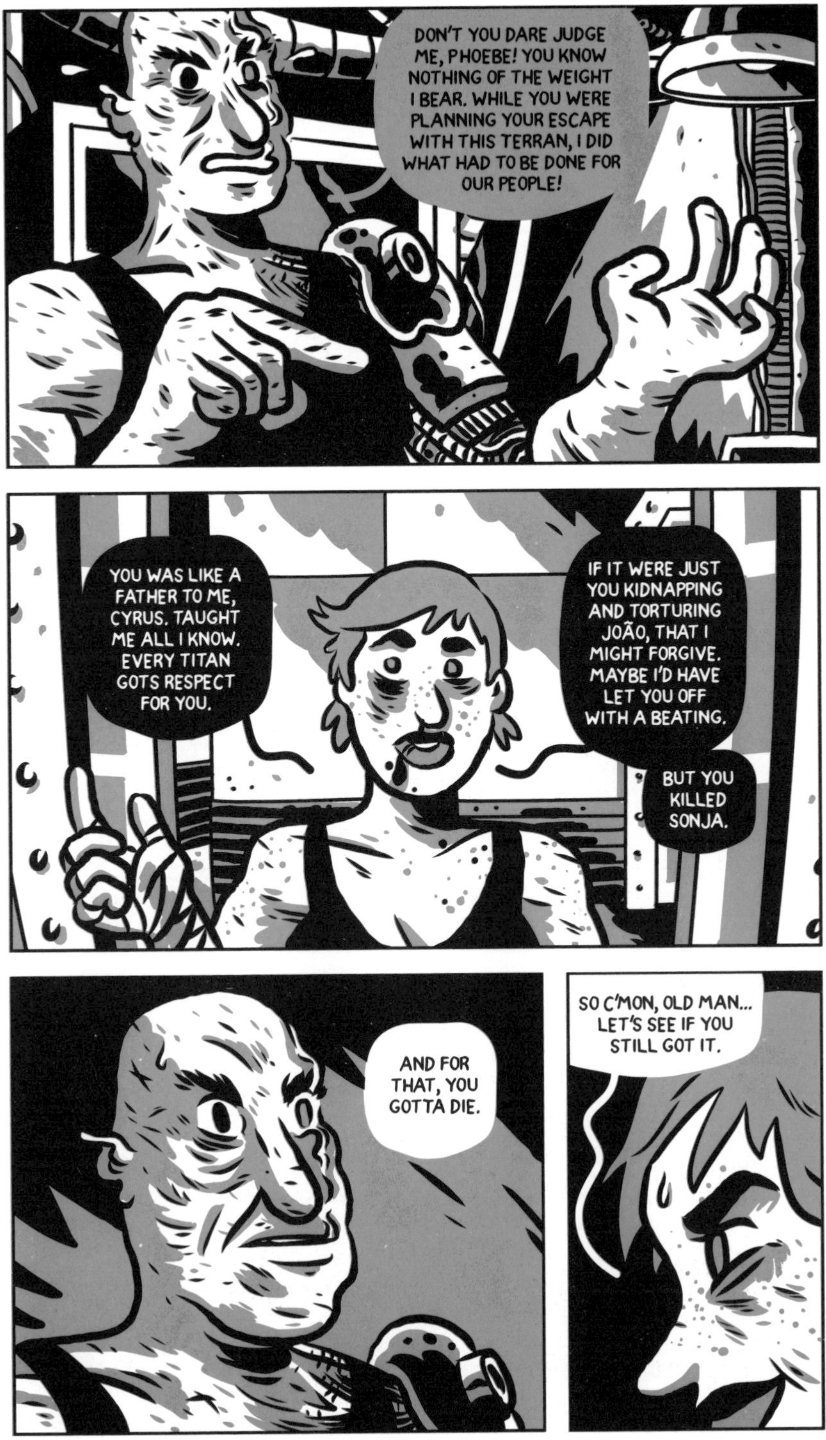
DON'T YOU DARE JUDGE ME, PHOEBE! YOU KNOW NOTHING OF THE WEIGHT I BEAR. WHILE YOU WERE PLANNING YOUR ESCAPE WITH THIS TERRAN, I DID WHAT HAD TO BE DONE FOR OUR PEOPLE!
YOU WAS LIKE A FATHER TO ME, CYRUS. TAUGHT ME ALL I KNOW. EVERY TITAN GOTS RESPECT FOR YOU.
IF IT WERE JUST YOU KIDNAPPING AND TORTURING JOÃO, THAT I MIGHT FORGIVE. MAYBE I'D HAVE LET YOU OFF WITH A BEATING.
BUT YOU KILLED SONJA.
AND FOR THAT, YOU GOTTA DIE.
SO C'MON, OLD MAN... LET'S SEE IF YOU STILL GOT IT.

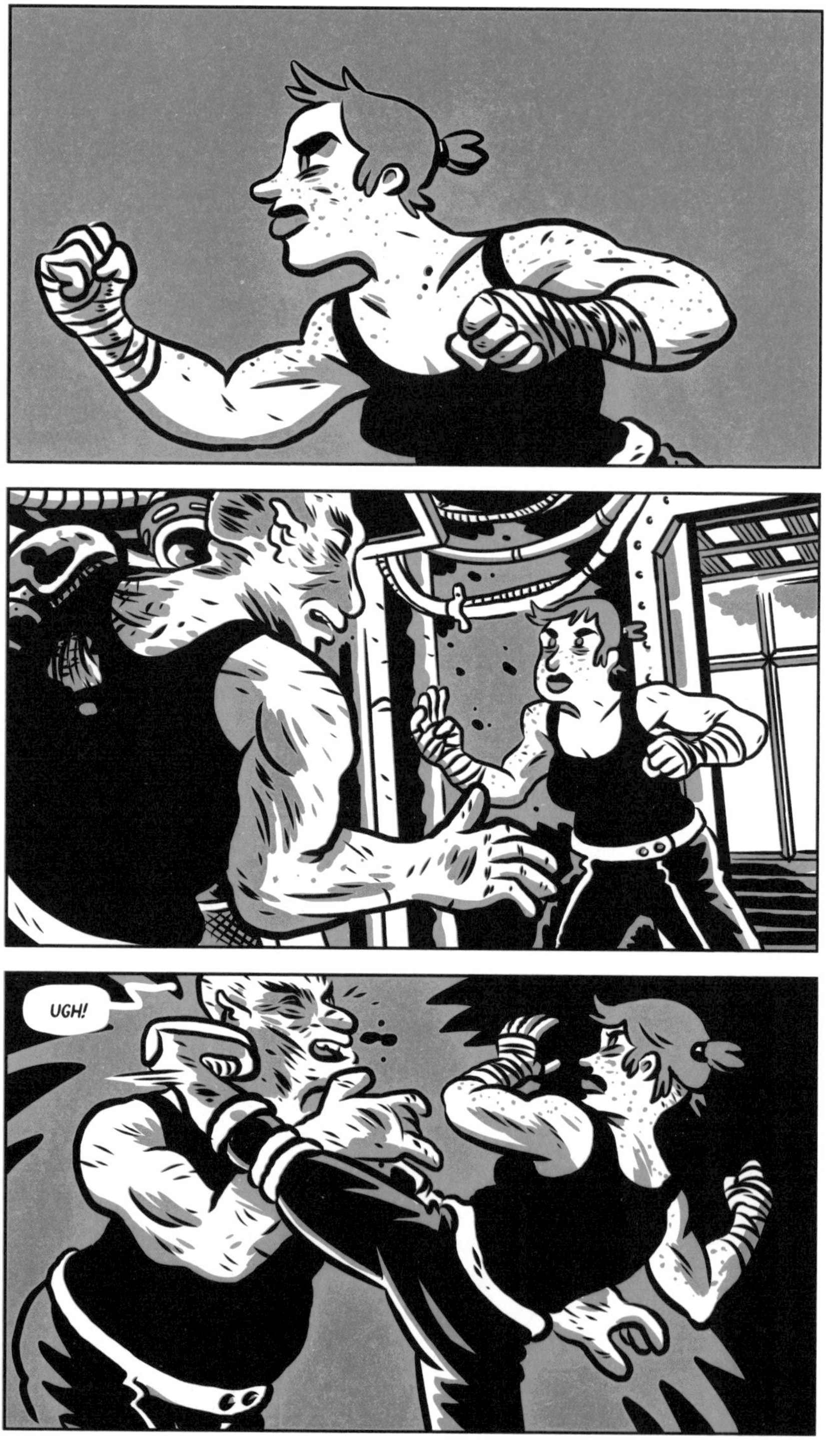
UGH!

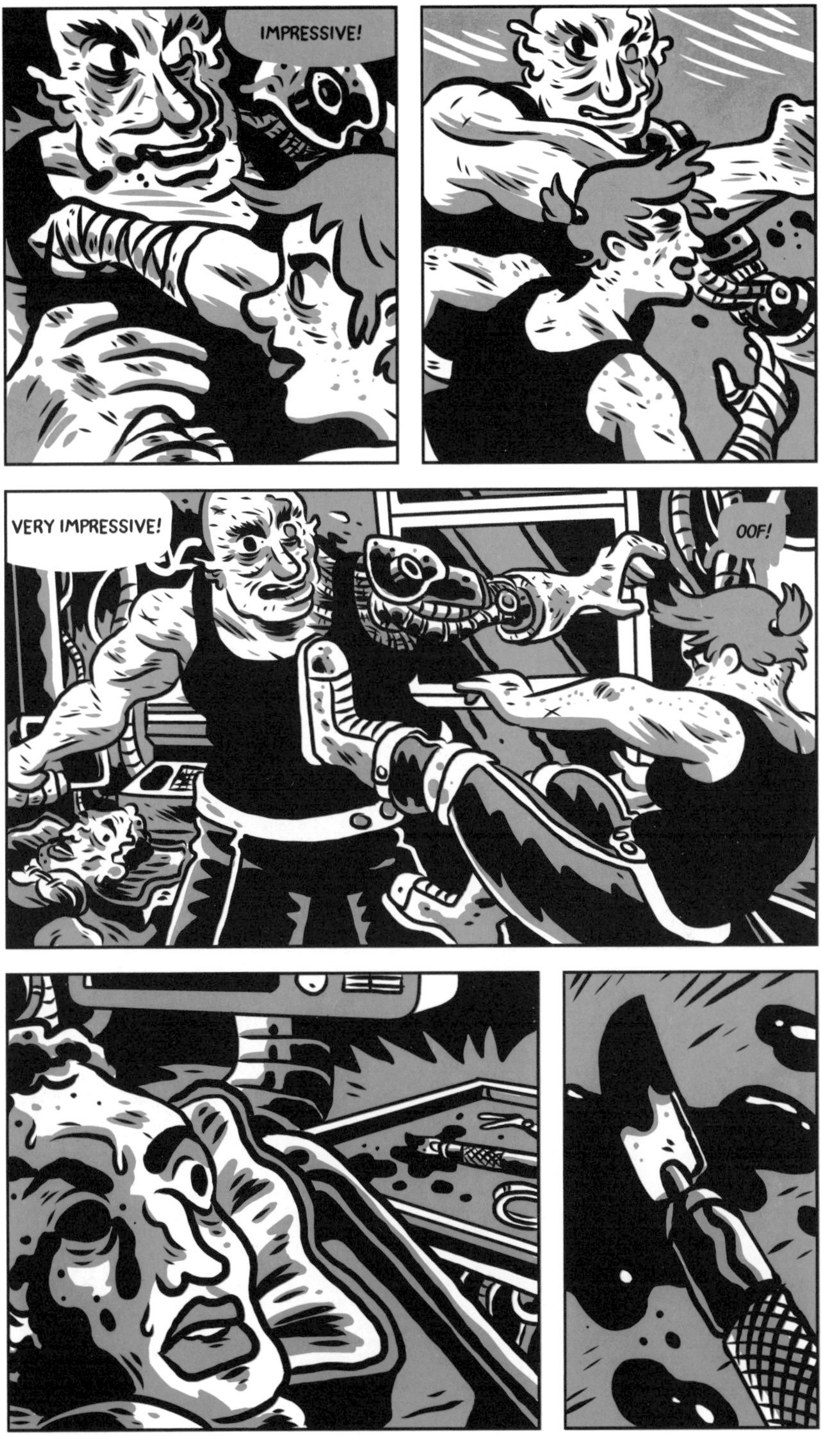
IMPRESSIVE!
VERY IMPRESSIVE!
OOF!

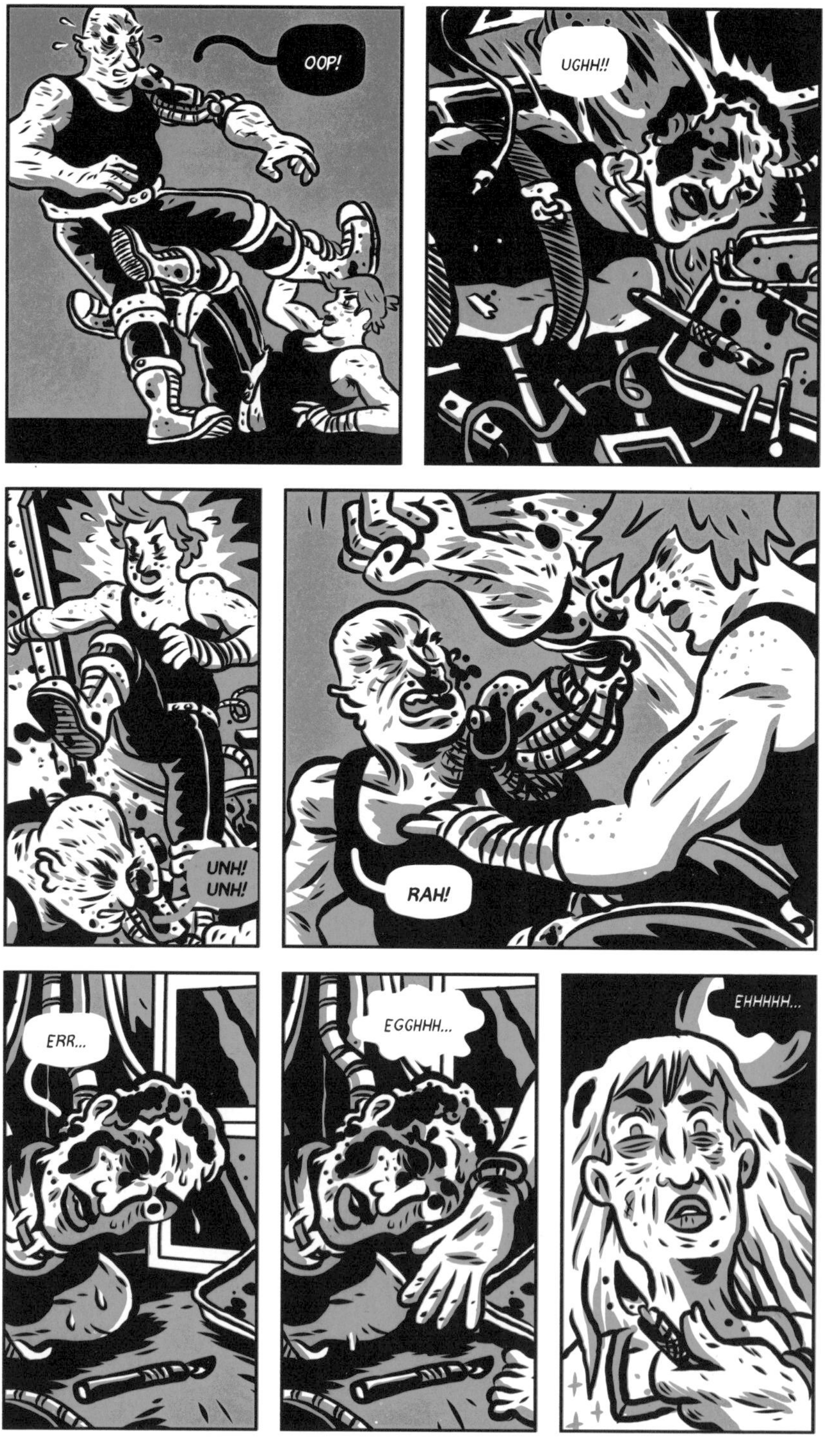
OOP!
UGHH!!
UNH! UNH!
RAH!
ERR...
EGGHHH...
EHHHHH...

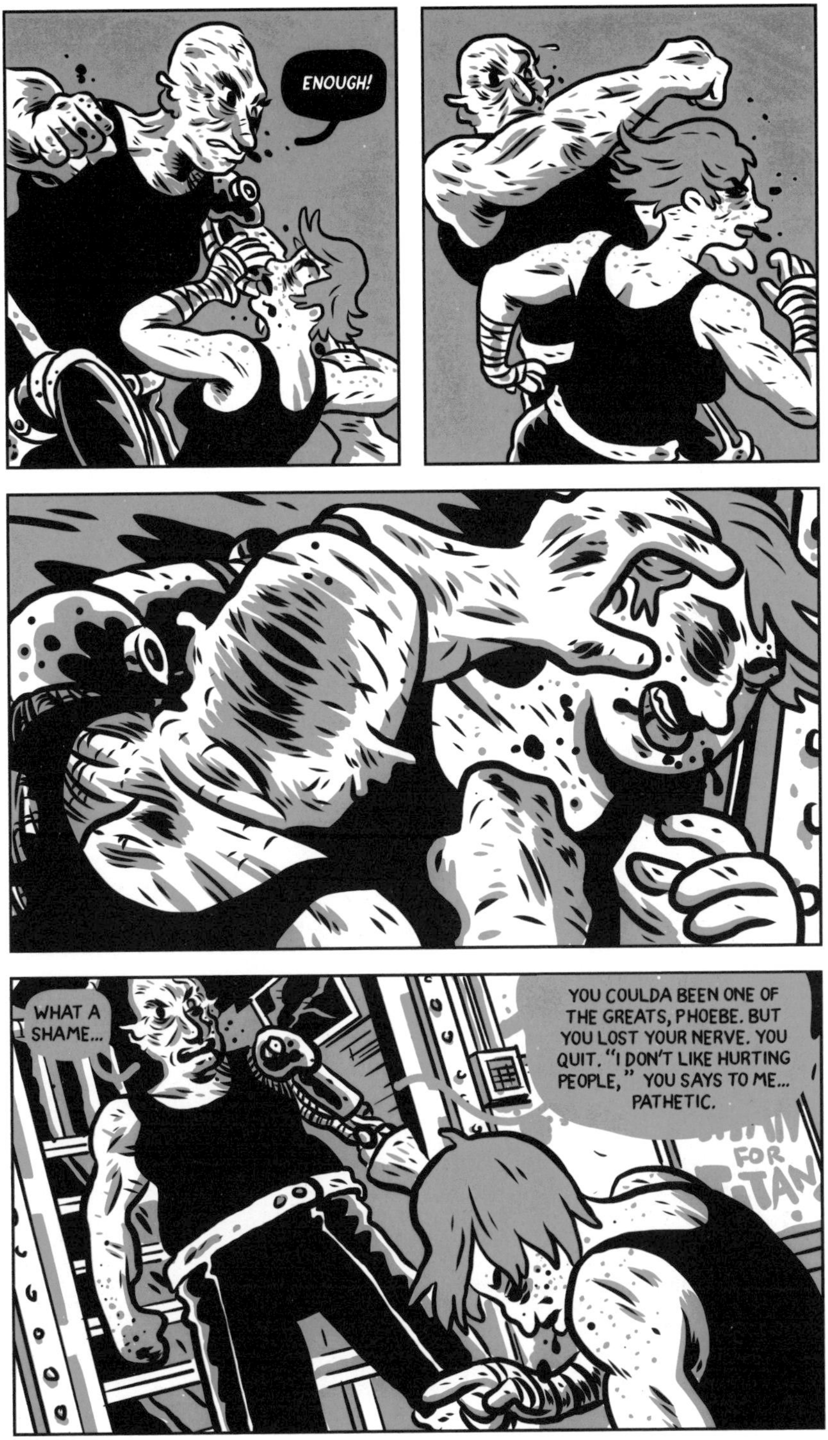
ENOUGH!
WHAT A SHAME...
YOU COULDA BEEN ONE OF THE GREATS, PHOEBE. BUT YOU LOST YOUR NERVE. YOU QUIT. "I DON'T LIKE HURTING PEOPLE," YOU SAYS TO ME... PATHETIC.
FOR

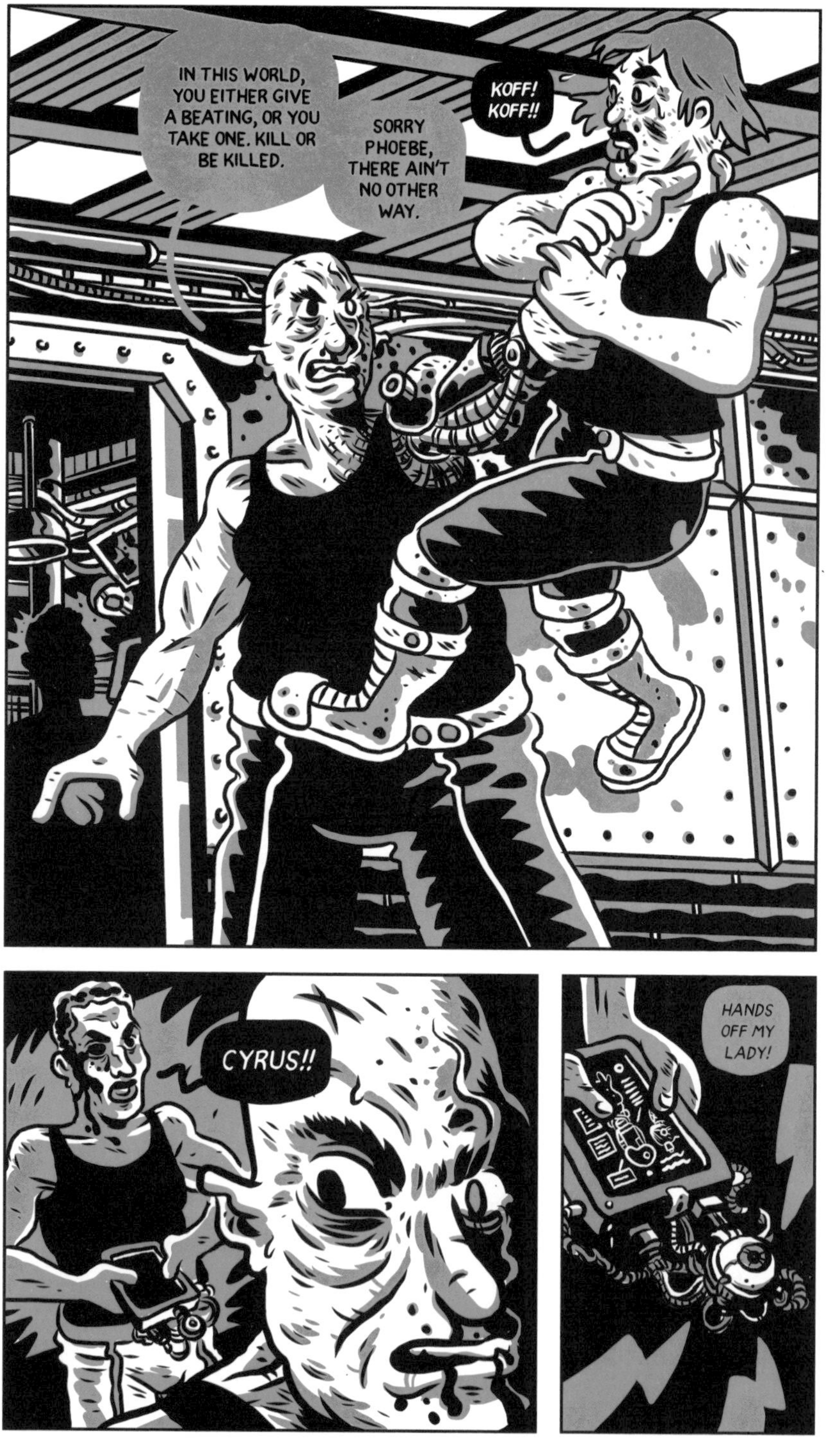
IN THIS WORLD, YOU EITHER GIVE A BEATING, OR YOU TAKE ONE. KILL OR BE KILLED.
SORRY PHOEBE, THERE AIN'T NO OTHER WAY.
KOFF! KOFF!!
CYRUS!!
HANDS OFF MY LADY!

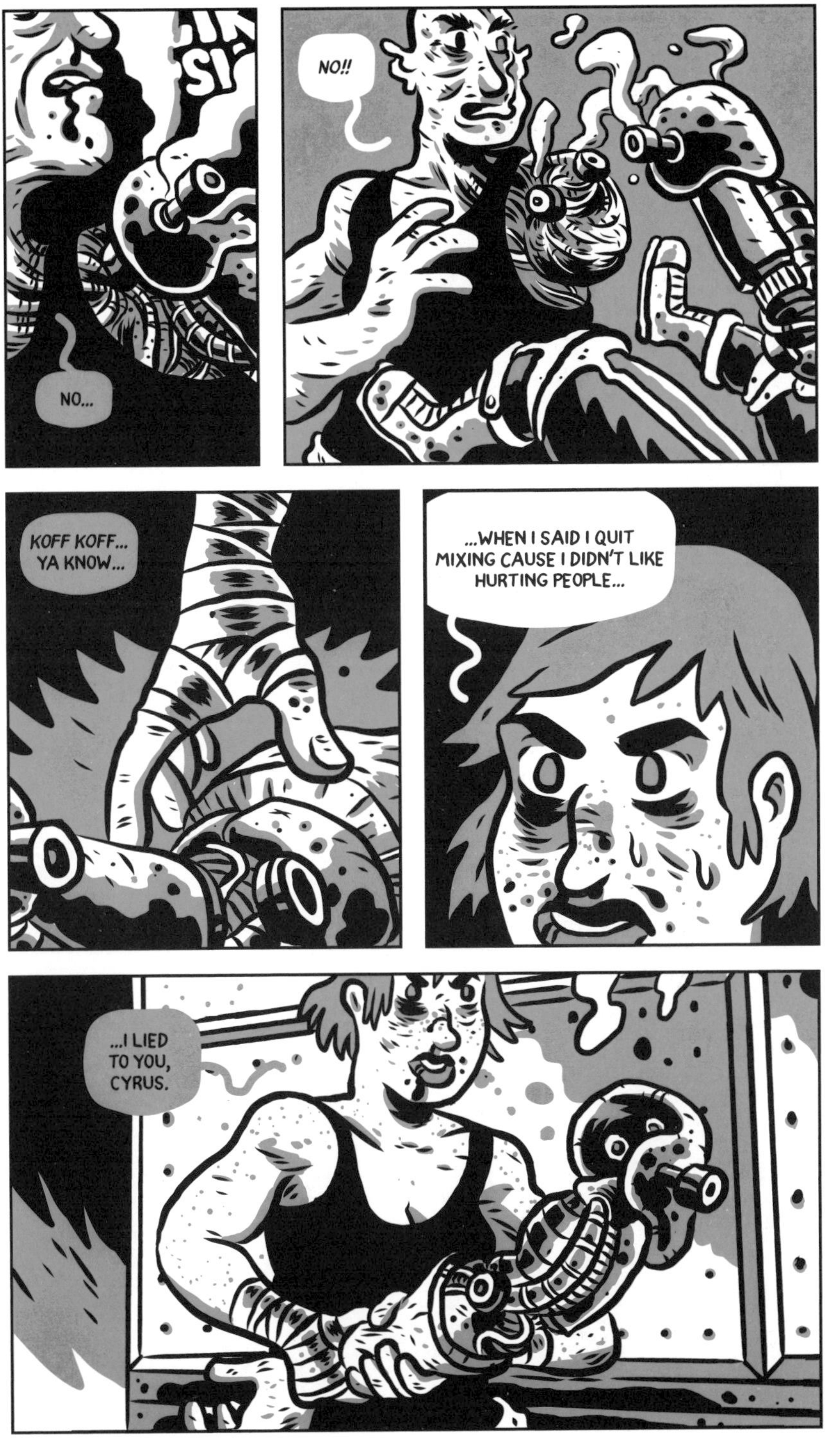
NO...
NO!!
KOFF KOFF... YA KNOW...
...WHEN I SAID I QUIT MIXING CAUSE I DIDN'T LIKE HURTING PEOPLE...
...I LIED TO YOU, CYRUS.

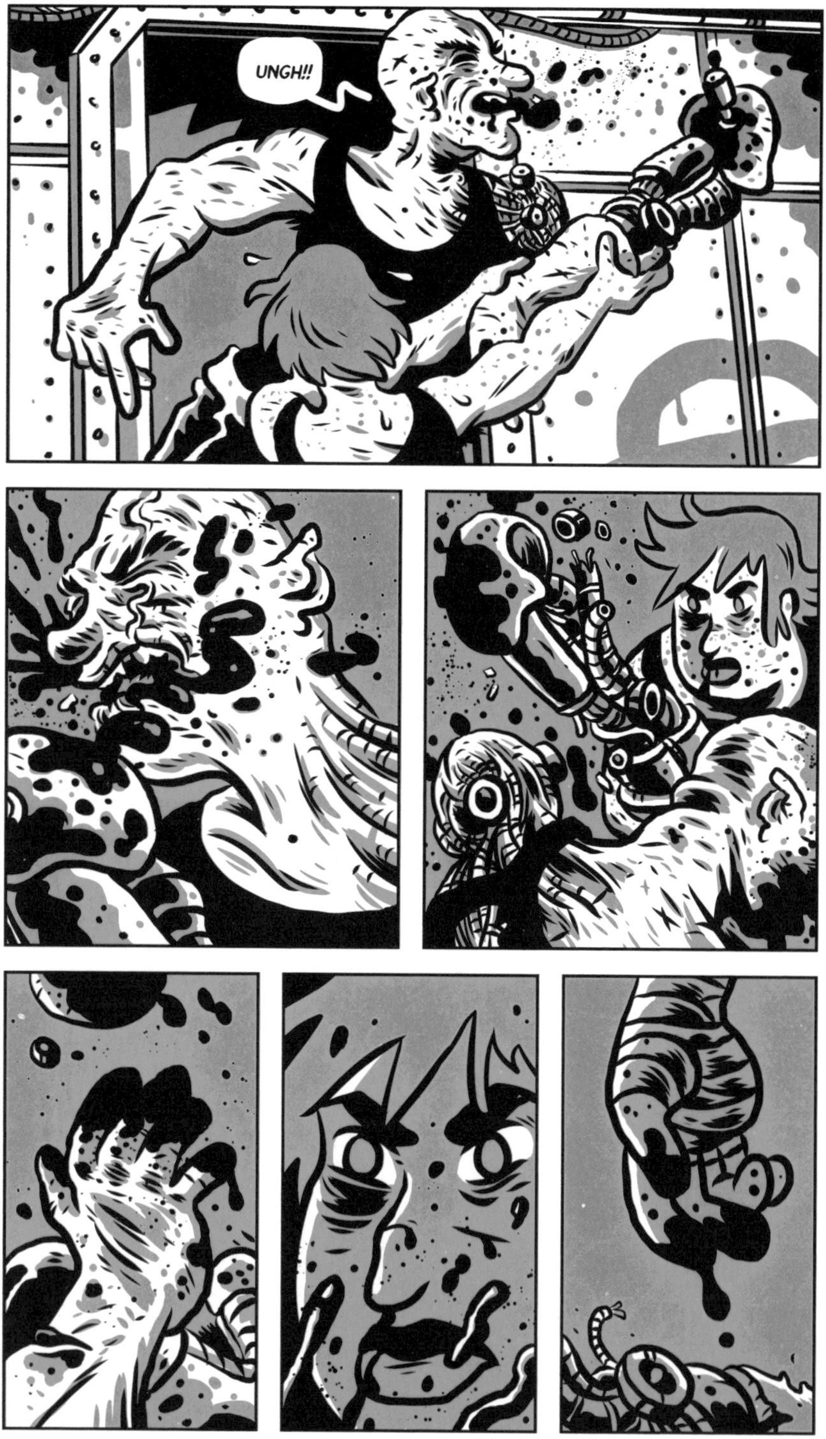
UNGH!!

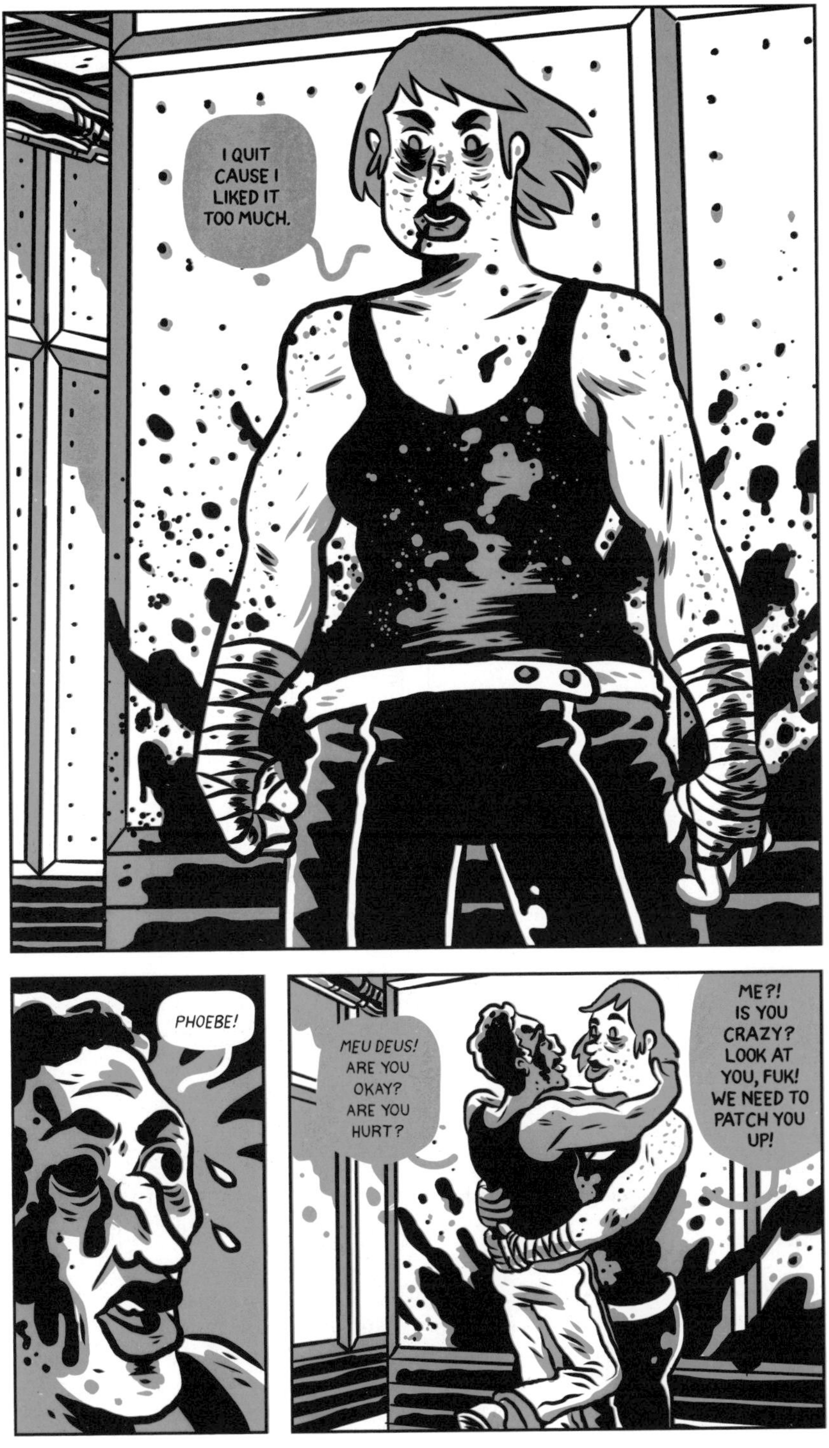
I QUIT CAUSE I LIKED IT TOO MUCH.
PHOEBE!
MEU DEUS! ARE YOU OKAY? ARE YOU HURT?
ME?! IS YOU CRAZY? LOOK AT YOU, FUK! WE NEED TO PATCH YOU UP!

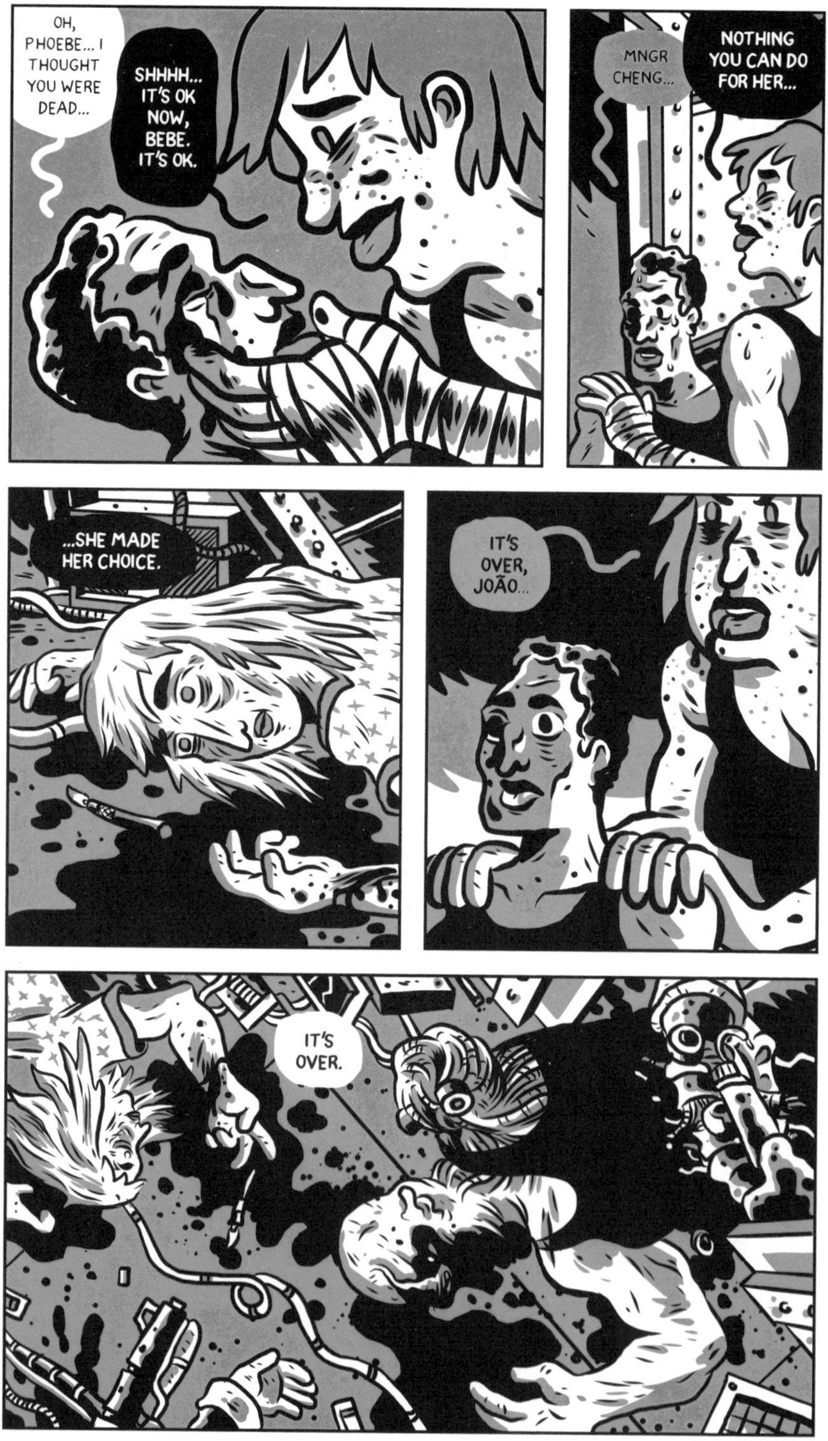
OH, PHOEBE... I THOUGHT YOU WERE DEAD...
SHHHH... IT'S OK NOW, BEBE. IT'S OK.
MNGR CHENG...
NOTHING YOU CAN DO FOR HER...
...SHE MADE HER CHOICE.
IT'S OVER, JOÃO...
IT'S OVER.

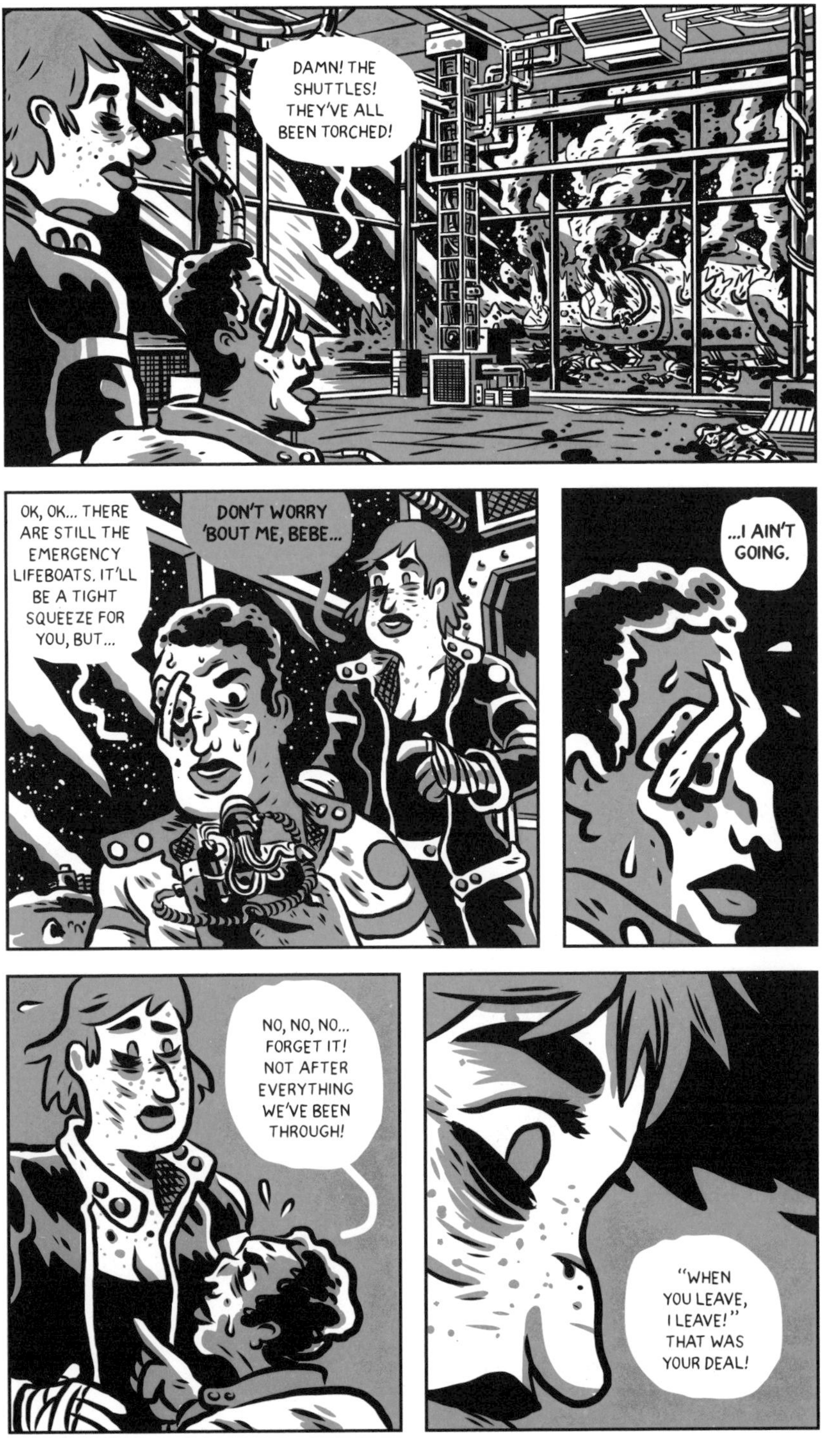
DAMN! THE SHUTTLES! THEY'VE ALL BEEN TORCHED!
OK, OK... THERE ARE STILL THE EMERGENCY LIFEBOATS. IT'LL BE A TIGHT SQUEEZE FOR YOU, BUT...
DON'T WORRY 'BOUT ME, BEBE...
...I AIN'T GOING.
NO, NO, NO... FORGET IT! NOT AFTER EVERYTHING WE'VE BEEN THROUGH!
"WHEN YOU LEAVE, I LEAVE!" THAT WAS YOUR DEAL!

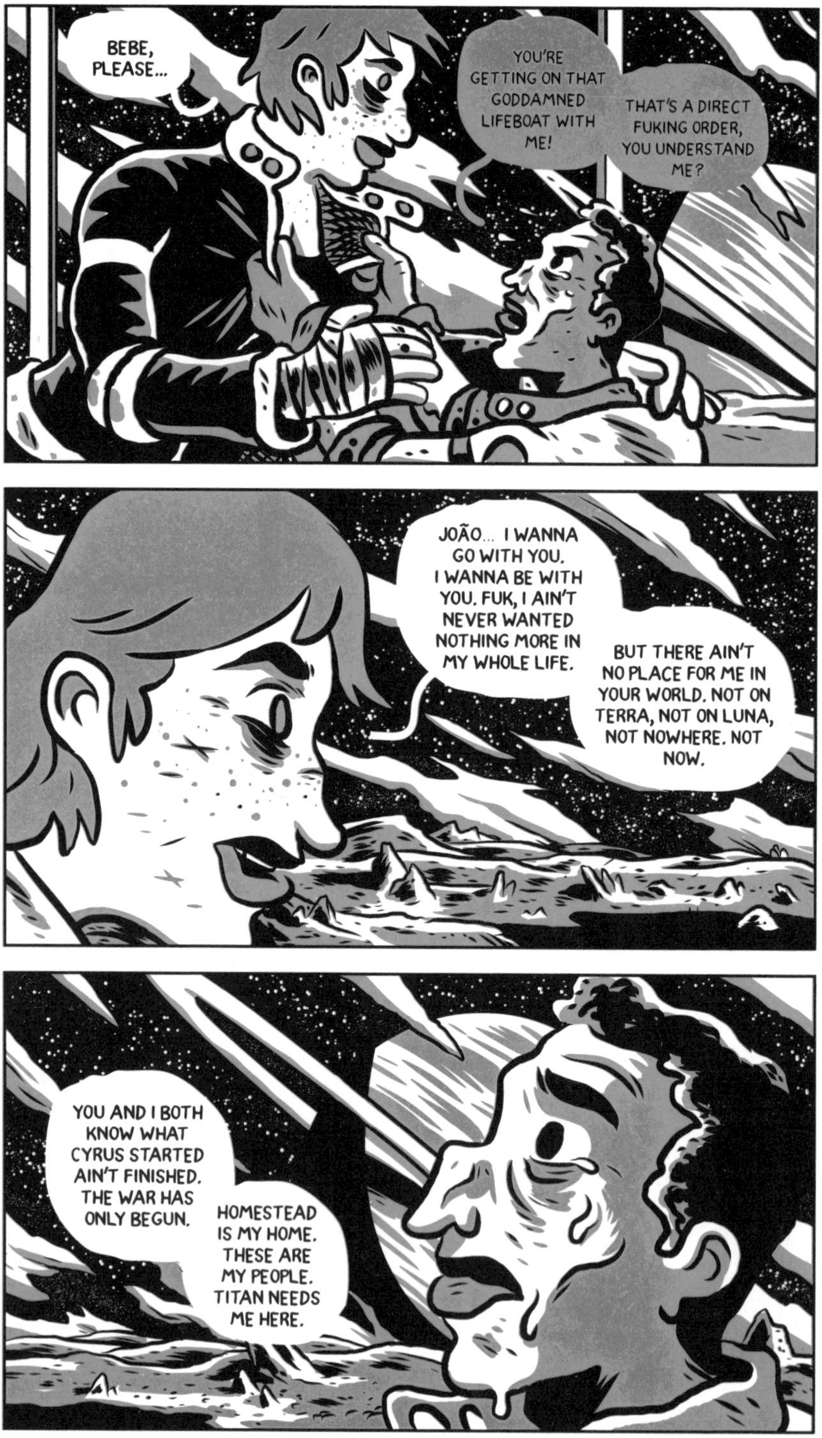
BEBE, PLEASE...
YOU'RE GETTING ON THAT GODDAMNED LIFEBOAT WITH ME!
THAT'S A DIRECT FUKING ORDER, YOU UNDERSTAND ME?
JOÃO... I WANNA GO WITH YOU. I WANNA BE WITH YOU. FUK, I AIN'T NEVER WANTED NOTHING MORE IN MY WHOLE LIFE.
BUT THERE AIN'T NO PLACE FOR ME IN YOUR WORLD. NOT ON TERRA, NOT ON LUNA, NOT NOWHERE. NOT NOW.
YOU AND I BOTH KNOW WHAT CYRUS STARTED AIN'T FINISHED. THE WAR HAS ONLY BEGUN.
HOMESTEAD IS MY HOME. THESE ARE MY PEOPLE. TITAN NEEDS ME HERE.

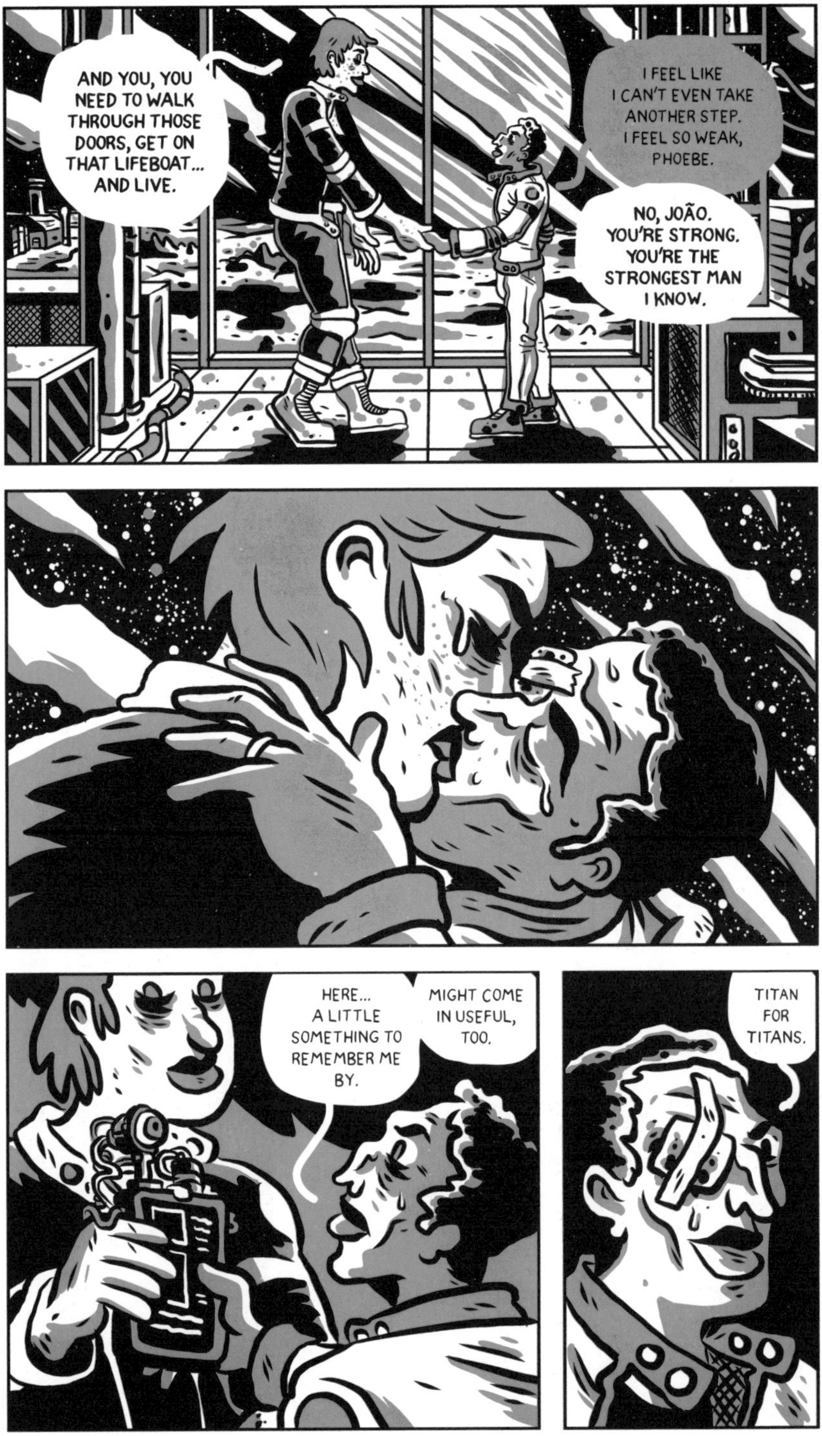
AND YOU, YOU NEED TO WALK THROUGH THOSE DOORS, GET ON THAT LIFEBOAT... AND LIVE.
I FEEL LIKE I CAN'T EVEN TAKE ANOTHER STEP. I FEEL SO WEAK, PHOEBE.
NO, JOÃO. YOU'RE STRONG. YOU'RE THE STRONGEST MAN I KNOW.
HERE... A LITTLE SOMETHING TO REMEMBER ME BY.
MIGHT COME IN USEFUL, TOO.
TITAN FOR TITANS.

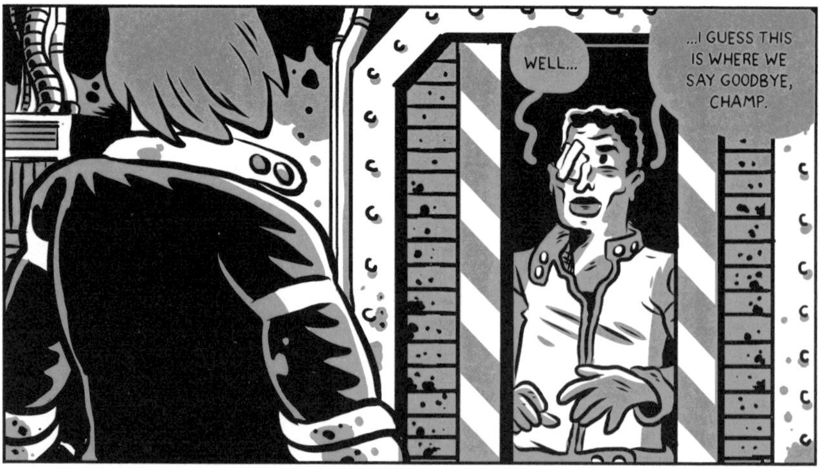
WELL...
...I GUESS THIS IS WHERE WE SAY GOODBYE, CHAMP.

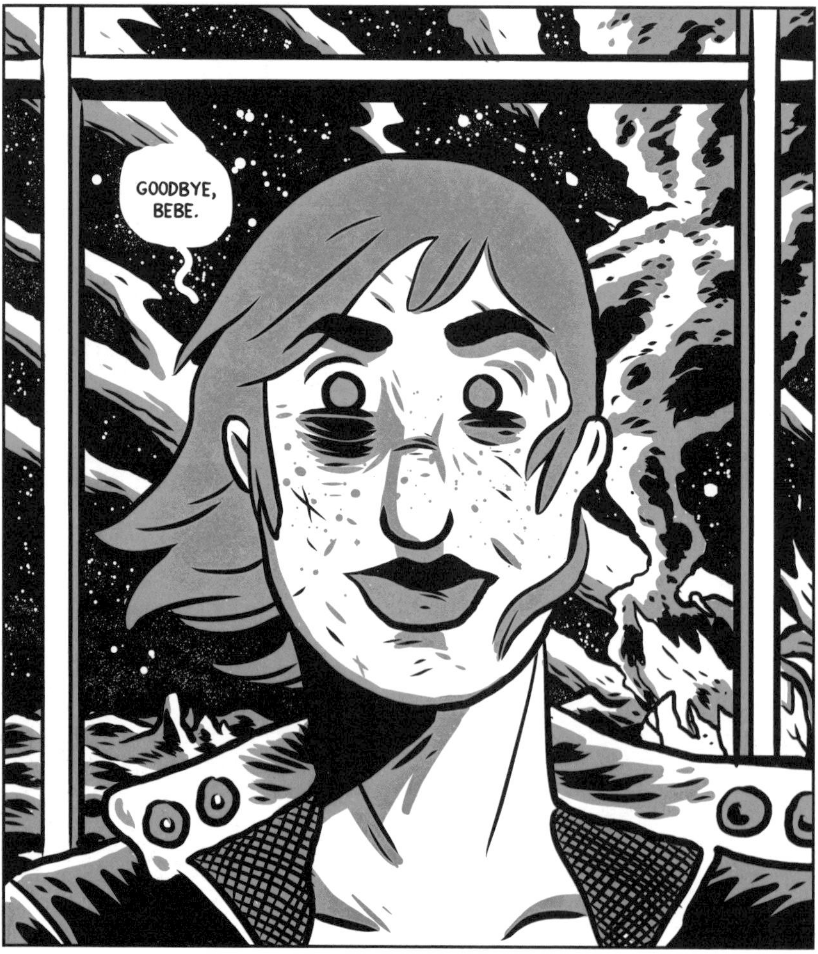
GOODBYE, BEBE.

PART 12: AFTER THE GOLD RUSH

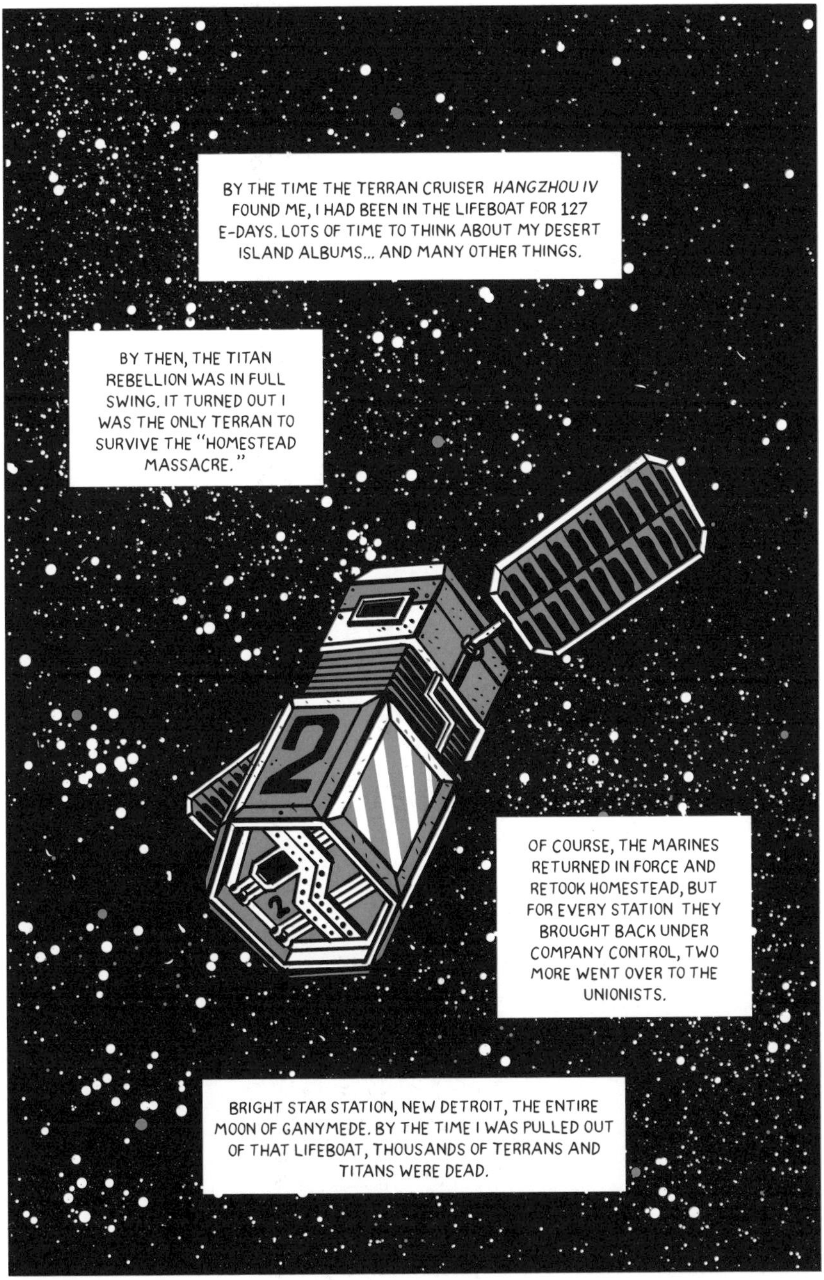
BY THE TIME THE TERRAN CRUISER *HANGZHOU IV* FOUND ME, I HAD BEEN IN THE LIFEBOAT FOR 127 E-DAYS. LOTS OF TIME TO THINK ABOUT MY DESERT ISLAND ALBUMS... AND MANY OTHER THINGS.
BY THEN, THE TITAN REBELLION WAS IN FULL SWING. IT TURNED OUT I WAS THE ONLY TERRAN TO SURVIVE THE "HOMESTEAD MASSACRE."
2
2
OF COURSE, THE MARINES RETURNED IN FORCE AND RETOOK HOMESTEAD, BUT FOR EVERY STATION THEY BROUGHT BACK UNDER COMPANY CONTROL, TWO MORE WENT OVER TO THE UNIONISTS.
BRIGHT STAR STATION, NEW DETROIT, THE ENTIRE MOON OF GANYMEDE. BY THE TIME I WAS PULLED OUT OF THAT LIFEBOAT, THOUSANDS OF TERRANS AND TITANS WERE DEAD.

THE UNIONISTS WERE ALWAYS ON THE MOVE. THERE WERE THOUSANDS OF REBELS SPREAD OVER MILLIONS OF KILOMETERS OF SPACE, ON MOONS AND FREIGHTERS AND THE COUNTLESS ASTEROIDS OF THE BELT.

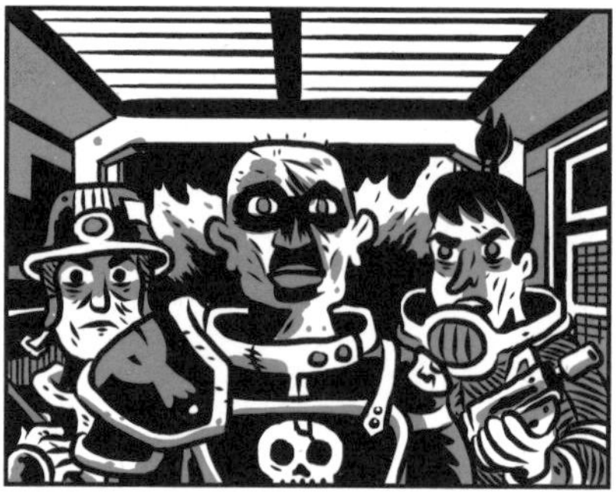

AND OF COURSE, THE TITANS HAD THEIR VERY OWN WARSHIP NOW: THE CAPTURED *USS MERLYN*, RECHRISTENED AFTER THEIR GREATEST MARTYR...

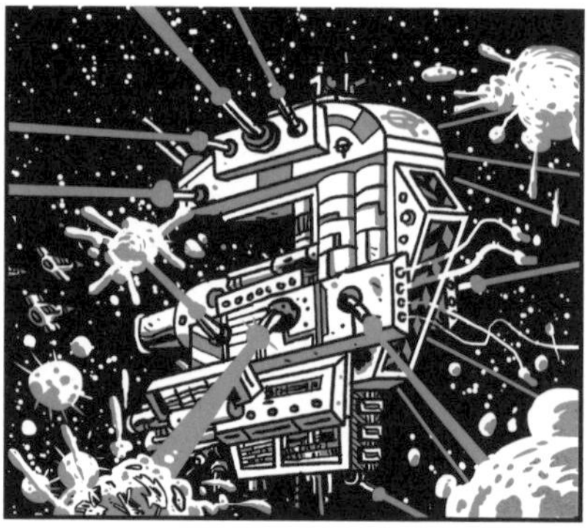

...CYRUS THE GREAT, THE CHAMPION OF TITAN, FATHER OF THE REVOLUTION. LAID LOW BY THE TREACHERY OF THE TERRAN MNGR JOÃO DA SILVA.

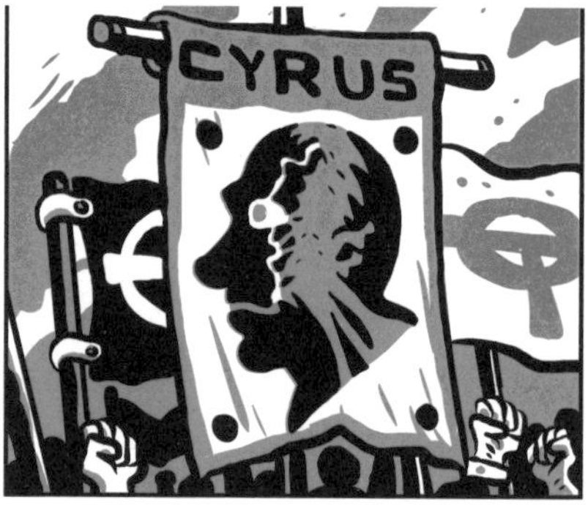
CYRUS

YES, THE TITANS BELIEVED I HAD KILLED CYRUS. AND I IMAGINE PHOEBE DID LITTLE TO DISSUADE THEM FROM THIS LIE. IN FACT, SHE MUST HAVE BEEN THE ONE WHO STARTED IT.

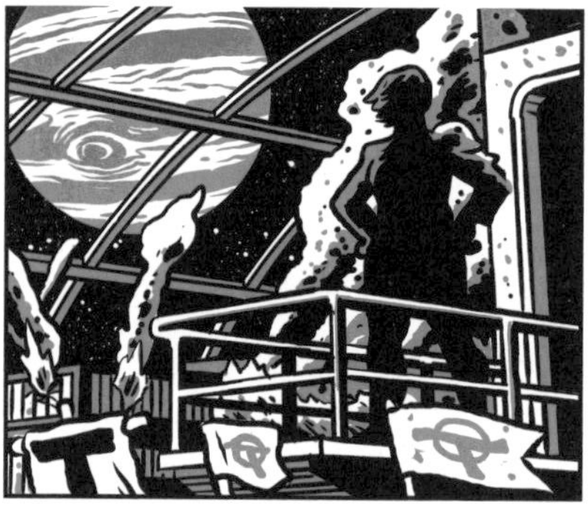

AND THE TITANS WEREN'T THE ONLY ONES WHO BOUGHT THE STORY. FOR MY PART, I WAS WELCOMED BACK TO TERRA AS A WAR HERO. JOÃO THE GIANT KILLER! THE HERO OF HOMESTEAD! IT MADE ME SICK.

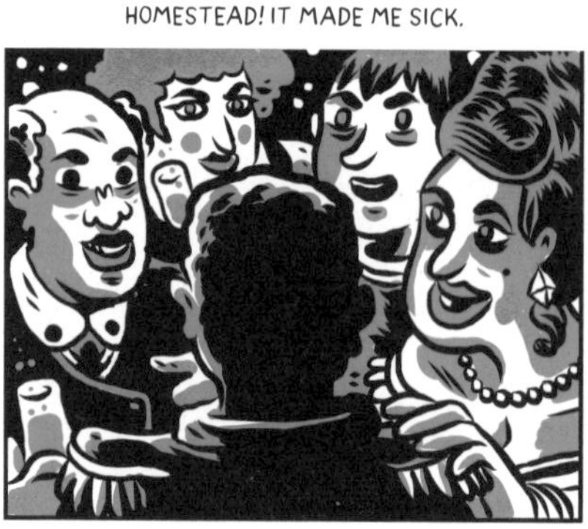

MOST OF MY FELLOW TERRANS STILL THOUGHT IT WAS A JUST A LITTLE REVOLT. HIT THE TITAN SCUM HARD ENOUGH, AND THEY WOULD FALL BACK IN LINE.

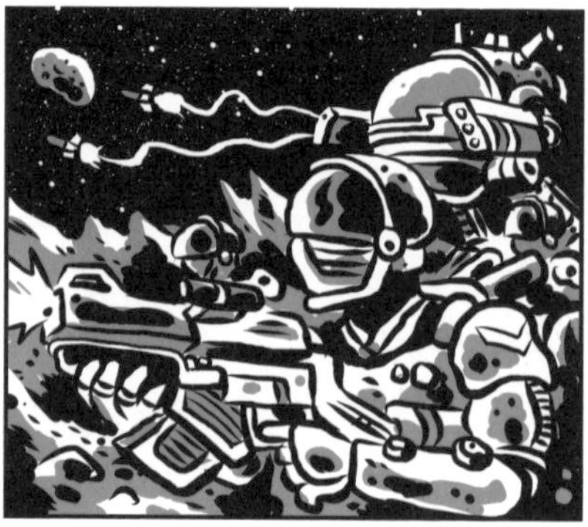

THAT WAS BEFORE THE FIRST "HAMMERS" FELL.
ALL THINGS CONSIDERED, WE GOT OFF EASY.
A FEW RANDOM STRIKES, AND THE TITANS DIDN'T
SEND ANYTHING BIGGER THAN 500 METERS.
NO MAJOR URBAN CENTERS WERE HIT.
JUST OVER TWO MILLION DEAD, PLANET WIDE.

TRUE, TERRA'S ORBITAL DEFENSES COULD CATCH
NEARLY EVERYTHING THEY THREW AT US. BUT
THERE WOULD ALWAYS BE GAPS. WITH MILLIONS
OF ASTEROIDS TO CHOOSE FROM, THE UNIONISTS
COULD THREATEN ALL LIFE ON TERRA AND MARS.

THE TITANS HAVE A SAYING:
"THE WINNER AIN'T THE ONE WHO CAN
HIT THE HARDEST, BUT THE ONE WHO CAN TAKE
THE HARDEST HIT."

IT DIDN'T MATTER HOW HARD WE RETALIATED,
HOW MANY STATIONS WE BURNED TO THE
GROUND, THE TITANS WOULD FIGHT TO THE
DEATH... THEY HAD NOTHING TO LOSE.

BUT YOU TRY TELLING ELEVEN BILLION TERRAN
CITIZENS THAT HOLDING ONTO SOME ROCKS IN THE
DEPTHS OF SPACE IS WORTH THE CHANCE
A RANDOM ASTEROID ATTACK MIGHT VAPORIZE
THE CITY THEY LIVE IN.

AND SO, TOMORROW, NEW YEAR'S EVE 2199, THE
TREATY OF TRANQUILITY WILL BE SIGNED ON
LUNA, AND PEACE WILL BE DECLARED. AFTER
SEVEN BLOODY YEARS OF WAR, THE TITAN UNION
WILL BE FREE.

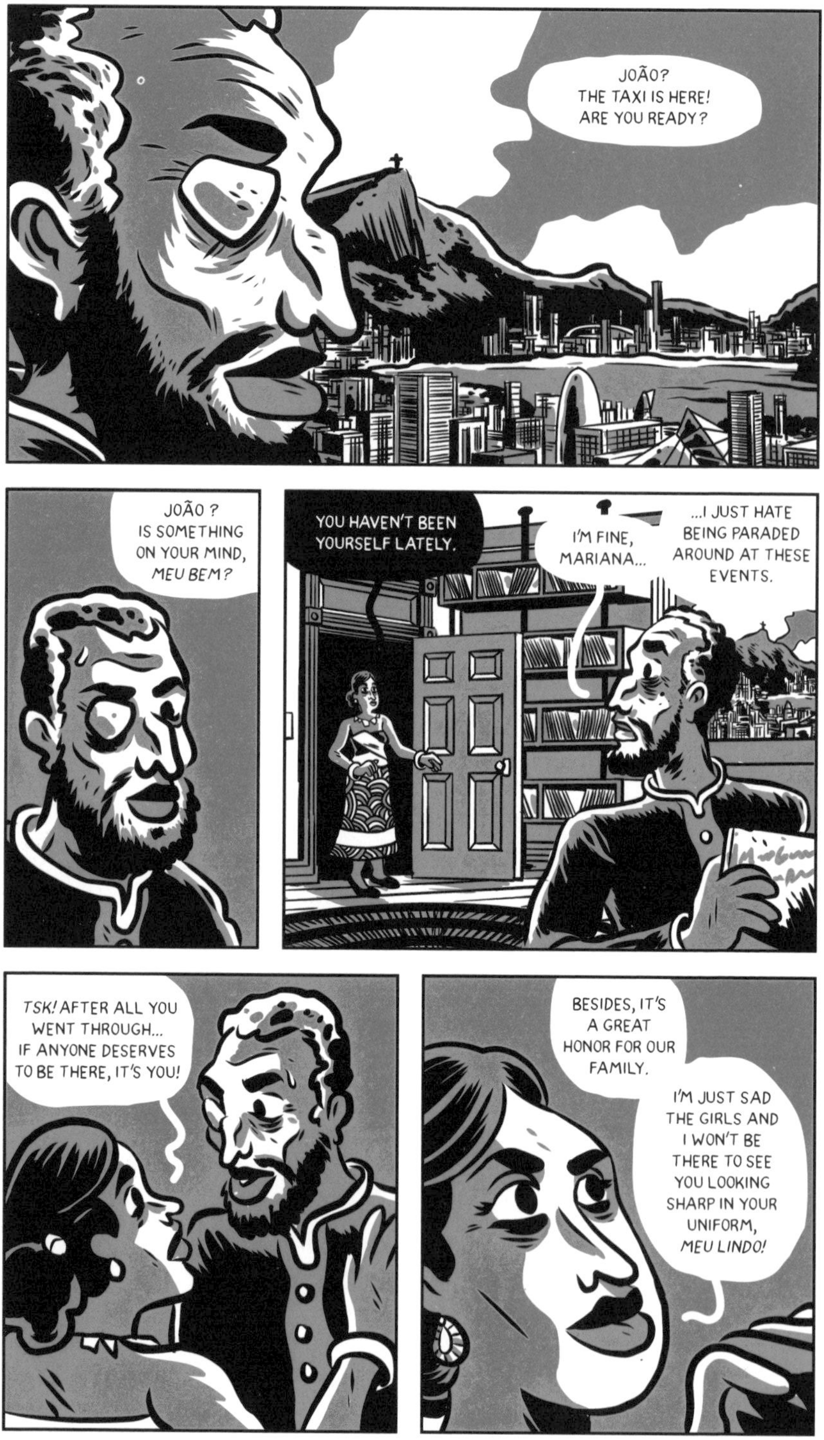
JOÃO?
THE TAXI IS HERE!
ARE YOU READY?
JOÃO ?
IS SOMETHING ON YOUR MIND, *MEU BEM?*
YOU HAVEN'T BEEN YOURSELF LATELY.
I'M FINE, MARIANA...
...I JUST HATE BEING PARADED AROUND AT THESE EVENTS.
TSK! AFTER ALL YOU WENT THROUGH... IF ANYONE DESERVES TO BE THERE, IT'S YOU!
BESIDES, IT'S A GREAT HONOR FOR OUR FAMILY.
I'M JUST SAD THE GIRLS AND I WON'T BE THERE TO SEE YOU LOOKING SHARP IN YOUR UNIFORM, *MEU LINDO!*

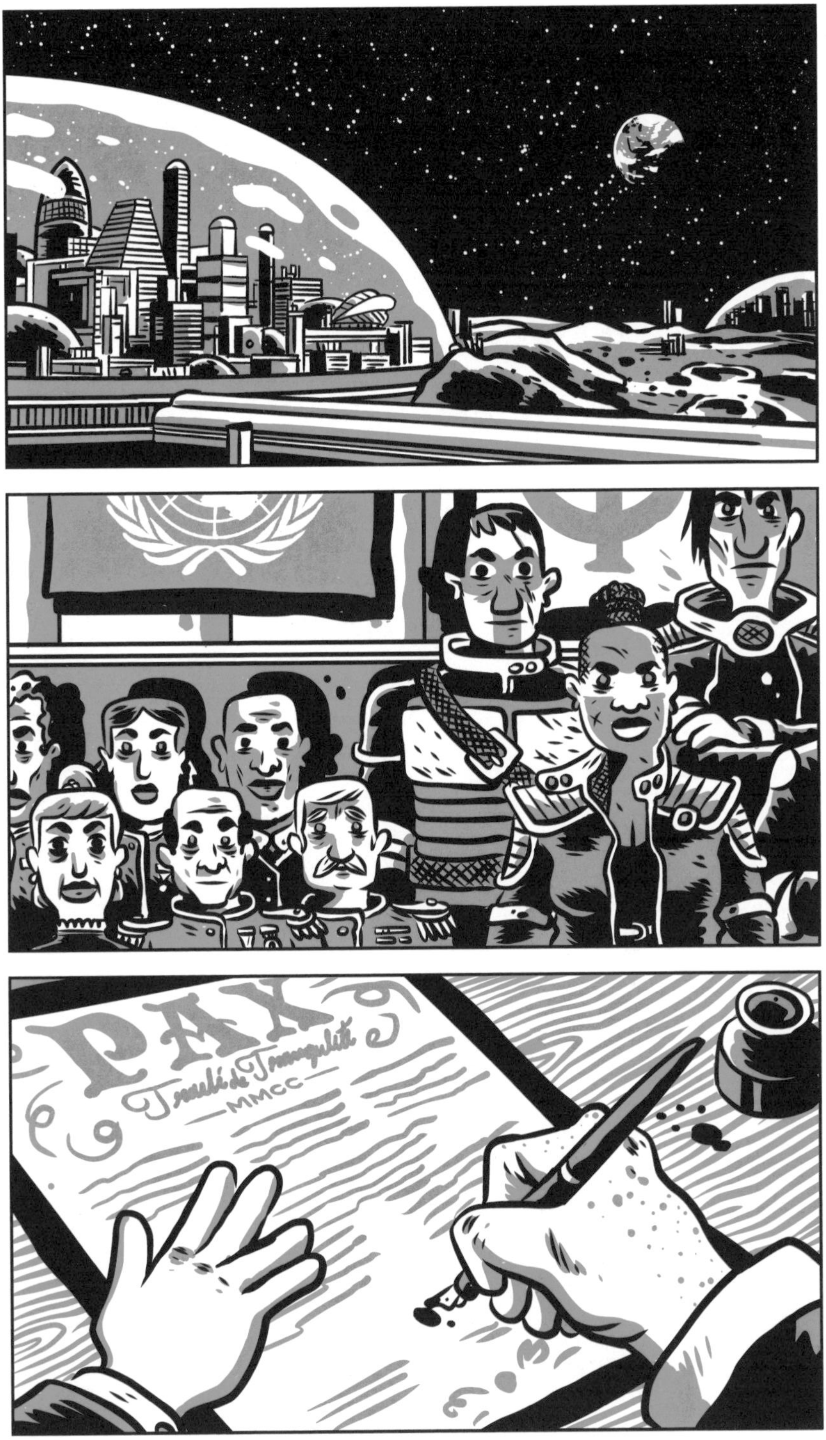
PAX
MMCC

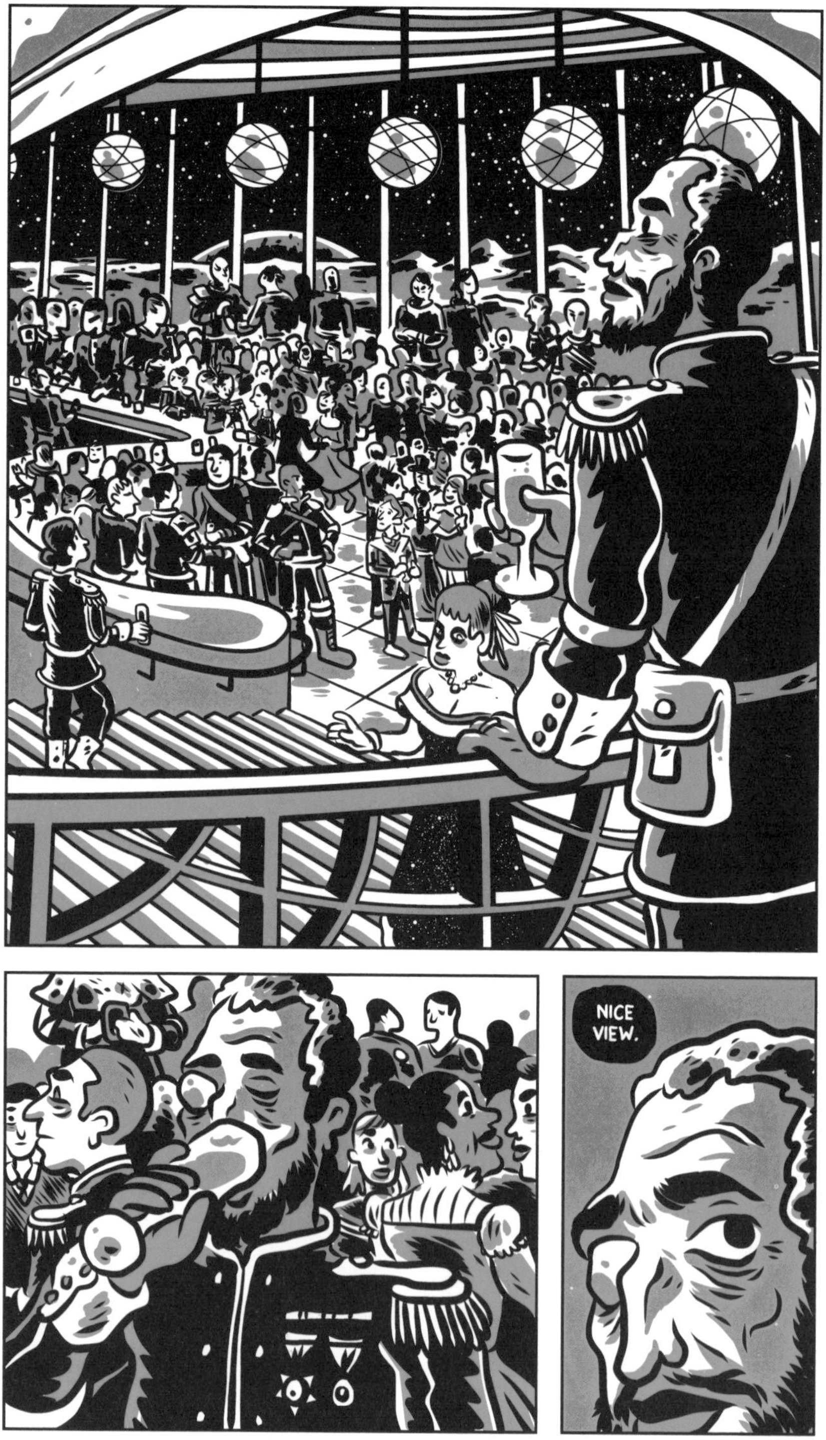
NICE
VIEW.

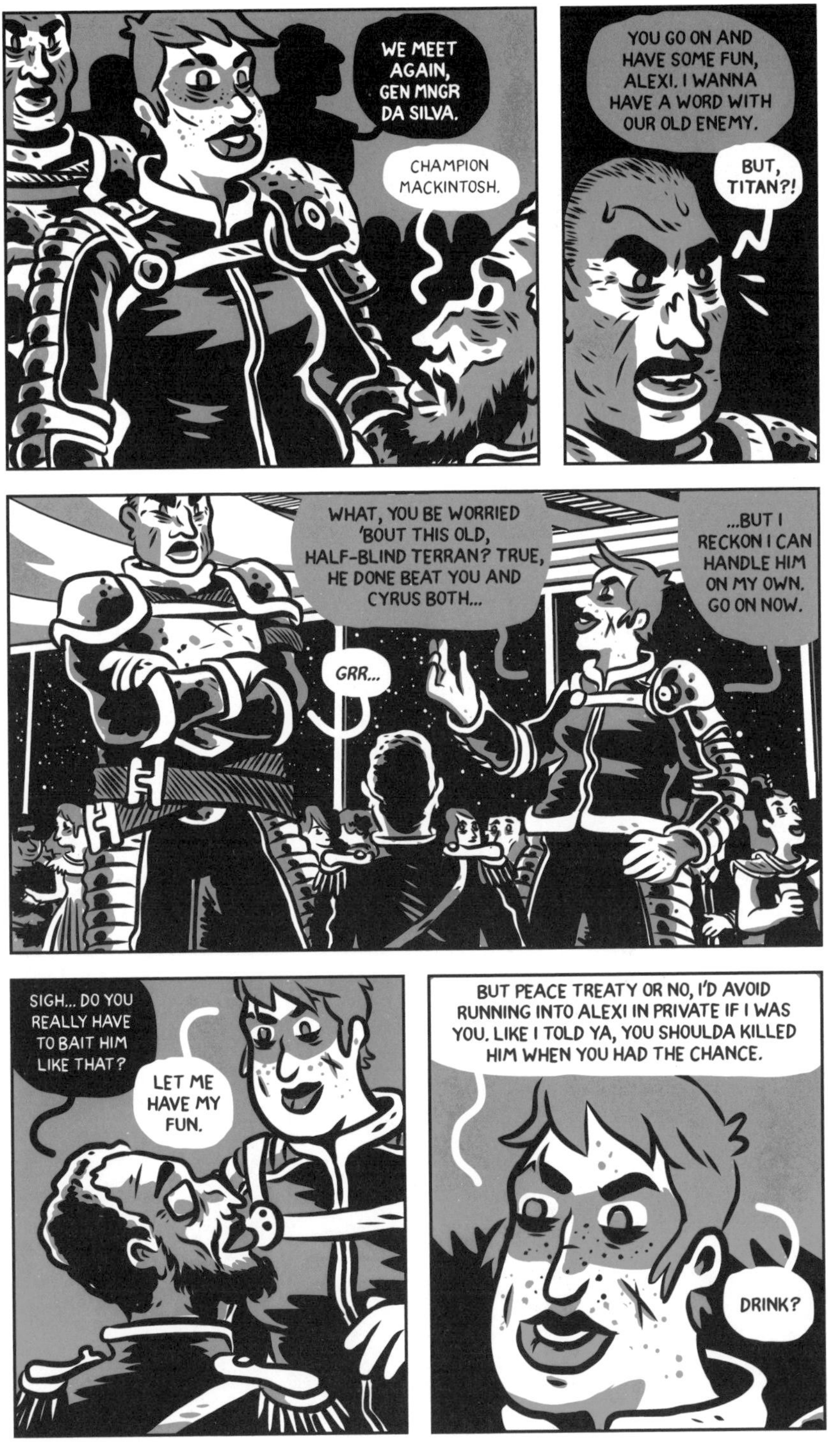
WE MEET AGAIN, GEN MNGR DA SILVA.
CHAMPION MACKINTOSH.
YOU GO ON AND HAVE SOME FUN, ALEXI. I WANNA HAVE A WORD WITH OUR OLD ENEMY.
BUT, TITAN?!
WHAT, YOU BE WORRIED 'BOUT THIS OLD, HALF-BLIND TERRAN? TRUE, HE DONE BEAT YOU AND CYRUS BOTH...
GRR...
...BUT I RECKON I CAN HANDLE HIM ON MY OWN. GO ON NOW.
SIGH... DO YOU REALLY HAVE TO BAIT HIM LIKE THAT?
LET ME HAVE MY FUN.
BUT PEACE TREATY OR NO, I'D AVOID RUNNING INTO ALEXI IN PRIVATE IF I WAS YOU. LIKE I TOLD YA, YOU SHOULDA KILLED HIM WHEN YOU HAD THE CHANCE.
DRINK?

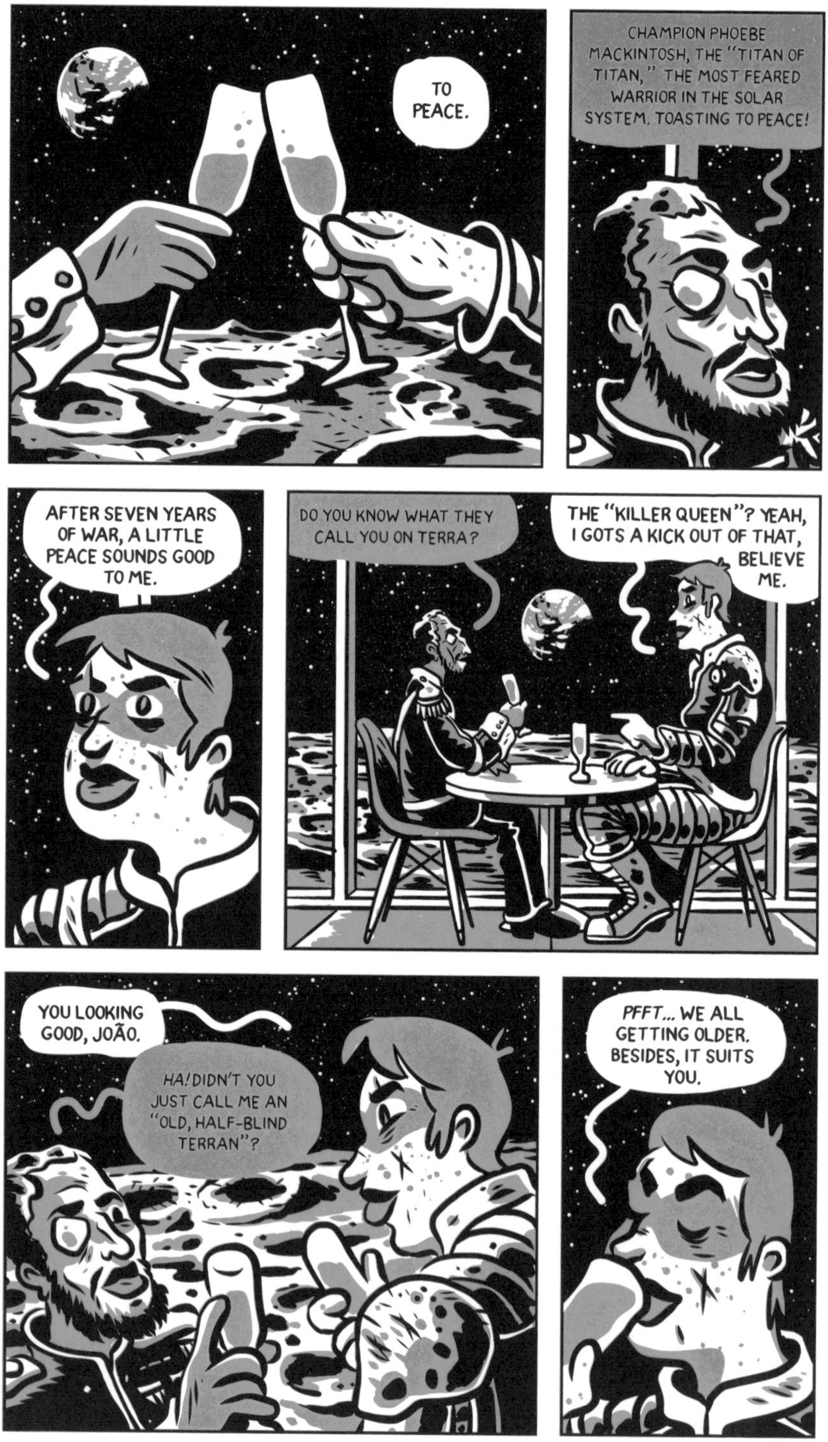
TO PEACE.
CHAMPION PHOEBE MACKINTOSH, THE "TITAN OF TITAN," THE MOST FEARED WARRIOR IN THE SOLAR SYSTEM. TOASTING TO PEACE!
AFTER SEVEN YEARS OF WAR, A LITTLE PEACE SOUNDS GOOD TO ME.
DO YOU KNOW WHAT THEY CALL YOU ON TERRA?
THE "KILLER QUEEN"? YEAH, I GOTS A KICK OUT OF THAT, BELIEVE ME.
YOU LOOKING GOOD, JOÃO.
HA! DIDN'T YOU JUST CALL ME AN "OLD, HALF-BLIND TERRAN"?
PFFT... WE ALL GETTING OLDER. BESIDES, IT SUITS YOU.

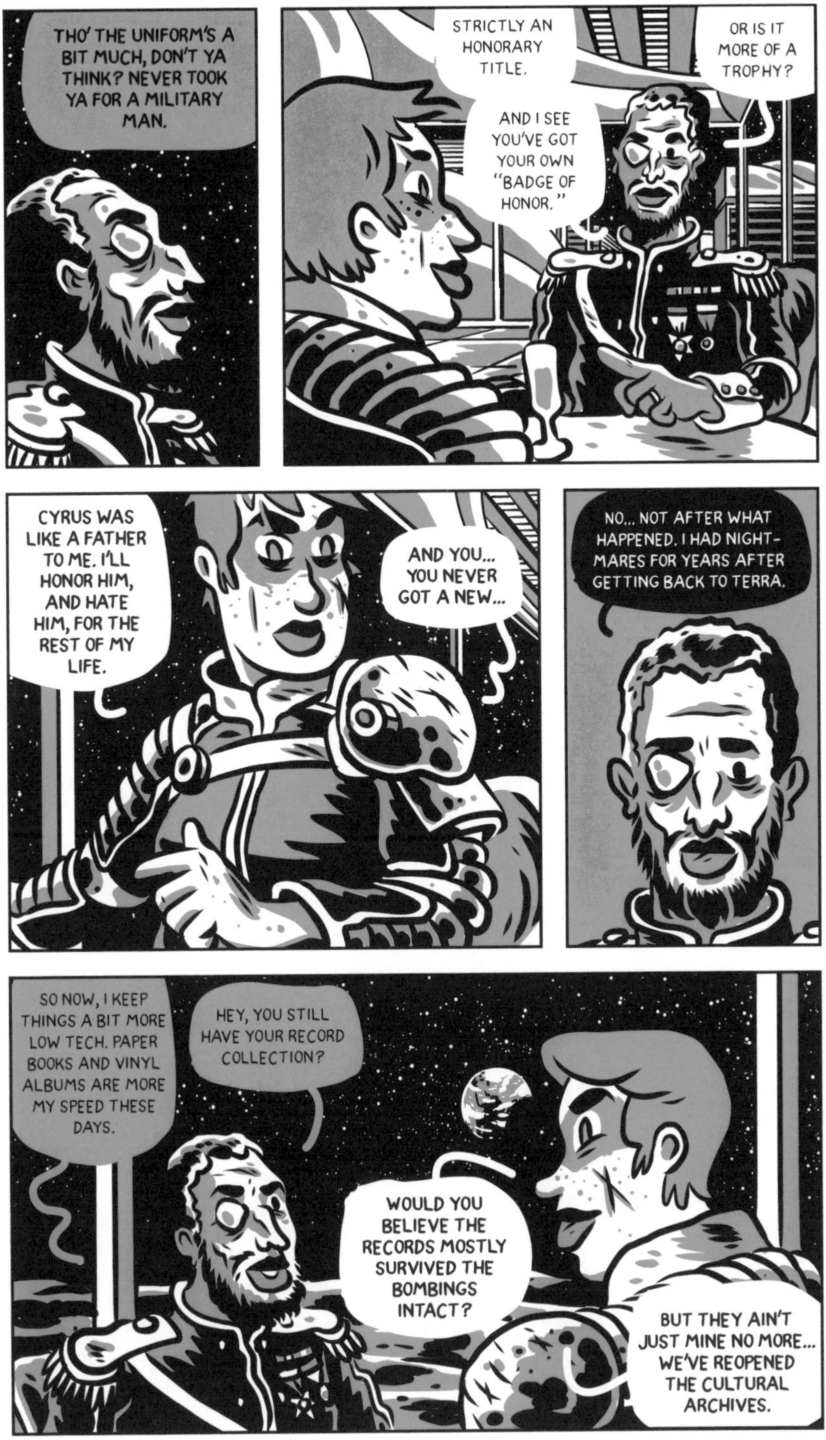
THO' THE UNIFORM'S A BIT MUCH, DON'T YA THINK? NEVER TOOK YA FOR A MILITARY MAN.
STRICTLY AN HONORARY TITLE.
OR IS IT MORE OF A TROPHY?
AND I SEE YOU'VE GOT YOUR OWN "BADGE OF HONOR."
CYRUS WAS LIKE A FATHER TO ME. I'LL HONOR HIM, AND HATE HIM, FOR THE REST OF MY LIFE.
AND YOU... YOU NEVER GOT A NEW...
NO... NOT AFTER WHAT HAPPENED. I HAD NIGHT-MARES FOR YEARS AFTER GETTING BACK TO TERRA.
SO NOW, I KEEP THINGS A BIT MORE LOW TECH. PAPER BOOKS AND VINYL ALBUMS ARE MORE MY SPEED THESE DAYS.
HEY, YOU STILL HAVE YOUR RECORD COLLECTION?
WOULD YOU BELIEVE THE RECORDS MOSTLY SURVIVED THE BOMBINGS INTACT?
BUT THEY AIN'T JUST MINE NO MORE... WE'VE REOPENED THE CULTURAL ARCHIVES.

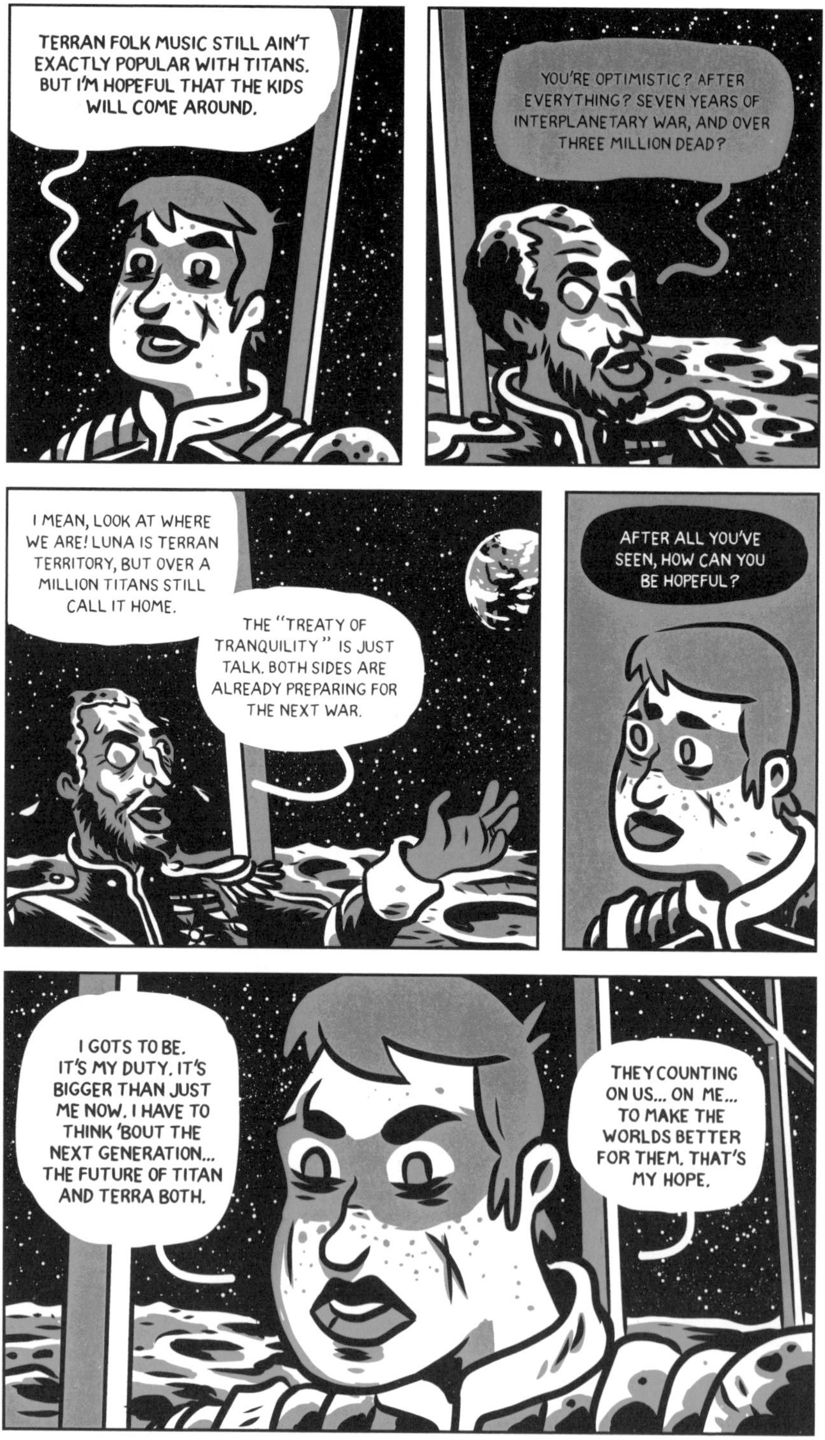
TERRAN FOLK MUSIC STILL AIN'T EXACTLY POPULAR WITH TITANS. BUT I'M HOPEFUL THAT THE KIDS WILL COME AROUND.
YOU'RE OPTIMISTIC? AFTER EVERYTHING? SEVEN YEARS OF INTERPLANETARY WAR, AND OVER THREE MILLION DEAD?
I MEAN, LOOK AT WHERE WE ARE! LUNA IS TERRAN TERRITORY, BUT OVER A MILLION TITANS STILL CALL IT HOME.
THE "TREATY OF TRANQUILITY" IS JUST TALK. BOTH SIDES ARE ALREADY PREPARING FOR THE NEXT WAR.
AFTER ALL YOU'VE SEEN, HOW CAN YOU BE HOPEFUL?
I GOTS TO BE. IT'S MY DUTY. IT'S BIGGER THAN JUST ME NOW. I HAVE TO THINK 'BOUT THE NEXT GENERATION... THE FUTURE OF TITAN AND TERRA BOTH.
THEY COUNTING ON US... ON ME... TO MAKE THE WORLDS BETTER FOR THEM. THAT'S MY HOPE.

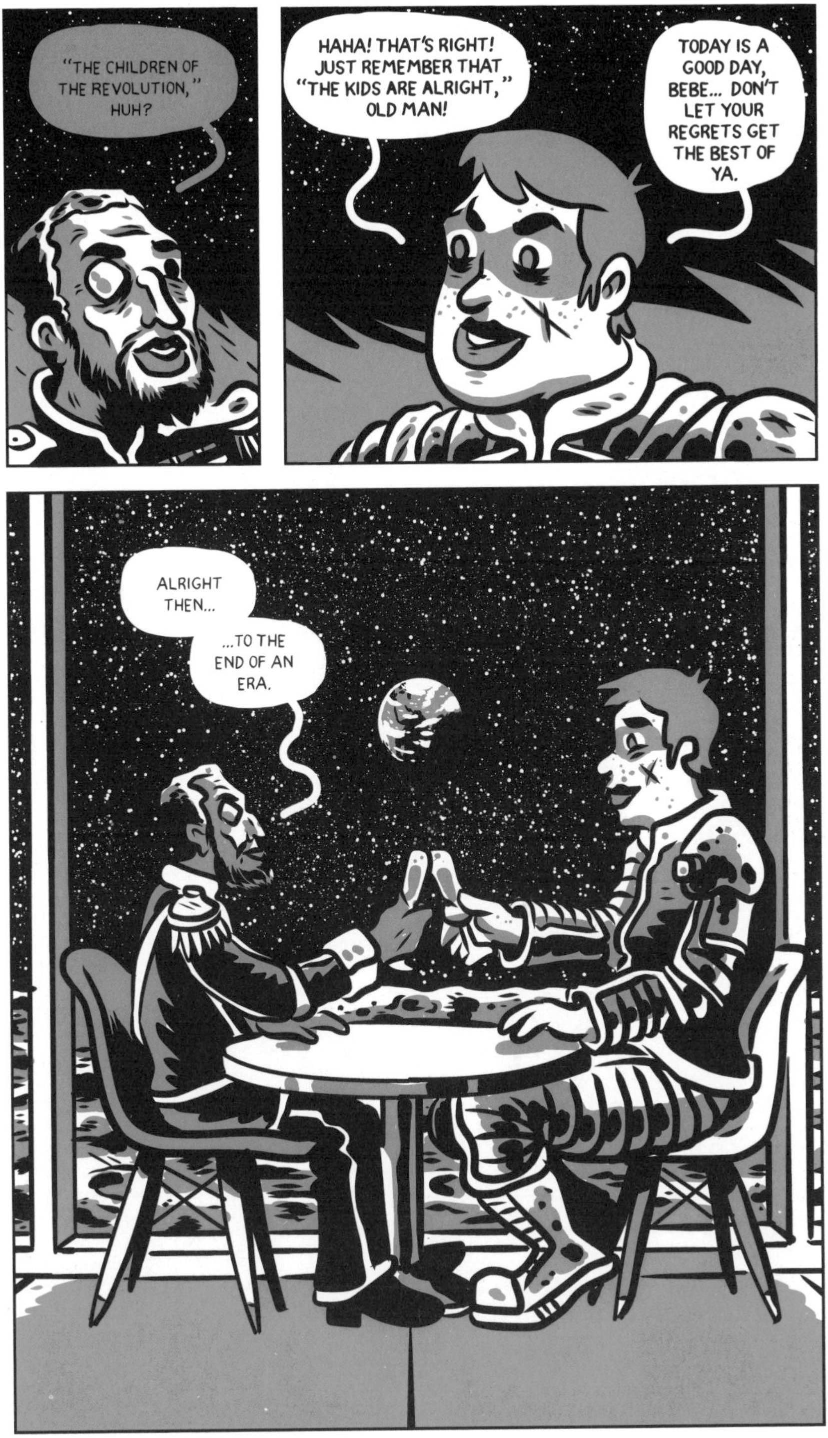

"THE CHILDREN OF THE REVOLUTION," HUH?
HAHA! THAT'S RIGHT! JUST REMEMBER THAT "THE KIDS ARE ALRIGHT," OLD MAN!
TODAY IS A GOOD DAY, BEBE... DON'T LET YOUR REGRETS GET THE BEST OF YA.
ALRIGHT THEN...
...TO THE END OF AN ERA.

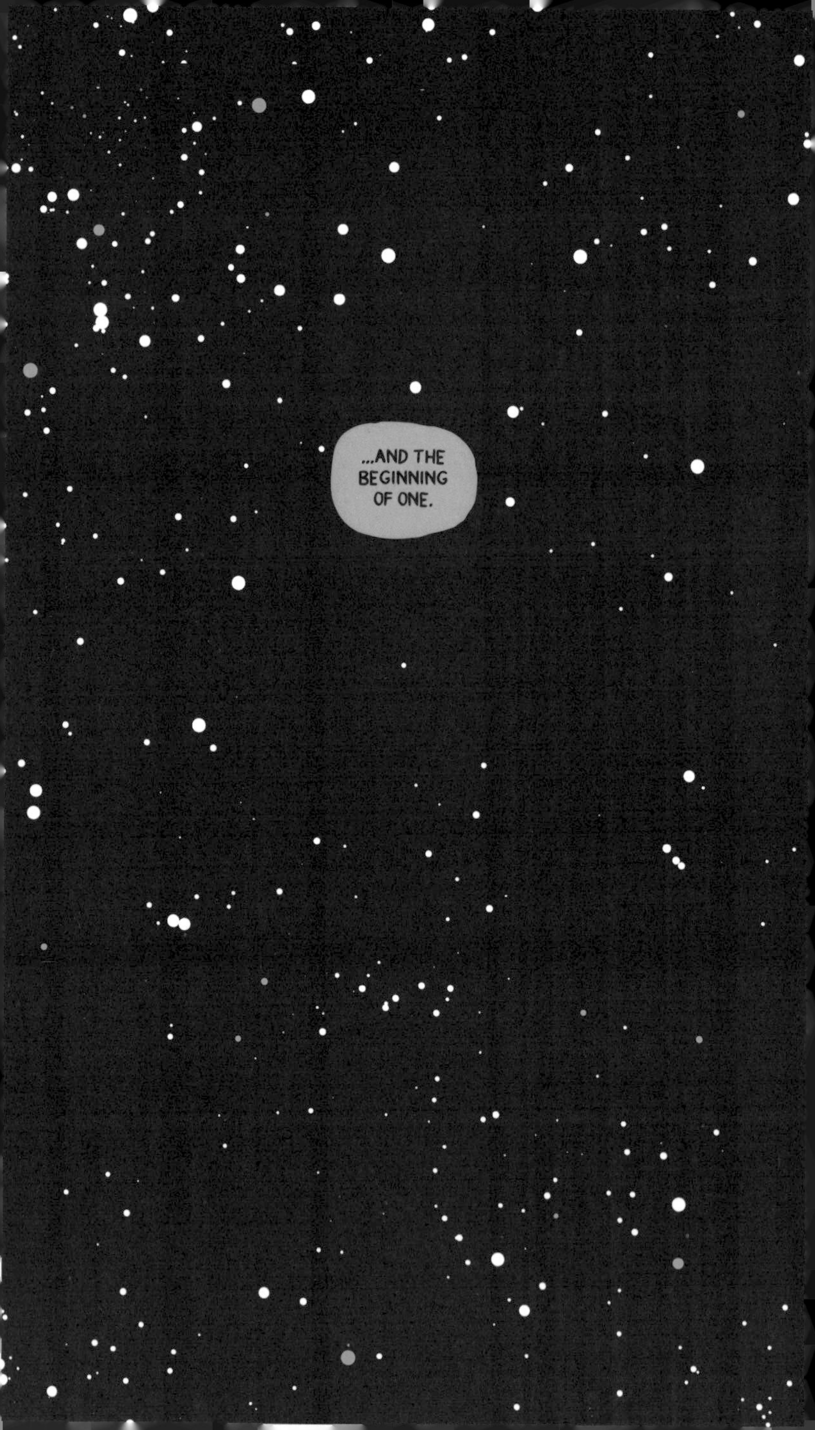
...AND THE BEGINNING OF ONE.

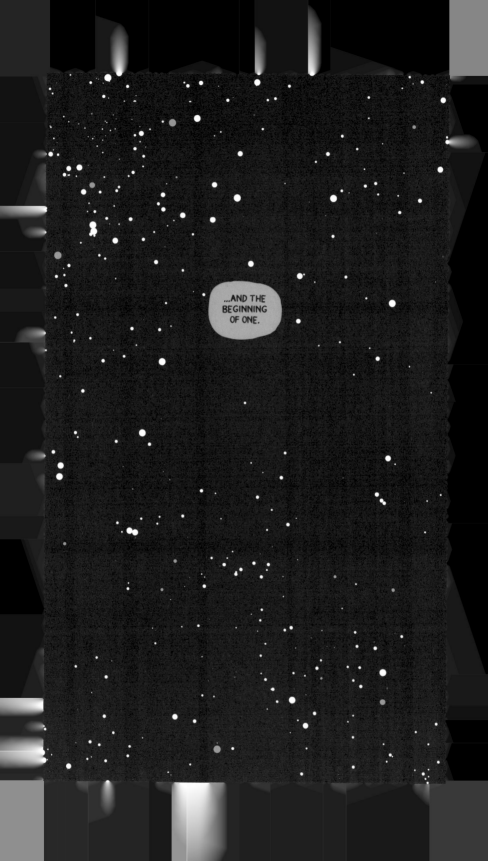

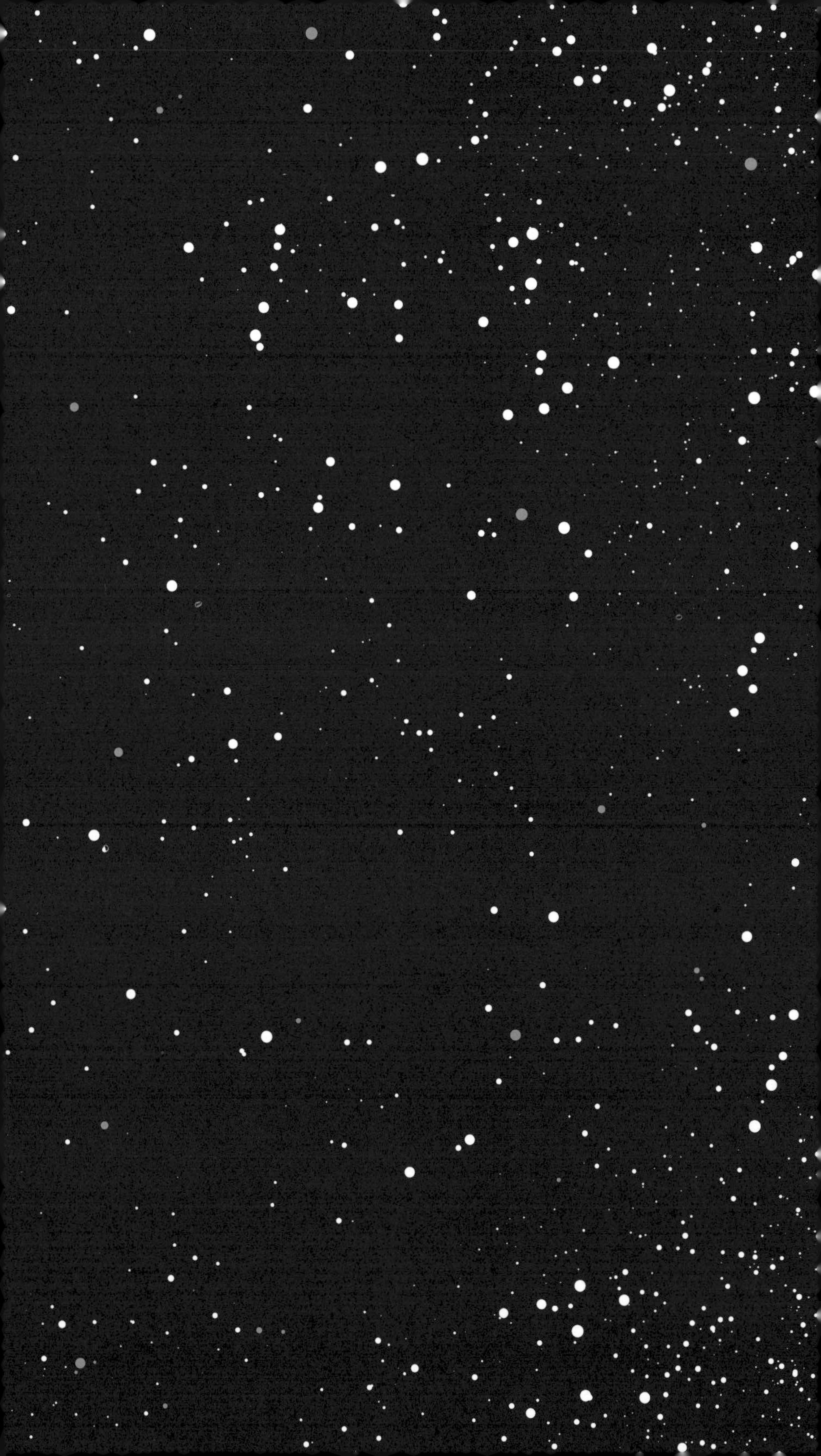

MUSICAL SELECTION

PART 01 "Far, Far Away," Wilco, *Being There*, 1996
PART 02 "99 Problems," Jay-Z, *The Black Album*, 2003
PART 03 "Hard Headed Woman," Cat Stevens (Yusuf Islam), *Tea for the Tillerman*, 1970
"Johnny B. Goode," Chuck Berry, 1958
PART 04 "I Think We're Alone Now," Tommy James & the Shondells, 1967
"Terra," Caetano Veloso, *Muito*, 1978
PART 05 "Just Like Honey," The Jesus and Mary Chain, *Psychocandy*, 1985
"Sunday Mornin'," Margo Guryan, *Take a Picture*, 1968
PART 06 "Serve the Servants," Nirvana, *In Utero*, 1993
PART 07 "Life During Wartime," Talking Heads, *Fear of Music*, 1979
PART 08 "My Moon My Man," Feist, *The Reminder*, 2007
PART 09 "Stand By Me," Ben E. King, 1961
PART 10 "Oh! You Pretty Things," David Bowie, *Hunky Dory*, 1971
PART 11 "The Greatest," Cat Power, *The Greatest*, 2006
PART 12 "After the Gold Rush," Neil Young, *After the Gold Rush*, 1970